LIBRARY OF HEBREW BIBLE/ OLD TESTAMENT STUDIES

457

Formerly Journal for the Study of the Old Testament Supplement Series

Editors
Claudia V. Camp, Texas Christian University
Andrew Mein, Westcott House, Cambridge

SACRED CONJECTURES

The Context and Legacy of Robert Lowth and Jean Astruc

edited by

John Jarick

t&t clark

NEW YORK • LONDON

T & T Clark International, 80 Maiden Lane, New York, NY 10038

T & T Clark International, The Tower Building, 11 York Road, London SE1 7NX

T & T Clark International is a Continuum imprint.

Library of Congress Cataloging-in-Publication Data
Sacred conjectures : the context and legacy of Robert Lowth and Jean Astruc / edited by
    John Jarick.
        p. cm. -- (The library of Hebrew Bible/Old Testament studies ; 457)
    Includes bibliographical references and index.
    ISBN-13: 978-0-567-02932-4 (hardcover : alk. paper)
    ISBN-10: 0-567-02932-8 (hardcover : alk. paper)
    1. Bible. O.T.--Criticism, interpretation, etc.--History--Congresses. 2. Lowth, Robert,
    1710-1787. De sacra poesi Hebraeorum--Congresses. 3. Hebrew poetry,
    Biblical--History and criticism--Congresses. 4. Astruc, Jean, 1684-1766. Conjectures
    sur la Génèse--Congresses. 5. Bible. O.T. Genesis--Criticism, interpretation,
    etc.--History--Congresses. I. Jarick, John.

BS1160.S23 2007
220.6092'2--dc22

                                                                    2006039365

06 07 08 09 10   10 9 8 7 6 5 4 3 2 1

CONTENTS

Part B
ON THE CONTEXT AND LEGACY OF JEAN ASTRUC'S *CONJECTURES* ON GENESIS

PREFACE

The year 1753 saw the publication of two major works of Old Testament scholarship: Robert Lowth's *On the Sacred Poetry of the Hebrews* (based on his renowned lectures as Professor of Poetry at the University of Oxford) and Jean Astruc's *Conjectures* on Genesis (published anonymously when the author was Professor of Medicine at the College Royal in Paris). Both these works have had considerable repercussions in biblical study down to the present day. Indeed they may be said to have inaugurated modern critical approaches to the poetry and prose respectively of the Old Testament.

To mark and reflect upon the 250th anniversary of the publication of the *Sacred Poetry* and the *Conjectures*, Oxford hosted a "Sacred Conjectures" conference at St Catherine's College and at New College (Lowth's own college) on 8th–10th April 2003. An international group of scholars gathered to discuss the context and legacy of Lowth's and Astruc's seminal contributions to the field of biblical scholarship, and now the majority of the papers presented at the conference are re-presented in the present volume. The collection aims to provide for both Robert Lowth and Jean Astruc not only an account and evaluation of their life and work but also an understanding of the wider intellectual context of their scholarship and the reception and influence of their work ever since.

The "Sacred Conjectures" conference was convened by John Barton, Hugh Williamson, John Day, and John Jarick, and was held under the auspices of the Faculty of Theology and the Faculty of Oriental Studies at the University of Oxford, with the support of the British Academy and the Pusey & Ellerton Fund, and in association with the Society for Old Testament Study. The support of all those bodies is gratefully acknowledged.

The *Sacred Conjectures* volume is published in the Library of Hebrew Bible/Old Testament Studies. Everyone associated with the project is indebted to the series editors Andrew Mein and Claudia Camp for so readily agreeing to accept the volume in the Library, and to copy-editor Duncan Burns for so skilfully bringing the work to publication. Credit is also due to Melissa Jackson for reading and making useful suggestions on a number of the essays.

Through the collective efforts of all involved, it is hoped that this set of studies on the context and legacy of Robert Lowth and Jean Astruc can help to serve the same aim that Lowth described for the study of poetry in general and biblical poetry in particular (*On the Sacred Poetry of the Hebrews*, 3): "to discover and relish those delicate touches of grace and elegance that lie beyond the reach of vulgar apprehension."

John Jarick

ABSTRACTS

Part A
ON THE CONTEXT AND LEGACY OF ROBERT LOWTH'S
SACRED POETRY OF THE HEBREWS

Biblical Scholarship at Oxford in the Mid-Eighteenth Century:
Local Contexts for Robert Lowth's De sacra poesi Hebraeorum

Scott Mandelbrote

Director of Studies in History at Peterhouse, Cambridge

This essay discusses an incident which helped to launch the career of Robert Lowth and provided the immediate setting for the reception of the publication of his lectures on Hebrew sacred poetry. The incident was a dispute over the appointment of the Principal of Hertford College, Oxford, which reveals the influence within the University of Oxford in 1753 of the ideas of John Hutchinson. The polemical, Trinitarian divinity of Hutchinson, his followers, and fellow travellers provides a context against which to set the work of Lowth. In particular, the essay describes the on-going debate between Lowth's mentor, Thomas Hunt, the Laudian Professor of Arabic and Regius Professor of Hebrew, and the Hutchinsonians, setting out the basis of the dispute (which focussed on the etymology of Hebrew words and the contextual meaning of passages of the Old Testament) in order to provide the setting for the reception of Lowth's book. This was not only a debate about divinity, but one which had profound implications for the future direction of the Church of England, particularly in terms of its willingness to tolerate anti-Trinitarian dissent. Lowth's intellectual success was mirrored by a political triumph at the polls in Oxford in 1754, engineered in part by his ally, Benjamin Kennicott. The resulting boost helped to launch Lowth's highly successful clerical career.

Original Poetry: Robert Lowth and Eighteenth-Century Poetics

Anna Cullhed

Researcher in the Department of Literature, Uppsala University

This essay suggests that Robert Lowth's *De sacra poesi Hebraeorum* should be understood as a series of lectures on poetics, even as a defence of poetry. As Professor of Poetry, Lowth exclusively discussed the poetical parts of the Old Testament. Parallelism, an implicit proof of a metrical system, made it possible to distinguish poetry from prose. To Lowth, poetry was superior to oratory mainly because of its strong emotional appeal. Hebrew poetry turned from being a special case, deviating from the poetical tradition of ancient Greece and Rome, to the foundation of poetry. Further, Lowth's definition of poetry as a passionate and originally religious expression brought the poetry of the Old Testament to the very centre of the eighteenth-century literary canon. Lowth's lectures were structured according to standard topics of poetics: he followed the Aristotelian and Horatian tradition in his definitions of the subject matter, and compared poetry to a number of neighbouring disciplines; Greek and Roman poetry remained the point of departure for the generic system, but Hebrew poetry surpassed even the masterpieces of Classical Antiquity, according to Lowth. The essay concludes with a discussion of Lowth's impact on mainstream poetics in Germany: with support from Lowth, lyric poetry became appreciated as the highest genre in the 1770s and the 1780s; however, with the Jena romantics in Germany Hebrew poetry lost its position in the lyrical canon, mainly due to their reinterpretation of the generic system, based on the poetry of ancient Greece.

Robert Lowth and the Idea of Biblical Tradition

Stephen Prickett

Margaret Root Brown Professor, for Browning Studies and
Victorian Poetry, and Director of the Armstrong, Browning Library,
Baylor University, Waco, Texas

From the perspective of the twenty-first century, it is easy to read Lowth's *Lectures on the Sacred Poetry of the Hebrews* as not merely a key event in the history of biblical criticism, but also as a key exploration of biblical tradition. Yet, in fact, he uses the word "tradition" only three times in the text, and always in a negative or sceptical context. This does not seem to be part of an anti-Catholic prejudice, since he openly stresses his indebtedness to the old Latin Bible, to the Vulgate, and to Catholic biblical writings. Nor can this be seen as a "modernist" scholarly inclination for documentation over poetic hyperbole, since, when in doubt, Lowth openly stresses his preference for literary as against narrowly historical readings. Nevertheless, Lowth's sense of historical context, both in biblical texts and in his own reading of them, meant that the missing term in this dialogue was undergoing profound historical changes. In a post-Reformation, post-Civil War context of political and religious pluralism, the *idea* of tradition (however absent verbally from debate) was inevitably modified by competing narratives—"traditions" rather than the "tradition." At the same time, Lowth's stress on the poetic value of the Hebrew scriptures helped prepare the ground in Germany for the Kantian and Romantic interest in aesthetics (and therefore of "aesthetic tradition") that was to be so important an aspect of the nineteenth- and twentieth-century concepts of tradition that were to bring the word back into widespread usage.

After Horace: Sacred Poetry at the Centre of the Hebrew Bible

Christoph Bultmann

Professor of Biblical Studies at the University of Erfurt

Starting from the observation that it was his appointment as Professor of Poetry in Oxford in 1741 which allowed Robert Lowth to pursue his investigation of Hebrew (Old Testament) poetry, this essay tries to recover some aspects of the historical constellation in which Lowth decided to lecture on poetry from ancient Israelite culture rather than on classical Roman poetry. While Lowth recognized some special status of the canonical Scriptures, he adopted the notion of the sublime in order to approach religious poetry in the Bible from the perspective of literary criticism. The essay shows that for an assessment of the theological significance of Lowth's lectures on Hebrew poetry, the poetry of Horace as well as Longinus's treatise on the sublime should be taken into account. It becomes clear that for Lowth biblical poems are not just objects for scholarly description and classification; poetic texts have a specific force and significance that should elicit a response from every individual reader.

Charles-François Houbigant: His Background, Work and Importance for Lowth

John Rogerson

Emeritus Professor of Biblical Studies at the University of Sheffield

Charles-François Houbigant's *Biblia Sacra* of 1753 is a neglected masterpiece of biblical scholarship, although its value was recognized by scholars such as Robert Lowth, Benjamin Kennicott and Alexander Geddes. The essay outlines Houbigant's methods and how and why he proposed some 5000 emendations to the text of the Bible in Hebrew, some of which have become standard in modern biblical scholarship and many of which were used by Lowth in his new translation and notes on Isaiah. A consideration of Lowth's enthusiasm for the work of Houbigant enables us to place Lowth more securely in his context in the world of eighteenth-century scholarship: while he did not go so far as Houbigant in advocating that Hebrew should be read other than according to the Masoretic punctuation, he did nonetheless express the view that greater progress would have been made in the study of the Old Testament if the Masoretic punctuation had been considered as an assistant and not an infallible guide. In demonstrating how much Lowth owed to his French Catholic colleague, this essay may also help to rescue Houbigant himself from an obscurity that he has not deserved.

Die literarische Gattung des Buches Hiob: Robert Lowth und seine Erben

Markus Witte

Professor of Old Testament at the University of Frankfurt am Main

This essay first describes the treatment of the book of Job in Robert Lowth's *Praelectiones de sacra poesi Hebraeorum* (1753) against the background of the literary-historical and aesthetical research of the eighteenth century, showing the influence of Lowth's work on poetical and form-critical studies from Johann Gottfried Herder's *Vom Geist der Ebräischen Poesie* (1782/83) to the present. Thereby the historical contexts and the hermeneutical implications of the classifications of the book of Job as *drama, epic, didactic poetry, sapiential dispute, lament, lawsuit, comedy* and *work sui generis* are presented in detail. Three topics of research are especially pointed out: (1) the tradition-historical question of the genres in the book (laments, hymns, sentences, juridical phrases) and the setting of the book in a specific cultural context or origin (cult, wisdom, law), i.e. the question of its *Sitz im Leben*; (2) the composition-historical question of the use (and misuse) of these genres in the book, i.e. the question of the *Sitz im Buch*; and (3) the reception-esthetical and semiotical question of the position of the book in the world of the readers. Furthermore, Witte demonstrates how the literary-critical question of the relation between the narrative frame and the poetic main body, and a comparison with Near Eastern and old Greek theodicy-poetry, determines the interpretation of the form and forms of the book of Job. Finally, the present status of poetical and form-critical research is considered, as well as the methodology of exegesis of the book of Job: the book reveals its form and forms in a dialogue of the readers with the traditions and redactions in the work, with the historical and social situations which created the work and with the intertextual associations established by the book.

The Study of Hebrew Poetry: Past–Present–Future

Wilfred G. E. Watson

Visiting Fellow at the University of Newcastle upon Tyne

After a brief survey of past studies, the focus here is on the contribution to Hebrew poetry by scholars since Robert Lowth. Modern analysis of Hebrew verse is considered to have progressed, partly due to the discovery of ancient Near Eastern literature and languages after his time. Further factors include the study of formula and theme, as in Homeric verse, and the application of modern linguistics to Hebrew. Present work on Hebrew verse is shown to concern topics such as the differentiation between prose and poetry, delimitation criticism (i.e. the examination of manuscript traditions for indications of poetic divisions in a text), parallelism and metre. As illustration, some passages from Hebrew and Ugaritic poetry are discussed. Then, suggestions for future study are provided, including the analysis of synthetic parallelism, additional comparison with ancient Near Eastern poetry and further study of the divisions in the Masoretic text and the versions. To close, some proposals for the analysis of poetic language are listed.

Part B
ON THE CONTEXT AND LEGACY OF JEAN ASTRUC'S *CONJECTURES* ON GENESIS

Jean Astruc: A Physician as a Biblical Scholar

Rudolf Smend

Professor of Old Testament at the University of Göttingen

This essay gives a brief survey of the life and work of Jean Astruc, about whom unfortunately no full biography as yet exists. It is interesting to consider him in his double role as physician and biblical scholar. His textbooks had a wide circulation and cover not only all branches of medicine but also natural history and other subjects. As teacher at the Collège Royal de France and at the Sorbonne, he had a wide influence, and he enjoyed a prominent position in Parisian society, not least as Louis XV's personal physician. His interest in the Old Testament may perhaps have to do with his surmised Jewish origin; something can undoubtedly be put down to the lasting influence of his father, a Reformed pastor who, however, in connection with the revocation of the Edict of Nantes, had gone over to the Catholic church. The *Conjectures* on Genesis are apologetic in intention: they presuppose that Moses was the author of the Pentateuch, and attempt to prove that he deserves complete trust in every respect (that is to say, as historian as well); all the objections to this postulate raised by Hobbes, Spinoza, Simon and others are disposed of by Astruc's hypothesis about the earlier documents which Moses took as the foundation for his work. The final part of the essay treats the book's reception and influence: in France it met with almost no response, and in Germany it was not immediately understood, but was then made the basis for the "documentary hypothesis," which for generations formed the backbone of the critical analysis of the Pentateuch.

De l'intuition à l'évidence: la multiplicité documentaire dans la Genèse chez H. B. Witter et Jean Astruc

Pierre Gibert

Professor of Bible at the Catholic Theological Faculty of Lyon

Following the insights of Andreas Masius, Isaac de la Peyrère and Jacques Bonfrère, the biblical commentators Jean le Clerc, Baruch

Spinoza and Richard Simon established, during the second half of the seventeenth century, the principle of the composite character of the Pentateuch. According to this theory, the work of Moses involved the integration of older documents while allowing for later additions. Henning Bernhard Witter's intuition (1711) that led him to distinguish two creation accounts in the beginning of Genesis, and Jean Astruc's theory (1753) that Moses made use of different "memoirs" in writing Genesis, demonstrated, each in a different way, the reality of the composite character in accounting for both the composition and the final state of the book of Genesis.

Jean Astruc and Source Criticism in the Book of Genesis

Jan Christian Gertz

Professor of Old Testament at the University of Heidelberg

By means of a literary analysis of the Flood story in Gen 6–9, this essay brings Jean Astruc (1684–1766) into conversation with Benno Jacob (1862–1945), who energetically denied the legitimacy of source criticism and its results. Astruc's *Conjectures sur les Mémoires originaux* are characterized by a remarkable internal coherence and conceptual logic. Older observations are integrated into methodologically consistent analyses and a scientific hypothesis. The latter is formulated stringently but also leaves space for new evidence regarding the fragmentary character of the sources. The apologetic aim of the work is unmistakable. Proof for "documents" in Genesis serves to defend the authority of the Pentateuch. It transforms the traditional view of its Mosaic authorship into an historical thesis: with the discovery of Moses as an "inspired historian," the doctrine of the inspiration of Scripture assumes a new character. Astruc has contributed immensely to biblical research insofar as his work laid the foundation for an historical and independent reading of the Old Testament and Israel's religion. In this way, Astruc has become unwittingly the father of modern pentateuchal research. Benno Jacob's appeal for the literary unity of the Pentateuch is conversely not apologetic. Although his arguments for unity are not convincing, his search for coherence contributed unintentionally to the development of composition history, a method which focuses on the entire formation of the Pentateuch rather than just the earliest sources.

The Mémoires *of Moses and the Genesis of Method in Biblical Criticism: Astruc's Contribution*

Aulikki Nahkola

Principal Lecturer in Old Testament at Newbold College in Bracknell, Berkshire

This essay argues that in Astruc's *Conjectures* on Genesis we also have the genesis of method in biblical scholarship. It is in Astruc's work that we see the first systematic, if embryonic, presentation of the procedures for determining compositional layers in biblical traditions, which became the hallmark of Old Testament criticism for nearly two centuries, as well as an articulation of the presuppositions on which these procedures are based. The essay outlines Astruc's critical approach and assesses its contribution to the developing Old Testament scholarship. It does this by employing three perspectives. First, it looks at the paradigm shift in the study and use of the Bible which took place at the time of the Enlightenment: the academic study of the Bible for its own sake emerged at this time, thus instigating a new discipline, eventually to be clearly demarcated from other realms of study, and Astruc's work is seminal in this development. Secondly, the essay focuses on the specific contribution of the *Conjectures* as a "first case" of explicitly articulated method in biblical studies for the study of a biblical book: the purpose of Astruc's *Conjectures* was to find a way of explaining the inconsistencies and repetitions in the biblical text which were vexing the scholars of the time, and he accomplished this by positing that these phenomena witness to the process of composition in Genesis (i.e. the author's use of sources or *Mémoires*). And finally, the essay reflects on the notion of method in biblical studies and the nature of the discipline as a quintessentially Enlightenment, i.e. modern, enterprise.

An Heir of Astruc in a Remote German University: *Hermann Hupfeld and the "New Documentary Hypothesis"*

Otto Kaiser

Emeritus Professor of Old Testament at the University of Marburg

The beginnings of historical criticism in the then remote German University of Marburg in Northern Hessia are especially connected with the names of Albert Jacob Arnoldi (1750–1835) and Hermann Hupfeld

(1796–1866). Arnoldi, in his time one of the most renowned orientalists and Old Testament scholars, left only two small volumes of text-critical studies, giving evidence not only that he owned an almost complete library of the new genre of critical biblical and oriental studies but also that he had made use of Robert Lowth's insight into the basic law of Hebrew poetry, the so-called *parallelismus membrorum*. Through his rationalistic lectures, in which he declared the concept of verbal inspiration of Scripture to be a disadvantage for biblical exegesis, he led his most gifted student, Hermann Hupfeld, into a deep crisis, which the latter mastered only when he had finished his studies. Reading the "classics" from Michaelis, Astruc, Lowth, Eichhorn to Herder, he became convinced that historical criticism is unavoidable, while the romance of W. M. L. de Wette's "Theobald oder des Zweiflers Weihe" ("Theobald or the Consecration of the Sceptic") gave him a more liberal concept of faith. That enabled him afterwards, when he had moved from his Marburg chair to that of Wilhelm Gesenius (1786–1842) at the University of Halle, to become in 1853 the founder of the Documentary Hypothesis and to publish between 1855 and 1861 one of the most voluminous and influential commentaries on the book of Psalms.

Part A

ON THE CONTEXT AND LEGACY OF ROBERT LOWTH'S
SACRED POETRY OF THE HEBREWS

BIBLICAL SCHOLARSHIP AT OXFORD IN THE MID-EIGHTEENTH CENTURY: LOCAL CONTEXTS FOR ROBERT LOWTH'S *DE SACRA POESI HEBRAEORUM**

Scott Mandelbrote

On Monday, June 11, 1753, a strange scene took place in Oxford's newest college. Hertford College was effectively the personal creation of Richard Newton (1676–1753), who, as Principal of Hart Hall from 1710, had set about a process of educational reform that culminated in his winning of a charter for a new college in 1740. Newton's statutes for Hertford College made stern reading. They were careful to preserve a great deal of power in the hands of the Principal (a legacy perhaps of the almost dictatorial control that the heads of private halls enjoyed); they prescribed in detail the duties of everyone else, in particular the tutors and the scholars. Newton spared no detail and even his consideration of the tasks of the College porter was coloured by a proper concern for Christian charity. Colleges were not inns, he argued, and in this particular, very poor College, individual students would be employed to keep the gate, even though the demands of their studies required that they should be in bed by 10pm.[1]

In common with many a martinet, Newton was no stranger to controversy. In the 1720s, he had fought a public battle with Exeter College to secure the institutional independence of Hart Hall.[2] At the same time,

---

* I should like to thank Nigel Aston for his kindness in commenting on a draft of this essay.

1. Richard Newton, *Rules and Statutes for the Government of Hertford College* (London, 1747), 76–77; cf. [Richard Newton], *A Scheme of Discipline with Statutes Intended to be Established by a Royal Charter for the Education of Youth in Hart-Hall in the University of Oxford* ([Oxford], 1720); see also Sidney Graves Hamilton, *Hertford College* (London: F. E. Robinson, 1903), 64–84; Bodleian Library, Oxford [hereafter, Bodl.], Ms. Rawlinson J fol. 4, ff. 147–51.

2. Richard Newton, *A Letter to the Revd. Dr Holmes* (London, 1734); idem, *The Grounds of Complaint of the Principal of Hart-Hall, Concerning the Obstruction Given to the Incorporation of his Society, by Exeter-College and their Visitor*

he had struggled to reform the University and to be allowed to take on students from other societies.[3] In these endeavours to establish his new College, Newton felt the need for allies, whom he found among some of the men that he picked by hand to be his tutors. At the same time, he made significant enemies, as the events of June 11, 1753 made apparent. *Jackson's Oxford Journal*, a periodical more noted for the tradesmen's advertisements that it carried than for its reporting of academic gossip, but at this stage engaged politically for the Whig "New Interest," described the day:

> On Monday last the Right Rev. the Lord Bishop of Bristol [John Conybeare], as Dean of Christ Church, attended by the Canons, and several of the Students of that Society, went to Hertford College in Oxford, and admitted the Rev. William Sharp, M.A. into the Office of Principal of Hertford College, upon which the new admitted Principal spoke a Latin Speech in the Hall, in praise of the late Principal and Founder, Dr. Newton. He then took the Oaths prescribed by the Statutes, and proceeded to his Seat in the Chapel, where he read the first Service, and the second at the Communion Table; as also received the Sacrament himself, and then gave it to the Bishop of Bristol, the Canons, and all of the Society that were present. When the Dean presented Mr. Sharp to the Society, Mr. Fowler Comings, in Presence of a Notary Public, protested against their Proceedings by virtue of his being nominated to the said Office by the Earl of Arran, Chancellor to the University.[4]

It is worth trying to make sense of this incident, since it is full of ironies and carries a number of hints for understanding the politics of scholarship and biblical criticism in Oxford in 1753. That was also the year of the publication of Robert Lowth's *De sacra poesi Hebraeorum*.[5] Lowth had composed the lectures that made up that volume while he held the Professorship of Poetry from 1741 to 1751. During that decade, he graduated from being a writer of polite verses for the in-crowd at Winchester and New College, promoted in particular by his predecessor as Professor of Poetry, Joseph Spence.[6] Lowth's lectures laid the

(London, 1735); cf. John Conybeare, *Calumny Refuted; Or, an Answer to the Personal Slanders Published by Dr. Richard Newton, in his Letter to Dr. Holmes* (London, 1735).

3. Richard Newton, *University Education* (London, 1726).

4. *Jackson's Oxford Journal*, 7 (16 June 1753).

5. Lowth was anxious about the printing of *De sacra poesi Hebraeorum* by the Clarendon Press, and organized the distribution of presentation copies through the leading London publisher, Robert Dodsley: see British Library, London, Ms. Add. 35339, ff. 1–10; Edinburgh University Library, Ms. Gen. 2127/9.

6. Cf. [Robert Lowth], *The Genealogy of Christ; As it is Represented in the East-Window in the College Chapel at Winchester. A Poem* (London, 1729); Peter Hall

foundations for an international reputation for erudition.[7] They made his name familiar to a wider world of scholars and churchmen, and drew him more closely into the circle of the Bishop of Oxford and future Archbishop of Canterbury, Thomas Secker (1693–1768), who had ordained him in December 1741.[8] The esteem in which Lowth was held derived from his success in settling the debate over the structure of Hebrew poetry. In the broader world of scholarship, Lowth's achievements were judged against the metrical theories of Marcus Meibomius or Francis Hare.[9] But, in the local context of Oxford University, Lowth's work had meaning as part of an intellectual debate about the best method for reading Hebrew that itself reflected many of the political and ecclesiastical divisions of mid-eighteenth-century Britain.[10] The events at Hertford College formed a part of that exchange, and, like much of the rest of it, they derived some of their edge from contemporary reactions to the work

(ed.), *Sermons, and Other Remains, of Robert Lowth, D.D.* (London, 1834), 16–17, 443–97; Henry E. Huntington Library, San Marino, California, Rare Book shelfmark 131213: Joseph Spence, *Anecdotes, Observations, and Characters, of Books and Men* (ed. Samuel Weller Singer; 4 vols.; London, 1820), interleaved with letters of Lowth and his friends, at I, p. xxxix; IV, 414, 431–35; Bodl., Mss. Eng. Lett. c. 574, ff. 117–23; Eng. Misc. c. 816, ff. 1–47.

7. For international scholarly interest in Lowth's work, see Robert Lowth, *De sacra poesi Hebraeorum* (ed. Johann David Michaelis; 2 vols.; Göttingen, 1758–61); Bibliotheek der Universiteit, Leiden, Ms. BPL 245 (VIII); Bodl., Mss. Eng. Lett. c. 573, ff. 39–42; Eng. Lett. c. 574, ff. 32–39, 58–65; Lambeth Palace Library, London, Ms. 2020, ff. 69–74; J. van den Berg, "The Leiden Professors of the Schultens Family and their Contacts with British Scholars," *Durham University Journal* 75 (1982–83): 1–14; Rudolf Smend, *Epochen der Bibelkritik* (Gesammelte Studien Band 3; Munich: Chr. Kaiser, 1991), 43–62

8. See John S. Macauley and R. W. Greaves, eds., *The Autobiography of Thomas Secker* (Lawrence: University of Kansas Libraries, 1988), 33, 50; Bodl., Mss. Eng. Lett. c. 574, ff. 67–74; Eng. Misc. c. 816, f. 126r; Lambeth Palace Library, London, Mss. 2559, 2569, 2596.

9. See James L. Kugel, *The Idea of Biblical Poetry* (New Haven: Yale University Press, 1981), especially pp. 12–15, 274–86; Marcus Meibomius, *Davidis psalmi duodecim et totidem sacrae scripturae veteris testamenti integra capita* (Amsterdam, 1698); Francis Hare, ed., *Psalmorum liber in versiculos metrice divisus* (2 vols.; London, 1736). Cf. the earlier criticism of Meibomius by Augustin Calmet, *Antiquities Sacred and Profane* (trans. N. Tindal; London, 1724), 19–36, which was known to Lowth and other Oxford scholars.

10. D. Patterson, "Hebrew Studies," in *The History of the University of Oxford*. Vol. 5, *The Eighteenth Century* (ed. L. S. Sutherland and L. G. Mitchell; Oxford: Clarendon, 1986), 535–50, largely concerns the provision and competence of teaching in the language; cf. W. R. Ward, *Georgian Oxford: University Politics in the Eighteenth Century* (Oxford: Oxford University Press, 1958), especially 161–91.

of John Hutchinson (1674–1737). Hutchinson was a critic of the natural
philosophy of Isaac Newton who advanced an alternative theory of God
and nature based on an idiosyncratic reading of the Hebrew Bible. This
ignored the vowel points and advanced a metaphorical reinterpretation of
the relationship between words with similar consonantal roots. The popularity of Hutchinson's ideas at Oxford provided part of the background
for the incident that took place at Hertford College on June 11, 1753.[11]

   An initial irony, that would surely not have been lost on some of those
present, concerns the Dean of Christ Church and Bishop of Bristol, John
Conybeare. During the 1730s, he had been one of Richard Newton's

---

   11. V. H. H. Green, "Religion in the Colleges 1715–1800," in Sutherland and
Mitchell, eds., *The History of the University of Oxford*, 5:425–67 (456–57), briefly
mentions the popularity of Hutchinsonian ideas at Oxford in 1753. On Hutchinsonianism more generally, see Nigel Aston, "Horne and Heterodoxy: The Defence of
Anglican Beliefs in the Late Enlightenment," *English Historical Review* 108 (1993):
895–919; Nigel Aston, "From Personality to Party: The Creation and Transmission
of Hutchinsonianism, c. 1725–1750," *Studies in History and Philosophy of Science*
35 (2004): 625–44; Geoffrey Cantor, "Revelation and the Cyclical Cosmos of John
Hutchinson," in *Images of the Earth* (ed. Ludmilla Jordanova and Roy Porter; 2d
ed.; Chalfont St. Giles, 1997), 17–35; John C. English, "John Hutchinson's Critique
of Newtonian Heterodoxy," *Church History* 68 (1999): 581–97; Patricia Fara,
Sympathetic Attractions (Princeton, N.J.: Princeton University Press, 1996), 24–30,
146–207; Derya Gürses, "The Hutchinsonian Defence of an Old Testament
Trinitarian Christianity: The Controversy Over Elahim, 1735–1773," *History of
European Ideas* 29 (2003): 393–409; idem, "Paradigm Regained: The Hutchinsonian
Reconstruction of Trinitarian Protestant Christianity (1724–1806)" (Ph.D. diss.,
Bilkent University, 2003); David S. Katz, "The Hutchinsonians and Hebraic
Fundamentalism in Eighteenth-Century England," in *Sceptics, Millenarians and
Jews* (ed. David S. Katz and Jonathan I. Israel; Leiden: Brill, 1990), 237–55; idem,
"'Moses's Principia': Hutchinsonianism and Newton's Critics," in *The Books of
Nature and Scripture* (ed. James E. Force and Richard H. Popkin; Dordrecht:
Kluwer Academic Publishers, 1994), 201–11; idem, "The Occult Bible: Hebraic
Millenarianism in Eighteenth-Century England," in *The Millenarian Turn* (ed. James
E. Force and Richard H. Popkin; Dordrecht: Kluwer Academic Publishers, 2001),
119–32; idem, *God's Last Words* (New Haven: Yale University Press, 2004), 159–
65; A. J. Kuhn, "Glory or Gravity: Hutchinson vs. Newton," *Journal of the History
of Ideas* 22 (1961): 303–22; C. D. A. Leighton, "Hutchinsonianism: A Counter-
Enlightenment Reform Movement," *Journal of Religious History* 23 (1999): 168–
84; idem, "'Knowledge of divine things': A Study of Hutchinsonianism," *History
of European Ideas* 26 (2000): 159–75; Gavin White, "Hutchinsonianism in Eighteenth-Century Scotland," *Records of Scottish Church History Society* 21 (1981–83):
157–69; C. B. Wilde, "Hutchinsonianism, Natural Philosophy and Religious
Controversy in Eighteenth Century Britain," *History of Science* 18 (1980): 1–24;
idem, "Matter and Spirit as Natural Symbols in Eighteenth-Century British Natural
Philosophy," *British Journal for the History of Science* 15 (1982): 99–131.

strongest opponents, as a protagonist of the rights of Exeter College.[12] Perhaps the two men had been reconciled following Newton's preferment to a canonry at Christ Church towards the end of his life; it seems more likely, however, that Conybeare was now acting in the cause of the "New Interest" that his College espoused. Certainly, Conybeare's nominee at Hertford, William Sharpe, proved a suitably scholarly successor to Newton.[13] In particular, Sharpe encouraged the careers of three tutors who followed in Lowth's footsteps as biblical critics: David Durell, Benjamin Blayney and William Newcome. In their respective publications, these three scholars would later build on the crowning achievement of Lowth's editorial work, his edition of Isaiah, with further critical studies of the Major and Minor Prophets.[14] They also helped to put into reality hopes that Lowth shared for an improved edition of the English Bible. These were reflected in the editorial work that Blayney carried out under commission from Durell during the latter's tenure as Vice-Chancellor of Oxford University and Delegate of the University Press.[15]

In June 1753, the Christ Church interest, represented by Conybeare and Sharpe, prevailed at Hertford against Comings and his patron, the Earl of Arran.[16] But apart from its later impact on the careers of a few hopeful young men, what did this victory mean for Oxford biblical

---

12. See n. 2 above.

13. Hamilton, *Hertford College*, 85–87.

14. Robert Lowth, *Isaiah: A New Translation* (London, 1778); cf. David Durell, *Critical Remarks on the Books of Job, Proverbs, Psalms, Ecclesiastes, and Canticles* (Oxford, 1772); Benjamin Blayney, *Jeremiah and Lamentations: A New Translation* (Oxford, 1784); idem, *Zechariah: A New Translation* (Oxford, 1797); William Newcome, *An Attempt Towards an Improved Version, a Metrical Arrangement, and an Explanation of the Twelve Minor Prophets* (Dublin, 1785); William Newcome, *An Attempt Towards an Improved Version, a Metrical Arrangement, and an Explanation of the Prophet Ezekiel* (Dublin, 1788). See also Lambeth Palace Library, London, Mss. 2580 (notes by Durell on biblical prophecy); 2577, 2579, 2581–88 (papers of Blayney); Bodl., uncatalogued manuscript of Durell's "[Critic]al Remarks on Passages in the Old Testament."

15. *The Gentleman's Magazine* 39 (1769): 517–19; "Diary of David Durell, 1765–8," entries for 12 June and 28 June 1766. I am grateful to the late Mrs D. V. Durell for giving me access to manuscripts in her possession. For Lowth's interest in the revision of the Bible and in the work of Durell and Blayney, see his *Isaiah: A New Translation* (2d ed.; London, 1779), lxix–lxxi; Bodl., Ms. Eng. Th. c. 94, ff. 18, 29–36; National Library of Scotland, Edinburgh, Ms. 25299, ff. 43–4; Scottish Catholic Archives, Edinburgh, Ms. BL 3/355/14, and especially Bodl., Ms. Kennicott c. 12, f. 92v (Lowth to Benjamin Kennicott, May 23, 1758).

16. For Arran's support of Comings, see *The London Evening Post*, 3584 (29–31 May 1753).

criticism in 1753? Arran (1671–1758), was the younger brother of the second Duke of Ormonde and had been elected Chancellor of the University on his brother's flight to exile at the Jacobite court in 1715.[17] Fowler Comings (b. 1728) was himself a Hebrew scholar and former tutor at Hertford, but of a rather different bent from the young men who would find favour with Sharpe. In the early spring of 1753, Comings had quarrelled with Newton, who had just appointed him to a tutorship even though there was no obvious vacancy and urged him to take on undergraduates. On March 9, Newton had sent for Comings "and told him that he thought it would hurt his College, to have (what he call'd) an Hutchinsonian tutor in it..." To this, Comings asked "whether he had been represented...as a despiser of all human learning: a thing, he apprehended, not rarely, tho' very unjustly objected to in those gentlemen, who read Mr. *Hutchinson*'s writings." His defiance did him no good, for on March 24, Newton deprived him of his tutorship, saying that "he was resolv'd...that no Hutchinsonian shou'd be a tutor in his house." Comings left in a huff, convinced that Newton was in breach of his own statutes and complaining that

> If I have been charg'd with a contempt of human learning; the charge is false: I am, within proper bounds, daily pursuing it myself, and daily recommending it to others. If I have been represented as a sectary: the representation is false: I believe every article and every doctrine of the church of England; and I read the writings of Mr. *Hutchinson*, as I do the works of Dr. *Hammond*, Dr. *Whitby*, or any other learned commentator upon the sacred scriptures...

With the aid of the Duke of Beaufort, on May 26, Comings, then aged 24, persuaded Arran to nominate him to be Newton's successor as Principal.[18]

Later events in 1753 suggest that Comings was being more than a little disingenuous in what he said about his relations with Newton. On August 20, Comings advertised his freshly published *The Printed Hebrew Text of the Old Testament Vindicated*, stating that the printing had been finished much earlier in the summer "but were delay'd on Account of

17.   Ward, *Georgian Oxford*, 52–82; P. Langford, "Tories and Jacobites 1714–1751," and L. S. Sutherland, "Political Respectability 1751–1771," both in Sutherland and Mitchell, eds., *The History of the University of Oxford*, 5:99–127 and 129–61 respectively, at 103, 105, 113, 124, 144 especially.

18.   Bodl., Ms. Rawlinson J fol. 2, ff. 412–16; quotations from ff. 415–16, *The State of the Case between Dr. Newton Principal, and Mr Comings A.M. of Hertford College, Oxford* ([Oxford, 1753)]. Henry Hammond and Daniel Whitby were well-known commentators on the New Testament.

Business of some Importance to the Author, with which the World has been already somewhat acquainted."[19] Comings was replying to an essay by Benjamin Kennicott (1718–83), a Fellow of Exeter College, entitled *The State of the Printed Hebrew Text of the Old Testament Considered.* Kennicott's work included a dissertation on the later part of the twenty-third chapter of the second book of Samuel, and exemplified his conviction, which had been growing since 1748, "that our Hebrew Text had suffered from transcribers, at least as much as the copies of other ancient writings; and that there are now such corruptions in this sacred volume, as affect the Sense greatly in many instances."[20] The person who had initially suggested the study of this particular text, from which sprang Kennicott's subsequent project of collating the variants in the Hebrew manuscripts of the Old Testament that occupied him for the rest of his life, was Robert Lowth.[21] What then did Comings have to say about Kennicott's initial discoveries, made among the manuscripts of the Bodleian Library in Oxford, about the variability of the transmission of the Hebrew text of the Old Testament and the state of printed Hebrew Bibles? He was severe on "the Method which must, in the End, most effectually destroy the Evidence of the Scriptures" and its consequences which were "the giving to each Man a liberty of correcting the Sacred Text at Pleasure," leading it to "dwindle away into an human Composition." In conclusion, he turned on Kennicott's "wicked new-fangled

19. Advertisement bound into copies of [Fowler Comings], *The Printed Hebrew Text of the Old Testament Vindicated. An Answer to Mr. Kennicott's Dissertation* (Oxford, 1753).

20. Benjamin Kennicott, *The Ten Annual Accounts of the Collation of Hebrew Mss of the Old Testament* (Oxford, 1770), 7. Cf. idem, *The State of the Printed Hebrew Text of the Old Testament Considered* (Oxford, 1753), 7–18; a second part of this work was published in 1759. On Kennicott, see Bodl., Ms. Rawlinson J fol. 3, f. 372; William McKane, "Benjamin Kennicott: An Eighteenth-Century Researcher," *Journal of Theological Studies* n.s. 28 (1977): 445–63; David S. Katz, "The Chinese Jews and the Problem of Biblical Authority in Eighteenth- and Nineteenth-Century England," *English Historical Review* 105 (1990): 893–919; David B. Ruderman, *Jewish Enlightenment in an English Key* (Princeton, N.J.: Princeton University Press, 2000), 23–56.

21. Kennicott, *The Ten Annual Accounts*, 7; cf. Lowth, *De sacra poesi Hebraeorum*, 168–69; idem, *A Sermon Preached at the Visitation of the Honourable and Right Reverend Lord Bishop of Durham* (London, 1758), 16. Kennicott, *The State of the Printed Hebrew Text*, 2:ix, indicates that Hunt had also suggested him as a possible collator of the Hebrew manuscripts in the Bodleian Library in 1757. See also Bodl., Ms. Kennicott c. 12, ff. 89–90. Lowth's later influence on Kennicott is apparent in, for example, Bodl., Ms. Eng. Lett. c. 573, ff. 113–16; Lambeth Palace Library, London, Ms. 1921; Hall, ed., *Sermons, and Other Remains*, 32.

Method," which, he argued, would replace the doctrines of God with those of men.[22]

It is tempting to read Comings' comments as the unlearned response of a precritical biblical literalist. However, to do so would not be entirely fair. There is no doubting against whom Comings was writing. In the events at Hertford, he had attempted to play the card of high Tory patronage, which had been in the ascendant at Oxford since the University election in 1751, in order to win a plum job for himself and secure revenge on the shade of Richard Newton, the man who had earlier misled and abused him. Comings' opponent, Kennicott, was a Whig in politics and behind him lurked stronger proponents of Whig policies within the University and the Church.[23] One of these was indeed Robert Lowth.[24]

Lowth's ecclesiastical preferment in the 1740s and early 1750s had come largely as a result of the efforts of the then Bishop of Winchester, Benjamin Hoadly, whose extreme Erastianism had long before made him the bête noire of even the most faint-hearted of High Churchmen.[25] Lowth's political patron, his surrogate brother from childhood, and the dedicatee of the newly published *De sacra poesi Hebraeorum*, was Henry Bilson-Legge, a major Hampshire landowner, MP and former client of Robert Walpole.[26] Legge had taken Lowth on embassy with him to Berlin in 1748 (perhaps introducing him to George II at Hanover) and may have had a hand in his appointment as tutor to the Cavendish

22. [Comings], *The Printed Hebrew Text of the Old Testament Vindicated*, 4, 129.

23. For clear evidence of Kennicott's politics, see Exeter College, Oxford, Ms. L.IV. 7, folders C and F.

24. Jonathan Lamb, *The Rhetoric of Suffering: Reading the Book of Job in the Eighteenth Century* (Oxford: Oxford University Press, 1995), 119, makes the extraordinary suggestion that Lowth was "an Oxford Tory" and even a Jacobite.

25. Bodl., Mss. Eng. Misc. c. 816, ff. 108–13; Eng. Misc. d. 1236/1–4. On Hoadly, see Norman Sykes, "Benjamin Hoadly, Bishop of Bangor," in *The Social and Political Ideas of Some English Thinkers of the Augustan Age* (ed. F. J. C. Hearnshaw; London: G. G. Harrap, 1928), 122–56; idem, *Church and State in England in the XVIIIth Century* (Cambridge: Cambridge University Press, 1934), 332–62; Ernest Gordon Rupp, *Religion in England 1688–1791* (Oxford: Clarendon, 1986), 88–101; William Gibson, *Enlightenment Prelate: Benjamin Hoadly, 1676–1761* (Cambridge: James Clarke, 2004).

26. For the close friendship between Lowth and Legge, see Nottingham University Library, Ms. Ne C (Newcastle [Clumber] Collection), 665/1–2; Lewis Walpole Library, Farmington, Connecticut, Ms. Sir Charles Hanbury Williams Papers 51–10909, f. 277. I am extremely grateful to P. J. Kulisheck for supplying me with these references and for providing additional information about Legge. See also Bodl., Ms. Eng. Misc. c. 816, f. 31r-v.

children on their Grand Tour in 1749.[27] He was one of the principal supporters of Lowth's later appointment in 1755 as chaplain to the Marquis of Hartington, Lord Lieutenant in Ireland. Lowth's tenure of this post precipitated his ascent of the pole of preferment within the Church of England.[28] But Lowth was not the only source of intellectual inspiration or political fellow-feeling in whom Comings' barbed attack on Kennicott might also have raised a smart.

A more serious target, and, at this stage, a more important political and still more significant intellectual figure, was Thomas Hunt (1696–1774). Hunt had been Laudian Professor of Arabic since 1738. He also became Regius Professor of Hebrew and a Canon of Christ Church in 1747. From as early as 1718, Hunt had served as a tutor at Hart Hall, having been appointed by Newton.[29] His first publications, a lecture, *De antiquitate, elegantia, utilitate, linguae arabicae* (Oxford, 1739) and *A Dissertation on Proverbs VII. 22, 23* (Oxford, 1743), had both been published under the seal of Hertford College, as testimony to the learning for which the new foundation would stand. From 1728, Hunt was chaplain to Thomas Parker (1666–1732), Earl of Macclesfield and former Lord Chancellor of England, who had used his ecclesiastical patronage prudently in the Whig interest.[30] In addition to teaching Hebrew to such men as Kennicott, Hunt had been tutor to the children of the second Earl of Macclesfield. The latter had been largely responsible for the change in the calendar in 1752 and was a leading patron of the Oxford astronomer, James Bradley.[31] If, as Comings alleged, Richard Newton's "knowledge in the Hebrew language was not sufficient to enable him to be a judge," then Hunt's qualifications for the quarrels of 1753 ought not to have been

27. Bodl., Mss. Eng. Misc. c. 816, f. 126v; Eng. Misc. c. 817, ff. 7–8, 41–47; University of Wales, Lampeter, Founder's Library, Ms. 30 (Accession number 30841), Robert Lowth to Philip Barton, April 16, 1750.

28. Bodl., Ms. Eng. Lett. c. 572, ff. 3–115.

29. Bodl., Ms. Rawlinson J fol. 3, ff. 326–30. I am grateful to Colin Wakefield for discussions and information about Hunt's career. See also [Daniel Prince], *A Catalogue of the Library of the Rev. Thomas Hunt, DD* (Oxford, 1775); Newton, *A Letter to the Revd. Dr Holmes*, 24.

30. Norman Sykes, *Edmund Gibson: Bishop of London* (London: Oxford University Press, 1926), 112–13. Both Hunt and Richard Newton maintained friendly relations with the prominent moderate dissenter, Philip Doddridge; see Geoffrey F. Nuttall, *Calendar of the Correspondence of Philip Doddridge DD (1702–1751)* (London: Her Majesty's Stationery Office, 1979), 190–91, 194, 219–20, 229, 243, 272, 293.

31. See Robert Poole, "'Give us our Eleven Days!': Calendar Reform in Eighteenth-Century England," *Past and Present* 149 (1995): 95–139.

in question.[32] At the conclusion of *De sacra poesi Hebraeorum*, Lowth
called on his listeners not to neglect the proper study of Hebrew and
pointed out to them that in this calling they had a leader, whose authority, example, teachings and assiduousness were at their service.[33] This
paragon was Hunt. Yet Hunt was pilloried by Tory Oxford. In November
1727, the antiquary and Jacobite sympathiser, Thomas Hearne, recounted
with glee the story of "Mrs Sarah Adkins, a large comely Laundress"
who "proved with child & was delivered of a Boy, the Father of w[hi]ch
is Mr. Thomas Hunt, M.A., a clergyman & a Tutor in Hart Hall, to whom
the said Sarah Adkins was a Laundress. After she was delivered, Mr.
Hunt (as is reported) married her, the least he could do."[34] Although
Hearne mocked the immorality and hypocrisy that Tories commonly
associated with Whig clerics, he conceded that "Mr. Hunt is a man well
versed in the Oriental Tongues, & was looked upon (before this Thing)
as a virtuous man, tho' I have heard of other sly Intriegues of his with
Girls."[35] The Hutchinsonians were less generous to Hunt's academic
achievements.[36]

Hunt's slim scholarly publications, based mostly on lectures delivered
in Oxford, testified to his commitment to seeing the Hebrew text of the
Old Testament in historical context. This meant, first, situating the text
within Eastern culture and, secondly, considering the linguistic changes
that had occurred over time in Hebrew, and that needed to be unpicked to
provide a proper lexicon for the comprehension of the Bible. In this
respect, Hunt rather than Lowth was the true inspiration for Kennicott's
later work, and it was indeed Hunt whose ideas and reading provided the
immediate background for Lowth's lectures on Hebrew poetry and then
for his later work on Isaiah. One example may suffice to demonstrate
this. In March 1754, Hunt had already encountered Charles-François

---

32. Bodl., Ms. Rawlinson J fol. 2, ff. 415–16.

33. Robert Lowth, *De sacra poesi Hebraeorum* (Oxford, 1753), 341–43.

34. *Remarks and Collections of Thomas Hearne* (ed. C. E. Doble et al.; 11 vols.;
Oxford: Oxford Historical Society, 1884–1918), 10:376. There is some uncertainty
over the truth of Hearne's allegations. Hunt's will mentions no children and, on
October 8, 1743, he was able to marry Hannah Hatrell. See National Archives,
London, PROB 11/1002; Bodl., Ms. Rawlinson Letters 96, f. 144; A.J. Tilson (ed.),
Newcastle-under-Lyme Parish Register (2 vols.; n.p., [1931–39]), 2:180.

35. *Remarks and Collections of Thomas Hearne*, 10:376.

36. Julius Bate, *Michah v. 2 and Mat. ii. 6 Reconciled; with some Remarks on
Dr. Hunt's Latin Oration at Oxford* (London, 1749); Bodl., Ms. Eng. Lett. d. 122, f.
67r (Benjamin Holloway to Nicholas Brett, January 12, 1751); Benjamin Holloway,
The Primaevity and Preeminence of the Sacred Hebrew (Oxford, 1754). Cf. Bodl.,
Ms. Rawlinson Letters 96, ff. 302–3.

Houbigant's *Prolegomena* and had also seen the first volumes of his translation and commentary on the Hebrew Bible.[37] He commented that

> tho' I am by no means a bigot to the absolute integrity of the printed Hebrew Copy, yet I think my great Predecessor's Rule a very good one, *Haud temerè solicitanda est recepta lectio*: a Rule, which I perceived Pere Houbigant often offended against... When I read his Prolegomena, I thought he had sometimes recourse to his Various Lections, where a truly skilful person would have easily made out the sense without that help.[38]

Hunt perceived Houbigant's usefulness, without doubt, but he also embodied what seems to us the careful conservatism of eighteenth-century English biblical criticism.

To his contemporaries, however, Hunt was anything but conservative. In his *Dissertation on Proverbs VII. 22, 23* (1743), Hunt had taken a text of Hebrew poetry, which he analysed much in the manner that Lowth would later make familiar. Verse 22 read, in the translation of the Authorised Version that Hunt used, "He goeth after her straightway, As an ox goeth to the slaughter, Or as a fool to the correction of the stocks."[39] In what appears to be a beautiful emendation (particularly given the device of Hertford College that was printed on the work's title-page), Hunt deployed the evidence of the Septuagint, the Chaldee Paraphrast, and of Syriac and Arabic texts, to read the word that the Authorised Version had translated "fool" (made up of the Hebrew consonants aleph, waw, yod, lamed) as "hart" (made up of the Hebrew consonants aleph, yod, yod, lamed), thus restoring a parallelism in the original poem. In 1743, Hunt did not set out his text typographically in the manner pioneered by Lowth, nevertheless he had clearly seen some of the ways in which an unpointed Hebrew text, if understood historically, could be

37. Charles-François Houbigant, *Prolegomena in scripturam sacram* (Paris, 1746); Houbigant, ed., *Biblia hebraica* (4 vols.; Paris, 1753). See also Mireille Hadas-Lebel, "Le P. Houbigant et la critique textuelle," in *Le siècle des Lumières et la Bible* (ed. Yvon Belaval and Dominique Bourel; Paris: Beauchesne, 1986), 103–12; Françoise Deconinck-Brossard, "England and France in the Eighteenth Century," in *Reading the Text: Biblical Criticism and Literary Theory* (ed. Stephen Prickett Oxford: Blackwell, 1991), 136–81. Manuscripts relating to Houbigant's version of the Bible may be found in the Archives de l'Oratoire, Paris, Mss. Fol. 10–14.

38. Bodl., Ms. Eng. Lett. d. 146, f. 91v; cf. ff. 74–75, 88–89, 93–94. Hunt was presumably referring to a rule of Edward Pococke that "one should not lightly disturb the received reading," cf. Pococke's comments in *A Commentary on the Prophecy of Micah* (Oxford, 1677), sig. *3r–4v, and in *A Commentary on the Prophecy of Hosea* (Oxford, 1685), sig. *4v.

39. Thomas Hunt, *A Dissertation on Proverbs VII. 22, 23: Being a Specimen of Critical Dissertations on the Proverbs of Solomon* (Oxford, 1743), 3–8.

structured. Not long afterwards, when Hunt prepared a second edition of his *Dissertation*, which was eventually published by Kennicott in 1775, he drew attention to the "Hemistichs" of Hebrew poetry, and referred to the way in which they had been set out in print by John Ernest Grabe in his edition of the Septuagint text, based on Codex Alexandrinus. This was again surely an influence on Lowth.[40]

This insight about the structure of Hebrew poetry led Lowth to the discoveries of *De sacra poesi Hebraeorum* and, together with Hunt's followers, Durell, Blayney and Newcome, he later applied it to the verse forms of prophecy. Similarly, Hunt's treatment of Job, in a brief discussion in the dedication to his *Dissertation*, was strongly reminiscent of the principles that Lowth would deploy in his own lecture on that book. Hunt discussed "the light that was continually darting in upon it from the windows of the *East*; and that not only with regard to particular words and phrases, but likewise to whole sentences and paragraphs."[41] He had at one stage intended a translation of all of Job and was convinced that it was "capable of receiving light from the *Arabic* and the other dialects."[42] Hunt was not completely original in this. His Cambridge colleague, Leonard Chappelow, had similar ideas about the provenance of Job and, like Lowth, was critical of attempts to demonstrate that the book was written in metre.[43] All three Englishmen also owed a debt to the ideas of the Dutch scholar, Albert Schultens.[44] Nevertheless, Hunt's work must

---

40.   Thomas Hunt, *Observations on Several Passages in the Book of Proverbs; with Two Sermons* (ed. Benjamin Kennicott; Oxford, 1775), iv–vi, 59–165; John Ernest Grabe, ed., *Septuaginta Interpretum* (4 vols.; Oxford, 1707–20), IV, sig. d1v– f2v. On Grabe, see George Every, "Dr. Grabe and his Manuscripts," *Journal of Theological Studies* n.s. 8 (1957): 280–92; Günther Thomann, "John Ernest Grabe (1666–1711): Lutheran Syncretist and Anglican Patristic Scholar," *Journal of Ecclesiastical History* 43 (1992): 414–27; Jean-Louis Quantin, "*Apocryphorum nimis studiosi?* Dodwell, Mill, Grabe et le problème du canon néo-testamentaire au tournant du XVIIe et du XVIIIe siècle," in *Apocryphité. Histoire d'un concept transversal aux religions du livre* (ed. Simon Claude Mimouni; Turnhout: Brepols, 2002), 285–306.
41.   Hunt, *A Dissertation on Proverbs VII. 22, 23*, vi; cf. idem, *Observations*, 7. Cf. Lowth, *De sacra poesi Hebreorum*, 309–19; Lambeth Palace Library, London, Ms. 2602, f. 1r.
42.   Hunt, *A Dissertation on Proverbs VII. 22, 23*, vi; cf. idem, *Observations*, 7.
43.   Leonard Chappelow, *A Commentary on the Book of Job* (2 vols.; Cambridge, 1752). Cf. Lowth, *De sacra poesi Hebraeorum*, 328–43; Lambeth Palace Library, London, Ms. 1721.
44.   Albert Schultens, *Origines hebraeae* (2 vols.; Franeker, 1724–38); Schultens, ed., *Liber Jobi* (2 vols.; Leiden, 1737). Cf. Chappelow, *Commentary on the Book of*

surely have been one of the influences on Lowth's startling treatment of Job as a historical, poetic and dramatic text, which marked the climax of his lectures on Hebrew poetry and precipitated a pamphlet war with William Warburton, the Bishop of Gloucester and the leading allegorical interpreter of Job.[45] Given his influence on Oxford criticism, it was no surprise that Hunt should welcome the intellectual coups delivered by his protégés. In February 1753, he wrote:

> I have just had a present of Mr Lowth's Poetry Lectures, to which are annexed his Confutation of B[isho]p Hare's Metre, and his Oration on our Oxford Benefactors; from the reading of all which I promise my self a great deal of Pleasure. Have you seen Mr. Kennicott's book? It has struck out a new field of sacred criticism, and is well worth your reading.[46]

In 1748, Hunt extended his earlier claims for the antiquity of Arabic and for its value in interpreting the Old Testament in a further lecture, *De usu dialectorum orientalium, ac praecipue Arabicae, in Hebraico codice interpretando*.

It was this text, and the influence that it had on Kennicott's work, that really inflamed the embittered and rejected Fowler Comings and his Hutchinsonian allies. Hunt's recourse to Arabic was the method that Comings scorned and that led him to ask: "What Doctrines, however damnable, will not this VAGUE, ANTICHRISTIAN Language be able to father upon the Word of the most High!"[47] Yet Comings' criticism of Kennicott, Hunt and Lowth was not simply a product of intellectual conservatism. The author of *The Printed Hebrew of the Old Testament Vindicated* was not ignorant of contemporary ideas in Hebrew grammar, nor indeed did he know nothing of other oriental languages. Richard Newton may have libelled Comings as a Hutchinsonian, as a result of his

---

Job, 1:i–iv; *De usu dialectorum orientalium, ac praecipue Arabicae, in Hebraico codice interpretando* (Oxford, 1748), 24; Lowth, *De sacra poesi Hebraeorum*, 315.

45. Lowth, *De sacra poesi Hebraeorum*, 309–43; [Robert Lowth], *A Letter to the Right Reverend Author of* The Divine Legation of Moses Demonstrated (Oxford, 1765) and 4th ed. (London, 1766); [John Towne (ed.)], *Remarks on Dr Lowth's Letter to the Bishop of Gloucester* (London, 1766); [J. Brown], *A Letter to the Rev. Dr. Lowth* (Newcastle-upon-Tyne, 1766); Bodl., Mss. Eng. Lett. c. 572, ff. 128–89; Eng. Lett. c. 574, ff. 74–89; Eng. Misc. c. 817, ff. 17d–e; British Library, London, Mss. Add. 4297, ff. 62–67; Add. 42560, ff. 145–54; National Library of Scotland, Edinburgh, Mss. 962, f. 159r–v; 1002, ff. 165–66; Bibliotheek der Universiteit, Leiden, Ms. Remonstrantsch Seminarium 45/10.

46. Bodl., Ms. Eng. Lett. d. 146, f. 37v.

47. [Comings], *The Printed Hebrew Text of the Old Testament Vindicated*, 96; see also the works cited in n. 36 above.

antagonism towards contemporary Oxford oriental scholarship and its practitioners. But Comings' book did not have the appearance of even the most careful and temperate of Hutchinsonian arguments, concentrating, as it did, on attacking the use of conjectural emendations in biblical exegesis, rather than on propounding an alternative system of reading Hebrew grammar and orthography.[48]

Hutchinson's followers, on the other hand, were prominent both in mid-eighteenth-century Oxford and among the critics of Hunt and his followers. Indeed Hunt's entire intellectual programme, like that of many of the better scholars of oriental literature of the time, was inimicable to Hutchinsonianism. In particular, it ridiculed Hutchinson's claim to have uncovered the true meaning of the Old Testament through a complete rejection of the orthography of the Masoretes and its substitution by a new structure of meanings for the consonantal roots of the Hebrew language. It similarly scorned Hutchinson's belief that his system of reading represented the only way to demonstrate the authority and eternity of the divine Trinity, revealed in the Old Testament as well as the New. Those who had an orthodox training in Hebrew, and particularly those who also knew something about other oriental languages, tended to regard Hutchinsonian scholarship as absurd.

For example, James Bate (1703–1775), parson of Deptford and the elder brother of Hutchinson's client and editor, Julius Bate (1711–1771), rector of Sutton, told Kennicott with typical sibling feeling that

> I being the elder Branch, and so—having a right to think for myself, can assure you, that Hutchinsonianism, does not run in the blood of the *whole* Family. For upon a carefull Examination of their Scheme, I found it to be, *in general*, an arrant Peice of Nonsense;—diametrically opposite to the real System of the World,—as well as to all the Rules of true Oriental Criticism.[49]

Hunt attacked the Hutchinsonians' "absurd conceits."[50] Hunt's correspondent, Gregory Sharpe (1713–1771), chaplain to Frederick, Prince of Wales, even characterized Hutchinson's attempt to underpin the doctrine of the Trinity through Old Testament references, which was one of the principal reasons for the popularity of his system with orthodox divines, as a "scheme of Idolatry."[51]

---

48. In his otherwise sensitive discussion of Kennicott and Lowth, Alun David is perhaps too ready to accept that Comings really was a Hutchinsonian: Alun Morris David, "Christopher Smart and the Hebrew Bible: Poetry and Biblical Criticism in England (1682–1771)" (Ph.D. diss., Cambridge University, 1994), 67–98 (85–86).
49. Bodl., Ms. Kennicott c. 12, f. 9r.
50. Bodl., Ms. Eng. Lett. d. 145, ff. 115–16.
51. Bodl., Ms. Eng. Lett. d. 145, f. 44v.

Most educated people, however, kept a more open mind than this, and with good reason. Hutchinsonian criticism of the use of vowel points in the Masoretic text of the Hebrew Bible represented an extreme version of the contemporary scholarly consensus that this version (or at least the received text of the Old Testament that embodied it) was indeed unreliable. That conviction was at least partly responsible for the project of collating all the extant manuscripts of the Hebrew Bible upon which Kennicott had just embarked.[52] It also helped to explain why Hunt, Lowth and others insisted on printing the unpointed Hebrew text as the basis for their own criticism. Hunt, in addition, encouraged the work of Gregory Sharpe, who developed critical theories of the origin of the Hebrew language and the manner of its vocalization that were based in part on the work of the seventeenth-century Oxford oriental scholar, Thomas Hyde.[53] George Horne, later Bishop of Norwich, but at the time sympathetic to Hutchinsonianism, dismissed the vowel points used in contemporary Hebrew Bibles in the following manner: "Dr. Hunt calls [the]m the impedimenta sacrarum literarum—Dr. Sharp will not undertake [th]e defence of [the]m. The [Septuagint] were without [th]em— [th]e Jews own [the]m made at Tiberias."[54] The dispute between the Oxonian Hebraists and Arabists and their Hutchinsonian contemporaries was not, therefore, an argument about the antiquity or authority of the Masoretic text. Both sides denied that the Masoretic text had any

52. The initial idea for this project occurred to Kennicott in 1751, he embarked in earnest on the collation in 1760; see Benjamin Kennicott, ed., *Vetus testamentum hebraicum cum variis lectionibus* (2 vols.; Oxford, 1776–80), vol. 2 ("Dissertatio generalis").

53. Gregory Sharpe, *Two Dissertations. I. Upon the Origin, Construction, Division, and Relation of Languages. II. Upon the Original Power of Letters; Wherein is Proved... that the Hebrew Ought to be Read without Points* (London, 1751); cf. Bodl., Ms. Eng. Lett. d. 145, ff. 8–9; Thomas Hyde, *Syntagma dissertationum* (ed. Gregory Sharpe; 2 vols.; Oxford, 1767). Hunt and Sharpe later fell out over this edition of Hyde. Although Lowth praised Sharpe, his use of conjectures based on Arabic was, however, perceived to be excessive; see James Merrick, *Annotations on the Psalms* (Reading, 1768) [a work to which both Lowth and Secker contributed], 313–33, and [Gregory Sharpe], *A Letter to the Right Reverend the Lord Bishop of Oxford, from the Master of the Temple. Containing Remarks upon some Strictures made by His Grace the Late Archbishop of Canterbury, in the Revd. Mr. Merrick's Annotations on the Psalms* (London, 1769).

54. Cambridge University Library, Ms. Add. 8134/B1, p. 109. Horne was probably referring to Thomas Sharp, Archdeacon of Northumberland, and author of *Two Dissertations concerning the Etymology and Scripture-Meaning of the Hebrew Words Elohim and Berith* (London, 1751), and of other attacks on Hutchinsonian divinity, rather than to Gregory Sharpe.

special status.[55] Nor, indeed, did the two parties disagree that the text of
the Bible had been altered while in the care of the Jews, in order to
obscure the coherence of the Old Testament with Christianity. Instead,
this quarrel focussed on questions of history, nature and scholarship.

The most important issue in the dispute related to the role that other
oriental languages, in particular Arabic, might play in reconstructing the
past of the Hebrew text. Following from this, debate focussed on the
function of historical criticism in recreating the living setting through
which that text could be understood. At stake were not just scholarly
practice but doctrinal rectitude and the future direction of the Church of
England. In particular, the findings of historical criticism might raise
questions about the doctrine of the Trinity and, consequently, about the
relationship between conforming Churchmen and dissenters. The controversy to which *De sacra poesi Hebraeorum* made a decisive contribution, by showing the power of contextual scholarship to recreate a
previously undreamed of past for the Bible, was certainly over politics as
well as erudition. That may explain why conservative Churchmen like
Comings, or, indeed, Thomas Randolph, could sound like Hutchinsonians during the heated debate of the early 1750s. Randolph was President
of Corpus Christi College, Oxford; a future Vice-Chancellor of the
University, and a former protégé of the late Archbishop of Canterbury,
John Potter. In his attack on Hunt, Kennicott and Lowth, published in
1755 as *Four Letters Concerning the Study of the Hebrew Scriptures*,
Randolph supported Hutchinson "whom he looks upon as a restorer of
true and valuable learning; one who seems to have done as much in
behalf of the *Hebrew* Scriptures, as *Erasmus*, and other learned men did
before him, in favour of the Greek."[56]

Beyond the narrow confines of Oxford and the quarrels over academic
advancement that were engendered there, what really mattered to divines
like Comings or Randolph was the contemporary state of the Church of
England. Its seminaries, the universities, were barometers for the pres-
sures that faced the Church as a whole. Shortly after Archbishop Potter's
death in 1747, the new primate, Thomas Herring (1693–1757), consulted
a number of leading Churchmen, including Thomas Secker.[57] One of the
main issues that faced the contemporary hierarchy was the problem of

55. See Ruderman, *Jewish Enlightenment in an English Key*, 57–88 (75). Some
Hutchinsonians were also able to praise several of Lowth's conclusions, see [Robert
Spearman], *Letters to a Friend Concerning the Septuagint Translation and the
Heathen Mythology* (Edinburgh, 1759), 27–28, 166.
56. [Thomas Randolph], *Four Letters Concerning the Study of the Hebrew
Scriptures* (London, 1755), sig. A2v, see also pp. 28–29.
57. Lambeth Palace Library, London, Ms. Secker Papers, vol. 2, ff. 158–82.

accommodating dissenters, which inevitably implied consideration of the issue of subscription to the Thirty-Nine Articles. Although this was not as violent a topic for debate in the Church during the late 1740s and early 1750s as it became during the 1760s and 1770s, when Lowth was much more closely involved in advising the ecclesiastical hierarchy, nevertheless discussions taking place at Cambridge about the alleged heterodoxy of Edmund Law and his disciples at Peterhouse made it a matter of current concern.[58] Closely linked to dissenting attitudes to the authority of the Church was what Herring described as "the want of a better translation" of the Bible than the Authorised Version.[59] At a time of Low Church and Whig political dominance through the ecclesiastical patronage of the Duke of Newcastle, conservative and High Church concern might easily be provoked by the scholarship of men such as Hunt, Kennicott and Lowth, whose achievements provided even cautious proponents of reform with evidence of the need for revision of the Authorised Version.[60] Comings commented "God...forbid!" that legislators should ever deliberate a new translation based on the discoveries and conjectures of Oxford oriental scholarship, which would lead to a text "corrupted in the Manner we have now seen."[61]

Hutchinsonian ideas provided a way out in such times. The heart of Hutchinson's doctrine had been the discovery of previously hidden references to the activity of Christ and the Holy Ghost and to their membership of the Godhead in the Hebrew Old Testament. Hutchinsonians such as Julius Bate and their sympathisers, in particular Benjamin Holloway (1691–1759), who was a client of the Duke of Marlborough, were first into the lists to attack Hunt. In 1749, Bate published *Michah v. 2 and Mat. ii. 6 Reconciled; with some Remarks on Dr. Hunt's Latin Oration at Oxford*, in which he turned on Hunt's account of the confusion of tongues.[62] In January 1751, Holloway promised to print a letter

58. B. W. Young, *Religion and Enlightenment in Eighteenth-Century England* (Oxford: Clarendon, 1998), 45–80; cf. John Stephens, "The London Ministers and Subscription, 1772–1779," *Enlightenment and Dissent* 1 (1982): 43–71.

59. Lambeth Palace Library, London, Ms. Secker Papers, vol. 2, f. 165; Neil W. Hitchin, "The Politics of English Bible Translation in Georgian Britain," *Transactions of the Royal Historical Society*, 6th series 9 (1999): 67–92.

60. Stephen Taylor, "'The Fac Totum in Ecclesiastic Affairs'? The Duke of Newcastle and the Crown's Ecclesiastical Patronage," *Albion* 24 (1992): 409–33; idem, "Whigs, Bishops and America: The Politics of Church Reform in Mid-Eighteenth-Century England," *The Historical Journal* 36 (1993): 331–56.

61. [Comings], *The Printed Hebrew Text of the Old Testament Vindicated*, 124.

62. See n. 36 above; cf. Hunt, *De usu dialectorum orientalium, ac praecipue Arabicae*, 49–52, where Hunt depended on work that he and Gregory Sharpe had been carrying out on Hyde's papers.

"on [th]e Primevity of [th]e Heb[rew] Tongue &c, in Ans[we]r to...Dr. Hunt &c.."[63] When this eventually appeared in 1754, having been held up by several more substantial publications in support of Hutchinsonian divinity from Holloway's pen, it included the remarkable and telling phrase that Arabic was "A *Language* contriv'd for *Unitarianism.*"[64] Holloway attacked "the Jumble" of Hunt's oratory and railed against those who denied Hutchinsonian typology.[65] Walter Hodges, Provost of Oriel and a former Vice-Chancellor of the University, asserted a typological reading of Job, linking the meaning of the Old Testament directly to Christ. He went on to defend Hutchinson's account of the relationship of Hebrew and Arabic and to portray Hunt as being "influenced by too common a passion, and weakness...a desire of exalting, and dignifying his subject, at the expence and prejudice of others, without duly attending to, or weighing the pernicious consequences that might follow."[66] With sentiments like these circulating in the University throughout the time when Lowth delivered his lectures, and coming to the fore in the months immediately before and after their publication, when even *The Gentleman's Magazine* commented on the disputes between the Hutchinsonians and Hunt and his circle, it is remarkable how distant the criticism in *De sacra poesi Hebraeorum* remains.[67]

63. Bodl., Ms. Eng. Lett. d. 122, ff. 66–67, at f. 67r. Holloway was particularly incensed at the use made of Houbigant's ideas by Oxford oriental scholars; cf. Benjamin Holloway, *Letter and Spirit, or Annotations upon the Holy Scriptures According to Both* (Oxford, 1753).

64. Holloway, *The Primaevity and Preeminence of the Sacred Hebrew*, p. xxii. Holloway's stated opponents appeared in print to be Kennicott and Samuel Shuckford, rather than Hunt. He had already targeted another ally of Hunt, George Costard, as well as Thomas Sharp, in *Marginal Animadversions on Mr. Costard's Two Late Dissertations on the Kesitah and the Hermai* (London, 1750), and *Remarks on Dr Sharp's Pieces on the Words Elohim and Berith* (Oxford, 1751).

65. Holloway, *The Primaevity and Preeminence of the Sacred Hebrew*, 67–88 (68).

66. Walter Hodges, *Elihu; Or an Enquiry into the Principal Scope and Design of the Book of Job* (London, 1750); Walter Hodges, *The Christian Plan Exhibited in the Interpretation of Elohim* (Oxford, 1752). The quotation comes from the enlarged, second edition of *The Christian Plan*, p. 213.

67. Further contributions to the debate from the Hutchinsonian side included George Horne, *A Fair, Candid, and Impartial State of the Case between Sir Isaac Newton and Mr. Hutchinson* (Oxford, 1753). For Horne's debt to Holloway and his comments on Hunt, as well as his later and more favourable reaction to Lowth, see Cambridge University Library, Mss. Add. 8134A/1; Add. 8134A/2, p. 90; Add. 8134B/1, pp. 22, 35–36, 109, 327–29. See also *The Gentleman's Magazine* 21 (1751): 317–18; 22 (1752), 168–69, 205–6, 259–61, 316–17, 254–57, 415–17, 463–64, 521, 548–50; 23 (1753), 150, 155–57, 202, 223–24, 298, 410–11.

There is no doubting the general effect on the debate of Lowth's careful deployment of ancient canons of literary taste to recreate a lost world of Hebrew poetry and drama. Despite this, some readers found Lowth's unfamiliar description of the style and structure of Hebrew poetry hard to follow. As one of Kennicott's correspondents commented: "I read Lowth over and over again must my Ears perceive any Cadence in the Hebrew Verse...if they must I am ruined for ever for I cannot yet feel the least tinkling I only see one Verse is longer th[a]n the other..."[68] No-one could be under any illusion, however, about the incompatibility of Lowth's work with that of the Hutchinsonians. Yet Lowth was himself reluctant to consider the arguments of individual Hutchinsonian authors. His caution may have derived from the realization that nothing more was to be gained from further descent into controversy with authors who denied the foundations of the critical method that he and his scholarly colleagues adopted. As Hunt told Gregory Sharpe in June 1751,

> You can get no credit, and are sure to draw upon Your self a great deal of ill language, by meddling with such a wrong-headed set of men. Their absurd conceits, if there be any such thing as true philosophy, or serious regard to the propriety & dignity of the sacred language left, must, in spite of the outrageous zeal, with which they are obtruded on mankind, soon fall to the ground of their own Accord.[69]

Despite such private optimism, Hunt, Lowth and Kennicott knew that the defeat of Hutchinsonianism and the triumph of more orthodox Church-manship were far from being foregone conclusions. In August 1752, Tory or "Old Interest" candidates had been chosen to contest the Oxford-shire seats at the forthcoming elections. This represented an exception-ally early decision and created the circumstances in which a prolonged campaign would be fought, politicizing many local issues, including the affairs of Hertford College, that might otherwise have attracted rather less attention.[70] During 1753, political life in any case exploded as a result of the debate over the Pelham administration's short-lived Jewish Naturalization Act. This briefly removed the bar of the religious test that excluded Jews resident in Britain from citizenship and would have allowed them some participation in politics and public life. It was a meas-ure that seemed to many High Churchmen to presage the dismantling of those other tests, aimed at Dissenters and Roman Catholics, which

68. Bodl., Ms. Kennicott c. 12, f. 14r-v (Burrows to Kennicott, March 9, 1765).
69. Bodl., Ms. Eng. Lett. d. 145, ff. 115–16.
70. Robert Poole, "Making Up for Lost Time," *History Today* 49, no. 12 (1999): 40–46; R. J. Robson, *The Oxfordshire Election of 1754* (London: Oxford University Press, 1949).

preserved the exclusive nature of the Anglican establishment. The political temperature was also raised by the debate in the first half of 1753
over Lord Hardwicke's Marriage Act, which seemed to threaten some
aspects of the ecclesiastical settlement, in particular the powers of the
Church courts and some of the rights and freedoms of the lesser clergy.[71]
The Oxford critics and scholars whose careers during the late 1740s and
early 1750s have been followed in this essay jumped in predictable ways
over these issues, often with serious effects for their future prospects.
Benjamin Holloway, for example, was so incensed by the support of the
Duke of Marlborough for the ministry that he voted against Marlborough's candidate in the Oxfordshire election of 1754, thus losing his
principal patron.[72] The furore over the "Jew Bill" provided the background for a decisive push by the "New Interest" in Oxford University
politics, and the consolidation of the intellectual and political authority of
Hunt and Kennicott. This was the setting for the reception of Lowth's
ideas in the wider world and part of the background to their favourable
political and intellectual reception. The political and intellectual manoeu-
vres of Fowler Comings and his allies were thus a feint in a larger
contest.

Robert Lowth married in December 1752 and may have spent much of
the following two years in the country. Certainly, he complained in
March 1755 that his "affairs seemed to be at a dead stand."[73] Yet in truth
those years saw the transformation of his intellectual as well as his personal standing, and formed the background for the political, clerical and
intellectual ascent that marked the remainder of his career. Events in
Oxford were a key to this and Lowth's friends, Thomas Hunt and, above
all, Benjamin Kennicott, could be found at the heart of the action.
Although it did not have any immediate effect on the internal politics of
the University, the Oxfordshire election of 1754 consolidated the political reputation of the "New Interest" and cemented the ties of its proponents with the ministry and with Secker, the future Archbishop of
Canterbury. Its consequences led their opponents to feel exposed to

71. See David Lemmings, "Marriage and the Law in the Eighteenth Century:
Hardwicke's Marriage Act of 1753," *The Historical Journal* 39 (1996): 339–60;
Leah Leneman, "The Scottish Case that Led to Harwicke's Marriage Act," *Law and
History Review* 17 (1999): 161–69; R. B. Outhwaite, *Clandestine Marriage in
England, 1500–1850* (London: Hambledon, 1995), 75–112.

72. Thomas W. Perry, *Public Opinion, Propaganda, and Politics in Eighteenth-
Century England* (Cambridge, Mass.: Harvard University Press, 1962).

73. Bodl., Mss. Eng. Misc. c. 816, f. 126v; Eng. Lett. c. 572, ff. 1–127, quotation
at ff. 9–10.

the charge of being disaffected with "their superiors and Governors."[74] The hotly contested 1754 election was eventually settled in April 1755 through scrutiny of the ballot in Parliament. This led to the election of Sir Edward Turner and his running mate, Thomas, Lord Parker, eldest son of the second Earl of Macclesfield, who had stood for the "New Interest." Naturally enough, Thomas Hunt supported his old pupil's ambitions throughout the campaign, as did Kennicott, who was instrumental in the lengthy propaganda war waged by Exeter College on behalf of Turner and Parker. During the vote itself, the Rector and Fellows of Exeter fought their battles with ballots as well as words. Using the College's direct access to Broad Street, where the poll was held, they ensured that voters for the "New Interest," borne along with the mob of their fellows in Turl Street, could escape the rival crowd of their opponents in the Broad and reach the booths.[75] Although the contest initially seemed to have brought a narrow victory to the "Old Interest," the propaganda battle that took place both before and after the poll turned the political tide in Oxford, where Kennicott recorded, *"the very streets... were pav'd with Jacobitism,"* and helped to justify the award of the election to the "New Interest" in a Parliament dominated by Whigs.[76] This political and rhetorical success vindicated Hunt and Kennicott much more efficiently than erudite argument. It reminded powerful patrons that there were Oxford scholars who were reliable men, worthy of promotion. Pre-eminent among these, as a result of the printing of *De sacra poesi Hebraeorum*, was Robert Lowth.

Lowth's future career derived significant benefit from the nexus of personal relationships that have been brought out in this consideration of Oxford erudition and intellectual politics in the years immediately before and after the publication of *De sacra poesi Hebraeorum*. With the support of the ministry, and with Legge's encouragement, his clerical career

74. Hodges, *The Christian Plan*, 2d ed., Advertisement. For the later disillusionment of Oxford Hutchinsonians with their intellectual forbears, see Derya Gürses, "Academic Hutchinsonians and their Quest for Relevance, 1734–1790," *History of European Ideas* 31 (2005): 408–27.

75. See Robson, *The Oxfordshire Election of 1754*; Ward, *Georgian Oxford*, 192–206; Sutherland, "Political Respectability 1751–1771," 129–42; Elaine Chalus, "The Rag Plot: The Politics of Influence in Oxford, 1754," in *Women and Urban Life in Eighteenth-Century England* (ed. Rosemary Sweet and Penelope Lane; Aldershot: Ashgate, 2003), 43–63; Guy Rowlands, "Scholarship and Sleaze: Exeter College and the Oxfordshire Election of 1754," *Exeter College Association Register* (1997): 58–69; Exeter College, Oxford, Mss. L.III.1; L.IV.7; David Durell to Thomas Durell, April 27, 1754 (unpublished correspondence, private collection).

76. Exeter College, Oxford, Ms. L.IV.7, folder C, number 68.

took off from October 1755. He moved first to a prebendal stall at
Durham and later to the sees of St David's and Oxford. Despite the
opprobrium generated by his very public quarrels with Warburton,
Lowth remained on close terms with Secker during the latter's primacy.
His scholarly career also flourished, in collaboration with the young men
whom Hunt had trained—Durell, Blayney, Newcome and above all
Kennicott, all of whom themselves found that their careers now
advanced at Oxford. The local context tells only part of the story, but
debate at Oxford in the late 1740s and early 1750s nevertheless provided
the arena in which Lowth's career was transformed.

ORIGINAL POETRY:
ROBERT LOWTH AND EIGHTEENTH-CENTURY POETICS

Anna Cullhed

1. *Introduction*

Robert Lowth's lectures from the 1740s on the sacred poetry of the Hebrews, printed as *De sacra poesi Hebraeorum* in 1753, are well known to biblical scholars, but not as familiar to literary scholars. With no intention of neglecting the importance of Lowth to biblical study, I wish to draw attention to two circumstances concerning the disciplinary identity of the lectures. Lowth was, in fact, Professor of Poetry, not Professor of Hebrew. Second, he lectured on Hebrew poetry only—not on the entire Old Testament, but exclusively on the poetical writings of the Hebrews.

The word "poetry" is crucial to my argument. Lowth's lectures could be described as primarily a poetics, a series of lectures on the nature of poetry, on criticism, on the division of poetry into genres, on poetical inspiration, and on similar subjects commonly discussed in poetical theory ever since its Aristotelian and Horatian beginnings. With this focus, the tradition of poetics becomes the principal point of comparison. Lowth's contribution in *De sacra poesi Hebraeorum* is in no way diminished by this context. Read as a series of lectures on poetics, it is seminal in its definition of poetry as a passionate expression of emotions, primarily religious emotions. His careful analysis of Hebrew poetry as an expression formed by a specific cultural setting shook the monolithic standard of taste, with its basis in Greek and Roman poetry. Furthermore, Lowth's importance to the history of poetics is not merely a construction in hindsight. In the second half of the eighteenth century, Lowth's lectures were appreciated in German poetics and constituted a standard reference in handbooks and encyclopaedias of poetics and the fine arts. They highlighted lyric poetry as the most passionate genre. The present study develops along these two lines of argument: first, I propose a reassessment of Lowth's lectures within the context of eighteenth-century poetics, and second, I emphasize their bearing on late eighteenth-century German poetics.

2. *Parallelism, Rhetoric, and Poetics*

Lowth's fame rests first of all on one discovery in biblical criticism: he is the father of parallelism. Parallelism designates a way of organizing poetry in sections of two lines, where the second line echoes the first according to different patterns of similarity, variation or even contrast. Lowth himself distinguishes between three major kinds of parallelism.[1] Although Lowth had precursors, the concept of parallelism became generally accepted as a main stylistic feature of Hebrew poetry through his lectures. However, as James L. Kugel is keen to point out, the parallelism functions as the evidence for a lost metrical system.[2] It is not the parallelism as such, but its function as an implicit proof of a forgotten system of Hebrew verse that makes it important for Lowth. Without it, he could not have decided so emphatically on the distinction between poetry and prose in the Old Testament.

It is obvious that Lowth's use of parallelism is crucial for our understanding of his lectures as a poetics. With help of this stylistic trait, Lowth divides the Old Testament texts into two categories: poetical texts, which are discussed in *De sacra poesi Hebraeorum*, and non-poetical texts, which are excluded from the discussion because of their prose form. Lowth thus follows eighteenth-century practice and separates poetics from rhetoric. Writings in verse belonged to the realm of poetics, while prose was discussed in terms of rhetoric.[3]

In a recent study, Scott Harshbarger discusses Lowth's lectures in connection with oral romantic rhetoric.[4] It is difficult to support the notion

---

1. Namely, the synonymous, the antithetic and the synthetic parallelism. Robert Lowth, *Lectures on the Sacred Poetry of the Hebrews* (trans. G. Gregory; 4th ed.; London, 1839), 205–14. Stephen Prickett counts eight different kinds of parallelism. Stephen Prickett, *Words and* The Word; see *Language, Poetics and Biblical Interpretation* (Cambridge: Cambridge University Press, 1986), 110.

2. James L. Kugel, *The Idea of Biblical Poetry: Parallelism and Its History* (New Haven: Yale University Press, 1981), 74.

3. On the discussion on the difference between verse and prose, poetics and rhetoric, see Lars Gustafsson, *Romanens väg till poesin: En linje i klassicistisk, romantisk och postromantisk romanteori* (Acta Universitatis Upsaliensis: Historia litterarum 23; Uppsala, 2002), 37–66.

4. Scott Harshbarger, "Robert Lowth's *Sacred Hebrew Poetry* and the Oral Dimension of Romantic Rhetoric," in *Rhetorical Traditions and British Romantic*

that Lowth's lectures should be interpreted as a rhetorical theory. In the eighteenth century, poetics and rhetoric were seen as acquainted disciplines—often described as brother and sister, but sometimes as stepsisters. According to Lars Gustafsson's historical outline, two lines of thought were present in the rhetorical and poetological tradition.[5] The relation between poetry and prose could be described in Aristotelian terms. To Aristotle, it was not the criterion of verse but the ontological status as a representation of the possible that defined poetry in contrast to the rhetorical genres. The Ciceronian tradition, on the other hand, understood rhetoric and poetics as two forms of eloquence, intimately connected, but separated by the formal aspect. Poetics of the eighteenth century turned to the origin of poetry in search of its nature, and Gustafsson mentions Lowth's lectures as an example of the "primitive" tendency that defined poetry as essentially different from prose. It is reasonable to conclude that Lowth's discussion of Hebrew poetry rather accentuated the differences between the forms of expression, and that the lectures belong to the domain of poetics.

Harshbarger argues that Lowth's lectures form an important stepping stone en route to a romantic rhetorical theory, "an oral rhetorical countercurrent."[6] On many points I agree with Harshbarger's interpretation of Lowth, but the insistence on rhetoric as the primary context leads to an unhistorical conclusion. Certainly, poetics and rhetoric share many conceptual tools for stylistic analysis, and they both thrive on and challenge a classical tradition from ancient Greece and Rome, but it is still important to recognize the differences between eloquence and poetry, as they were understood in the eighteenth century.

Rhetoric remained a premeditated occupation, a theory of how to convince an audience either as an orator or in writing. Poetry certainly performed the office of persuasion in the classical tradition of poetics, but tended to exceed this function. Poetry could also be defined by other qualities, which did not primarily focus on the verse–prose distinction. In the discussion from the Renaissance to the eighteenth century, a whole set of criteria were available. Poetry was characterized as fiction, as imitation, or as displaying a figurative and daring language.[7] In eighteenth-century poetics, poetry held several offices and made alliances with disciplines other than the purely linguistic. Poetry showed affinity with

Literature (ed. Don H. Bialostosky and Lawrence D. Needham; Bloomington: Indiana University Press, 1995), 199–214.

5. The following account refers to Gustafsson, *Romanens väg till poesin*, 37–60.
6. Harshbarger, "Robert Lowth's *Sacred Hebrew Poetry*," 200.
7. Gustafsson, *Romanens väg till poesin*, 54–58.

music, it turned into the mother tongue of mankind or even into the voice of God.

Lowth makes the distinction between poetry and eloquence quite clear in his first lecture, in a passage on the lyric poetry of the Hebrews. He compares a ballad, or a convivial song, to the speeches by the "Tyrannicides" after Caesar's death, and argues that "one stanza of this simple ballad of Hermodius would have been more effectual than all the Philippics of Cicero."[8] Harshbarger quotes this section and concludes as follows: "In posing a 'simple ballad' against 'all the Philippics of Cicero' Lowth brings head to head the two competing rhetorics deeply embedded in the history of Western discourse, leaving little doubt as to which, in the long run, is more socially powerful."[9] Far from contrasting "the two competing rhetorics," Lowth distinguishes the power of poetry, that is, the ballad, from rhetoric, even though performed by one of the main authorities, Cicero. The poem is superior, especially since it belongs to the most passionate genre, lyric poetry.

Lowth builds the definition of poetry, as a contrast to rhetoric, by giving special prominence to the lyric genre, since it constitutes the most passionate of all poetical kinds. So far, his discussion draws on the examples of classical antiquity:

> The amazing power of Lyric poetry, in directing the passions, in forming the manners, in maintaining civil life, and particularly in exciting and cherishing that generous elevation of sentiment on which the very existence of public virtue seems to depend, will be sufficiently apparent by only contemplating those monuments of genius which Greece has bequeathed to posterity.[10]

In Lowth's defence of poetry, lyric poetry is appreciated for its ability to affect the audience and encourage virtue with its passionate approach. In this sense, poetry, even lyric poetry, is persuasion in the same way as common speech. But Lowth's distinction between the ballad and the speech is a distinction between natural expressions of the passions and the appeal to reason—to Lowth it is a difference that can change the world.

In fact, Lowth comments on the neighbouring disciplines on several occasions. In the fourth lecture, he criticizes grammarians for not distinguishing "between poetical and common language."[11] Further on, he offers the following characteristic of rhetoric: "It would be a no less

8. Lowth, *Lectures on the Sacred Poetry*, 13.
9. Harshbarger, "Robert Lowth's *Sacred Hebrew Poetry*," 207–8.
10. Lowth, *Lectures on the Sacred Poetry*, 10.
11. Ibid., 37–38.

indolent and trifling occupation to post through all those forms of tropes and figures which the teachers of rhetoric have pompously (not to say uselessly) heaped together."[12] Lowth's purpose is to analyse "the peculiar marks and characters of the Hebrew poetry," and not to conceive a grammar of Hebrew as a language or to collect tropes that could be found in any kind of text.[13] In the fourteenth lecture, Lowth continues with his characterization of rhetoricians as "pompous," this time criticizing them for attributing that to art, "which above all things is due to nature alone."[14] According to Lowth, the passions speak poetically, and the specific kind of expression—rich in imagery and vehemence—is the direct result of the emotional agitation. In this way, Lowth seems anxious to place poetics closer to eighteenth-century philosophy and psychology than to rhetoric, which is perceived as a technical science, scrupulously collecting isolated stylistic traits.

Harshbarger is well aware of Lowth's rather acid comments on rhetoric and rhetoricians, but he interprets them as criticism from within the discipline.[15] He observes that Lowth depends on the terminology of classical rhetoric but puts special emphasis on Lowth's recourse to the oral aspects of Hebrew poetry. To Harshbarger, this is the key that opens the door to romantic rhetoric.[16] I suggest that the strong interest in "original" or "primitive" poetry in the eighteenth century should be understood in the context of the discipline of poetics. The oral features of this admired kind of poetry are in many eighteenth-century sources connected with music and dance, and not primarily with rhetoric. The oral aspect is merely regarded as a historical fact, together with features such as the standard subjects of "original" poetry: praise of the gods and heroes, expressions of gratitude, and so forth.[17] The mnemotechnic quality of oral poetry is commonly mentioned, but the arguments for the superiority of "original" poetry are generally based on its emotional warmth and authenticity, far from the cold deliberation of civilized mankind. The fact that original poetry is oral does not play a major part in the arguments of eighteenth-century poetics.

12. Ibid., 38.

13. Ibid., 38.

14. Ibid., 150. See also his comments (p. 155) on the "officious grammarian": "for this is a very diligent race of beings, and sometimes more than sufficiently exact and scrupulous."

15. Harshbarger, "Robert Lowth's *Sacred Hebrew Poetry*," 202.

16. Ibid., 205–9.

17. Anna Cullhed, *The Language of Passion: The Order of Poetics and the Construction of a Lyric Genre* (Frankfurt am Main: Peter Lang, 2002; Ph.D. diss., Uppsala, 2001), 285.

As Harshbarger points out, Lowth certainly does comment on stylistic traits in Hebrew poetry, but first of all he insists on a broad "cultural" interpretation of Hebrew poetry, in contrast to many of his predecessors. To understand the imagery and the expressions of the Hebrews, we have to study their culture, their beliefs, and their every-day conditions, according to Lowth. But this is not enough, and he continues: "we must even investigate their inmost sentiments, the manner and connexion of their thoughts; in one word, we must see all things with their eyes, estimate all things by their opinions; we must endeavour as much as possible to read Hebrew as the Hebrews would have read it."[18] In fact, Lowth introduces an extreme relativism in terms of poetical values by this statement, which is remarkable also within the context of classical poetics. The Bible had previously been compared with a standard based on classical Greek and Roman poetry, and consequently been criticized for "obscurity," for its strange figurative language and so forth.[19] Hebrew poetry did not conform to the traditional levels of style, according to which "high" subjects should be represented in an elevated language. That the Holy Scripture showed such lack of a *decorum* was a stumbling block to criticism. The historical argument, posed by Lowth, made it possible to recognize the sublimity of Hebrew poetry even in the perceived clash between the divine truths and the poetical imagery of every-day life.[20] In the eighteenth century, the stylistic range was broadened and the qualities of various allegedly "primitive" kinds of literature were recognized. Biblical poetry was happily mentioned along with "original" poetry from all parts of the world—Peru, China, Arabia, and poetry from the ancient Celtic and Germanic tribes.[21] The classical standard was not relinquished, but extended with "original" poetry which was said to display qualities like sublimity, emotional authenticity, and the freshness of expression peculiar to primeval man.

Lowth's contribution to poetics lies foremost in two, seemingly contradictory, lines of thought. First, his consistent sensitivity to cultural circumstances in the interpretation of Hebrew poetry allows for an

---

18. Lowth, *Lectures on the Sacred Poetry*, 56.

19. See Rolf P. Lessenich, *Dichtungsgeschmack und althebräische Bibelpoesie im 18. Jahrhundert: Zur Geschichte der englischen Literaturkritik* (Köln: Böhlau, 1967), passim.

20. David B. Morris, *The Religious Sublime: Christian Poetry and Critical Tradition in 18th-Century England* (Lexington: University Press of Kentucky, 1972), 163.

21. See Lessenich, *Dichtungsgeschmack und althebräische Bibelpoesie*, 233, also Cullhed, *The Language of Passion*, 271.

appreciation of formerly despised stylistic traits. Second, his transformation of Old Testament poetry from a special case to the foundation for a general definition of poetry is seminal since it accentuates the emotional quality of poetry and clears the road for an appreciation of the lyric genre. Hebrew poetry is "original" in terms of age, and in the sense that it performs the "original" function of poetry in a religious context. The cultural reading leads to relativism in terms of style, but the focus on passionate, especially religious, poetry brings together poems from different stylistic schools into a literary canon, based on the quality of expression. And the primary emotional expression of poetry is the praise of God, according to Lowth.

3. *The Structure of the Lectures*

From G. Gregory, the translator of *De sacra poesi Hebraeorum* into English, we know that Lowth had very little time to prepare his lectures. He was appointed Professor of Poetry less than three weeks before he addressed his audience for the first time.[22] Even though the first lecture is framed by conventional expressions of humility and of a certain hesitation concerning the future plan for the lectures, it contains essential definitions of great consequence for the whole series of lectures. As Stephen Prickett writes, the introductory lecture does not suggest "some of his most epoch-making conclusions," but it entails a complete definition of poetry and poses sacred poetry as the oldest as well as the most admirable and commendable kind of poetry.[23] The first two introductory lectures support the idea that Lowth's lectures are conceived as a series of lectures on poetics, since they are faithful to the conventions within the discipline, formed by a long tradition since the days of Aristotle.

The first lecture, "Of the Uses and Design of Poetry," is habitual in terms of structure, when compared to other lectures on poetics. It contains a definition of the subject matter, poetry, in essence and in relation to other disciplines, its purpose, its subdivision into different poetical genres, and ends with arguing specifically for the study of sacred poetry.[24]

Lowth begins by asserting the significance of poetry in relation to the other arts and sciences studied at the University of Oxford: "For, can there be any thing of more real importance to literature itself, can any

22. See Gregory's note in Lowth, *Lectures on the Sacred Poetry*, 1.
23. Prickett, *Words and* The Word, 105.
24. On the structure of handbooks and lectures in poetics, see, Cullhed, *The Language of Passion*, 28–40.

thing be more consistent with the ends for which this University was
founded, than that the art, of whose assistance every other art and profession has so greatly availed itself, should be assigned a place among the
rest?"[25] At least since the Renaissance, university professors began their
lectures by examining the location of their subject matter in relation to
the other arts and sciences.[26] Lowth further conforms to an ancient definition of poetry as an instrumental science, or even a universal science,
since it contributes to all other disciplines.[27] In this initial praise of poetry
as a subject of higher education, Lowth also indicates the more immediate results of training in poetry. The student shall learn to "discover and
relish those delicate touches of grace and elegance that lie beyond the
reach of vulgar apprehension." With the words "taste" and "judgment,"
Lowth points at useful skills and he concludes by once more confirming
"the alliance between Philosophy and the Muses."[28] Poetics had emphasized either the production of poetry or the judgment of poetry since
classical antiquity, with a stronger leaning toward the creative aspects in
the wake of romanticism.[29] Lowth's introductory lecture primarily
concentrates on the training of discerning readers and hints that the study
of poetry will open almost any door to them.

From this glorious prospect, Lowth performs one of the most fundamental duties of a true poetics, that of defining "the end and utility of
the poetic art."[30] Without mentioning Horace's *Ars poetica* as the source,
Lowth repeats one of the commonplaces of Western poetics: "Poetry is
commonly understood to have two objects in view, namely, advantage
and pleasure, or rather an union of both."[31] The general definition is
somewhat qualified, as utility becomes the "ultimate object," and pleasure "the means." In a standard comparison between poetry and philosophy, Lowth concludes the superiority of the former, since "the writings
of the poet are more useful than those of the philosopher, inasmuch as
they are more agreeable."[32] The conclusion is further supported by
exempla, Roman poets and philosophers such as Epicurus, Lucretius and

25. Lowth, *Lectures on the Sacred Poetry*, 3.
26. Cullhed, *The Language of Passion*, 30.
27. For further discussions on poetry as an instrumental or universal science, see
the references in ibid., 31.
28. Lowth, *Lectures on the Sacred Poetry*, 3.
29. Cullhed, *The Language of Passion*, 40; M. H. Abrams, *The Mirror and the
Lamp: Romantic Theory and the Critical Tradition* (repr.; Oxford: Oxford
University Press, 1971 [1953]), 3–29.
30. Lowth, *Lectures on the Sacred Poetry*, 4.
31. Ibid., 4.
32. Ibid., 4.

Virgil, and poetry is described in terms of yet another commonplace of poetics, the sugar-coated pill.[33] The doctor knows that the pill is beneficial, but its bitter taste must be made agreeable to the patient. In a similar way, a "bitter" message has to borrow the "sweetness" of poetry to gain its wholesome end.

Having defined poetry in general, Lowth turns to a subdivision of poetry into different genres. He begins with "heroic poetry," or the epic, with Homer as the most prominent example. The comparison between poetry and philosophy is extended with history, and since poetry "calls the passions to her aid," she is more successful than the competing forms of discourse.[34] Lowth's arguments on the qualities of poetry lean on a definition of poetics not only as a universal science in terms of a linguistic branch, but as part of moral philosophy.[35]

From the epic, Lowth continues to tragedy, described as "philosophy introduced upon the stage."[36] Aristotle's *Poetics* and the three great masters of Greek tragedy, Aeschylus, Sophocles and Euripides, are the major points of departure, defining the genre on a theoretical level and indicating a canon of tragedies worthy of imitation. However, it is to Shakespeare, who in the early eighteenth century had not yet gained footing in the canon of tragedy, Lowth offers the top position. Drama (or tragedy) should not only arouse passions, but "temper and regulate the passions," and the dramas of Shakespeare describe passions—jealousy is Lowth's example—"more satisfactorily...than in all the disputations of the schools of philosophy."[37]

Aristotle had provided poetics with a comparison between history and poetry. Because of its recourse not only to actual events, but to the imaginative level, poetry gained a higher level of truth, according to the Greek philosopher. Lowth echoes this argument since it has become part of the tradition of poetics. History, Lowth points out, "relates things as they really were, it traces events under the guidance of authority; it must exhibit what has happened, not what might or ought to have happened."[38] Poetry, on the other hand, treats subjects that are "infinite and universal."[39] With the help of Aristotle, and with further support from Bacon, Lowth argues for the advantages of poetry compared to history.

33. Ibid., 5–6. On poetry compared to a sugar-coated pill, see the references in Cullhed, *The Language of Passion*, 60.
34. Lowth, *Lectures on the Sacred Poetry*, 6–7.
35. Cullhed, *The Language of Passion*, 118–19.
36. Lowth, *Lectures on the Sacred Poetry*, 7.
37. Ibid., 8.
38. Ibid., 8.
39. Ibid., 8.

From the epic and tragedy, Lowth continues with a section on the ode.
As we have seen in the discussion on the relation between rhetoric and
poetics, and the example of the ballad compared to a Ciceronian speech,
Lowth puts great faith in the ode, or lyric poetry. Tragedy and epic were
traditionally defined as the highest genres, but in the eighteenth century,
the appreciation of the ode led to the formation of a lyric genre that was
raised to the same level as epic and drama.[40] The ode, Lowth writes,
"yields to none in force, ardour, and sometimes even in dignity and
solemnity," it is "a flash of lightning, which instantaneously bursts
forth."[41] Lyric poetry is described as the most passionate genre, a genre
with great power to affect an audience. Lowth's examples are, as usual,
Greek, and belong to a standard canon of lyric poets, established already
in antiquity: Pindar, Stesichorus and Alcaeus.[42]

Lowth discusses the elegy, and touches upon the usefulness even of
the "lighter kinds of poetry." The climax of the first lecture consists of its
concluding remarks on sacred poetry. Lowth has already established the
importance of poetry, which "must be allowed to stand eminent among
the other liberal arts," but sacred poetry reaches even higher: "But, after
all, we shall think more humbly of poetry than it deserves, unless we
direct our attention to that quarter where its importance is most emi-
nently conspicuous; unless we contemplate it as employed on sacred
subjects, and in subservience to religion."[43] To Lowth, this is "the original office and destination of poetry," and the best example of this "natural
splendour" is found in Hebrew poetry.[44] As we know, Lowth had based
his previous remarks on the nature of poetry and the different genres on
examples from Greek and Roman poetry, the models of antiquity that
had formed poetical ideals ever since. At this point, Lowth not only
observes that Hebrew poetry is older than Greek poetry; it also outshines
it in terms of sublimity.[45] In this praise of the poetry from the Old Testament, Lowth emphasizes qualities that make Hebrew poetry the model
for all kinds of poetry. It is an "original" poetry in the sense that it displays authentic emotions, it is "animated by that inspiration, which, on
other occasions, is spoken of without being felt," and it displays stylistic

40. Cullhed, *The Language of Passion*, passim.
41. Lowth, *Lectures on the Sacred Poetry*, 10.
42. Ibid., 10–11. See also Anna Cullhed, "Nio greker, en herdinna och Goethe:
Om lyrikens kanon" [Nine Greeks, a shepherdess, and Goethe: On the Lyrical
Canon], *Tidskrift för litteraturvetenskap* (issue 3 for 2001): 3–15 (5), and *The
Language of Passion*, 217–33.
43. Lowth, *Lectures on the Sacred Poetry*, 17–18.
44. Ibid., 18.
45. Ibid., 18.

features caused by its passionate nature, such as interruptions and excla-mations.[46]

The second lecture, "The design and arrangement of these lectures," addresses a more delicate question, that of whether sacred poetry can be subjected to the rules of criticism. Lowth's answer is in the affirmative, even though the poems of the Hebrews "boast a much higher origin, and are justly attributed to the inspiration of the Holy Spirit."[47] To understand the immense power of this kind of poetry, it is to Lowth necessary to turn both to "nature" and "art": "if we wish to understand its power in excit-ing the human affections, we must have recourse to both; for we must consider what those affections are, and by what means they are to be excited."[48] Lowth makes an important statement on the nature of poetical theory in this section. Even though the poet does not consciously apply any rules—he could even be directly inspired by the Holy Spirit—it is possible to form a notion of poetry by close study of poetical practice. Writes Lowth: "Moreover, as in all other branches of science, so in poetry, art or theory consists in a certain knowledge derived from the careful observation of nature, and confirmed by practice and experi-ence."[49] Observations are "reduced…to an established order or method: whence it is evident, that art deduces its origin from the works of genius, not that genius has been formed or directed by art."[50] Poetry precedes poetics, in Lowth's lectures, and this is one of the reasons why even sacred poetry can be part of criticism.

Hebrew poetry holds its position as the oldest and most excellent kind of poetry in Lowth's lecture. While the first lecture formed a definition of poetry supported by excellent examples of poetry from classical Greece and Rome, the second lecture makes a comparison, which raises Hebrew poetry to an even higher level: "It would not be easy, indeed, to assign a reason, why the writings of Homer, of Pindar, and of Horace should engross our attention and monopolise our praise, while those of Moses, of David, and Isaiah, pass totally unregarded."[51] Not only are the lectures concerned with poetry, they discuss the kind of poetry which even sur-passes the classical canon. From Lowth's enumeration it seems reason-able to suggest that the three Hebrew names correspond directly to the

46. Ibid., 18.
47. Ibid., 22.
48. Ibid., 23.
49. Ibid., 23.
50. Ibid., 23. On a similar "reduction" of observations into principles in Charles Batteux' poetics from 1746, see Cullhed, *The Language of Passion*, 40–49.
51. Lowth, *Lectures on the Sacred Poetry*, 22.

Greek authors and that each poet represents a certain kind of poetry. Moses turns into an epic poet eclipsing Homer and the Psalms of David outshine the odes of Pindar as hymns of praise. The last pair, Isaiah and Horace, is not as easily joined together. Perhaps their similarity could be described as an insistent poetic diction of praise and blame directed toward a specific audience. In a later characterization of Isaiah, Lowth describes his merit as follows: "He is at once elegant and sublime, forcible and ornamented; he unites energy with copiousness, and dignity with variety."[52] Further, the prophet is lauded for several qualities, combining majesty, propriety, beauty and clearness.[53] The features are in some respects similar to the ones ascribed to Horace in eighteenth-century poetics, especially the combination of propriety with elegance.[54] Isaiah's superiority to Horace is indisputable to Lowth.

Lowth is not without predecessors in the comparison between Greek and Hebrew poets. A definition of lyric poetry as praise of the gods puts the Psalms in a key position and suggests a kinship between David and Pindar. The parallel is evident in Elizabethan England and the most famous comparison between the two is found in Boileau's *L'Art poétique* (1674). In the eighteenth century, David and Pindar became incorporated in the canon of lyric poetry, and were appreciated as two individual poets of equal merit.[55]

Lowth is keen to point out that he reads his series of lectures as Professor of Poetry: "In other words, it is not my intention to expound to the student of theology the oracles of Divine truth, but to recommend to the notice of the youth who is addicted to the politer sciences, and studious of the elegancies of composition some of the first and choicest specimens of poetic taste."[56]

The second lecture ends with a brief outline of the entire series. The first part following the introductory lectures is devoted to Hebrew metre, followed by an analysis of poetic style, and finally a number of lectures discussing the different genres of Hebrew poetry.

As we have seen from the introduction, Lowth uses the poetry of Greece and Rome as a useful background to Hebrew poetry and his generic division of Old Testament poetry follows the norm of poetics to

---

52. Ibid., 228.
53. Ibid., 228.
54. Cullhed, *The Language of Passion*, 221.
55. Ibid., 288–89, on English poetics, see O. B. Hardison Jr., *The Enduring Monument: A Study of the Ideas of Praise in Renaissance Literary Theory and Practice* (Chapel Hill: University of North Carolina Press, 1962), 95–96.
56. Lowth, *Lectures on the Sacred Poetry*, 25.

a certain point. Hebrew poetry is fitted into the categories of prophetic poetry, elegiac poetry, didactic poetry, lyric poetry, hymn and dramatic poetry. Only one category, prophetic poetry, does not belong to the generic core of classical poetics. Lowth argues that the prophetic parts of the Old Testament are poetical, in the sense that they display the specific traits of Hebrew poetry, such as parallelism.

The point of comparison in traditional poetics is calculated to set off Hebrew poetry to an even greater advantage, but occasionally turns into a framework that cannot account for the poetry of the Old Testament. It is evident that Lowth encounters certain difficulties when trying to fit the book of Job into the box labelled drama. Certainly, he concludes that the Aristotelian definition of tragedy is in many ways alien to the poem of Job, but after considering the matter in three full lectures, he concludes that the book of Job nevertheless possesses "things in common with the perfect drama."[57]

With this rather detailed study of the two introductory lectures and of the general structure of the whole series I have shown that Lowth was well prepared to address his audience as Professor of Poetry. Interpreted within the context of eighteenth-century poetics, *De sacra poesi Hebraeorum* forms a mainstream example of instructional poetics. Of course, the choice of Hebrew poetry as the object of study is notable, but the manner of treating the subject is formed by a long tradition. Lowth's lectures display typical features of a poetics, in terms of structure and in many detailed definitions and arguments that have been commonplaces of poetics since Aristotle. For example, he positions his subject matter within the circle of sciences, he reflects on the method to form rules by observation of nature, he defines poetry in relation to utility and pleasure in a Horatian manner, refers to Aristotle's comparison between history and poetry to set off the advantages of poetry, and employs Greek and Roman poetry as the model for his generic subdivision of poetry and for establishing a canon within each genre. And it is against this weighty tradition that Lowth makes the poetry of the Hebrews stand out in unsurpassed splendour.

4. *Hebrew Poetry, Classicism, and Romanticism*

From the discussion on Lowth's initial statements in his lectures we are already familiar with some aspects of his definition of poetry, especially his emphasis on the passionate character of poetry. I have pointed out that Lowth's views are founded in traditional poetics, but little has been

57. Ibid., 379.

said on his position in the history of poetics in relation to the two major competing epochal labels of the late eighteenth century, classicism and romanticism. Harshbarger's notion of Lowth as a contributor to an oral romantic rhetoric has, so far, been commented on only in relation to the concepts of "oral" and "rhetoric." With reference to Abrams' *The Mirror and the Lamp*, Harshbarger observes that Lowth's lectures have been embraced by the definition of romantic poetics as "expressive," but prefers to interpret them as anthropological investigations of consequence to romantic rhetoric.[58]

Likewise, Prickett has studied the legacy of Lowth in England within the context of poetics, and traces the poetic ideals of Wordsworth and his generation back to Lowth.[59] Hugh Blair, the Edinburgh Professor of Rhetoric and Belles Lettres, stands as the most important link between them, since he included a summary of Lowth's *De sacra poesi Hebraeorum* in his own lectures from the 1750s, printed in 1783.[60] It is to Blair, Prickett writes, that Wordsworth owes much of his poetical manifesto in the *Lyrical Ballads*.[61]

To begin with, Prickett argues that Lowth's lectures, albeit indirectly, encouraged the tendency to diminish the difference between poetry and prose, as argued by Wordsworth.[62] Since Lowth remarked that a prose translation of Hebrew poetry retained most of the poetic quality of the original, Prickett takes it in evidence for a development that ignored differences between prose and verse, and defined poetry according to other criteria, such as its passionate qualities. In a later discussion on Gerard Manley Hopkins and the ideas of poetry in the mid-nineteenth century, Prickett returns to Lowth and biblical poetry: "For Hopkins the rediscovery of the Bible as 'poetry' did not mean the progressive obliteration of formal distinctions between verse and prose so much as a rediscovery of the *meaning* behind the traditional constructs."[63]

The second remark by Prickett is important, and I suggest that much of it is true also for the late eighteenth century. Lowth's distinction between poetry and prose declares that poetry is the natural way to express strong emotions, since the agitated mind functions in a special

58. Harshbarger, "Robert Lowth's *Sacred Hebrew Poetry*," 206–7; Abrams, *The Mirror and the Lamp*, 21–26, 76–78. Abrams draws a direct line from Lowth to Keble and Herder.
59. Prickett, *Words and* The Word, 41–45.
60. Hugh Blair, *Lectures on Rhetoric and Belles Lettres* (London, 1783), I–II.
61. Prickett, *Words and* The Word, 43.
62. Ibid., 43.
63. Ibid., 119.

way. The ensuing form is characterized by leaps, interruptions, meta-phorical language, boldness and so forth. Writes Lowth: "The language of the passions is totally different: the conceptions burst out into a turbid stream, expressive in a manner of the internal conflict; the more vehement break out in hasty confusion; they catch (without search or study) whatever is impetuous, vivid, or energetic."[64] It is quite obvious that this idea of poetry is not just a mechanical distinction between two linguistic forms, but a theory that relies on a specific understanding of the workings of the mind, and the relation between emotions and language.

Lowth claims that poetry stands apart from other "kinds of composition" and it follows that the fourth lecture, with the unpromising title "Of the parabolic or poetical style of the Hebrews," is not just a registration of tropes, but contains a general survey of the origin of poetry and its early history.[65] Style turns into a broad anthropological concept, connecting the linguistic expressions to the affections, to the primeval unity of poetry, song and dance, and finally to the functions of poetry in the early stages of society: "to depict the great, the beautiful, the becoming, the virtuous; to embellish and recommend the precepts of religion and virtue; to transmit to posterity excellent and sublime actions and sayings; to celebrate the works of the Deity, his beneficence, his wisdom; to record the memorials of the past, and the predictions of the future."[66]

The "primitive" line of argument, as suggested above, is combined with references to more up-to-date contributors to the philosophy of man, or "psychology," as we would say. With support from Hobbes and Locke, Lowth separates two major faculties, judgment and imagination, in the twelfth lecture, "Of the Comparison." While judgment discovers "in things which have in general a very strong resemblance, some partial disagreement," the second concept, imagination—which Lowth sometimes calls genius or fancy—"is entitled to the highest commendation, when in those objects which upon the whole have the least agreement, some striking similarity is traced out."[67] The connection of ideas, in terms of creating a novel imagery by an unexpected but pleasing simile, is defined as a basic trait of poetry in Lowth's lectures. This second reflection on a stylistic feature of poetry is founded in a philosophical tradition, to which Lowth had added other attractive discourses, such as the speculations on the origins of man and language.

---

64. Lowth, *Lectures on the Sacred Poetry*, 150.
65. Ibid., 16, 37–43.
66. Ibid., 40–41.
67. Ibid., 128.

The specific quality of poetry stands unquestioned in Lowth's lectures. His concession concerning the poetical aspects of a prose translation only confirms that Hebrew poetry relies on parallelism, and not on the versification of the Western tradition. It does not revoke the separation between verse and prose, poetry and rhetoric, it only points out that poetic diction takes different paths in different cultural settings, while the original office and function of poetry, and its emotional nature, remain constant.

The distinction between verse and prose (and the ensuing understanding of style) is not, in itself, a clue to designations such as classicism or romanticism. Far from necessarily being a mechanical principle of classification, the subdivision could suggest a new theory of poetry. However, the examples discussed above serve as a reminder of the difficulties in interpreting eighteenth-century poetics in terms of "old" and "new," of "classicism" and "romanticism."

To add a further example of this dilemma, it is obvious that Lowth's analysis of Hebrew poetry in many ways depends on the understanding of poetry as the means to a certain end, which would disqualify him from the rank of "romantic" in most histories of poetics. The poetics of *Wirkung* (effect) of classicism is generally contrasted to the poetics of *Schöpfung* (creation) of romanticism.[68] Still, this framework which poetics shares with rhetoric well into the eighteenth century, does not exclude an understanding of poetry as a primarily emotional category. On the contrary, the *pathology* shared by rhetoric and poetics offered a powerful foundation for persuasion, well-known to every poet or orator since antiquity.

As we have seen, Lowth tries to draw the line between theology and criticism already in his first lecture on Hebrew poetry. The understanding of the Old Testament not only as a concern for theology, but also for poetics, is also deemed important to the classicism–romanticism debate. Prickett summarizes some of Lowth's contributions, seminal to romanticism. "To Lowth," he writes, "we owe the rediscovery of the Bible as a work of literature within the context of ancient Hebrew life," and not primarily as "a timeless compendium of divinely inspired revelation."[69] Further on he qualifies the picture of Lowth as a "materialist" and as "one of the prime agents of secularization," in a careful analysis that brings out the complexity of Lowth's standpoints.[70] Prickett points out

68. See the references in Cullhed, *The Language of Passion*, 39–40.
69. Prickett, *Words and* The Word, 105.
70. Ibid., 111, with references to Abrams, *The Mirror and the Lamp*, and to Brian Hepworth, *Robert Lowth* (Boston: Twayne, 1978).

that "the Bible was still regarded by Lowth as having 'one common author'—in the person of the Holy Spirit."[71] It would seem that Lowth combines an aesthetic and historical view of Hebrew poetry with a tacit acceptance of the Bible as a sacred and inspired scripture. These views are commonly ascribed to romanticism, and to the legacy of classicism, respectively.

To some extent, it proves a difficult task to handle the question of verbal inspiration within a secular poetics.[72] On the one hand, Lowth wants to discuss Hebrew poetry in comparison to any other kind of poetry, but on the other hand, it is because of its dignity as revelation— Hebrew poetry is "justly attributed to the inspiration of the Holy Spirit"—that Old Testament poetry acquires the top position, compared to all other kinds.[73] The very definition of poetry ties it closely to the religious sphere. In Lowth's opinion, religion is not only the "original office and destination of poetry," but its very source.[74] And the origin of poetry tends to be equated with the essence of poetry. In this sense, the Holy Spirit stands as a guarantee for authenticity and true enthusiasm.

The link between poetry and religion in the form of enthusiasm can be traced back to Plato's dialogue, *Ion*. To Plato, the "divine madness" was far from desirable, since it transformed the poet into a mere plaything of the gods, an instrument who did not possess any real knowledge.[75] Enthusiasm retained much of its negative value, and was despised by the rationalist philosophers of the seventeenth century and the view prevailed into the eighteenth century.[76] Treatises on poetry displayed many attempts to separate "true" enthusiasm from "false" inspiration, thus maintaining the barrier between Hebrew poetry and secular poetry of a later date. However, the interest in original and authentic poetry in the eighteenth century led to two adjustments in poetic theory. First of all, enthusiasm became reassessed as a quality of poetry, and second, "divine" and "natural" forces tended to become interchangeable in eighteenth-century criticism.[77] The passionate and sublime style of original

71. Prickett, *Words and* The Word, 110–11.

72. For a summary of the discussion of biblical enthusiasm compared to poetical enthusiasm in general, see Lessenich, *Dichtungsgeschmack und althebräische Bibelpoesie*, 13–23.

73. Lowth, *Lectures on the Sacred Poetry*, 22.

74. Ibid., 18.

75. For a discussion on the Platonic source and the eighteenth-century discussion, see Cullhed, *The Language of Passion*, 286–89.

76. Lessenich, *Dichtungsgeschmack und althebräische Bibelpoesie*, 13–15.

77. Ibid., 21–23, 234.

poetry was defined as a direct result of enthusiasm, of the inspired poet, and the concepts were closely tied together.

In fact, Lowth discusses the interaction between the "Divine Spirit" and the poet in the sixteenth lecture, "Of Sublimity of Sentiment," and comments on the Platonic view of enthusiasm:

> I am indeed of opinion, that the Divine Spirit by no means takes such an entire possession of the mind of the prophet, as to subdue or extinguish the character and genius of the man; the natural powers of the mind are in general elevated and refined, they are neither eradicated nor totally obscured: and though the writings of Moses, of David, and of Isaiah, always bear the marks of a divine and celestial impulse, we may nevertheless plainly discover in them the particular characters of their respective authors.[78]

Lowth's argument indicates an emerging separation between two levels in the eighteenth-century discussion on enthusiasm and sublimity. While the content was still assigned to a divine origin, the poetical form was interpreted as man made.[79]

Lowth's position in the history of poetics is conceived in relation to an epochal shift between classicism and romanticism. Critics tend to identify single views as belonging to one or the other epoch. Depending on how these specific views are evaluated, Lowth is placed closer to one of the two opposite poles of classicism and romanticism. He is a "liberal classicist" according to Lessenich, and his views of the sublime reveal "revolutionary possibilities," according to Morris, while Joachim Dyck characterizes him as a "typical figure of transition."[80] Without doubt, closeness to romanticism suggests a higher esteem, in a historical framework implying progression.

Many of the changes within eighteenth-century poetics took place within a traditional framework. They can also be understood as conflicting impulses within a discipline that relied not on one, but on many theories of man, language and the universe. Poetics, as an instructional discipline, had in the eighteenth century incorporated not only the authorities of classical antiquity, but lectures and treatises from the Renaissance and onwards. Professors tended to approach their subject matter in an eclectical manner, at times combining incompatible points of departure

---

78. Lowth, *Lectures on the Sacred Poetry*, 168–69.

79. Cullhed, *The Language of Passion*, 288.

80. Lessenich, *Dichtungsgeschmack und althebräische Bibelpoesie*, 237; Morris, *The Religious Sublime*, 163; Joachim Dyck, *Athen und Jerusalem: Die Tradition der argumentativen Verknüpfung von Bibel und Poesie im 17. und 18. Jahrhundert* (Munich: Beck, 1977), 99.

in the same lecture. In this sense, innovations often took place by subtle displacements of emphasis, or by reinterpretations of an age-old terminology. The romantic generation, on the other hand, tended to view themselves as an avant-garde. The novelty of their contributions was at times exaggerated, perhaps just as much as the previous generations saw their eclectic contributions as part of the tradition.[81] A discipline with a long academic repute does not change easily. The basic Aristotelian outline of instructional poetics took certain elements for granted, even though the theoretical foundation had changed radically from within. These tensions were in no way dissolved in romantic poetics, but prevailed well into the nineteenth century, a fact which makes a clear-cut opposition between classicist and romantic poetics difficult to maintain.

In the eighteenth century, sensual theories stood at the centre of philosophy and the rising discipline of psychology. Poetical theory included an ancient *pathology* that was dislocated by the new trends. At the same time, poetics relied on certain calculable linguistic operations in order to attain certain effects, but this legacy tended to clash with the increasing interest in primitive, emotional and enthusiastic expressions, a trend that accounts for the sudden importance invested in the lyric genre.

Lowth's contribution to the history of poetics rests not least on his appraisal of Hebrew lyric poetry. All the major qualities of poetry—enthusiasm, naturalness, sublimity, emotional warmth, metaphorical language, boldness of expression—run together in this genre. Supported by the argument that the oldest poetical expressions of mankind were essentially lyrical, Lowth makes way for an important transformation of genre poetics. The ode had hitherto been recognized as a high genre in generic outlines based on three levels of style. Few poetics mentioned a lyric genre and different kinds of songs and short poems were scattered in the generic outlines in a first sorting according to stylistic level. When the emotional and original aspects of poetry were emphasized, these minor kinds were united in a separate genre. The lyric genre, which strived to take up a position alongside the core genres of epic and tragedy, turned into the most important genre in eighteenth-century poetics, recognized as the origin as well as the essence of poetry.[82]

5. *Lowth and the Lyrical Canon*

Lowth's impact on eighteenth-century poetics is not as recognized as his influence on biblical criticism. His name is mentioned in very general

---

81. Cullhed, *The Language of Passion*, 308–17.
82. Ibid., passim.

terms as a representative of historical criticism or "primitive" trends in eighteenth-century poetics. It is to Prickett we owe an exhaustive account of the legacy of Lowth in English criticism.[83] With the exception of Hugh Blair, the following discussion concerns how Lowth's theory of the Hebrew ode supports the construction of a lyric genre in German instructional poetics and comments on the standpoints of the early German romantics.[84]

If we turn to the poetics of the second half of the eighteenth century, it is but natural to begin with Hugh Blair and his *Lectures on Rhetoric and Belles Lettres*, printed in 1783, but delivered from the 1750s and onward. This is a rare example of a general poetics that includes a lecture exclusively on Hebrew poetry. Blair pays tribute to Lowth and elegantly summarizes the principal arguments of the *Praelectiones* into one single lecture. He shares Lowth's high appreciation of the original, passionate and sublime qualities of Hebrew poetry. Lowth's "cultural" interpretation of Hebrew poetry, the idea that we should read as if we were Hebrews of biblical times, is driven to a rather sad conclusion in Blair's lectures. While Lowth claimed that more information of the customs of the ancient Hebrews would inevitably add to our appreciation of their poetry, Blair mourns our lack of information—"and how much of this beauty must now be lost to us, through our imperfect acquaintance with many particulars of the Hebrew history, and Hebrew rites."[85] Neither of them seems to bear in mind the possibility that more knowledge could result in a negative verdict of Hebrew poetry, that better acquaintance with Hebrew culture could, in fact, put the poetry of the Bible in a less advantageous light.

If we turn to some of the most wide-spread poetics in Germany from the 1770s and the 1780s, Lowth's name was mentioned in a number of contexts. Lowth's recognition of a separate lyric genre had a decisive impact on lyric theory in Germany. The Hebrew ode, or lyric poetry, could boast of two essential qualities, that of being the most ancient kind of poetry known and that of being the most perfect model for modern poets. Lyric poetry of the Old Testament became the very origin, and at the same time, the very best example of the genre.

Johann Georg Sulzer published his encyclopaedia of the fine arts, the *Allgemeine Theorie der schönen Künste* between 1772 and 1774. His

83. Prickett, *Words and* The Word, esp. 104–23.

84. See also Cullhed, "Nio greker, en herdinna och Goethe," 7, 12–13; idem, *The Language of Passion*, 217–33 (230).

85. Blair, *Lectures on Rhetoric*, II, Lecture XLI, "The Poetry of the Hebrews," 390.

article on the ode directs the reader to Lowth's lectures on lyric poetry, lecture XXV to XXVIII. Sulzer describes the odes of the Hebrews as the most ancient, and at the same time the most perfect odes of all, in complete accordance with Lowth.[86] As Joachim Dyck points out, the appreciation of biblical poetry is connected to the concept of genius in the eighteenth century, and he quotes Sulzer's article *"Begeisterung,"* enthusiasm. To Sulzer, a poet in the state of enthusiasm expresses himself in the form of hymns, odes, or elegies—in short, in lyric poetry—and the Hebrew odes are confirmed as the most enthusiastic models for the lyric genre.[87]

In a similar way, Johann Joachim Eschenburg explicitly refers to Lowth's lectures on lyric poetry and highlights the odes of the Bible as the *"Muster,"* or model, for the kind of poetry in question.[88] With direct support from Lowth's lectures, the Hebrew odes became established as part of the lyrical canon. Their position remained stable until the end of eighteenth century. However, the fame of Hebrew lyric poetry came to a very decisive and sudden end in the poetics of the early romantics in Jena. In August Wilhelm Schlegel's lectures held in Jena in 1798–99 and in Berlin in 1801–3, the lyrical content of the Bible is completely disregarded in favour of Greek poetry, which is discussed at considerable length. The same omission of Hebrew poetry is evident in several of the poetics from around 1800, such as Schelling's *Philosophie der Kunst,* Friedrich Ast's *System der Kunstlehre* and Friedrich Bouterwek's *Aesthetik.*[89]

Why is Hebrew poetry, and in this case the Hebrew lyric, suddenly wiped out from the list of canonical lyric authors? One explanation could be the concentration on Greek poetry in early German romantic literary theory. Greece is not only the admired source of poetry, but the history of Greek poetry tends to constitute the perfect union between the historical

86. Johann Georg Sulzer, *Allgemeine Theorie der schönen Künste*, vols. 1–4 (Leipzig, 1792–94; repr. Hildesheim: Olms, 1994), here 3:548.
87. Dyck, *Athen und Jerusalem*, 123: "Dichter, die in diesem Zustand ihre Empfindungen äußern wollen, ergreifen die Leyer, und singen Hymnen, Oden oder Elegien. Nirgend sieht man alle diese Würkungen lebhafter, als in den Oden und Elegien der Propheten des jüdischen Volks"; Sulzer, *Allgemeine Theorie der schönen Künste*, 1:351.
88. Johann Joachim Eschenburg, *Entwurf einer Theorie und Literatur der schönen Wissenschaften* (Berlin, 1783; repr. Hildesheim: Olms, 1976), 110.
89. See, for example, Friedrich Wilhelm Joseph von Schelling, *Philosophie der Kunst* in *Sämmtliche Werke*, 1:V (ed. K. F. A. Schelling; Stuttgart, Augsburg, 1859), 353–736; Friedrich Ast, *System der Kunstlehre* (Leipzig, 1805); and Friedrich Bouterwek, *Aesthetik* (Leipzig, 1806).

and the theoretical level of early romantic poetics. There is simply no space left for predecessors, such as the Hebrews. The theoretical construction of the generic system is based on and proved by Greek poetry, according to the Schlegel brothers, Schelling and their supporters.

It is somewhat surprising that the same generation that made the study of Sanskrit and other Oriental languages a university discipline should be the very persons to exclude Hebrew poetry from the canon. However, the acknowledgment of the Hebrew odes was closely tied to a specific view of poetry, which hailed supposedly "primitive" expressions of a sublime character. This "primitivism" lasted for a few decades in the second half of the eighteenth century and could successfully draw on Lowth's investigations of Hebrew poetry. It would seem that the following generation—just as many other vanguard generations—decided on a negative verdict of all the favourites of the preceding era. Friedrich Schlegel is an exception from this complete silence on biblical poetry. In his lectures, *Geschichte der alten und neuen Literatur* from 1812, he comments on Hebrew poetry, and with great appreciation.[90] However, in Schlegel'w view, Hebrew poetry has lost its position as the origin and model for emotional poetry, and occupies a somewhat awkward position, squeezed in between Roman poetry and Indian poetry in the fourth lecture.

Schlegel begins his series of lectures with an outline of Greek poetry. The poetry of the Bible does not fit into his system derived from Greece, in spite of its historical precedence. The importance of Hebrew poetry lies, not least, in its influence for succeeding centuries, and this accounts for its position within the historical framework. To Schlegel, a true history of literature should incorporate "das göttliche," the divine.[91] The union between sacred and secular poetry is not complete, however. Further on, Schlegel qualifies his system of poetry and points out the differences between "poetry" (or "art") and "religion." The epic, the oldest genre, is completed in the highest genre, drama, according to Schlegel's general outline of the history of poetry, but the lyric genre, and especially the hymn, takes precedence within a religious context.[92]

90. Friedrich Schlegel, *Kritische Friedrich-Schlegel-Ausgabe*. Vol. 6, *Geschichte der alten und neuen Literatur* (Munich: Ferdinand Schöningh; Zurich: Thomas-Verlag, 1961). See Dyck, *Athen und Jerusalem*, 125–30, for an analysis of Schlegel's lectures as an epoch-making contribution to literary history.

91. Schlegel, *Geschichte der alten und neuen Literatur*, 103: "denn was wäre das für eine Literatur, für eine Erklärung und Geschichte des Worts und seiner Entfaltung in menschlicher Erkenntnis und Darstellung, von welcher nur das göttliche ausgeschlossen sein sollte?"

92. "Für die Poesie überhaupt ist hieraus einleuchtend, warum unter allen Gattungen, während die epische, historisch genommen, die erste und älteste, und

Two generic standards ensue from this remark, which still suggests a separation between the two realms. The lyric of the Bible fails to achieve the position it was given in late eighteenth-century poetics, and once more becomes a special case in the category of religious poetry. On other points, Schlegel's comments on Hebrew poetry show similarities to Lowth. He discusses parallelism as a stylistic trait of biblical poetry, and interprets it as a sign of an enthusiastic soul—without mentioning his predecessor—and he admires the passionate quality of Hebrew lyric poetry.[93]

The systematic grid had changed fundamentally in poetics after 1800, and the poetry of the Bible had been expelled from the general literary canon.[94] However, it is also evident that the interest in Oriental studies provided Hebrew poetry with a widened context and that the emerging literary history occasionally tried to find room for the poetry of the Old Testament. But students at the universities of Germany no longer heard lectures on lyric poetry which hailed the Psalms as the most perfect models of the genre. Their place had been taken back by the Greeks. Ironically, the historical argument that helped Lowth to turn biblical lyric into the essence of poetry, also undermined the notion of a poetical canon, valid for all times. The road from classicism to romanticism could perhaps be perceived as a roundabout, or a cul-de-sac. In a sense, Lowth's transitional poetics encouraged the obliteration of his own ideas.

Urquell aller andern ist, die dramatische aus der Standpunkte der Kunst als die letzte Stufe, Krone und Vollendung des Ganzen gilt, für die Religion doch die lyrische Gattung die höchste, die angemessenste und würdigste bleibt, wie in dieser Hinsicht selbst in der Poesie der heidnischen Völker die Hymnen die erste Stelle einnehmen" (Schlegel, *Geschichte der alten und neuen Literatur*, 110).

93. Ibid., 110–11.

94. See also G. W. F. Hegel, *Vorlesungen über die Ästhetik*, vol. 3 (Werke in Zwanzig Bänden 15; ed. Eva Moldenhauer and Karl Markus Richter; 1970; Frankfurt am Main: Suhrkamp, 1980), 452–53. Hegel mentions the "sublime Psalms" but does not grant them the same appreciation as we have seen in Lowth's lectures.

Robert Lowth and the
Idea of Biblical Tradition

Stephen Prickett

If we consult a record of historical etymology such as the *Oxford English Dictionary* we find that, at first sight, there has been remarkably little change in the meaning of the word "tradition" since Tertullian and the Church Fathers wrote of the *Traditio evangelica*—or *Catholica*. Thus we find the standard ecclesiastical definition, that of "bequeathing any Doctrine to posterity from age to age" more or less unaffected by its translation into English and the Reformation—and, indeed, of course, playing a significant part in the rhetoric of the post-1688 Anglican settlement. Whether the Church of Rome is viewed as that of the Antichrist, a corrupted and withered branch of the true vine, or merely a thriving but parallel stem, it is repeatedly emphasized that the Church of England, at any rate, is a legitimate historical descendent of the original Apostolic Church. Unlike those nonconformist Protestants who sought authority solely from the Bible, the inner light or even from direct divine inspiration, the idea of tradition lay at the very heart of the eighteenth-century Anglican claim to legitimacy and authority. A first reading of Lowth's *Sacred Poetry of the Hebrews* and, more significantly, his *New Translation of Isaiah*, would suggest that both supported this sense of partaking in an ongoing apostolic tradition reaching back to the early Church, and through that to the prophetic tradition of the Old Testament itself.

But if that word "tradition," and the concept it conveys, seems entirely familiar to the modern reader, there are other meanings of the word that may be less so. Consider, for instance, Watson's claim in 1601 that "A priest is made by the tradition of the Chalice, Patten and Host into his hands." We understand (we think) what is being said, but the context seems, shall we say, odd. There is, we may suspect, a technical or perhaps obsolete connotation to the word that is intruding. This suspicion is, of course, justified when we turn to the primary meaning of the English word, which is essentially legal, and concerns the conveyancing or "handing over" of something from one person or body to another. It reminds us, too, of the close historical connections between legal and ecclesiastical terminology both in English, and in the *lingua franca* of Latin before that.

Indeed, despite the New Testament distinctions between the "law" and the "spirit," the concepts of legal and religious traditions have always been closely tied, even if, like the poles of a magnet, they have usually represented opposite aspects of that historical transmission. Not least of the ties that bind these odd partners is a deeply ambiguous attitude to the past. Take the case of law. On the one hand, it seeks to claim an inherited body of wisdom—to embody stability, order and eternal values, such as truth, fair play and justice. The costumes and rituals of the courtroom are visual symbols of the history, continuity and dignity of its administration. Yet, on the other hand, at the same time, we are all aware that it is in fact in a continual process of change, by both case law and legislation, as it attempts (usually belatedly) to address new needs and new situations. Indeed, the concept of English common law *depends* not on its immutability, but on just such a process of continual modification and adaptation.

The case of the Church is strangely parallel. One the one hand, it has the strongest of all claims to be charged with an inherited body of unchanging wisdom and truth—that provided by divine revelation itself. On the other, it has continually found itself called to speak prophetically to the contemporary scene, to interpret the words of scripture to its own day, and to draw from them a meaning appropriate to very different cultural contexts. Reverence for the past has sometimes gone hand-in-hand with radical judgments on the present. Even where such radicalism was notably absent—and the Established Church in the 1740s was scarcely a hotbed of prophetic fervour—there was always a perceived gap between the world of the New Testament (let alone the Old) and the English Church of the period that needed some kind of explanation—and a great deal of religious apologetic, direct or more often oblique, was devoted to explaining the difference between the apparent words of scripture and the interpretations placed on them by later authorities. To give the most obvious example: since at least the time of Constantine, every established Church has found it necessary to gloss the Commandment "Thou shalt not kill" with some kind of releasing clause at least for times of war. As numerous commentators have pointed out, reading the Bible has *always* been a hermeneutic as well as a textual activity.

For whatever reason, however, "tradition" is *not* a word that occurs often in Robert Lowth's vocabulary. Given the nature of his subject, it is little short of astonishing how *absent* the word (or even the concept) is from either the *Lectures*, or from *Isaiah*. A careful count reveals only *one* use of the word in the former, and *two* in the latter.[1] Moreover, the sole use in the *Lectures* is both adjectival and—by implication—negative. Citing the authority of Tacitus, he comments that the Germans "had no records or annals but the traditional poems, in which they celebrated the heroic exploits of their ancestors."[2] Not surprisingly, one feels at times that Lowth actually goes out of his way to avoid the word and its associations altogether, preferring to write in purely technical terms of the texts and their "transmission" "down to the present time." "All writings transmitted to us," he writes in the Preliminary Dissertation to Isaiah,

> …from early times, the original copies of which have long ago perished, have suffered in their passage to us by the mistakes of many transcribers, through whose hands we have received them; errors continually accumulating in proportion to the number of the transcripts, and the stream generally becoming more impure, the more distant it is from its source.[3]

This watery metaphor of a stream, once pure at its source, and becoming progressively more polluted by time and distance from its original spring, is one that explicitly or implicitly dominates Lowth's whole principle of translation in *Isaiah*. It is the role of the translator to filter or purify the corruptions of time, and so *restore* it to its original quality. Though this nominally retains the legal and ecclesiastical notion of "handing down" a precious legacy, the implications of this are, of course, the very opposite of the accepted ecclesiastical tradition on which the 1688 Anglican settlement was as much dependent as its Catholic rival, and is far closer to the assumptions of the more radical Protestant reformers of the sixteenth and seventeenth centuries, who had wished to "restore" the structures of a now-lost primitive Church.

Now it is, of course, possible that Lowth felt that the word "tradition," with its associations of an ongoing body of hermeneutic commentary and practice in the interpretation of scripture, was potentially too Catholic for comfort, and might, as it were, be seen as selling the pass to Rome. But not merely is there no evidence of such ideological nervousness on

1. I owe this labour to my research assistant, Dana White.
2. Robert Lowth, *Lectures on the Sacred Poetry of the Hebrews* (trans. G. Gregory; 2 vols., London, 1787), 1:84–86.
3. Robert Lowth, *Isaiah: A New Translation* (1778; repr., London: Routledge/Thoemmes Press, 1995), lvii.

Lowth's part, there is overwhelming evidence of his interest in consulting *all* possible rival traditions in the interests of textual accuracy. In *Isaiah*, the primacy of the Vulgate, and even its old Latin predecessor, is dismissed not on polemical grounds, but simply as being already too far from the source—"being for the most part the Translation of Jerom, made in the Fourth Century, [it] is of service…in proportion to its antiquity."[4] Instead, he is happy to invoke authorities from whatever traditions may be appropriate, ranging from the scholarly conjectures of the sixteenth-century Mantuan Jewish authority, Rabbi Azarias,[5] to the "learned Mr Woide," a Coptic scholar, and Chaldean, Syriac and three early Greek texts, besides that of the Septuagint. Particular acknowledgment is made to Benjamin Kennicott's magisterial variorum edition of the Hebrew Bible, the *Dissertatio Generalis*, which was in preparation at the same time that Lowth was at work on his own translation.

It is, therefore, revealing that the first time in Lowth's *Isaiah* where the word "tradition" *is* used is in a context of doubtful authority at the beginning of the "Notes"—which are, incidentally, more extensive than the entire Preliminary Dissertation and the actual text of Isaiah combined. Lowth writes:

> Isaiah exercised the Prophetical Office during a long period of time, if he lived to the reign of Manasseh; for the lowest computation, beginning from the year in which Uzziah died, when some suppose him to have received his first appointment to that office, brings it to 61 years. But the Tradition of the Jews, that he was put to death by Manasseh, is very uncertain; and one of their principal Rabbins (Aben Ezra…) seems rather to think, that he died before Hezekiah, which is indeed more probable.[6]

"Tradition" in other words is *inherently* suspect—it consists of an oral sequence of transmission for which, unlike written texts, one only has the latest version. Even where this may not be strictly true (one suspects in this case that this has been for some time a written rather than an oral tradition), it is still to be contrasted with the more reliable opinions of specific scholarly authorities, such as, in this case, Aben Ezra. Another use of the word, at the end of the Notes to Isa 1, occurs in the gloss to v. 30, where the "revolters and sinners" shall be "as a garden, wherein is no water." Here, we are told, "there never was a more stupendous work of this kind, than the reservoir of Saba, or Merab, in Arabia Felix. According to the tradition of the country, it was the work of Balkis, that queen of Sheba, who visited Solomon":

4. Ibid., lxix.
5. Ibid., xli–xlviii.
6. Ibid., Notes, 1.

It was a vast lake formed by the collection of the waters of a torrent in a valley, where, at a narrow pass between two mountains, a very high mole, or dam, was built. The water of the lake so formed had near twenty fathom depth; and there were three sluices at different heights, by which, at whatever height the lake flood, the plain below might be watered. By conduits and canals from these sluices the water was constantly distributed in due proportion to the several lands; so that the whole country for many miles became a perfect paradise. The city of Saba, or Merab, was situated immediately below the great dam; a great flood came, and raised the lake above its usual height: the dam gave way in the middle of the night; the waters burst forth at once, and overwhelmed the whole city, with the neighbouring towns, and people. The remains of the eight tribes were forced to abandon their dwelling, and the beautiful valley became a morass and a desert. This fatal catastrophe happened long before the time of Mohammed, who mentions it in the Koran, Chap. xxxiv.[7]

Apart from the fact that Lowth is prepared to cite the Koran, what is interesting about this passage is its sheer irrelevance to the text under discussion. No English reader, even from the soggiest bit of fenland around Oxford's greatest rival, was really going to have trouble with the image of a garden without water. Nevertheless, in a piece of almost unequalled overkill, Lowth insists "That the reader may have a clear notion of this matter, it will be necessary to give some account of the management of their gardens in this respect"—and follows it with no less than three and half pages on the irrigation of Near Eastern gardens, beginning with that of Eden.[8] Even by Lowthian standards of scholarship, this is surely excessive.

While this may be simply an example of an academic never letting a good footnote get away, a literary critic might also observe that this fascination with hydraulics in the Notes is entirely of a piece with the water imagery running throughout the Preliminary Dissertation. The river of life, beginning with the rivers in the Garden of Eden, is a constant precious flow through the text—and, for us, down to the present. As Lowth is at pains to stress, it is the lifeblood, the artery, that nourishes all civilization, all life. Under proper control, it makes all else possible; without it, without the dam and sluices that deliver and hand on the water supply, the land is dead and barren—made worse, in Isaiah's imagery, because it was once a green and fertile garden.

7. Ibid., 20.
8. Ibid., 17–20.

Whether or not such trains—or should one say "flow"?—of imagery
was in any way conscious in Lowth's mind, it may also go some way to
clarify his own attitude to the biblical tradition he was attempting to
expound.

> The first and principal business of a Translator is to give us the plain literal
> and grammatical sense of his author; the obvious meaning of his words,
> phrases, and sentences, and to express them in the language into which he
> translates, as far as may be, in equivalent words, phrases, and sentences...
> This is peculiarly so in subjects of high importance such as the Holy
> Scriptures, in which so much depends on the phrase and expression; and
> particularly in the Prophetical books of scripture; where from the letter are
> often deduced deep and recondite senses, which must all owe their weight
> and solidity to the just and accurate interpretation of the words of the
> Prophecy. For whatever senses are supposed to be included in the
> Prophet's words, Spiritual, Mystical, Allegorical, Anagogical, or the like,
> they must all entirely depend on the Literal Sense.[9]

Now it is possible to hear in such declarations the voice of proto-moder-
nity, of the new-style textual scholar paying ironic lip-service to the
flummery of typological and allegorical readings even while secretly
dismissing them to the scrap-heap of history. But I believe this is a
profound mis-reading of Lowth. First, this is evidently such an important
point that he repeats it again, almost verbatim, at the conclusion of the
Preliminary Dissertation.[10] Second, he himself is quite clearly drawn,
over and over again, towards the very "deep and recondite senses" that
he modestly assigns to others. If we look only as far as Isa 1:29—the
verse before the "garden, wherein is no water"—we find this:

> For ye shall be ashamed of the ilexes, which ye have desired; and ye shall
> blush for the gardens, which ye have chosen: when ye shall be as an ilex,
> whose leaves are blasted...

This draws from Lowth over a page and a half of notes concerning the
exact tree intended—which is translated by the King James Bible as
"oak." Some of this does indeed concern the precise meaning of the
Hebrew, which most commentators have interpreted as Terebinth, but
Lowth rejects this not on textual, but on overtly symbolic grounds.

> ...I think neither the Oak, nor the Terebinth, will do in this place of
> Isaiah... [because of] their being deciduous; where the Prophet's design
> seems to me to require an ever-green: otherwise the casting of its leaves
> would be nothing out of the common established course of nature, and no

9. Ibid., lii.
10. Ibid., lxxiii–lxxiv.

> proper image of extreme distress, and total desolation; parallel to that of a garden without water, that is, wholly burnt up and destroyed... Upon the whole, I have chosen to make it the Ilex; which word Voffius...derives from the [same Hebrew word]; that, whether the word itself be rightly rendered or not, I might at least preserve the propriety of the poetical image.[11]

In other words, where there is any doubt, the "poetical" takes precedence over the literal mechanics of textual scholarship. Nor, in practice, does Lowth neglect the allegorical. Here, for instance, is his note to Isa 52:13, which he translates as "Behold, my servant shall prosper; he shall be raised aloft, and magnified, and very highly exalted":

> The subject of Isaiah's Prophecy, from the Fortieth Chapter inclusive, has hitherto been, in general, the Deliverance of the people of God. This includes in it three distinct parts; which, however, have a close connection with one another: that is, the deliverance of the Jews from the captivity of Babylon; the deliverance of the Gentiles from their miserable state of ignorance and idolatry; and the deliverance of Mankind from the captivity of sin and death. These three subjects are subordinate to one another; and the latter two are shadowed out under the image of the former. They are covered by it as by a vail; which however is transparent, and suffers them to appear through it... Now these three subjects having a very near relation to one another; for, as the agent, who was to effect the two later deliverances, that is, the Messiah, was to be born a Jew, with particular limitations of time, family, and other circumstances; the first deliverance was necessary in the order of Providence, and according to the determinate counsel of God, to the accomplishment of the two latter deliverances; and the second deliverance was necessary to the third, or rather, was involved in it, and made an essential part of it: this being the case, Isaiah has not treated the three subjects as quite distinct and separate in a methodical and orderly manner, like a philosopher or a logician, but has taken them in their connective view; he has handled them as a prophet and poet; he hath allegorised the former, and under the image of it has shadowed out the two latter; he has thrown them all together, has mixed one with another, has passed from this to that with rapid transitions, and has painted the whole with the strongest and boldest imagery.

Perhaps sensing at this point that he has allowed himself to be carried away by the awe-inspiring reach of the allegorical meaning of this relatively straightforward-seeming verse, Lowth suddenly reverts to his plain man just-clearing-the-ground style:

> This seems to me to be the nature and the true design of this part of Isaiah's Prophecies; and this view of them seems to afford the best method of resolving difficulties, in which Expositors are frequently engaged, being

11. Ibid., 17.

much divided between what is called the Literal, and the Mystical sense, not very properly; for the mystical or spiritual sense is very often the most literal sense of all.

Nevertheless, the cat is out of the bag. For all the "modernism" of his polyglot scholarship and his careful respect for the text, Lowth is very much a man of his time in his belief in the Mosaic authorship of the Pentateuch, the inspiration of the Holy Spirit, and in the possibility of multi-layered allegorical and typological readings. Perhaps we should look again at the huge commentary constructed around the "garden, wherein is no water" (Isa 1:30). Here too is, in effect, an allegorical structure as elaborate as anything in Augustine or any of the Church Fathers. The difference, of course, is that it is superficially composed of scholarly references (even drawing in the Koran) rather than other biblical texts. In that respect, however, it is not so very different from other, contemporary, eighteenth-century biblical commentaries which, even before Lowth, were an increasingly eclectic patchwork of previous authorities. The real difference is that even as Lowth attempts to set his material in its literary and historical context, his imagery is reaching out to create a much more poetic and symbolic frame of reference.

And here, of course, however we may construe Lowth's seeming reluctance to use the *word* "tradition," he is actually being at his most traditional. Whatever may have been the Latin legal meaning of tradition, for the *Hebrew* world tradition was not only a "handing on," it was an on-going debate and commentary on what was being conveyed. "'What is Torah?' runs the traditional question: 'It is *midrash* Torah.'"[12] The law is incomplete without the associated tradition of reflection and discussion by which it was acclimatized and absorbed by each Jewish community, wherever it was to be found. Nor was this only a post-biblical phenomenon. As David Jeffrey has pointed out:

> Isaiah, as a book of prophecy, is itself a powerful "reading" of another book, the Torah, and…its unity comes from the established shape of the canonical transmission of Hebrew Scripture and history—the implied as well as explicit rhetorical patterning of its foundational texts. And this, then, is essential perspective for reading Hebrew prophetic literature: one is required to read it with one eye on the first five books of the Bible.[13]

12. See Michael Wadsworth, "Making and Interpreting Scripture," in *Ways of Reading the Bible* (ed. Michael Wadsworth; Brighton: Harvester, 1981).
13. David Lyle Jeffrey, *The People of the Book: Christian Identity and Literary Culture* (Grand Rapids: Eerdmans, 1996), 35.

This may also be one reason, at least, for the seemingly vast weight of
notes and commentary in which Lowth had embedded his "new translation." If we see it *simply* as a new translation, separated from the
Preliminary Dissertation which, together with the 283 pages of Notes,
make up the bulk of the 1783 volume, we miss what is, in effect, the
grand midrashic design of the whole. Lowth's *Isaiah* is in many ways as
much a commentary as it is a translation. The Preliminary Dissertation
not merely summarizes the insights of the earlier *Lectures on the Sacred
Poetry of the Hebrews*, but adds twenty-five years of reflection and
research since their publication in 1753, revealing that he himself has
been profoundly influenced by the Higher Criticism that he had helped to
create. He is, if anything, more alive to the problems presented by
corrupt texts. In addition to a vastly increased list of primary sources, he
also cites, with respect, the ideas of the pioneer German biblical scholar
Johann David Michaelis who had republished Lowth's Lectures in the
original Latin in Göttingen in 1758, with extensive further notes in
German.[14] It was Michaelis who was one of his principal sources for the
notes on the waterworks of Arabia Felix. At the same time, Lowth is, as
we have observed, noticeably *more* aware of the poetic possibilities—not
to mention those "deep and recondite meanings"—that can co-exist in a
single passage of scripture. Alongside the rediscovery of the Bible within
a historical context, runs the no less important rediscovery of the Hebrew
prophets *as poetry*. Unlike his German contemporaries, Eichhorn or
Reimarus, there is in Lowth, as we have seen, no sense that historical
criticism diminishes or displaces poetic sensibility.

Lowth's *Isaiah* is, therefore, a deeply traditional work in the Hebrew
and biblical sense. But time does not stand still. As Julius Hare was to
observe some forty years later, no work stands alone:

> Goethe in 1800 does not write just as Shakespeare wrote in 1600: but
> neither would Shakespeare in 1800 have written just as he wrote in 1600.
> For the frame and aspect of society are different; the world which would
> act on him, and on which he would have to act, is another world. True
> poetical genius lives in communion with the world, in a perpetual recipro-
> cation of influences, inbibing feeling and knowledge, and pouring out what
> it has inbibed in words of power and gladness and wisdom. It is not, at least
> when highest it is not, as Wordsworth describes Milton to have been "like
> a star dwelling apart"... In short, Genius is not an independent and insu-
> lated, but a social and continental, or at all events a peninsular power...[15]

14. See Stephen Prickett, *Words and* The Word: *Language, Poetics and Biblical
Interpretation* (Cambridge: Cambridge University Press, 1986), 49–50, 111–13.
15. Julius and Augustus Hare, *Guesses at Truth* (2 vols.; London, 1827), 2:136–
38.

If this is true of Goethe or Shakespeare, how much more true is it of a work expressly written within the Judeo-Christian tradition? For if, in the sense in which I have been outlining, Lowth's work can be seen as an eighteenth-century continuation of the "literary" and midrashic tradition of the Hebrew Bible, there are other senses in which, notwithstanding, it also *has* to be seen as a quite different kind of work. To begin with the obvious, it is a *Christian*, not a Jewish work. Lowth's Isaiah is most certainly a Hebrew document, but for him, however much it must be read within the context of the Hebrew Bible, it is always also part of the Old Testament. Structurally it may well look backward to a reading of the Torah, but, equally, its prophecies look forward to the coming of Christ and the salvation of all humanity. Similarly, the mystical and recondite layers of interpretation belong to a specifically Christian tradition of hermeneutics by which the Hebrew Bible was appropriated and re-structured to point beyond itself to a fulfilment in the New Testament. Typological and allegorical readings, though not entirely absent from the Hebrew scriptures, belong more to the Hellenistic world, leading back to Augustine and to the Church Fathers, not to the world of the Hebrew prophets.

But no less importantly, Lowth is always aware that his work is of its time: eighteenth-century England. This is not merely a matter of the vastly increased range of the scholarly tools then becoming available—of which the Kennicott Bible was but one. Nor is it simply that of the new horizons opened up by the Enlightenment—essential though these also were. What was also unique to Lowth's England was that it was the world's first *pluralistic* society. As Peter Harrison has argued, it was only in the late seventeenth century, after the Reformation, Civil War and the Restoration of 1668, that people became fully aware of "religion" as a word encompassing radically different possibilities—in short, as a word with a plural form.[16] Or, as Locke had put it in one of his more deadpan moments: the kings and queens of post-Reformation England had been "of such different minds in point of religion, and enjoined thereupon such different things," that no "sincere and upright worshipper of God could, with a safe conscience, obey their several decrees."[17] What had changed, however, with the coming of pluralism was not merely a new meaning to "religion," but with it, a whole clutch of words whose

16. Peter Harrison, *"Religion" and Religions in the English Enlightenment* (Cambridge: Cambridge University Press, 1990).

17. J. Locke, *A Letter Concerning Toleration*, in *Treatise of Civil Government and A Letter Concerning Toleration* (ed. Charles L. Sherman; New York: Appleton-Century-Crofts, 1965), 191.

meanings had to modify and change in response. One such word was "tradition" itself.

I began by citing the *OED* to the effect that there has been no substantial change in the meaning of the word "tradition" over the past three hundred years, and in lexicographical terms this is no doubt true. But religious pluralism not merely brought a plural form to "religion," it also gave one to "tradition." A single religious grand narrative had little or no need for different or competing "traditions." Even the violent polemics of the Reformation (together with its no less violent actions) did not necessarily portend competing traditions. For those not prepared to overthrow the established Episcopal structures, the battle was for *possession* of the one true Apostolic tradition, not over how to divide it up. There might be fierce debate as to who best represented that tradition, but no one suggested there might be different Apostolic traditions. As we have noted, Lowth rarely uses the word "tradition," but he *never* to my knowledge uses the word in its plural form at all.

Yet between 1753 and 1778 other changes were occurring that made the plural form meaningful for perhaps the first time. If the Church of England and the Church of Rome could fight over possession of the Christian Apostolic tradition, could it be said that the Lutherans (whom Lowth was now much more aware of than in 1743) must fight the Anglicans over the same territory? With a Sovereign who was head of the Anglican Church south of the border, but a Presbyterian if ever he was to enter Scotland (which none did until the Prince Regent made his famous visit), in what sense did two such different churches *share* a tradition? Unlike the 1743 *Lectures*, which had been prepared in a great hurry, Lowth had had thirty-five years—in effect, a life's work—to study Catholic, Coptic, Orthodox and Old Syriac, not to mention Jewish and Muslim sources for his understanding of Isaiah. All had long and scholarly traditions. If, in the past, the concept of tradition had been a matter for dispute between religious polemicists and the evidence of historical scholars, by the late eighteenth century that very evidence was making it increasingly clear that there could be, in effect, *many* traditions, and more than one way of understanding and conveying the wisdom, rituals and spiritual experience of the former ages down to the present day. Small wonder that Lowth so carefully confined his use of the word to the singular, and then only to the distant past—to Josephus or the writings of pre-Islamic Arabs.

Finally, and perhaps most importantly, a new meaning to the word "tradition" had been, in effect, created by Lowth himself twenty-five years before with the publication of the *Lectures*. The revolutionary identification of prophecy with poetry in the Hebrew Scriptures had, as we know, set in motion a new critical aesthetics that was to find its culmination in the romantic movement—in England, Blake, Wordsworth, Coleridge and Shelley; in Germany, Herder, Lessing, Novalis, Schiller, Schleiermacher and the Schlegels—both groups, in this respect, as I have elsewhere called them, "the children of Lowth."[18] In the growth of the new concept we can see at work what Coleridge was to call the process of "de-synonymy," whereby what was originally thought of as a single concept is divided into two separate, if related, notions—which require the coinage of new words to describe the separation.[19]

The new word here is, of course, "aesthetics," first used in its modern sense of "criticism of taste" in Germany in the second half of the eighteenth century, and, despite Kant's opposition,[20] rapidly taken up by the German Romantics. Only a few years later it had passed into regular currency in less theoretical Britain because of a similar need.[21] It is difficult for the modern reader, thoroughly secularized and acclimatized to the academic division between literary and biblical studies, to recapture the mental set in which the two disciplines could not yet be experienced as requiring separate ways of thinking. Yet, if we look at the criticism of the eighteenth century—Dennis, Jacob, Trapp, not to mention Watts, or even Burke himself—poetry is taken for granted as "the natural language of religion."[22] The very idea of poetic sublimity was inconceivable without reference to religious awe. The idea of an aesthetic tradition entirely separable from its religious roots was almost impossible to contemplate, and at first sight Lowth seems no different from his fellow-critics in the 1740s and '50s. But simply by emphasizing the central role of poetic technique—parallelism etc.—in the creation of prophecy, Lowth turned poetry from being the handmaid of religion to its partner.

18. See Prickett, *Words and* The Word, Chapter 3.

19. S. T. Coleridge, *Philosophical Lectures (1818–1819)* (ed. K. Coburn; London: Routledge, 1949).

20. First used by Baumgarten in his *Aesthetica* (1750–58). Kant, however, applied it in what he believed was its "correct" sense of "the science which treats of the conditions of sensuous perception" in the *Critique of Pure Reason* (1781) and thereafter in his *Critique of Judgement*.

21. See S. T. Coleridge: "I wish I could find a more familiar word than aesthetic, for works of taste and criticism" (*Blackwood's Magazine* 10 [1821]: 254).

22. John Dennis, *The Grounds of Criticism in Poetry* (1704); Giles Jacob, *An Historical Account of the Lives and Writings of our most Considerable English Poets* (1720); Joseph Trapp, *Lectures on Poetry* (trans. William Bowyes; 1742); Isaac Watts, Preface to *Horae Lyricae* (1709); Edmund Burke, *A Philosophical Enquiry into our Ideas of the Sublime and the Beautiful* (1757).

Form influenced content, and vice versa. If, on the one hand, Lowth's *Lectures* had re-awakened poets to their prophetic role, he had also paved the way for the idea of a secular aesthetics. Shelley's *Defence of Poetry*, with its blurring of the distinction between poetry and prose and stress on poets as "the unacknowledged legislators of mankind," is, in this sense, simply a linear development of Lowthian principles.[23] But, as in this case, the separation of aesthetics from religion, so far from being a clean divorce, has meant that each has returned to haunt the other. If aesthetics has suffered from what I have elsewhere called an "ache in its missing limb,"[24] theology without aesthetics has, as Kierkegaard recognized, become a bumbling, blundering thing, blind to awe and wonder, confused by the poetic, baffled and irritated by irony.

Lowth's *Isaiah* is, in effect, the greatest monument of traditional biblical scholarship of his century, and with it, he was to blow wide open the very meaning of the word "tradition" itself. It is, for him, almost the word that dare not speak its name; the dog that did not bark. From 1778 onwards, the debate has raged not so much over who has, or has not, the biblical or Apostolic tradition, as over the *meaning* of the word itself, of the relationship between religion and aesthetics, and how that can be understood (if at all) in an increasingly pluralistic society. That was the issue as much for Coleridge as for Julius Hare in the 1820s; that was to be the question that was to divide the University of Oxford in the 1830s, in the wake of Keble's Assize Sermon of 1833; that was the problem with which Newman was to wrestle in the 1840s, and was to be explored over and over again in his works from the 1845 *Essay on the Development of Christian Doctrine*, to his *Letter to the Duke of Norfolk* thirty years later. It was the stumbling-block to Keble's godson, Matthew Arnold. It was to give new inspiration to F. D. Maurice, the Unitarian convert to Anglicanism and author of *The Kingdom of Christ*. It was the cause of George Tyrrell's agonies over his Catholic faith in *Through Scylla and Charybdis* (1907). By the twentieth century, still as much a literary as a theological problem, it was to be as central to T. S. Eliot's aesthetics as it was to his theology—and to read his 1919 essay, *Tradition and the Individual Talent*, without an awareness of how its arguments were to affect his conversion to Christianity seven years later, is also to miss how central the idea of tradition is to *Ash Wednesday* and the *Four Quartets*.

---

23. P. B. Shelley, *A Defence of Poetry* (1840).

24. See Stephen Prickett, *Narrative, Religion and Science: Fundamentalism versus Irony* 1700–1999 (Cambridge: Cambridge University Press, 2002), Chapter 5.

We are not yet far into the twenty-first century, but already it is clear that we are in a world where the question of what constitutes religious tradition, and how it is to be understood, incredible as it might have seemed two hundred and fifty years ago, may even be central to the peace of the world.

AFTER HORACE: SACRED POETRY AT THE CENTRE OF THE HEBREW BIBLE

Christoph Bultmann

> The odes of *David* are among the densest lyric poems ever written. The allusions are rich and subtle, and the tone is so iridescent, that readers can never be quite sure of it, and find endless pleasure in disagreeing with each other about it. Translation of poetry is always impossible but translation of *David's* odes is inconceivable.

This quotation is not a newly discovered apocryphal statement of Robert Lowth's about the Psalms. Neither is it taken from some recent commentary on the Psalms, and even after a quarter-century of postmodernism it would be difficult to imagine biblical scholars find "endless pleasure in disagreeing with each other" about the tone of David's poetic compositions. The quotation is quite prosaically from the "Translator's Note" in David West's new translation of the odes of Horace.[1] In my adaptation, the name of *Horace* has been exchanged for that of *David* in order to indicate what distance there is between biblical and literary studies. Studying David and Horace as poets in the same sense of the word may seem to many to be a vain and futile endeavour. And Lowth himself was wise enough not to push direct comparison too far. Nevertheless, the question needs to be asked what idea of poetry might justify the convention in biblical scholarship to call a certain number of texts in the Hebrew Bible "poetic," and if we look back for this to the eighteenth century, the name of Horace must not be ignored.

1. *Lowth, the Oxford Professor of Poetry*

From the perspective of intellectual history, one is still impressed by Lowth's bold decision to devote his lectures as the Oxford Professor of

---

1. Horace, *The Complete Odes and Epodes* (trans. D. West; Oxford: Oxford University Press, 1997), xxvii.

Poetry from 1741 to the "Sacred Poetry of the Hebrews." For there must have been two strong reasons against such a choice of subject. The first of these is that it was Horace who could be called the patron saint of English literary culture in the eighteenth century, and a professor of poetry might duly have been expected to offer lectures on poets of the classical tradition.[2] The second is that poetry, although it does in fact have its place in the Bible, must be considered an awkward element in a religion which is based on doctrine. Was it naïvety which made Lowth disregard such objections? Was he carried away by that kind of light-hearted inquisitiveness which—perhaps not least due to the influence of Horace—characterized not a few of eighteenth-century debates in history and philosophy? It seems more likely that the reason for his choice of subject was a deep concern with the religious potential of a poetic language. The edifice of a classicist theory of poetry was not altogether a place to feel at home for someone who subscribed to (Pseudo-)Long-inus's ideas about the sublime, and while doctrine, controversy and ritual will be considered in every ecclesiastical tradition to be the central aspects of Christian identity, biblical poetry may have a liberating force since it raises an awareness of God at an even more fundamental level of religious faith and human sentiment.[3]

260 years ago, the time was also just right for someone to embark on a scholarly study of Old Testament poetry. In 1736, Francis Hare had published his *Psalmorum Liber, in versiculos metrice divisus, et cum aliis critices subsidiis, tum paecipue metrices ope multis in locis integritati suae restitutus*, an edition of the Psalms in metrical divisions. Someone had to answer this critic's learned obsession with Trochaic ($-\smallsmile$) and Jambic ($\smallsmile-$) verses as well as his peculiar appropriation of the popular catch-all rule which says that the closer the arts are to their beginnings,

---

2. A pragmatic reason for Lowth's choice of subject is suggested by S. Prickett, *Words and* The Word*: Language, Poetics and Biblical Interpretation* (Cambridge: Cambridge University Press, 1986), 105. For Lowth and the Oxford chair of poetry, see L. S. Sutherland and L. G. Mitchell, eds., *The Eighteenth Century* (The History of the University of Oxford 5; Oxford: Clarendon, 1986), especially the contributions by M. L. Clarke, D. Patterson and D. Fairer, and the list of incumbents in the appendix. The notion of a "*literarischer Schutzpatron*" is borrowed from R. Sühnel, "Ars Horatiana in England," in *Zeitgenosse Horaz: Der Dichter und seine Leser seit zwei Jahrtausenden* (ed. H. Krasser and E. A. Schmidt; Tübingen: Gunter Narr, 1996), 153–81 (173).

3. For the issue of biblical poetry generally see, e.g., J. Kugel, *The Idea of Biblical Poetry: Parallelism and Its History* (Baltimore: The Johns Hopkins University Press, 1981; repr. 1998); R. Alter, *The Art of Biblical Poetry* (Edinburgh: T. & T. Clark, 1990 [1st ed. 1985]); Prickett, *Words and* The Word.

the simpler they are ("*quo initiis propiores, eo rudiores*"). In his third
lecture as well as in an appendix to his book and again in a separate
pamphlet of 1766, Lowth rejected the metrical theories of Hare.[4] Despite
the failure of Hare's analysis of Hebrew metre—which makes a striking
contrast to the lasting success of Lowth's investigation of Hebrew parallelism[5]—he may still have the merit to have put poetry back on the
agenda of biblical exegesis. In the introduction to his book, Hare not
only reminded the readers of a forgotten seventeenth-century controversy
between the Groningen scholar Franciscus Gomarus and the Saumur
scholar Louis Cappel about Greek and Roman metre in biblical poetry,[6]
he also revived faded recollections of a debate about biblical poetry in
the Patristic tradition and notably Jerome's assertions concerning the
biblical poets. While Jerome is not entirely consistent in his view of
poetry in the Bible, his praise of David as the biblical counterpart to the
great Greek and Roman poets remained a challenge for biblical critics. If,
as Jerome states on several occasions, David is no less a poet than were.
for example, Pindar or Horace, and if poetry matters at all, as is implied
not least by Jerome's references and allusions to Horace, it follows that

4.   F. Hare, *Psalmorum Liber in Versiculos Metrice Divisus* (London: S. Buckley
& T. Longman, 1736), xxxii. On Francis Hare (1671–1740) see the entry in DNB 24.
365–66; ODNB 25, 246–48, and D. Norton, *A History of the Bible as Literature*
(2 vols.; Cambridge: Cambridge University Press, 1993), 2:72. R. Lowth, *De sacra
poesi Hebraeorum praelectiones academicae Oxonii habitae* ([1753]; repr. of 3d ed.
1775; ed. D. A. Reibel; London: Routledge/Thoemmes, 1995), 31–43 "Praelectio
tertia: רומזמ sive de metris Hebræis," 469–76 "Metricæ Harianæ brevis confutatio";
English ed.: *Lectures on the Sacred Poetry of the Hebrews* ([1787]; 2 vols.; repr.,
London: Routledge/Thoemmes, 1995), 1:55–73, 2:436–46; *A larger Confutation of
Bishop Hare's system of Hebrew metre in a letter to Rev. Dr. Edwards, in answer to
his Latin epistle* [1766], in R. Lowth, *Sermons and other Remains of Robert Lowth*
(ed. P. Hall [1834]; repr., London: Routledge/Thoemmes, 1995), 373–442.
5.   For an earlier analysis of Hebrew parallelism, see Erasmus's commentaries
on Ps 1 and Ps 2: Erasmus, *Enarratio Allegorica in Primum Psalmum Beatus Vir*
([1515]; ed. A. Godin); *Commentarius in Psalmum II Quare Fremuerunt Gentes*
([1522]; ed. S. Dresden); *Opera Omnia* 5/2 (Amsterdam: North Holland; Oxford:
Elsevier, 1985), 19–80 and 81–159 (74 and 108–9); English version *Collected Works*,
63 (trans. M. J. Heath; Toronto: University of Toronto Press, 1997), 1–63 and 65–
146 (55–56 and 86).
6.   See the article on Cappel in J. H. Hayes, ed., *Dictionary of Biblical Interpretation* (2 vols.; Nashville: Abingdon, 1999), 2:167–68. Among the authors quoted
by Hare is Johann Gottlob Carpzov (1679–1767), who, in his survey of biblical
poetry, also refers to that controversy: J. G. Carpzov, *Introductio ad libros poeticos
Bibliorum Veteris Testamenti* (Introductio ad libros canonicos Bibliorum Veteris
Testamenti omnes 2; Leipzig: Lankisius, 1720), 12.

the poetic character of certain biblical texts must become a proper issue in exegesis.[7]

For a further, and probably the most decisive, aspect of Lowth's scholarly initiative, reference must be made to what was arguably the biggest issue in theology in his day, that of natural religion.[8] For the sake of convenience, I would like to illustrate this point with a few quotations from the writings of Robert Lowth's father. In 1692, William Lowth published a *Vindication of the Divine Authority and Inspiration of the Old and New Testament*, a book to be followed in 1708 by *Directions for the Profitable Reading of the Holy Scriptures*. Whereas the first of these works engaged in a controversy about Scripture with Jean le Clerc, the second was designed to prevent ordinary readers of the Bible from being moved away "*from the hope of the Gospel* by the little cavils and exceptions of *Scepticks* and *Infidels*, which we may be bold to say proceed from their not knowing the Scriptures."[9] Although these apologetic writings would have been seriously weakened by Anthony Collins's *Discourse of the Grounds and Reasons of the Christian Religion* of 1724, a third edition of the *Directions* was published in 1726, and a fourth in 1735. Most pertinent to the question of the theological background of Robert Lowth's *Lectures* is what William Lowth says about the book of

---

7. The three *loci classici* for the first aspect (which are quoted by Hare) are in Jerome's preface to his translation of Euseb's Chronicon (GCS 47, 1–7), in his letter to Paulinus (ep. 53: CSEL 54, 442–65, esp. 461) and in his preface to Job (see current editions of the Vulgate). For the second aspect see, for example, the letter to Pammachius (ep. 57: CSEL 54, 503–526, esp. 509–10) and the Commentary on Amos (on Amos1.2: CCL 76, 215). Jerome's renunciation of the classical tradition in his letter to Eustachium (ep. 22: CSEL 54, 143–211, esp. 188–91) must be seen in its proper context. See Kugel, *The Idea of Biblical Poetry*, 149–56; P. L. Schmidt, "Horaz," in *RAC* 16 (Stuttgart: Hiersemann, 1994), 491–524; R. Henke, "Quid facit cum psalterio Horatius? Zur Horaz-Nutzung in der frühchristlichen Literatur," in *Alvarium: Festschrift für Christian Gnilka* (ed. W. Blümer et al.; JACSup 33; Münster: Aschendorff, 2002), 173–86; M. Marin, "La presenza di Orazio nei Padri latini: Ambrogio, Girolamo, Agostino. Note introductive," in *Atti del Convegno Nazionale di Studi su Orazio* (ed. R. Uglione; Turin: Regione Piemonte, Assessorato ai Beni Culturali, 1993), 259–71; H. Hagendahl and J. H. Waszink, "Hieronymus," in *RAC* 15 (Stuttgart: Hiersemann, 1991), 117–39. Jerome's rhetoric is echoed in the "Preface to the Reader" in B. Ugolino's massive collection of writings on biblical poetry (including Gomarus, Hare, and Lowth), *Thesaurus Antiquitatum Sacrarum*, 31, no. 1 (Venice, 1766).

8. A good introduction to this issue is P. Byrne, *Natural Religion and the Nature of Religion: The Legacy of Deism* (London: Routledge, 1989).

9. W. Lowth, *Directions for the Profitable Reading of the Holy Scriptures* ([1708]; 3d ed.; London, 1726), Preface (no page).

Job. The author defends the divine inspiration of this book which had
been attacked by le Clerc for its poetic character as well as for the
unrestrained passionate sentiments which it contains. Having first
appealed to the great "Speeches in Old Tragedies" as an analogy to Job's
effusions, William Lowth then goes on:

> I see no Reason why God might not in this as well as other things, suffer
> the Holy Writers to comply so far with their own Genius, and the Humour
> which then prevail'd among the grave Sages of the World, as to deliver
> Great and Weighty Truths in Poetical numbers and Expressions, both to
> recommend them to the more Curious and Nice Readers, and to convince
> the Wise men of the World, who are apt to despise the Plainness of the
> Scriptures, that there are to be found as Elevated Thoughts, and as Noble
> Expressions in the Holy Writings, as any *Greece* or *Rome* can boast of.[10]

As a summary of the book of Job, the author offers some mildly pious
reflections when he describes its "principal and obvious Designs" as "the
Powerful Comforts this Book affords to the Afflicted, and the submission
it teaches us to yield to God's Will, and to Adore the Unsearchableness
of his Judgements." In addition to this, however, he emphasizes a theo-
logically more challenging aspect and states, "'tis likewise of excellent
Use upon another account, *viz.* as it gives us a True Idea of *Natural
Religion*, when it was in its Prime, and as it was practis'd in those early
Ages, before the Tradition of the Creation was lost, or the World quite
overrun with Idolatry."[11] Thus we find an almost Longinian emphasis on
"elevated thoughts" and "noble expressions" in the Bible, the suggestion
of a comparison between Job and Greek tragedy, and the concept of an
uncorrupted natural religion in the early ages of human history, which
had found expression in a poetic language. The poetry of the book of
Job, it would seem, is a testimony to a kind of religious insight which
was not based on any particular historical revelation. However, this interpretation of William Lowth's understanding of Job must not be taken too
far, because his ideas about an early "natural religion" are obviously
linked to a concept of a tradition of ancient theology which goes back to
the time of the creation.[12] Furthermore, although the passage on natural

10. W. Lowth, *A Vindication of the Divine Authority and Inspiration of the Old
and New Testament* (Oxford, 1692; 2d ed., London, 1699) [also on *Early English
Books Online*], 1692, 229.

11. Ibid., 239.

12. On the issue of a primeval tradition, a *"prisca theologia,"* see D. P. Walker,
*The Ancient Theology: Studies in Christian Platonism from the Fifteenth to the
Eighteenth Century* (London: Duckworth, 1972); H. B. Nisbet, "Die naturphiloso-
phische Bedeutung von Herders 'Aeltester Urkunde des Menschengeschlechts,'" in
Bückeburger Gespräche über Johann Gottfried Herder 1988: Älteste Urkunde des

religion in Job is repeated almost verbatim in the *Directions* of 1708, and although Pss 8; 19; 33; 103; 104; 107, and 148 are listed there as compositions about God's *"excellent greatness*, as 'tis made manifest in the works of creation and providence,"[13] the more extended discussion of revelation and natural religion in this second book focuses on the question of a moral law—and the difficulty of reading such a law off the human heart such as it is without the help of divine revelation.

The issue of natural religion acquired a new significance in the early decades of the eighteenth century when it became a central tenet in the philosophy of religion that it was possible to demonstrate the existence and attributes of God from observations of nature. In 1713, for example, William Derham published his Boyle Lectures under the title of *Physico-Theology, or a Demonstration of the Being and Attributes of God, from his Works of Creation.*[14] Although Derham does not seek much support from the Bible for his argument, he does refer to the poetic lines on the ravens and the ostrich in Job 38–39 where he comes to speak of the food of animals or the incubation of birds.[15] He also quotes Ps 19:3–4 against the atheist, and since he uses the translation of the King James Version, he finds an effective argument in this text for the universality of the possibility for human beings to discern God the creator from his works:

> For as *there is no Speech nor Language where their Voice is not heard, their Line is gone out through all the Earth, and their Words to the End of the World*: So all, even the barbarous Nations, that never heard of *God*, have from these his Works inferred the Existence of a Deity, and paid their Homages to some Deity, although they have been under great Mistakes in their Notions and Conclusions about him.[16]

It is obvious that poetic texts in the Bible such as Job, Ps 104 or Ps 148 were seen to have a particular affinity to the philosophical issue of natural religion.

Menschengeschlechts (ed. B. Poschmann; Rinteln: Verlag C. Bösendahl, 1989), 210–26; R. Häfner, "Die Weisheit des Ursprungs. Zur Überlieferung des Wissens in Herders Geschichtsphilosophie," *Herder Jahrbuch/Herder Yearbook 1994* (Stuttgart: J. B. Metzler, 1994), 77–101.

13. Lowth, *Directions*, 67, 72.

14. 12th ed. 1754 (which edition was not the last!).

15. W. Derham, *Physico-Theology, or a Demonstration of the Being and Attributes of God, from his Works of Creation* (3d ed.; Boyle Lectures 1711/12; London: W. Innys, 1714), 184, for the ravens (Job 38:41); 355–57, for the ostrich (Job 39:14–17); cf. 207 for the eagle (Job 39:27–29).

16. Ibid., 432; cf. the opening of W. Derham, *Astro-Theology, or a Demonstration of the Being and Attributes of God, from a Survey of the Heavens* (London: W. Innys, 1715), 1–2.

Turning from the theological background of Robert Lowth's *Lectures*
to literary history, a few hints will suffice to indicate the influence of
Horace on English literary criticism and literary theory from the sixteenth to the eighteenth century.[17] Philip Sidney, in his *Defense of Poesy*
of 1595, refers to the two most important statements by Horace on the
work of a poet which are also quoted or alluded to by Lowth. The first is
from the *Art of Poetry*: "The aim of a poet is either to benefit or to please
/ or to say what is both enjoyable and of service." The second is from
Epistles 1:2: "The poet shows what is fine and foul, what is advisable /
and what is not, more clearly and better than Chrysippus and Crantor."[18]
John Dryden confirms in 1685 that Horace's criticism was "the most
instructive of any that are written in this art," and Joseph Trapp, the first
Oxford Professor of Poetry, declares in his lectures that Horace's *Art of
Poetry* was a work "that ought to be got by Heart by all true Lovers of
Poetry." Alexander Pope praises Horace in his *Essay on Criticism* of
1711, and when the established critic John Dennis in his *Reflections
Critical and Satyrical, upon a Late Rhapsody, Call'd, An Essay upon
Criticism* opposes this new voice, he relies even more strongly on the
authority of Horace for his critique. Joseph Addison and Richard Steele
use almost 100 mottoes from Horace in their *Spectator*, introducing the
first issue in 1711 with two lines from the *Art of Poetry* about the poet:
"His aim is not to have smoke after a flash, but light / emerging from
smoke..."[19] In short, the attitude to Horace in the early decades of the

17. The following section is largely based on C. Goad, *Horace in the English
Literature of the Eighteenth Century* (Yale Studies in English 58; New Haven: Yale
University Press, 1918), and the articles in C. Martindale and D. Hopkins, eds.,
*Horace Made New: Horatian Influences on British Writing from the Renaissance to
the Twentieth Century* (Cambridge: Cambridge University Press, 1993); as well as in
Krasser and Schmidt, eds., *Zeitgenosse Horaz*. For Horace in early modern France,
see J. Marmier, *Horace en France, au dix-septième siècle* (Paris: Presses Univer-
sitaires de France, 1962).

18. P. Sidney, *An Apology for Poetry or The Defense of Poesy* ([1595]; ed. G.
Shepherd; Edinburgh: Nelson, 1965), 101, for *ars poetica* 333–34; 120, for *epistles*
1.2.3–4; the translation quoted is by Niall Rudd (with a reference in *ep.* 1.2 to
Homer): Horace, *Satires and Epistles* (trans. N. Rudd; London: Penguin, 1979). See
the first lecture in Lowth, *De sacra poesi*, 4 (*a.p.* 333) and 7 (*ep.* 1.2.3–4).

19. J. Dryden, *Essays* (ed. W. P. Ker; 2 vols.; Oxford: Clarendon, 1900), 1:266
(*Preface to Sylvae*); J. Trapp, *Lectures on Poetry* ([1742]; repr., London: Routledge/
Thoemmes, 1994), 200 (the lectures were first published in Latin in 1711–19);
A. Pope, *Works* (ed. P. Rogers; Oxford: Oxford University Press, 1993), 17–39; J.
Dennis, *The Critical Works* (ed. E. N. Hooker; 3d ed.; 2 vols.; Baltimore: The Johns
Hopkins University Press, 1967), 1:396–419; for Addison and Steele, see Goad,

eighteenth century is worlds apart from the nonchalance of a Laurence Sterne who, in 1759, brushes aside all Horatian (and other) rules for an aspiring author.[20]

Latin editions and English translations of Horace were published at a rapid pace throughout the sixteenth to eighteenth centuries and were catalogued, not for the first time, in commemoration of the tercentenary of the first printed edition of 1470.[21] To mention just a few, Thomas Grant, a contemporary of Philip Sidney, published the first English translation of the *Art of Poetry* in 1567. In 1640 this was followed by a translation by Ben Johnson, and the Earl of Roscommon, a contemporary of John Dryden, published a new translation in 1680. The *Odes* and other poetic works by Horace became available in an English verse translation by Thomas Creech in 1684, reprinted many times by the mid-eighteenth century when a new verse translation by Philip Francis was published in 1743. While the poetic merits of these achievements are more than questionable, they stand out from a broader background of numerous versions in prose. Another translator to be mentioned is Christopher Smart who not only published a prose translation of the *Odes* in 1755, to be followed by a verse translation in 1767, but also produced a translation of the psalms.[22] Earlier in the eighteenth century, again, Alexander Pope composes "imitations" of Horace's *Satires*, and the general appreciation of Horace's poems resounds in a letter of well-educated Thomas Burnet, a son of Gilbert Burnet, who, in 1716, tells his friend George Duckett: "I am now at my leisure hours reading Horace with some diligence and find the world was just the same then that it continues to be now."[23] Finally, at least one critical edition of Horace's works must be recalled: in 1711 Richard Bentley publishes a magisterial, though controversial, edition of Horace which consists of some 300 pages of the text, plus some 450

Horace in the English Literature, 26–89 and the Appendix, esp. 47 for the quotation from *ars poetica* 143–44.

20. L. Sterne, *The Life and Opinions of Tristram Shandy* (London: Penguin, 1985), 38 (vol. 1, Chapter 4), quoted in Goad, *Horace in the English Literature*, 221.

21. *Bibliotheca Horatiana sive Syllabus editionum Q. Horatii Flacii, interpretationum, versionum ab an. MCCCCLXX ad an. MDCCLXX* (Leipzig: W. G. Sommer, 1775).

22. See A. Sherbo, Introduction to C. Smart, *Verse Translation of Horace's Odes* (ed. A. Sherbo; Victoria, B.C.: University of Victoria, 1979), and C. Smart, *A Translation of the Psalms of David* (ed. M. Walsh; The Poetical Works 3; Oxford: Clarendon, 1987).

23. Pope, *Works*; incidentally, Lowth composed "An Ode to the People of Great Britain. In imitation of the 6th Ode of the 3rd book of Horace," see Lowth, *Sermons*, 472–76. Burnet's remark to Duckett is quoted by Sherbo, "Introduction," 6.

two-columned pages in small print of explanations of the almost 800
conjectural emendations which he suggests.[24]

An unexpected example of the presence of Horace in eighteenth-century intellectual life is provided by David Hume who resorts to a quotation from Horace—"expel nature with a fork; she'll keep on trotting back
/ relax—and she'll break triumphantly through your silly refinements"—
when, in an essay of 1741, he compares Machiavelli the politician and
Machiavelli the historian and states a major point in moral philosophy.[25]
There is no need to continue this list in the present context. However, in
order to complement the picture with just two references to literary life
in Germany in the 1750s, it may be mentioned that Voltaire in an address
to Frederick the Great in the "exorde" of his *Poème sur la loi naturelle*
of 1756 recollects their discussion of Horace: "*Nos premiers entretiens,
notre étude première, / Étaient, je m'en souviens, Horace avec Boileau. /
Vous y cherchiez le* vrai, *vous y goûtiez le* beau;..."[26] And Gotthold
Ephraim Lessing, in one of his earliest critical quarrels, published a dev-
astating review of a new translation of Horace's *Odes* into German, and
then demonstrates his commitment to the ancient Roman poet with a
further *Apology of Horace*, a substantial piece of literary criticism in
defence of Horace's moral character against philosophically ambitious,
but hermeneutically naïve critics.[27]

The reception history of Horace in European culture since the Renaissance is a vast field. Whether one looks, for example, to Erasmus's
Praise of Folly of 1511 or to Melanchthon's inaugural lecture at the University of Wittenberg of 1518, the presence of Horace cannot be ignored,

---

24. *Q. Horatius Flaccus ex recensione et cum notis atque emendationibus
Richardii Bentleii* (Cambridge, 1711). On Bentley as a textual critic of the New
Testament, see K. Haugen, "Transformations of the Trinity Doctrine in English
Scholarship: From the History of Beliefs to the History of Texts," *Archiv für
Religionsgeschichte* 3 (2001): 149–68.

25. D. Hume, *Essays Moral, Political and Literary* (ed. E. F. Miller; Indianapo-
lis: Liberty Classics, 1987), 567 (*Of the Study of History*); the translation of *epistles*
1.10.24–25 quoted is by Rudd (above, n. 18; one may object to the ring of line 25).

26. Voltaire, *Mélanges* (ed. J. van den Heuvel; Paris: Gallimard, 1961), 271–87
(273); the dismissive judgment on Horace in the continuation of this passage can
also be found in Voltaire's *Candide*, Chapter 25: Voltaire, *Romans et Contes* (ed. F.
Deloffre and J. van den Heuvel; Paris: Gallimard, 1979), 145–233 (217).

27. G. E. Lessing, *Werke 1751–1753* (ed. J. Stenzel; Werke und Briefe 2;
Frankfurt: Deutscher Klassiker Verlag, 1998), 705–9 (review, *in a printed letter*, of
1753) and 562 (*an announcement*, of 1753); *Werke 1754–1757* (ed. C. Wiedemann
et al.; Werke und Briefe 3; Frankfurt: Deutscher Klassiker Verlag, 2003), 105–46
(review, under the title, *Ein Vademecum*, of 1754) and 158–97 (*Rettungen des
Horaz*, of 1754).

and it may be assumed that not least authors such as these had a major impact on what looks like a rather stable cultural trend.[28] For good reasons, the reception history of this Augustan poet was the subject of at least two conferences in celebration of the Bimillennium of his death in 1992.[29] Needless to say that the name of Lowth does not occur in the index of either of the respective conference volumes, and needless, too, to emphasize that Horace was of course by no means the only classical authority for writers and scholars in the eighteenth century. However, my claim is that Lowth was very much aware of the significance of Horace as the foremost ancient Roman poet and critic no less than as a standard for English literature and criticism in his own time. I have already mentioned that he quotes the *"quid sit pulchrum, quid turpe, quid utile, quid non"* from *Epistles* 1:2 in his opening lecture, and he alludes to it again in the fourth lecture. The Horatian "to benefit and to please" resounds throughout his lectures, as does the *"feliciter audere"* (the invention of daring, but successful strokes) of *Epistles* 2:1. Even in his lectures 14–17 on the sublime, which are based on Longinus, he quotes a few lines from the *Art of Poetry* in order to explain the relationship between nature and art in poetry in an attempt to define "the true nature of poetry."[30] One could also ask whether Lowth shared the view of his predecessor Trapp who had claimed that "the Ode in its own Nature is chiefly adapted to the Sublime; and nothing can have more of that Quality than some of Horace's."[31] What, then, about David? In the introduction to his Lectures, Lowth asks the provocative question, *"...quid est cur Homeri,*

28. See Erasmus, *Encomium Moriae, id est Stultitiae Laus* ([1511]; ed. C. H. Miller; *Opera Omnia* 4/3; Amsterdam: North Holland Publishing Co., 1979); English version *Collected Works*, 27–28 (trans. B. Radice; Toronto: University of Toronto Press, 1986), and P. Melanchthon, *De corrigendis adolescentiae studiis* [1518], *Opera*, vol. 11, CR 11, 15–25. On Erasmus as a reader of Horace, see the introductions by Miller and Radice as well as E. Schäfer, "Erasmus und Horaz," *Antike und Abendland* 16 (1970): 54–67.

29. Martindale and Hopkins, eds., *Horace Made New*; Krasser and Schmidt, eds., *Zeitgenosse Horaz*; see also W. Ludwig, ed., *Horace: L'œuvre et les imitations. Un siècle d'interprétation* (Entretiens sur l'antiquité classique 39; Geneva: Fondation Hardt, 1993); R. Lindauer-Huber, "Rezeption und Interpretation des Horaz an der Universität Leipzig 1670–1730 zwischen Philologie, Philosophie und Poetik," in *Die Universität Leipzig und ihr gelehrtes Umfeld 1680–1780* (ed. H. Marti and D. Döring; Basel: Schwabe Verlag, 2004), 379–407; D. Money, "The Reception of Horace in the Seventeenth and Eighteenth Centuries," in *The Cambridge Companion to Horace* (ed. S. Harrison; Cambridge: Cambridge University Press, 2007), 318–33.

30. Lowth, *De sacra poesi*, 172; *Lectures on the Sacred Poetry*, 1:310.

31. Trapp, *Lectures on Poetry*, 212; see ibid., 5, for Trapp's view of "the inexpressible Sublimity" of "*Job, David*, and the other sacred Authors."

*Pindari, Horatii scriptis celebrandis omnique laude cumulandis toties
immoramur, Mosem interea, Davidem, Isaiam, silentio praeterimus?*"[32]
With some luck, therefore, or *felix curiositas*, it may be possible to find
some sense in reading biblical poetry "after Horace."

2. Horace, the Roman Poet of the Augustan Age

While it is clear that in the 1740s Lowth confronted a milieu of erudition
and taste which was deeply impregnated with Horatian literary ideals,
there is now a challenge to reverse as it were Lowth's question and ask
why it is that biblical scholars pass over *Horace* in silence. Is there
anything to be gained for biblical hermeneutics from a comparative
reading of non-biblical poems from antiquity? In order to illustrate this
question, *Odes* 2.9 and 1.34 may serve as examples. The first of these is
a piece of poetry as well as a piece of criticism, the second a piece of
poetry as well as a piece of theology (at least so it looks):[33]

> Rain is not always streaming down from the clouds
> on roughened fields, wild squalls
>> are not for ever vexing the Caspian sea,
>>> and not through every month of the year,
>
> my dear friend Valgius, does the ice stand motionless
> on the shores of Armenia, nor do the oaks of Garganus
>> labour in north winds nor are ash trees
>>> always being widowed of their leaves.
>
> But you are always harassing your lost lover Mystes
> with mournful melodies and your love never leaves you,
>> not when Vesper rises
>>> nor when he retreats from the scorching sun.

32. Lowth, *De sacra poesi*, 24; *Lectures on the Sacred Poetry*, 1:44.
33. For introductions to Horace and modern studies, see, e.g., D. C. Innes,
"Augustan Critics," in *The Cambridge History of Literary Criticism*. Vol. 1, *Classical Criticism* (ed. G. A. Kennedy; Cambridge: Cambridge University Press, 1989),
245–73; M. Fuhrmann, *Dichtungstheorie der Antike. Aristoteles-Horaz-"Longin"*
(2d ed.; Darmstadt: Wissenschaftliche Buchgesellschaft, 1992), 111–61; B. Kytzler,
Horaz. Eine Einführung (2d ed.; Stuttgart: Philipp Reclam, 1996); E. Oliensis,
Horace and the Rhetoric of Authority (Cambridge: Cambridge University Press,
1998); and the volumes edited by Ludwig (*Horace*); S. J. Harrison, ed., *Homage to
Horace: A Bimillenary Celebration* (Oxford: Clarendon, 1995); T. Woodman and
D. Feeney, eds., *Traditions and Contexts in the Poetry of Horace* (Cambridge: Cambridge University Press, 2002). A brief but brilliant survey of philosophical issues is
offered by N. Rudd, "Horace as a Moralist," in *Horace 2000: A Celebration. Essays
for the Bimillennium* (ed. N. Rudd; London: Duckworth, 1993), 64–88; see also the
relevant articles in Harrison (ed.), *The Cambridge Companion to Horace*.

But the old man who lived three lifetimes did not spend
all his years in mourning for his beloved Antilochus,
    and the Trojan parents and sisters
        of young Troilus did not always

weep for him. The time has come to give over
these soft complaints. Let us rather sing
    of the new trophies of Caesar Augustus,
        of the Niphates frozen hard,

of the Persian river joining its peoples in defeat
and lowering the crests of its rolling waves,
    of the Geloni in their reservation
        riding their horses in their narrow plains.

—Horace, *Odes* 2.9 "*Non semper imbres*"
(trans. David West)[34]

In his address to Valgius, a contemporary poet known not least as a
writer of elegies, Horace dismisses all undue exaggeration and perpetua-
tion of a certain kind of emotions and directs the poet's attention to
worthier subjects than that of a deceased or defected lover. In order to
give more force to his admonitions, he produces arguments from the
analogy of nature as well as from Greek and Roman canonical history. A
sequence of more or less specific images has been designed to make
Valgius aware of the unnatural agitation which underlies his poems, and
two references to classical moments in history further underline this
point. Horace then suggests his alternative to pointless poetry, or more
particularly to Valgius's preferred poetic genre. Deeply personal emotions, it seems, should be replaced by shared public feeling and a response
to political events: "Let us rather sing of the new trophies of Caesar
Augustus." The question may be asked whether the examples adduced in
the second half of the ode subvert the thrust of the first half since they
probably indicate an imposition of order in conditions which are likely to
burst all constraints. Even if such an interpretation is rejected, there
remains a certain ambiguity in this ode, for Horace devoted *Odes* 1.6 to
an apology for not wanting to sing the praises of Augustus and his
general Agrippa:[35]

34. West, trans., *The Complete Odes and Epodes*, 63–64. For the Latin text and
notes, see Horace, *The Odes* (ed. K. Quinn; London: Bristol Classical Press, 1996),
44, 213–15; for more extensive commentary, see R. G. M. Nisbet and M. Hubbard,
A Commentary on Horace: Odes, Book II (Oxford: Clarendon, 1978), 134–51.
35. West, trans., *The Complete Odes and Epodes*, 30–31; cf. Quinn, ed., *The
Odes*, 8–9, 132–35; R. G. M. Nisbet and M. Hubbard, *A Commentary on Horace:
Odes, Book I* (Oxford: Clarendon, 1970), 80–90.

> ...We are too slight for these large themes. Modesty
> and the Muse who commands the unwarlike lyre forbid us
> to diminish the praise of glorious Caesar and yourself
>   by our imperfect talent.

What follows from this poetic statement for the instruction "let us rather sing" of *Odes* 2.9? Readers may well find "endless pleasure in disagreeing with each other" about the tone of the ode, whether or not it has a tinge of irony to it, whether it is designed to console or to tease the affectionate elegiac poet, whether or not it defines political rhetoric as the true purpose of poetry. What seems clear is that Horace is critical of poetry as an expression of deeply felt emotions when he merely sees Valgius waste his love in soft complaints (*"molles querelae"*).

Ellen Oliensis argues in her *Horace and the Rhetoric of Authority* that *Odes* 2.9 was an example of that "emphasis on limit that lends Horatian lyric an 'imperial' character." Horace, she claims, "represents Augustan imperialism as an analogue of his own lyric practice—the imposition of order on unruly materials."[36] However, the question then arises: What materials? In *Odes* 1.6, the ode to general Agrippa, Horace asserts that the proper subjects for his pen were "drinking parties" and convivial battles between girls and young men. And even towards such social enjoyments he adopts an attitude of detachment and calls himself free, or if a little moved, then cheerfully and not exceeding the usual limits (*"nos...vacui, sive quid urimur, non praeter solitum leves"*). This self-image of the emotionally restrained poet is neatly summarized in *Odes* 1.6 in the two words *"tenues"* and *"grandia"*: being himself "too slight," the poet would not attempt to sing of "great themes." In its context, this gesture of modesty refers to epic praise of great heroes. Yet the notion of "great themes" also has a religious aspect since there would be no epic without references to or representations of Mars as the god of war. Accordingly, Horace asks the rhetorical question, "Who could write worthily of Mars girt in adamantine tunic...?" Does Horace, therefore, put those critics in the right who, when they speak of the "aesthetic appreciation" of a poetic text, presuppose the assumption that poetry was not about "great themes" anyway?

The rhetorical question in *Odes* 1.6 is not all Horace has to say about poetry and religion. The gods are present almost everywhere in his poetry—one would only have to think of the images in *Odes* 1.2 of Jupiter who sends hail and snow, who frightens with his lightnings the city of Rome and all the nations, and who would (and did, for Horace)

---

36. Oliensis, *Horace and the Rhetoric of Authority*, 107, 113.

entrust some divine or god-like saviour (Augustus, that is) with the task
of expiating the crime of the Roman civil war. On a similar note, we find
the poet in *Odes* 1.12 submit to conventional religion when he goes
through the pantheon, starting from Jupiter:[37]

> ...What can I do but follow custom and praise first
> the Father who governs from hour to hour
> the affairs of men and gods,
>> the land, and sea, and sky?

> None of his children is greater than himself.
> There is no living thing like him
> or second to him...

The ode which is probably the most explicit one on religious attitudes
is *Odes* 1.34. The poem is often seen to oscillate between Epicureanism
and Stoicism, but as Kenneth Quinn notes, there is "general agreement
that H[orace]'s recantation of Epicureanism is not wholly serious."[38] At
last, this would be a "great theme" in poetry, and the intersection of
philosophy, belief in miracles, and the issue of divine providence in this
ode deserves the reader's attention.

> I used to worship the gods grudgingly,
> and not often, a wanderer expert
>> in a crazy wisdom, but now I am forced
>>> to sail back and once again go over

> the course I had left behind. For Jupiter
> who usually parts the clouds with the fire
>> of his lightning has driven his horses
>>> and his flying chariot across a cloudless sky,

> shaking the dull earth and winding rivers,
> the Styx and the fearsome halls of hateful Taenarus,
>> and the Atlantean limits
>>> of the world. God has the power

> to exchange high and low, to humble the great,
> and bring forward the obscure. With a shrill cry
>> rapacious Fortune snatches the crown from one head
>>> and delights to lay it on another.

> —Horace, *Odes* 1.34 *"Parcus deorum cultor"*
> (trans. David West)[39]

37. West, trans., *The Complete Odes and Epodes*, 35–36; cf. Quinn, ed., *The Odes*, 13–15, 145–48; Nisbet and Hubbard, *Odes, Book I*, 142–69.
38. Quinn, ed., *The Odes*, 186; cf. Rudd, "Horace as a Moralist," and H. P. Syndikus, "Die Einheit des horazischen Lebenswerks" in Ludwig, ed., *Horace*, 207–55.
39. West, trans., *The Complete Odes and Epodes*, 51–52; cf. Quinn, ed., *The Odes*, 31–32, 186–87; Nisbet and Hubbard, *Odes, Book I*, 376–86.

Eclectic readers of Horace may content themselves with the opening line and take Horace as a model of religious indifference. Alternatively, they may appreciate the tone of resignation in the concluding lines on *"rapax Fortuna"* and her little delights. However, what are we to make of the poet who confesses to have been "forced to sail back" from a philosophical current through a miraculous meteorological phenomenon? Does he teach us to exchange what he calls "crazy wisdom" (*"insaniens sapientia"*) for superstitious credulity? Are his images of the thundering horses and flying chariot in a blue sky, of the shaking earth and trembling underworld a genuine, a sublime expression of a sense of being overwhelmed by the majesty and power of God? In other words, has the poet been converted who, in *Satires* 1.5, confidently rejects belief in a miracle with an unmitigated declaration:[40]

> ...Apella the Jew
> may believe it—not me, for I have learned that the gods live a life
> of calm, and that if nature performs a miracle, it's not
> sent down by the gods in anger from their high home in the sky.

It would seem that in *Odes* 1.34 the poet walks away and leaves his readers in the dark about what type of worshipper of the gods he has become and what philosophical orientation he would not regard as foolish.

In a study of the reception history of *Odes* 1.34, Helmut Krasser outlined a development in three stages of its interpretation.[41] The traditional view held that the ode was about the poet's repenting his temporary allegiance to Epicureanism. This view already goes back to commentators in antiquity whose comments were included in most of the early editions of Horace and invited a rather edifying reading of the poem. A new understanding was suggested by the French critics Tanaquil Faber and André Mercier in the seventeenth century who came to the conclusion that Horace was mocking the Stoics here who would revere Jupiter for his frequent miraculous interventions on bright and sunny days—a view admittedly facilitated by a syntactical irregularity in the Latin text of the ode, which later was correctly explained by Bentley in his 1711 edition. For a third position, Krasser refers to Lessing's *Apology for Horace* of 1754 in which this literary critic insists on a distinction between the poet himself and the first-person singular in lyric poetry. "The writer of odes in particular almost always speaks in the first person, but this *I* very rarely is his own *I*. From time to time he has to imagine

40. Rudd, "Horace as a Moralist," 65.
41. H. Krasser, "Büßer, Spötter oder Künstler. Zur Interpretationsgeschichte der Horazode 1,34," in Krasser and Schmidt, eds., *Zeitgenosse Horaz*, 311–43.

himself in the places of others, or rather he does so on purpose, in order to exercise his wit not only within but also outside the sphere of his own sentiments."[42] In Lessing's understanding what matters is the poem as a work of art, not as a delineation of a poet's moral character, and it is characteristic of good poetry to leave some room for interpretation rather than to impose a simple, single doctrine on the reader.

If such a reading of *Odes* 1.34 is plausible, Horace would again emerge as a poet who warns against too strong an emphasis on poetry as a means to convey serious emotions or insights. As far as I am aware, Horace nowhere in his writings specifically recommends subjects such as the power of God or divine providence as subjects for poetry. *"Tenues"* and *"grandia"*—the poet is "too slight" for attempting to sing of "great themes"—may be taken to be a fair expression of his view of this issue. As the *Odes* as well as the *Satires* and the *Epistles* make clear, there is enough to observe in human life to occupy a poet and entertain a reader, and although some touches of religious convention here and there may not distort the work of art, there is no need for a poet to go beyond an attitude of such restrained piety. Thus John Dryden was probably right when, in 1685, he noted that Horace "made use of gods and providence only to serve a turn in poetry."[43] What, if anything, does this mean for reading biblical poetry "after Horace"?

3. *Lowth, the Exegete of the Hebrew Bible*

In his two opening lectures, Robert Lowth[44] praises poetry in general and sketches a rising scale from enjoyment and rhetorical refinement to

42. Lessing, *Werke 1754–57*, 186 (my translation).

43. Dryden, *Essays*, 266; also quoted in Nisbet and Hubbard, *Odes, Book I*, 377, and Krasser, "Büßer, Spötter oder Künstler," 323.

44. Of recent studies of Lowth, in addition to those in the present volume, the following may be mentioned: Norton, *A History of the Bible as Literature*, 2:59–73; C. Bultmann, *Die biblische Urgeschichte in der Aufklärung: Johann Gottfried Herders Interpretation der Genesis als Antwort auf die Religionskritik David Humes* (BHTh 110; Tübingen: Mohr Siebeck, 1999), 75–81; G. Stansell, "Lowth's Isaiah Commentary and Romanticism"; P. K. Tull, "What's New in Lowth? Synchronic Reading in the Eighteenth and Twenty-First Centuries," in *SBL Seminar Papers, 2000* (SBLSP 136; Atlanta: Scholars Press, 2000), 148–82, 183–217 respectively; R. Smend, "Der Entdecker des Parallelismus: Robert Lowth (1710–1787)," in *Prophetie und Psalmen* (ed. B. Huwyler; AOAT 280; Münster: Ugarit-Verlag, 2001), 185–99; R. P. Gordon, "The Legacy of Lowth: Robert Lowth and the Book of Isaiah in Particular," in *Biblical Hebrews, Biblical Texts: Essays in Memory of Michael P. Weizman* (ed. A. Rapoport-Albert and G. Greenberg; JSOTSup 333; Sheffield: Sheffield Academic Press, 2001), 57–76.

moral education and further on to religious enlightenment. He suggests that "the goodness, the wisdom, and the greatness of the Almighty" (*"Dei Optimi Maximi bonitas, sapientia, et magnitudo"*) was the original subject matter of poetry and that the best specimens of such poetry were preserved in the Hebrew Bible.[45] Reading biblical poetry "after Horace," therefore, would mean for a critic to turn from moral philosophy to philosophy of religion. Lowth proposes an understanding of poetry as an adequate means to express a religious awareness of God.

At a more technical level, reading biblical poetry "after Horace" just means reading biblical texts with an acute sense of a poet's or a scribe's use of language and imagery. This may indeed, as is common, be called an enhanced "aesthetic appreciation" of biblical texts and of the style of the biblical authors. One could point out, for example, an analogy between the way in which Horace exploits certain features of nature in *Odes* 2.9 and Jeremiah's poetic strategy in Jer 18:13–17. The "ice on the shores of Armenia" and the "snow on the mountain range of Lebanon" have a similar effect on the imagination of the reader (even if the thrust of the argument in both cases goes in directly opposite directions). In this sense, Chapters 6–9 of Lowth's *Lectures* on biblical writers—"Of poetic imagery from the objects of nature" (*"de imaginibus poeticis, ex rebus naturalibus"*), "Of poetic imagery from common life" (*"de imaginibus ex communi vita"*), "Of poetic imagery from sacred topics" (*"de imaginibus ex rebus sacris"*), and "Of poetic imagery from the sacred history" (*"de imaginibus ex historia sacra"*)—offer a kind of analysis which readers of Horace would find equally useful. Poetic imagery from these four sources has its significance in ancient Judean poetry just as much as in Roman poetry, and, going beyond Lowth, even biblical narratives may usefully be approached from such a critical angle.

At another level, the genius of the biblical writers will be seen in a different light when "Moses, David, Isaiah" (to quote Lowth's favourite triad) become as it were members of the same guild of poets as Horace and all those other Greek and Latin writers. This aspect comes through strongest in Chapters 14–17 of Lowth's *Lectures*, which are devoted to the issue of the sublime—"Of the sublime in general…" (*"de sublimi genere…"*), "Of sublimity of expression" (*"de sublimitate dictionis"*), "Of sublimity of sentiment" (*"de sublimitate conceptuum"*), and "Of sublimity of passion" (*"de sublimitate affectuum"*). Referring to (Pseudo-) Longinus, Lowth defines sublimity as a

---

45. Lowth, *De sacra poesi*, 21; *Lectures on the Sacred Poetry*, 1:38.

force of composition, whatever it be, which strikes and overpowers the mind, which excites the passions, and which expresses ideas at once with perspicuity and elevation (*illa quaecunque sit orationis vis, quae mentem ferit et percellit, quae movet affectus, quae rerum imagines clare et eminenter exprimit*).[46]

"After Horace," and with Longinus, Lowth extends the narrow limits which Horace set for poetry as the voice of the passions and consequently acknowledges, especially in his lecture *De sublimitate affectuum*, that emotional turmoil was nothing unknown to biblical poets. Their individuality as sensitive human beings can be discovered behind the poetic compositions which they produced. The book of Job offers the foremost example of such sensitivity, but the "David" of the Psalms betrays an equally vivid character. The prophets are no weaker figures, even if Lowth has some reservations about Jeremiah as a man more of the "softer affections" ("*nec in hoc minus eminet Jeremias, etsi lenioribus affectibus magis fortasse idoneus*"), a point which he illustrates with a reference to the poem in Jer 4:19–21, that is, the poem with the opening: "My bowels, my bowels! I am pained at my very heart; my heart maketh a noise in me…" (thus the King James Version).[47] The literary critic and exegete would thus invite readers to relate to the writers of biblical poetry in a sympathetic way. Readers and scholars with an interest in prophetic biography should, however, remind themselves of Lessing's distinction between the poet himself and the first-person singular in lyric poetry. Furthermore, for a comparative study of biblical poetry one could also refer to certain philosophical *topoi* in non-biblical poetry and compare, for example, the "*non semper*" motif in Horace's *Odes* 2.9 and the mood swings in the Psalms, or the personification of "*rapax Fortuna*" in *Odes* 1.34 and the assertions about God in the Song of Hannah (1 Sam 2:1–10). The exploration of the poetic force of biblical texts is still a challenge for contemporary biblical studies.[48]

46. Lowth, *De sacra poesi*, 171; *Lectures on the Sacred Poetry*, 1:307; see Longinus, *On the Sublime* (ed. D. Russell; LCL 199; Cambridge, Mass.: Harvard University Press, 1995).

47. Lowth, *De sacra poesi*, 222; *Lectures on the Sacred Poetry*, 1:386–87 (Lowth quotes Jer 4:19–21 in conjunction with 4:23); cf. also Lowth, *De sacra poesi*, 283–84; *Lectures on the Sacred Poetry*, 2:87–89.

48. The conference in Oxford in April 2003 was the perfect occasion to be made aware of Hugh Williamson's contribution to the P. D. Miller *Festschrift*: H. G. M. Williamson, "Reading the Lament Psalms Backwards," in *A God So Near: Essays on Old Testament Theology in Honor of Patrick D. Miller* (ed. B. A. Strawn and N. R. Brown; Winona Lake, Ind.: Eisenbrauns, 2003), 3–15.

At a third level, reading biblical poetry "after Horace" takes us back to
the issue of natural religion, and this not just because Jupiter, too, sends
"fierce hail and snow" (*Odes* 1.2) or "brings back ugly winters and
removes them" (*Odes* 2.10). In his lecture *De sublimitate conceptuum*,
Lowth does not explicitly address this issue. Nevertheless, when he lists
divine attributes such as power and wisdom, this is clearly an echo of
contemporary preoccupations with the demonstration of "the being and
attributes of God from his works of creation." Job 38; Ps 33, and Isa 40
(one might add Jer 5:21–25, which Derham quotes in his Boyle Lectures)[49] are adduced to justify the claim that in regard to this theme "the
Hebrew writers have obtained an unrivalled pre-eminence" ("*unice
eminent et excellunt*").

> The greatness, the power, the justice, the immensity of God; the infinite
> wisdom of his works and of his dispensations, are the subjects in which
> the Hebrew Poetry is always conversant, and always excels. (*Dei magni-
> tudo, potentia, justitia, immensitas; divinorum factorum et consiliorum
> infinita sapientia; argumenta sunt, in quibus et perpetuo, et semper digne,
> versatur; in quibus plane triumphat, Hebraeorum Poesis.*)[50]

Lectures 25–29 on the ode and the hymn culminate in the praise of Ps 104
on the power, the wisdom and the providence of God. "There is nothing
of the kind extant, indeed nothing can be conceived, more perfect than
this hymn…" ("*hoc Hymno nihil extat, nihil cogitari potest, perfectius*").
And yet, the biblical poem allows further comparisons: the hymn to Zeus
by the Stoic philosopher Cleanthes is a poetic composition, Lowth states,
"replete with truths not less solid than magnificent" ("*pulcherrimum sane
antiquae sapientiae monumentum, sensibus magnificis, solidis, verisque
refertum*"). All of the philosopher's sentiments concerning the power of
God, natural law, human folly and the invocation of God "breathe so true
and unaffected a spirit of piety, that they seem, in some measure, to
approach the excellence of the sacred poetry" ("*haec omnia tam sano
minimeque fucato pietatis affectu animantur, ut ad Sacrorum etiam
Vatum spiritum aliquatenus videantur accedere*").[51] Thus, where a literary critic discovers grand and sublime themes in poetry, a meaningful
relationship between poetry and religion can be discussed. And religious

49. Derham, *Physico-Theology*, 434.
50. Lowth, *De sacra poesi*, 195; *Lectures on the Sacred Poetry*, 1:348.
51. Lowth, *De sacra poesi*, 387–88; *Lectures on the Sacred Poetry*, 2:280–82.
On Ps 104, see J. Barr, *Biblical Faith and Natural Theology* (Oxford: Clarendon,
1993), 81–85. For the Hymn of Cleanthes, see A. A. Long and D. N. Sedley, *The
Hellenistic Philosophers* (2 vols.; Cambridge: Cambridge University Press, 1987),
1:326–27 and 2:326–27; J. C. Thom, *Cleanthes' Hymn to Zeus* (Tübingen: Mohr
Siebeck, 2005).

poetry is quite obviously more than just a didactic vehicle for transmitting points of religious doctrine. In some cases, poetic texts from different cultures reveal themselves to be expressions of human perceptions of God. Every relevant poem, not only from the biblical tradition, would challenge the reader to engage in a dialogue with the poet about the kind of religious insight which found expression in his composition.

From the perspective of intellectual history it may seem doubtful whether my emphasis on the humanity of the poet and on natural religion does in fact do justice to Lowth's work. And the answer to this question may well be a negative one. More than one passage in the *Lectures* suggests a rather conventional frame of reference for Lowth's investigations of biblical poetry. So why emphasize the notion of sublimity when Lowth makes a distinction between a "natural" species of enthusiasm and a "wildly different one," of "a much higher origin," the "true and genuine enthusiasm...with which the sublimer poetry of the Hebrews, and particularly the prophetic, is animated"? ("*est certe longe diversus, et altioris quidem originis, verus ille et germanus εvθουσιασμος...quo solummodo Hebraeorum Poesis sublimior, ac maxime Prophetica, incitatur.*") "I shall endeavour to detract nothing from the dignity of that inspiration, which proceeds from higher causes...," Lowth declares ("*ut nihil derogemus Divini Spiritus afflatui*").[52] And finally, for all his groundbreaking investigation of prophetic poetry, he includes as Chapter 11 a lecture on "Mystical Allegory" in which he accepts the traditional theory about a specific kind of figurative speech to which the New Testament has given Christians the indispensable key. Lowth detects the basis for this allegorical character of Old Testament texts in "the nature of the Jewish economy" ("*fundamentum habet in ipsa Judaicae Religionis natura positum*"), which, accordingly, one could only regard as a prelude to Christianity.[53] Thus can the claim be defended that, following Lowth, we should recognize "sacred poetry" at the centre of the Hebrew Bible rather than, for example, the theme of promise which finds its christological fulfilment in the New Testament?

In my view, traditional conceptual and doctrinal definitions recede from the centre as the focus of exegetical interest shifts to the poetic texts in all their diversity. Lowth himself does not discuss all possible forms of a reader's engagement with biblical poetry. He just seems to rely on the two key notions of "sublimity" and, corresponding to this, "admiration." Thus he states,

52. Lowth, *De sacra poesi*, 209 and 194; *Lectures on the Sacred Poetry*, 1:367 and 347
53. Lowth, *De sacra poesi*, 134; *Lectures on the Sacred Poetry*, 1:238.

How much the sacred poetry of the Hebrews excels in exciting the
passions, and in directing them to their noblest end and aim;…how it
strikes and fires the admiration by the contemplation of the Divine
Majesty; and, forcing the affections of love, hope, and joy, from unworthy
and terrestrial objects, elevates them to the pursuit of the supreme
good;…is a subject which at present wants no illustration, and which,
though not unconnected with sublimity in a general view, would be
improperly introduced in this place. (*Quantum vero in Affectibus com-
movendis, et ad suum finem rite dirigendis, praestat sacra Hebraeorum
Poesis; quomodo…Admiratione per Divinae Majestatis contemplationem
animum percellit et incendit; Gaudium, Spem, Amorem, a rerum terrena-
rum et abjectarum amplexu revulsum, ad Summum Bonum traducit;…haec
omnia neque hic loci egent explicatione, nec, quanquam cum summa
Sublimitate plerumque conjuncta, et ad finem suum egregie perducta,
proprie ad rem praesentem faciunt.*)[54]

What is clear, however, is that for Lowth biblical poems are not just
objects for scholarly description and classification. The poetic texts have
a specific force and significance which would elicit a response by every
individual reader. Biblical poetry, therefore, does not depend on the two
"grand narratives" into which canonical tradition has placed it. In 1753,
Lowth could still accept and propound the argument that biblical poetry
was the most ancient poetry known and that in its origin it was—to
borrow Matthew Tindal's phrase—"as old as the creation." In 1753, too,
the christological unity of the Bible was still assured by the idea of
allegorical prophecy—in spite of Anthony Collins's criticism. When
sacred poetry moved into the centre of the Hebrew Bible in the mid-
eighteenth century, this change of emphasis would not necessarily represent an alternative to obsolete models of hermeneutics in the theological
tradition. Today, biblical poetry may have acquired an even greater
significance as the foundation of biblical faith than in Robert Lowth's
time. Biblical history, in turn, may be more properly considered a source
of poetic imagery than a subject for historical or theological investigation. If there is a reason to call Lowth's book a classic, it is the fact
that his analysis of biblical poetry still has the potential to develop a
momentum of its own.

54. Lowth, *De sacra poesi*, 211–12; *Lectures on the Sacred Poetry*, 1:375–76.

CHARLES-FRANÇOIS HOUBIGANT:
HIS BACKGROUND, WORK AND IMPORTANCE FOR LOWTH

John Rogerson

One, whom I honour as an author, and respect as a friend.

Thus did the Oxford hebraist Benjamin Kennicott describe Charles-François Houbigant; and commenting on Houbigant's *Biblia Hebraica* Kennicott wrote:

> It seems to proceed upon so just a plan, as to its main principles and to be executed (in the general) with so much skill and judgment, as to claim for its worthy author the applause of all the friends of Religion and Learning.[1]

Kennicott was not the only enthusiastic supporter of Houbigant. Writing in 1786 in his *Prospectus of a New Translation of the Holy Bible*, Alexander Geddes had the following to say about Houbigant's *Biblia Hebraica*:

> Nothing can exceed the purity, simplicity, perspicuity and energy of his translation; and if he has not always been equally happy in his conjectural emendation of the text, it cannot be denied that he has, at least, carried away the palm from all those who preceded him in the same career. The clamors [*sic*] that have been raised against him are the clamors of illiberal ignorance, or of partiality to a system which he had turned into ridicule. While his mode of interpreting is approved by a Lowth, a Kennicott, a Michaelis and a Starck, the barkings of inferior critics will not much injure him.[2]

The *Biblia Hebraica* over which Kennicott and Geddes were enthusing was a monumental work of scholarship which appeared in its complete form in 1753; and before I describe it, we must note an irony. The

---

1. Benjamin Kennicott, *The State of the Hebrew Text of the Old Testament considered*. Vol. 2, *Dissertation the Second* (Oxford, 1759), 471, 488.

2. Alexander Geddes, *Prospectus of a New Translation of the Holy Bible from corrected Texts of the Originals, compared with the Ancient Versions, with Various Readings, Explanatory Notes and Critical Observations* (London, 1786), 81.

purpose of this conference is to commemorate two works published in
1753—Astruc's *Conjectures* and Lowth's *Praelectiones*, both of which,
it can be fairly said, are dwarfed by Houbigant's *Biblia Hebraica*, at least
from the point of view of the range and depth of scholarship of the
respective works. Yet while a conference is being held to commemorate
Astruc and Lowth, Houbigant has virtually disappeared from the history
of Old Testament interpretation. While it comes as no surprise that he is
absent from Hans-Joachim Kraus's *Geschichte*,[3] the lack of reference to
him in Diestel is more unexpected.[4] Houbigant has suffered the same fate
in the otherwise comprehensive *Dictionary of Biblical Interpretation*
edited by John Hayes,[5] and although references to him can be found in
nineteenth-century Introductions to the Bible or the Old Testament, these
are usually dismissive of his work.[6] The reasons for Houbigant's descent
into obscurity will be considered after his life has been briefly outlined.[7]

Houbigant was born in Paris in 1686 and entered the Oratory there at
the age of eighteen.[8] After teaching in Juilly, Marseilles and Soissons he
was called by his superiors to work at the church of Saint Magloire in
Paris. Here, as a result of his labours in the church, he suffered the complete loss of his hearing, after which he seems to have devoted himself to
scholarship. He adopted the system of vocalizing Hebrew advocated by
François Masclef (died 1728), of which more later, and published in
1732 a work entitled *Racines Hebraiques sans points-voyelles* in which
he attacked the Masoretic text and its vowel points and appended a
dictionary of Hebrew verbs and their meanings.[9] All the principles of his

3. H.-J. Kraus, *Geschichte der historisch-kritischen Erforschung des Alten
Testaments* (2d ed.; Neukirchen–Vluyn: Neukirchener, 1969).

4. Ludwig Diestel, *Geschichte des Alten Testamentes in der christlichen Kirche*
(Jena, 1869).

5. J. H. Hayes, *Dictionary of Biblical Interpretation* (2 vols.; Nashville: Abingdon, 1999).

6. See, for example, T. H. Horne, *An Introduction to the Critical Study and
Knowledge of the Holy Scriptures* (5th ed.; 4 vols.; London, 1825), 2:224; E. Riehm,
Einleitung in das Alte Testament (2 vols.; Halle, 1889–90), 2:472.

7. For what follows, see *Dictionnaire de la Bible* (Paris: Letouzey et Ané, 1903),
765–66.

8. In fact, Houbigant's dates are disputed, and are given as c. 1686 or 1687–
c. 1783? or 1784 by Françoise Deconinck-Brossard, "England and France in the
Eighteenth Century," in *Reading the Text: Biblical Criticism and Literary Theory*
(ed. S. Prickett; Oxford: Blackwell, 1991), 137–81. She refers to A.-M.-P. Ingold,
ed., *Essai de bibliographie oratorienne* (Paris, 1880–82), 62–63, which I have been
unable to obtain.

9. C. F. Houbigant, *Racines Hebraiques sans points-voyelles ou Dictionaire
Hebraique par racines, Où sont expliquez, suivant les Anciens et Nouveaux*

later *Biblia Hebraica* were contained in this work. The *Biblia Hebraica* itself appeared in four magnificent folio volumes in 1753.[10] Volume I contained an Introduction of 190 pages which repeated Houbigant's reasons for distrusting the Masoretic text (MT) and its vowel points, and his reasons for preferring the Samaritan Pentateuch. Some of his arguments were based upon the existence of Hebrew manuscripts that differed from the MT; but he also made important observations about the textual history of the Samaritan Pentateuch. The main part of the Introduction, however, was devoted to classifying the mistakes that, in Houbigant's opinion, had crept into the MT, and to laying down principles for correcting them, including conjectural emendation.

The text of the Hebrew Bible itself was given without vowel points and followed the edition published in 1705 by Van der Hooght. For the Pentateuch it gave the readings of the Samaritan in the margin, where they differed from the MT. Opposite the Hebrew was a translation into Latin that was Houbigant's own, and following each chapter were extensive notes in Latin not only on the text and translation, but on critical matters. How these affected the work of Lowth will be discussed later, but several examples can be given here. The textual variations of the length of the lives of the patriarchs in Gen 5 are well known, and Houbigant did not hesitate to set out all the evidence fully, with comparative tables indicating the numbers given in the Hebrew, Greek and Samaritan versions.[11] There are also long discussions about reconciling the period of 430 years during which the Israelites sojourned in Egypt according to Exod 12:40, with other chronological and genealogical evidence, as well as of the chronology of the period of the Judges.[12] In making the lengths of the reigns of the kings of Judah and Israel add up to the same number, Houbigant assigned a reign of ten years and six months to Zechariah son of Jeroboam (2 Kgs 15:8 says that he reigned six months), and he also increased the length of Pekah's reign from twenty to thirty years (cf. 2 Kgs 15:27).[13] This exemplifies one of Houbigant's principles, that the text should make sense historically as well as grammatically and that if it

Interpretes touts les Mots Hebreux et Caldaïques du Texte Original des Livres Saints [whole title *sic*] (Paris, 1732).

10. C. F. Houbigant, *Biblia Hebraica cum notis criticis et versione Latina ad notas criticis facta* (4 vols.; Paris, 1753). Some authorities give 1747–53 as the dates of publication, but the copy that I consulted in Aberdeen gave the date of each of the four volumes as 1753, and this is also the information given in the British Library Catalogue.

11. Houbigant, *Biblia Hebraica*, 1:15–17.

12. Ibid., 2:xii–xiii, xvi–xxix.

13. Ibid., 2:xliv.

did not, this was because there was a mistake in the text that needed to be identified and corrected. Although entitled *Biblia Hebraica*, the work also included the books of the so-called Apocrypha. It can be said that the *Biblia Hebraica* is not only a monumental piece of scholarship, being in effect a textual and critical commentary and new translation of the whole of the Old Testament; it is also the work of a scholar who, if he had lived in later times, would arguably have been a radical historical critic. In fact, Houbigant was radical in the one area in which it was open to an orthodox Christian scholar of the first part of the eighteenth century to be radical, and that was in regard to the state of the Hebrew text of the Old Testament. But at times, as we shall see, this radicalism touched on historical matters. It says much for the Roman Catholic Church of that period that a work of scholarship that altered the text of the Old Testament so freely (a rough estimate is that Houbigant proposed around five thousand alterations), and that produced a new Latin translation in preference to the Vulgate, should have been rewarded by Pope Benedict XIV with two gold medals.[14] The production of such a monumental work must have left its mark upon the author, and apart from reissues of sections of the *Biblia Hebraica*, in the years that remained until his death in Paris on 31 October 1784, Houbigant's main publication was a critical examination of a French psalter prepared by the friars of the Capuchin order.

What were the causes of his decline into obscurity? In the first place he adopted and advocated the method of reading unpointed Hebrew that was introduced by François Masclef in his *Grammaire Hébraïque* of 1716. This made two assumptions: first, that a Hebrew consonant should be pronounced together with the vowel of its name, i.e. *beth* should be pronounced bé, *gimel* as gi, *dalet* as da etc.; second, that there were six written vowels in Hebrew, *aleph* pronounced "a," *he* pronounced "e," *vav* pronounced "i," *het* pronounced "u," *yod* pronounced "ai" (as in "raison" in French) and *ayin* pronounced "â."[15] In practice, this meant that *Moshe* would be pronounced *Mishe* and that the consonants *dalet*, *beth*, *resh* would be pronounced *daber*.

Anyone today used to speaking or reading Hebrew fluently may well be astonished that such a system could be taken seriously; but taken seriously it was, and the Norrisian Professor of Divinity in Cambridge, John Hey, could write of Masclef's grammar in his Divinity Lectures published in 1796 that

14. Kennicott, *State of the Hebrew Text*, 491.
15. Houbigant, *Racines*, lxxv–lxxvi. See also James Robertson, *Clavis Pentateuchi, sive Analysis omnium vocum hebraicarum suo ordine in Pentateucho Moseos occurentium. Una cum Versione Latina et Anglica* (Edinburgh, 1770), 80–81.

I know none more to be recommended; as it gives rules for the Chaldee, Syriac, and Samaritan, as well as for what is commonly called Hebrew.[16]

A modified version of Masclef's system was used in the Hebrew Grammar of Gregory Sharpe published in 1751, in which the *matres lectiones* gave the long vowels, the only other vowel being a short "e." "Thus you may read Hebrew fluently" Sharpe assured his readers.[17] Houbigant backed up his advocacy of using unpointed texts by reference, among other things, to the Samaritan Pentateuch, which lacked vowel points; and indeed, it was his high estimation of this version over the MT which provided his critics with ammunition against him. Another reason why his position was heavily criticized was because he believed that all printed editions of the Hebrew Bible were derived from one Rabbinic version. Also, his treatment of the Hebrew text seemed cavalier in the extreme in circles which still clung in some way to accepting that the MT was the divinely inspired original. At the end of the eighteenth century, E. F. K. Rosenmüller expressed an opinion that was to become standard, if not in such vivid language, in subsequent German Protestant scholarship. This, unfairly to my mind, spoke patronisingly of Houbigant's supposed incomplete competence as a linguist, and likened him to a physician who exaggerated the illnesses of his patients in order to make them more ready to accept his cures:

> *Gleich den medicinischen Charletans, welche die Krankheiten ihrer Patienten so viel, wie möglich, vergrößern, um ihr eigenes Verdienst desto geltender zu machen, sucht auch Houbigant das Verderbnis des hebräischen Textes recht groß vorzustellen, damit man die von ihm angebotenen und so sehr empfohlenen Hülfsmittel so begieriger annehme.*[18]

How fair this verdict was is a matter to be addressed, and before I consider the use made by Lowth of Houbigant's alterations, I shall consider several examples that are given in the Introduction to the *Biblia Hebraica*. In Gen 47:21 the Hebrew reads, of the action of Joseph towards the Egyptians העביר אתו לערים. This is rendered by the RV as "he removed them to the cities." For Houbigant this made no sense historically. If Joseph removed the people from the fields to the cities, how did he expect the fields to be sown? The simplest way to solve the problem was to follow the Samaritan and the LXX and to read העביד, "he made

16. John Hey, *Lectures in Divinity* (4 vols.; Cambridge, 1796–98), 1:23.

17. Quoted in Robertson, *Clavis Pentateuchi*, 83. See Gregory Sharpe, *Two Dissertations...to which is added...a Hebrew Grammar and Lexicon without points*, (London, 1751).

18. E. F. K. Rosenmüller, *Handbuch für die Literatur der biblischen Kritik und Exegese* (Göttingen, 1797), 500.

bondsmen of them."[19] Whether Houbigant was the first scholar to make this proposal I do not know. It was certainly not accepted by Delitzsch[20] or by Kalisch, who described the reading of the Samaritan as "without support or authority, and scarcely grammatical."[21] By the time we get to Skinner's ICC commentary of 1910, the reading proposed by Houbigant had been generally accepted, and it is found in all modern English translations including the conservative NIV and ESV.

An example of an emendation by Houbigant that has not found its way into subsequent scholarship is at Gen 9:5, but it is an excellent example of Houbigant's critical acumen. The passage in question says (RSV):

> For your lifeblood I will surely require a reckoning; of every beast I will require it and of man.

An explanation of the statement that God will require a reckoning of every beast that kills a man, is that this is envisaged in Exod 21:28, which commands the death penalty for an ox that gores a man or woman to death.[22] However, it can be argued against this that the law in Exodus is more directed towards the responsibilities of the owner of the ox than the misdeeds of the ox itself. For Houbigant, the passage is illogical. Is God going somehow to take vengeance on any lion or wolf that devours a human, he asks? Animals are not subject to laws, and therefore the law does not apply to them.[23] Houbigant's solution was to read, with the Samaritan, כל-חי, in the sense of "every living [person]," instead of כל-חיה. No commentary that I have perused draws attention to this possible difficulty, which certainly deserves consideration.

Having begun to introduce Houbigant's approach to the MT and its interpretation, I shall continue by discussing the use of Houbigant made by Lowth in his Commentary on Isaiah of 1779. So far as I have been able to tell, Houbigant's *Biblia Hebraica* appeared too late to affect Lowth's *Praelectiones*.[24] However, there are around forty references

19. Houbigant, *Biblia Hebraica*, 1:xxix.

20. F. Delitzsch, *Die Genesis ausgelegt* (Leipzig, 1853), 2:125.

21. M. M. Kalisch, *Historical and Critical Commentary on the Old Testament with a New Translation* (London, 1858), 707.

22. So S. R. Driver, *The Book of Genesis with Introduction and Notes* (Westminster Commentaries; London: Methuen, 1904), 97.

23. Houbigant, *Biblia Hebraica*, 1:xxxiii. "Num enim qui leones, aut qui lupi homines vivas devorant, ex iis Deus humanum sanguinem repetit, sanguinemque sanguine ulciscitur?... Nam ad bestias nihil de lege, de bestiis nihil ad legem pertinet."

24. R. Lowth, *Isaiah: A New Translation; with a Preliminary Dissertation and Notes, Critical, Philological, and Explanatory* (1779; new ed., Glasgow, 1822).

to Houbigant in Lowth's Isaiah commentary, and I shall discuss some specific examples and then make general observations before coming to a conclusion.

In Isa 7:17, part of the judgment passed upon Ahaz for refusing a sign from God is that

> The LORD will bring upon you and upon your people and upon your father's house such days as have not come since the day that Ephraim departed from Judah—the king of Assyria. (RSV)

In Houbigant's view the words "king of Assyria" were a marginal gloss meant to explain the phrase "the bee which is in the land of Assyria" which comes in the following verse, and which had inadvertently been copied into the main text. He based his argument upon the attempts of the Versions and older interpreters to make sense of the verse, none of which he found convincing.[25] Lowth accepted this:

> [T]hey do not join well in construction with the words preceding: as may be seen by the strange manner in which the ancient interpreters have taken them; and they very inelegantly forestall the mention of the king of Assyria, which comes in with great propriety in the 20th verse. I have therefore taken the liberty of omitting them in the translation.[26]

This textual alteration, which Houbigant seems to be the first to have proposed, has become standard in modern scholarship. Gray, in the ICC, indeed, credits Houbigant and Lowth with having been the first scholars to recognize the phrase "the king of Assyria" as a gloss. Wildberger, in the Biblischer Kommentar, notes that it is almost universally accepted as a gloss, and the phrase is omitted from the main text of the NEB and REB.[27] The Study Edition of the New Jerusalem Bible notes that "*the king of Assyria* is a gloss based on a misinterpretation."[28]

Another interesting example of Houbigant's work concerns Isa 25:7. The Hebrew reads ובלע בהר הזה פני הלוט הלוט על כל־העמים and is rendered literally by the RV as

> And he will destroy in this mountain the face of the covering that is cast over all peoples.

25. Houbigant, *Biblia Hebraica*, 4:20.

26. Lowth, *Isaiah*, 2:87.

27. G. B. Gray, *A Critical and Exegetical Commentary on the Book of Isaiah I–XXXIX* (Edinburgh: T. & T. Clark, 1912), 137; H. Wildberger, *Jesaja* (BKAT 10; Neukirchen–Vluyn: Neukirchener, 1969), 297.

28. *The New Jerusalem Bible, Study Edition* (London: Darton, Longman & Todd, 1994), 1201.

Houbigant conjectured that פֵֹני had become misplaced, and that it should
come after עַל.[29] Lowth noted that this was the reading found in the
Bodleian MS, and added

> The word פֵֹני has been removed from its right place into the line above,
> where it makes no sense; as Houbigant conjectured.[30]

Accordingly, Lowth rendered the verse

> And on this mountain shall he destroy.
> The covering that covers the face of all the peoples.[31]

Wildberger writes that this alteration has found "*wenig Zustimmung*" and
notes the attempts of Delitzsch and Naegelsbach to explain the MT,
attempts which he describes as "*Verlegenheitsauskünfte.*" He concludes,
"*Vermutlich haben Houbigant und Lowth das Richtige gesehen*"; yet
arguably, he is not completely fair to Houbigant. Wildberger gives the
impression that Houbigant and Lowth based their reading on one Hebrew
MS. In fact, Houbigant's suggestion was the result of his critical acumen,
which was subsequently supported by the Oxford MS to which Lowth
had access via Kennicott.[32]

Another emendation proposed by Houbigant that has found wide-
spread acceptance is at Isa 30:12. The Hebrew ותבטחו בעשק ונלוז is
rendered by the RV as "and trust in oppression and perverseness," translations also given by RSV and NRSV. Houbigant read בעקש, transposing
the consonants ש and ק and translating the word as "*in perverso.*"[33] Lowth
regarded this as "a very probable conjecture"[34] and in his own translation
rendered the phrase "And have trusted in obliquity and perversion."[35]
The NEB has "Trust in devious and dishonest practices," while Wildberger comments that עשק, meaning "oppression" or "exaction"

> *fügt sich nicht wohl in den Zusammenhang und ist keine befriedigende
> Parallele zum folgenden* נלוז. *Mit großer Einmütigkeit...ändern die Text-
> arbeiter in* עקש, *womit die Schwierigkeiten behoben sind.*[36]

Before I consider a case which shows evidence of the excesses of which
Houbigant's opponents complained, I want to discuss one other example

29. Houbigant, *Biblia Hebraica*, 4:65.
30. Lowth, *Isaiah*, 2:191.
31. Ibid., 1:74.
32. Wildberger, *Jesaja*, 959.
33. Houbigant, *Biblia Hebraica*, 4:81.
34. Lowth, *Isaiah*, 2:213.
35. Ibid., 1:91.
36. Wildberger, *Jesaja*, 1174.

of a conjecture which Lowth accepted. In Isa 28:4, the Hebrew has אשר
יראה הראה אותה, translated by the RV as "Which when he that looketh
upon it seeth it." Lowth commented that ירה taken with הראה made "a
miserable tautology" and accepted as "a happy conjecture of Houbigant"
the suggestion that יראה should be read as יארה by the transposition of
two consonants, with the rendering "he plucketh it."[37] This verb can be
found with this meaning at Song 5:1. The commentaries that I have
perused do not take this issue up, and while the RSV and NRSV avoid
producing a "miserable tautology," they accept the MT. The NEB, on the
other hand, has "pluck" for "see."

At Isa 11:4, Houbigant was troubled by the Hebrew phrase "the rod of
his mouth," שבט פיו. He argued that a rod could be used by the hand or
the arm, but not by a mouth. Consequently, he read שבת and posited a
noun meaning "blast" which he derived from the verb נשב, meaning "to
blow."[38] Lowth commented that the conjecture was ingenious and probable, that it seemed to be confirmed by the Septuagint and the Chaldee,
which had "word of his mouth," and that it was a perfect parallel to "the
breath of his lips" in the next line.[39] No commentary or translation that I
have seen finds any problem with "the rod of his mouth" and if, as is
likely, this is a poetic phrase, it is odd that the famous lecturer on the
poetry of the Hebrews did not see it as such. This is an example, then, of
one of Houbigant's extravagant conjectures, although my own rough
impression is that they were far outweighed by suggestions that have
either been adopted by subsequent scholarship, or which deserve serious
consideration.

A consideration of Lowth's enthusiasm for the work of Houbigant
enables us to place Lowth more securely in his context in the world of
eighteenth-century scholarship. While he did not go so far as Houbigant
in advocating that Hebrew should be read other than according to the
Masoretic punctuation, he did nonetheless express the view that greater
progress would have been made in the study of the scriptures of the Old
Testament if the Masoretic punctuation had been considered as an
assistant and not an infallible guide.[40] Again, if one reads Lowth's Preliminary Dissertation to the commentary on Isaiah having first read the
Prolegomena to Houbigant's *Biblia Hebraica*, it will become immediately obvious how much Lowth owed to his French Catholic colleague.

37. Lowth, *Isaiah*, 2:199–200. See Houbigant, *Biblia Hebraica*, 4:71, and
Racines, 12.
38. Houbigant, *Biblia Hebraica*, 4:32.
39. Lowth, *Isaiah*, 2:113.
40. Ibid., 1:lxxiii.

But I hope that this lecture will have done more than help to place Lowth more firmly within the world of eighteenth-century biblical scholarship. I hope that it will have helped to rescue Houbigant from an obscurity that he has not deserved; and there is obviously much more research that could be done on the links between Lowth, Kennicott and Houbigant on the basis of their correspondence, if that exists. Let, indeed, the last word come from Kennicott, who defended his friend against the criticism that Houbigant's *Biblia Hebraica* did not add the variant readings from Hebrew manuscripts, in the following noble tribute:

> When learned men consider, how very laborious a work is already executed, and what a very toilsome addition they would willingly pre-scribe further: should they not also consider the shortness of human life; and reflect, *what an heavy burden they would bind upon another, when they themselves* (it may be) *would not touch it with one of their fingers*? Instead therefore of censuring the author for what he has not done, and perhaps at his time of life could not do; it may be nobler and more just to be thankful for what he has performed, and thus usefully communicated to the world.[41]

---

41. Kennicott, *State of the Hebrew Text*, 489.

DIE LITERARISCHE GATTUNG DES BUCHES HIOB: ROBERT LOWTH UND SEINE ERBEN

Markus Witte

Niemand klassifiziert so gerne als der Mensch,
besonders der deutsche...

—Jean Paul[1]

Die Frage nach der literarischen Gattung (*genre*)[2] des Buches Hiob zu stellen, ist gefährlich. Bekanntlich wurde Theodor von Mopsuestia auf dem Konzil von Konstantinopel (533) unter anderem auch deshalb verurteilt, weil er das Buch Hiob als eine von einem heidnischen Weisen erfundene Dichtung im Stil einer griechischen Tragödie bezeichnet hatte (und daher aus dem Kanon der biblischen Schriften hatte ausschließen wollen).[3] Und selbst der eigentliche Begründer der alttestamentlichen Gattungsforschung, Hermann Gunkel (1862–1932), mußte sich vorwerfen lassen, seine Einordnung des Hiobbuches als Streitreden der Weisen klinge "fast kleinlaut."[4] Dennoch sollte der Frage nach der Gattung des Hiobbuches sowohl aus literaturgeschichtlichen als auch aus hermeneutischen Gründen nicht ausgewichen werden.

> In every respect the poem of *Job* stands in a class by itself. More than any other book in the Hebrew canon it needs bringing near to the modern

---

1. J. Paul, *Vorschule der Ästhetik* (ed. W. Henckmann; Philosophische Bibliothek 425; Hamburg: Meiner, 1967), 67.
2. Die begriffliche und sachliche Differenzierung zwischen Form und Gattung (*genre*) ist vor allem ein Problem in der neueren Forschung, vgl. dazu M. Rösel, "Formen/Gattungen," *RGG*[4] 3 (2000): 187.
3. *Patrologiae cursus completus* (Accurante J.-P. Migne ; Series Latina 66 ; 1864), 697–98; vgl. dazu L. Pirot, *L'Œuvre exégétique de Théodore de Mopsueste* (SPIB 8 ; Rome, 1913), 131–34; J. M. Vosté, "L'œuvre exégétique de Théodore de Mopsueste au IIe Concile de Constantinople," *RB* 38 (1929) : 390–93.
4. L. Köhler, *Der hebräische Mensch. Eine Skizze. Mit einem Anhang: Die hebräische Rechtsgemeinde* (Tübingen: J. C. B. Mohr/Paul Siebeck, 1953), 154, mit Bezug auf H. Gunkel, "Hiob," *RGG*[2] 2 (1928): 1929.

reader, untrained as he is in Oriental and especially in Semitic modes of
thought and imagination. Such a reader's first question will probably
relate to the poetic form of the book.[5] (Thomas K. Cheyne).

In den 1753 veröffentlichten *Praelectiones de sacra poesi Hebraeorum*
des Oxforder Professors für Poesie und späteren Lordbischofs von
London Robert Lowth nimmt die methodisch abgesicherte Auseinandersetzung mit der Formgeschichte des Buches Hiob, zumal mit der Frage
nach seiner übergreifenden literarischen Gattung, eine zentrale Stellung
ein. Mittels einer genauen Erfassung des poetischen Profils und eines
textorientierten Vergleichs mit analogen literarischen Werken der Antike
versucht Lowth, den Reichtum der hebräischen Poesie darzustellen, und
begründet in diesem Zusammenhang auch die neuzeitliche formgeschichtliche Arbeit am Buch Hiob. Im folgenden soll gezeigt werden,
wie die Forschung im Laufe ihrer Geschichte im direkten oder indirekten
Anschluß an Lowth die literarische Gattung des Hiobbuches grundsätzlich bestimmt hat, wie sie die jeweilige Einordnung begründet hat und
auf welche literaturgeschichtlichen Analogien sie dabei verwiesen hat.
Dabei werden auch das Verhältnis zwischen der literaturgeschichtlichen
Gattungsbestimmung und der Auslegung sowie die rezeptionsästhetischen Implikationen der formgeschichtlichen Einordnungen skizziert.

1. *Die* heilige *Form oder der Beitrag von Robert Lowth zur Formgeschichte des Buches Hiob*

1.1. Die Interpretation des Buches Hiob von Lowth bewegt sich zwischen zwei Fronten.[6] Auf der einen Seite steht der *Commentaire littéral
sur le livre de Job* (1712) des Benediktiners August Calmet (1672–
1757). Im Vorwort seines Kommentars referiert Calmet Versuche, das
Hiobbuch als Tragödie zu beschreiben. Es gebe Ausleger, die meinten,
die Erzählung von Hiob sei zur Unterhaltung ("à plaisir") verfaßt und die
Reden Hiobs und seiner Freunde seien "une piéce [*sic*] de Poësie, toute
de l'invention de quelqu'homme d'esprit, qui a voulu représenter, non ce
qui étoit en effet, mais ce qui pouvoit être."[7] Auch wenn Calmet die

---

5. Th. K. Cheyne, *Job and Solomon or the Wisdom of the Old Testament*
(London, 1887), 107.
   6. Instruktiv dafür ist der Briefwechsel zwischen R. Lowth und W. Warburton
aus dem Jahr 1756 "Letters between Dr Lowth and Dr Warburton," in *The Works of
the Right Reverend William Warburton: A New Edition in Twelve Volumes* (ed. R.
Hurd; London, 1812), 12 :444–66.
   7. A. Calmet, *Commentaire littéral sur tous les livres de l'Ancien et du Nouveau
Testament. Job* (Paris, 1712 ; 3d ed. 1724), ix. Im Hintergrund dieser Äußerung steht

Verwendung poetischer Elemente im Buch Hiob in formaler Hinsicht keineswegs bestritten, so bedeutet doch die Bezeichnung dieses Buches wesenhaft als Poesie für ihn Fiktion und dies heißt Widerspruch zu Historizität und zur Verbindlichkeit der heiligen Schrift. Poesie ist für Calmet daher letztlich keine angemessene Kategorie, die biblischen Schriften zu beschreiben.[8] Auf der anderen Seite steht die Hiobdeutung von William Warburton (1698–1779), der zur Zeit von Lowth zunächst Prediger von London und später Lordbischof von Gloucester war. In einem Exkurs zu seiner *Divine Legation of Moses* (1737–41) hatte Warburton die These vertreten, das Buch Hiob sei eine von Esra verfaßte, dramatisch angelegte Allegorie auf die unter dem babylonischen Exil und seinen Folgen leidenden Israeliten.[9] Negation der Poesie als

die Gegenüberstellung der Intentionen des Historikers und des Dichters in der Poetik des Aristoteles (c. 9): der Historiker teile das wirklich Geschehene mit (τὰ γενόμενα), der Dichter hingegen das, was geschehen könnte (οἶα ἂν γένοιτο). In der lateinischen Übersetzung *Commentarius literalis in omnes libros Veteris Testamenti* (ed. J. D. Mansi; Würzburg, 1791), 5:311, fehlen bezeichnenderweise die auch von Lowth im Briefwechsel mit Warburton (*Works*, 12:456) zitierten Wendungen "à plaisir" und "une piéce de Poësie." In den von Lowth selbst besorgten Ausgaben der *Sacra Poesis* von 1753 und 1763 wird Calmet nicht ausdrücklich genannt; die entsprechende Anmerkung in der von G. Gregory angefertigten Übersetzung *Lectures on the Sacred Poetry of the Hebrews* (London, 1787), 389, stammt vom Übersetzer.

8. Dabei ist allerdings zu berücksichtigen, daß Calmet zwischen natürlicher Poesie und künstlicher Poesie (i.e. Poesie im eigentlichen Sinne) unterscheidet, wobei die natürliche Poesie, zu der er auch die poetischen Elemente in der Bibel zählt, in die Urzeit der Menschheit zurückreiche. Vgl. dazu Chr. Bultmann, *Die biblische Urgeschichte in der Aufklärung. Johann Gottfried Herders Interpretation der Genesis als Antwort auf die Religionskritik David Humes* (BHTh 110; Tübingen: Mohr Siebeck, 1999), 29, und J. Dyck, *Athen und Jerusalem. Die Tradition der argumentativen Verknüpfung von Bibel und Poesie im 17. und 18. Jahrhundert* (Munich: Beck, 1977), 97ss. Zur Problematik eines äquivoken Poesiebegriffs siehe bereits J. A. Cramer, "Von dem Wesen der biblischen Poesie," in idem, *Poetische Übersetzung der Psalmen nebst Abhandlungen über dieselben*, (Leipzig, 1755.1759; 2d ed. 1764, hier zitiert nach idem, *Einleitung in die Psalmen. Neunzehn Abhandlungen, neue Ausgabe* [Gütersloh, 1850], 43–58), und J. G. Herder, *Briefe, das Studium der Theologie betreffend* (1780.1785), in *Sämmtliche Werke* (ed. B. Suphan; Berlin, 1879), 10:29.

9. Warburton, *The Divine Legation Demonstrated*, in *Works*, ed. Hurd, 5:298–384. Mit Warburton führte Lowth gerade über das Buch Hiob einen mehrjährigen literarischen Streit. Für dessen erste Phase steht der Briefwechsel von 1756. Eine Neuauflage erlebte die Auseinandersetzung anläßlich einer Ergänzung von Lowth zur 32. Vorlesung der *Sacra Poesis* (2d ed. 1763), auf die Warburton in einem Appendix zur *Divine Legation of Moses* (1765) reagierte und Lowth "A Letter to the Right Reverend Author of the Divine Legation of Moses Demonstrated" verfaßte

Kategorie für die biblischen Schriften einerseits, Bestreitung der Historizität und des hohen Alters des Hiobbuches andererseits: demgegenüber
versucht Lowth Geschichtlichkeit, Poesie, Kanonizität und Frühdat-
ierung im Blick auf das Buch Hiob zu vereinbaren.

1.2. Lowth befaßt sich im dritten und letzten Teil der *Sacra Poesis*, welcher der Darstellung der verschiedenen Arten (*species*) der hebräischen
Dichtungen gewidmet ist, und hier wiederum in den letzten drei Vorlesungen (XXXII–XXXIV) mit dem Hiobbuch. Durch diese Positionierung
wird schon äußerlich der besondere Rang deutlich, den dieses Buch für
Lowth im Rahmen der biblischen Schriften einnimmt. Ähnlich eröffnet
Johann David Michaelis, der die Lowth'schen *Praelectiones*, mit umfangreichen eigenen Anmerkungen versehen, 1758/61 herausgegeben und
dadurch—neben anderen—deren Rezeption von der deutschen Forschung
des 18. Jahrhunderts begründet hat,[10] seine *Deutsche Übersetzung des
Alten Testaments* (1769) und seine *Einleitung in die göttlichen Schriften*

(London, 1775). Zu diesem Streit siehe auch R. M. Ryley, *William Warburton*
(Boston: Twayne, 1984), 62–63, und R. Smend, "Der Entdecker des Parallelismus:
Robert Lowth (1710–1787)," in *Prophetie und Psalmen, FS K. Seybold* (ed. B.
Huwyler; AOAT 280; Münster: Ugarit-Verlag, 2001), 189–90.

    10. R. Lowth, *De sacra poesi Hebraeorum. Notas et epimetra adjecit Iohannes
David Michaelis* (Göttingen, 1758/61; 2nd edn. 1770). Erheblichen Anteil an der
Verbreitung des Werks von Lowth hatte auch die ausführliche Rezension von Moses
Mendelssohn in der *Bibliothek der schönen Wissenschaften und freien Künste*
(1757), in *Moses Mendelssohn's gesammelte Schriften* (ed. G. B. Mendelssohn
Leipzig, 1844), vol. 4/1, 171–210. Vgl. dazu A.-R. Löwenbrück, "Johann David
Michaelis' Verdienst um die philologisch-historische Bibelkritik," in *Historische
Kritik und biblischer Kanon in der deutschen Aufklärung* (ed. H. Graf Reventlow,
W. Sparn, und J. Woodbridge; Wolfenbütteler Forschungen 41; Wiesbaden:
Harrassowitz, 1988), 159–60; R. Smend, "Lowth in Deutschland," in idem, *Epochen
der Bibelkritik, Gesammelte Studien III* (BEvTh 109; Munich: Chr. Kaiser, 1991),
43–62. Gleichwohl mußte noch 1793 Carl Benjamin Schmidt feststellen, daß Lowths
Werk "vielleicht noch nicht genug bekannt…und gebraucht" sei. Schmidt fertigte
unter dem Titel *Auszug aus D. Robert Lowth's Lord Bischofs zu London Vorlesungen über die heilige Dichtkunst der Hebräer mit Herder's und Jones's Grundsätzen
verbunden. Ein Versuch, zur Beförderung des Bibelstudiums des alten Testaments,
und insbesondre der Propheten und Psalme. Nebst einigen vermischten Anhängen*
(Danzig, 1793) eine Paraphrase der *Praelectiones de sacra poesi Hebraeorum* an.
Während die *Sacra Poesis* ins Englische (1787), Französische (1812) und Italien-
ische (1832) übersetzt wurde, fehlt bis heute eine deutsche Übersetzung. Zu einer
frühen kritischen Auseinandersetzung mit den Lowth'schen Klassifikationen siehe
J. A. Cramer, "Von dem poetischen Charakter der Psalmen," in id., *Poetische
Übersetzung* (Leipzig, 1755/59; 2d ed. 1763/64), zitiert nach id., *Einleitung in die
Psalmen* (Gütersloh, 1850), 295–306.

des Alten Bundes (1787) mit dem Buch Hiob.[11] Nach einer Übersicht
über die prophetische (נבואה), die elegische (קינה) und die didaktische
Poesie (משלים) sowie die Ode (שיר) und den Hymnus bzw. das Idyll
(שיר) des Alten Testaments kommt Lowth zur dramatischen Dichtung
(*poemata dramatica*). Zu dieser rechnet er neben dem von ihm allego-
risch gedeuteten Hohenlied auch das Buch Hiob. Das im Bereich der
alttestamentlichen Literatur inhaltlich und formal einzigartige Hiobbuch
basiere auf einer *wahren Geschichte*. Es sei weder eine fiktive Trost-
schrift des Mose zur Erbauung der in Ägypten versklavten Israeliten, wie
es Michaelis vertrat,[12] noch eine Allegorie der nachexilischen Situation
Israels, wie es Warburton behauptete.[13] Das Buch sei *rein Hebräisch*
abgefaßt—hier verwirft Lowth ausdrücklich die im wichtigsten Hiobkommentar des 18. Jahrhunderts von Albert Schultens vertretene These
einer arabischen Grundform.[14] Als *Verfasser* komme aus sachlichen
(*res*), aus sprachlichen (*sermo*) und aus kompositionellen (*universus
character*) Gründen weder Elihu[15] noch Mose[16] noch Esra oder ein
anderer nachexilischer Autor[17] in Frage, sondern entweder Hiob selbst

11. J. D. Michaelis, *Deutsche Übersetzung des Alten Testaments mit Anmerkungen für Ungelehrte*, vol. 1 (Göttingen, 1769); idem, *Einleitung in die göttlichen
Schriften des Alten Bundes* (Hamburg, 1787). Den Beginn mit dem Hiobbuch
begründet Michaelis literaturgeschichtlich mit dem Hinweis auf das hohe Alter des
Hiobbuches ("das älteste unter allen biblischen Büchern") und inhaltlich, insofern
dieses die zentralen theologischen Fragen nach der Unsterblichkeit der Seele und
dem Ort der göttlichen Gerechtigkeit stelle (*Übersetzung*, 35*).

12. Michaelis, *Übersetzung*, 38*; idem, *Notae et Epimetra ad Lowthi Praelectiones de S. Hebraeorum Poesi* (1761; 2d ed. 1770) ed. E. F. C. Rosenmüller (Leipzig, 1815), 649–52; idem, *Einleitung*, 1–23, 72–106.

13. Warburton, in *Works*, ed. Hurd, 5:330–69, 6:145–54.

14. A. Schultens, *Liber Iobi cum nova versione ad Hebraeum fontem, et commentario perpetuo* (Leiden, 1737); G. I. L. Vogel, *Alberti Schultensi Commentarius
in librum Iobi. In compendium redegit et observationes criticas atque exegeticas
adspersit*, vols. 1–2 (Halle, 1773/74); vgl. auch J. J. Reiske, *Conjecturae in Jobum et
Proverbia Salomonis cum eiusdem oratione de studio arabice linguae* ([1749];
Leipzig, 1779).

15. J. Lightfoot, *Opera ominia* (ed. Joh. Leusden; 2d ed.; Ultrajecti, 1699),
1:24–25.

16. Michaelis, *Einleitung*, 72–106; zur Annahme der mosaischen Abfassung
im unmittelbaren Umfeld von Lowth siehe auch R. Grey, *Liber Iobi in versiculos
metrice divisus, cum versione Alberti Schultens Notisque ex eijus Commentario
excerptis. Edidit atque Annotationes suas ad metrum praecipue spectantes adjecit*
(London, 1741), 12, und B. Kennicott, *Remarks on Select Passages of the Old
Testament to which are added eight Sermons* (Oxford, 1787), 152.

17. Warburton, in *Works*, ed. Hurd, 5:370–84; Th. Heath, *An Essay Towards a
New English Version of the Book of Job* (London, 1756), viii.

oder einer seiner Zeitgenossen. Jedenfalls sei das Hiobbuch *das älteste Buch* des Alten Testaments—ein Urteil, das unter Verweis auf den Buchcharakter dieses Werks später Hermann Gunkel[18] wiederholen wird. Lowth erkennt deutliche *formale und tendenzielle Unterschiede* zwischen den narrativen Teilen in c. 1–2 und 42,7–17 einerseits und den Reden andererseits. Die stilistische Differenz zwischen der Rahmenerzählung und den Reden erscheint ihm wie der Unterschied zwischen Livius und Vergil oder zwischen Homer und Herodot.[19] Dennoch führt Lowth das Buch als Ganzes auf *einen* Autor zurück.[20] Ansätze zu einer literarkritischen Differenzierung, wie sie sich im Hiobkommentar von Thomas Heath (1756) und bei dem mit Lowth zusammenarbeitenden Benjamin Kennicott (1780/87) finden,[21] bietet er nicht. *Hauptziel der Hiobdichtung sei es, den Menschen über die eigene Schwäche und über die Stärke Gottes zu belehren sowie den Menschen zum Glauben an Gott und zur Unterwerfung unter Gott zu führen. Lehre der gesamten Hiobgeschichte* sei es, ein Beispiel für Geduld im Leid, die letztlich belohnt werde, zu geben. Lowth spürt eine gewisse Inkongruenz zwischen dem Ziel der Dichtung und dem Skopus des gesamten Buches. Er verzichtet aber angesichts vieler ihm noch dunkel erscheinender Stellen auf eine

18. H. Gunkel, "Die israelitische Literatur," in *Die Kultur der Gegenwart. Ihre Entwicklung und ihre Ziele, I/VII. Die orientalischen Literaturen* (ed. P. Hinneberg; Berlin: Teubner, 1906), 91.

19. Lowth, *De Sacra Poesi* (praelect. XIV), ed. Rosenmüller, 150.

20. Lowth zeigt sich in der entsprechenden Passage (ed. Rosenmüller, 365), die Gregory in seiner englischen Übersetzung (*Lectures*, 359–64) sehr viel eindeutiger in Richtung einer einheitlichen Verfasserschaft wiedergibt, mit den Thesen einer sekundären Rahmung der ursprünglich selbständigen Hiobdichtung vertraut, wie sie vor ihm R. Simon, *Histoire Critique du Vieux Testament* (1678), Nouvelle Edition (Amsterdam, 1685), 30, und A. Schultens, in der Vorrede zum Kommentar, XXXI-XXXIV, vertreten haben. Zu weiteren Vertretern siehe M. Witte, *Vom Leiden zur Lehre. Der dritte Redegang und die Redaktionsgeschichte des Hiobbuches* (BZAW 230; Berlin: de Gruyter, 1994), 192, und W. D. Syring, *Hiob und sein Anwalt. Die Prosatexte des Hiobbuches und ihre Rolle in seiner Redaktions- und Rezeptionsgeschichte* (BZAW 336; Berlin: de Gruyter, 2004), 25–28. Allerdings nennt Lowth keine entsprechenden Vertreter der von ihm bestrittenen These.

21. Heath rechnete mit einer mechanisch bedingten Vers- und Blattvertauschung und ordnete den Text in c. 31 und im Bereich von c. 38–42 neu an: 31,1–25.38. 40a.26–37.40b und 38,1–39,30; 40,15–42,6; 40,1–14; 42,7–17 (*Essay*, 128–31, 163–73). Kennicott, der Heath darin folgte, glaubte zusätzlich in 27,13–23 die Reste einer im Laufe der Textüberlieferung verlorengegangenen dritten Rede Zophars zu erkennen (*Remarks*, 162–71). Auch wenn Heath und Kennicott textgeschichtlich argumentierten, bilden ihre Beobachtungen doch die Voraussetzung zu späteren literarkritischen Lösungen der Probleme in 27,13–23 und 40,1–41,26.

abschließende Klärung und widmet sich dann der wirkungsgeschichtlich bedeutenderen Frage nach der literarischen Gattung des Hiobbuches.
Bereits in der Überschrift der entscheidenden 33. Vorlesung fällt das eingehend begründete Urteil: "*poema Iobi non esse iustum drama.*" Damit bestreitet Lowth eine im 16. und 17. Jahrhundert weit verbreitete formgeschichtliche Klassifikation des Buches Hiob.[22] Zunächst unterscheidet Lowth zwei *Definitionen von Drama*:

1. eine antike, derzufolge die dialogische Form das entscheidende Merkmal des Dramas sei,
2. eine moderne, derzufolge zum Dialog eine in diesem ausgeführte Handlung (*actio*) oder Geschichte (*fabula*) komme.

Der ersten Definition entspreche das Hiobbuch letztlich nicht, weil es eine Mischung aus Erzählung und Dialog darstelle, der zweiten entspreche es nicht, weil dem Hiobdialog die Handlung fehle und diese auch nicht durch die rahmende Erzählung kompensiert werde. Obgleich Lowth damit bereits die Problematik der Einordnung des Hiobbuches als Drama aufgezeigt hat, unterzieht er in einem zweiten Schritt die *Hiobdichtung* einer genauen Prüfung, und fragt, ob diese die wesentlichen *Kriterien eines echten Dramas* (nämlich [a] einen dramatischen Aufbau, [b] eine dramatische Katastrophe, [c] die Figur eines *deus ex machina* und [d] eine genaue Anzahl von Akten und Szenen) aufweise. Das Ergebnis für die Dramendeutung der Hiobdichtung ist negativ: die Hiobdichtung enthält die Nachahmung von Sitten, aber gerade nicht die für das Drama gemäß der Poetik des Aristoteles (c.6) entscheidende Nachahmung von Handlung. Für die Hiobdichtung gilt: "*nulla rerum motio aut conversio, nulla actio*"—und dies sei nicht nur formal nachweisbar, sondern auch inhaltlich durch das *argumentum* der Hiobdichtung ausgeschlossen. Dieser poetologisch und inhaltlich begründeten Abweisung der Anwendung des Dramenbegriffs fügt Lowth in einem dritten Abschnitt eine detaillierte Gegenüberstellung der Hiobdichtung

---

22. Vgl. exemplarisch J. Mercerus (Mercier), *Commentarius in librum Job* (Genf, 1573), praefatio: das Buch Hiob lasse sich in drei Teile oder Akte wie eine Tragödie gliedern (I: Die Heimsuchung Hiobs; II: Der Dialog Hiobs mit den Freunden; III: Die Entscheidung durch Gott). Man habe im Buch fünf Personen, durch die das Ganze wie in einer Tragödie oder besser noch—wegen des glücklichen Ausgangs (*laetum exitum*)—in einer Komödie verhandelt werde und als sechste Person Gott als Richter auftrete. Den Satan könne man noch als siebte Person hinzunehmen. Vgl. auch Th. Beza, *Iobus Commentario et Paraphrasi illustratus* (Genf, 1583), und J. Gerhard, *Loci Theologici* (ed. J. F. Cotta; Tübingen, 1762), vol. 5, §140: Das Buch Hiob kann wie das Drama in *protasis, epistasis* und *laeta catastropha* gegliedert werden.

mit den beiden *Oedipus-Tragödien* des *Sophokles* an. Daß Lowth gerade Sophokles auswählt, ist kein Zufall. Denn wie in der literaturgeschichtlichen Forschung des 18. Jahrhunderts *Homer* als Muster des Epos und *Pindar* (gefolgt von *Horaz*) als Paradigma der Lyrik galt, wurde Sophokles als *das* Beispiel für dramatische Dichtung angesehen.[23] Lowth's Vergleich gipfelt in dem Urteil, das Hiobbuch könne nur dann richtig mit einer griechischen Tragödie verglichen werden, wenn die Handlung entweder aus dem Drama eliminiert oder zum Hiobbuch addiert werde. Nach griechischer Poetik könne die Hiobdichtung eher noch als θρῆνος (*monody*) oder κομμός (*elegiac dialogue*) bezeichnet werden. In seiner vorliegenden Gestalt stelle das Buch Hiob eine *Größe eigener Art* dar, die nicht nach einer fremden Norm zu messen sei— letztlich sei es dann auch zweitrangig, ob es eher didaktisch oder ethisch oder pathetisch oder dramatisch genannt werde; entscheidend sei, daß diesem Werk der erste Platz in der hebräischen Dichtung eingeräumt werde—und daß es, so gemäß der grundsätzlichen Intention der *Praelectiones*, gelesen werde. Denn das Hiobbuch übertreffe alle anderen Monumente der hebräischen Dichtung hinsichtlich seiner poetischen Gesamtanlage, zu der nicht zuletzt die besonders schönen Parallelismen zählten.[24] Der Nachzeichnung der poetischen und kompositionellen Struktur des Hiobbuches ist die abschließende 34. Vorlesung *De poematis Iobi moribus, conceptionibus et stylo* gewidmet. Hier arbeitet Lowth dann auch, nach seiner prinzipiellen Ablehnung des Dramenbegriffs, durchaus dramatische Elemente in der Hiobdichtung heraus[25] und

---

23. S. Trappen, "Formen / Gattungen, I. Literaturwissenschaftlich," *RGG*[4] 3 (2000): 186; A. Cullhed, *The Language of Passion. The Order of Poetics and the Construction of a Lyric Genre 1746–1806* (European University Studies 18/104; Frankfurt am Main: Peter Lang, 2002), 185ss. Der kanonische Rang, den die griechischen und römischen Autoren in Fragen der Poetik im 18. Jahrhundert spielten, zeigt sich auch immer wieder bei Lowth (p.e. *De Sacra Poesi*, ed. Rosenmüller, 22, 345–346); siehe dazu auch J. L. Kugel, *The Idea of Biblical Poetry. Parallelism and its History* (Baltimore: Yale University Press, 1981; repr. 1998), 274.

24. In der Übersicht zu den drei Arten der Parallelismen (synonym, antithetisch, synthetisch/konstruktiv) in der *Preliminary Dissertation* zum Jesajakommentar von 1778 führt Lowth als besonders eindrückliche Beispiele aus dem Hiobbuch 3,4.6.9; 12,13–6 und 26,5 an. Typisch für das Hiobbuch seien synthetische / konstruktive Parallelismen (R. Lowth, *Isaiah: A New Translation with a Preliminary Dissertation and Notes Critical, Philological, and Explanatory* [London, 1778], wieder abgedruckt in Robert Lowth (1710–1787), *The Major Works* [ed. D. A. Reibel; vol. 1–8; London: Routledge/Thoemmes, 1995], xxviii).

25. Vgl. auch Lowth, *Isaiah*, in *Works*, ed. Reibel, xxvii: "The Poem of Job, being on a large plan, and in a high Tragic style…"; vgl. auch Schmidt, *Auszug*, 184.

weist einzelne ihrer Abschnitte den zuvor begründeten Gattungen (*genera*) und Dichtungsarten (*species*) zu.[26]

Der wesentliche Beitrag, den Lowth mit seinen *Praelectiones* zur Erhellung der Formgeschichte des Hiobbuches geleistet hat, besteht zunächst in zwei Punkten:

1. in der ausführlichen Begründung und Würdigung des Hiobbuches als *Poesie*. Dadurch wird die methodisch kontrollierte Anwendung poetologischer Kategorien und der gezielte literaturgeschichtliche Vergleich mit nichtbiblischen poetischen Texten möglich.

2. in dem Bemühen, das Buch Hiob sowohl in seiner Gesamtkomposition als auch in seinen Teilen einzelnen poetischen *Gattungen der hebräischen Dichtung* zuzuweisen. Damit wird der Weg zu einem methodisch begründeten literaturgeschichtlichen und ästhetischen Verstehen des Buches Hiob im *Kontext der biblischen Texte* eröffnet.[27]

2. *Die* richtige *Form oder der* status quaestionis *um 1800*

2.1. Kennzeichnend für die formgeschichtlichen Klassifikationen des Hiobbuches in den ersten Jahrzehnten nach Lowths Poetik ist die *Vielfalt der vorgeschlagenen Gattungen* und der *Korrelationen mit scheinbar analogen Literaturen*. Die grundsätzliche Beurteilung des Hiobbuches als Poesie wird von allen folgenden kritischen Exegeten geteilt, ohne daß diesen damit der Wahrheitsgehalt des Hiobbuches verloren geht. Nicht unerheblichen Anteil an dieser Einschätzung dürfte wie schon bei der Verbreitung der Lowth'schen Thesen in Deutschland das Urteil von Johann David Michaelis gehabt haben: "Hiobs und seiner Freunde Reden sind durch und durch Poesie, noch dazu die erhabenste und begeistertste Poesie, die wir in der an Gedichten so reichen Hebräischen Bibel haben."[28] Ein erheblicher Dissens besteht in der Frage, ob das Hiobbuch eher der epischen, lyrischen, dramatischen oder didaktischen Poesie zuzurechnen sei. Darin spiegelt sich die lebhafte gattungsgeschichtliche Diskussion, die in der gesamten Literaturwissenschaft der zweiten Hälfte des 18. Jahrhunderts geführt wurde.[29]

---

26. So bilden die Klagen Hiobs in c. 3; 6–7; 10; 14; 17; 19; 29–30 die schönsten Beispiele für die hebräische Elegie (קינה) (*De Sacra Poesi*, praelect. XXIII, ed. Rosenmüller, 264–65).

27. Siehe dazu auch die umfassende forschungsgeschichtliche Würdigung bei St. Prickett, *Words and* The Word*: Language, Poetics and Biblical Interpretation* (Cambridge: Cambridge University Press, 1986), 105ss.

28. Michaelis, *Einleitung*, 9.

29. Siehe dazu R. P. Lessenich, *Dichtungsgeschmack und althebräische*

2.2. Ohne Hinweis auf Lowth's Vorlesungen vertrat nur drei Jahre nach deren Publikation Thomas Heath in seinem in London erschienenen Hiobkommentar erneut die Einordnung als *Drama*—und auch Michaelis formulierte pathetisch: "So poetisch läßt man im Drama die auftretenden Personen reden… Wie Drama sieht es aus…"[30]—eine literaturgeschichtliche Klassifikation, die sich bis in die Gegenwart immer wieder findet.[31] Dabei stellte Heath das Hiobbuch einerseits den Tragödien des Euripides, andererseits den Komödien des Plautus zur Seite. Von diesen unterscheide sich die Hiobdichtung allerdings dadurch, daß sie nicht für die *Bühne*, die den Orientalen unbekannt gewesen sei, bestimmt war. Vielmehr führe der Hiobdichter die für die Handlung wichtigen Personen und die Lösung des Konflikts im Prolog und Epilog seines "tragical dialogue" selbst narrativ ein.[32]

2.3. Eine gewisse Inkonsistenz in der Argumentation von Lowth stellt dessen Forderung dar, einerseits die hebräische Poesie aus der hebräischen Literatur selbst zu verstehen, andererseits sein methodisches Vorgehen,

---

Bibelpoesie im 18. Jahrhundert. Zur Geschichte der englischen Literaturkritik (Anglistische Studien 4; Köln u. Graz: Böhlau, 1967), 149; K. R. Scherpe, *Gattungspoetik im 18. Jahrhundert. Historische Entwicklung von Gottsched bis Herder* (Studien zur Allgemeinen und Vergleichenden Literaturwissenschaft 2; Stuttgart: Metzler, 1968), 82–113; S. Trappen, *Gattungspoetik. Studien zur Poetik des 16. bis 19. Jahrhunderts und zur Geschichte der triadischen Gattungslehre* (Beihefte zum Euphorion 40; Heidelberg: Winter, 2001), 123ss.

30. Michaelis, *Einleitung*, 9–11; vgl. auch Hermann Samuel Reimarus (1698–1768) in den von G. E. Lessing herausgegebenen Fragmenten (1777) bei R. Smend, *Das Alte Testament im Protestantismus* (Grundtexte zur Kirchen- und Theologiegeschichte 3; Neukirchen–Vluyn: Neukirchener, 1995), 80–104, hier p.96.

31. An erster Stelle ist hier H. M. Kallen, *The Book of Job as a Greek Tragedy* (New York: Hill & Wang, 1918; rev. ed. 1959), zu nennen, der im Anschluß an Theodor von Mopsuestia (vgl. Anm. 3) im Hiobbuch eine nach dem Muster der Tragödien des Euripides gestaltete, mit einzelnen Chorliedern (Hi 28 nach c. 14; Hi 24,2–24 nach c. 21 und Hi 40,15–41,26 nach c. 31) versehene Komposition zu erkennen glaubte. Die jetzige, narrative Gestalt des Hiobbuches führte Kallen auf eine orthodoxe Redaktion zurück. Obgleich Kallen seine phantasievolle Neuordnung des hebräischen Textes und die angenommene Beeinflussung des Hiobdichters durch Euripides kaum näher begründete, blieb seine Hypothese nicht ohne Einfluß; vgl. die forschungsgeschichtliche Diskussion bei M. Hadas, *Hellenistic Culture. Fusion and Diffusion* (New York: Columbia University Press, 1959), 130–46; J. Steinmann, *Le livre de Job* (LecDiv 16 ; Paris: Les éditions du cerf, 1955), 23; J. Lévêque, *Job et son dieu. Essai d'exégèse et de théologie biblique* (EtB 1–2 ; Paris: Gabalda, 1970), 104–16.; A. de Wilde, *Das Buch Hiob. Eingeleitet, übersetzt und erläutert* (OTS 22; Leiden: Brill, 1981), 25–27, 60–61.

32. Heath, *Essay*, vii.

bei der Bestimmung der alttestamentlichen Gattungen immer wieder auf die Kategorien der griechischen und römischen Poetiken, vor allem von Aristoteles und Horaz zurückzugreifen. Genau dies wurde Lowth von Johann Gottfried Herder vorgeworfen:

> Er (*sc.* Lowth) gab nach Englands Weise Prälectionen, wollte seinen Gegenstand ab ovo aufnehmen und nach griechischer und römischer Art behandeln: er wählte also auch römische und griechische Namen, und beliebte das Fachwerk der neuern Poetik, obs gleich seinen uralten, morgenländischen, heiligen Objekten nicht immer angemessen war. Daher die manchmal unpassende Fragen und Gesichtspunkte: ob das Buch Hiob ein wahres Drama? das hohe Lied ein wahres theokritisches Hirtengedicht sey? und unter welche Classe von Oden und Gedichten jeder Psalm, jeder Prophet gehöre?[33]

Herders Werk *Vom Geist der Ebräischen Poesie* (1782/83) stellt nicht nur von seiner Konzeption her, sondern auch im Blick auf die Formgeschichte des Hiobbuches die fruchtbarste Auseinandersetzung und Weiterführung der Arbeiten von Lowth dar. "Durch Lowth ist Herder zu der Ansicht gekommen, daß man eine Poetologie der hebräischen Poesie schreiben müsse, und ebenso, daß man sie anders schreiben müsse, als Lowth es getan hat."[34] Das Hiobbuch wird bei Herder zum morgenländischen "*Consessus* einiger Weisen…die *pro* und *contra* die Sache der Gerechtigkeit des obersten Weltmonarchen verhandeln."[35] Herder kann sich bei der Nachzeichnung des Hiobbuches einzelner dramatischer Begriffe bedienen, wenn er von der "zwiefache(n) Szene, im Himmel und auf der Erde," oder von den "unsichtbaren Zuschauer(n)" und dem "Schauplatz des ganzen Buches" spricht.[36] Dennoch steht für ihn—wie für Lowth—fest, daß es "kein Drama"[37] ist. Deutlicher als Lowth verortet Herder das Buch im orientalischen Milieu: "Die Morgenländer lieben solche gelehrte *Consessus*, lange Reden in geflügelten Sprüchen, die sie geduldig aus- und anhören und denn in eben der Weise beantworten."[38] Herder teilt mit Lowth die Einschätzung des Hiobbuches als "älteste Kunstkomposition der Welt." Es zeigt sich bei Herder aber eine charakteristische Verschiebung in der Bestimmung des Verhältnisses von

33. Herder, *Studium*, 15, 29–30.
34. Bultmann, *Urgeschichte*, 82.
35. J. G. Herder, *Vom Geist der Ebräischen Poesie. Eine Anleitung für die Liebhaber derselben, und der ältesten Geschichte des menschlichen Geistes* (1782/83; 2d ed. 1787), in *Sämmtliche Werke* (ed. B. Suphan; Berlin, 1879), 11:314.
36. Herder, *Geist*, 316–17.
37. Ibid., 314.
38. Ibid., 315.

Poesie und Historizität. Für Calmet schloß der Begriff Poesie die Geschichtlichkeit des Dargestellten aus. Lowth versuchte Historizität und Poesie mittels der Zuordnung der hebräischen Dichtung zur Prophetie und mittels der Figur der heiligen, d.h. der göttlich inspirierten Poesie, zu vereinbaren. Herder hingegen liegt an der Geschichtlichkeit des Geschilderten nichts: für ihn macht die "starke und kräftige Poesie" das Hiobbuch zur Geschichte.[39] "Ob die Geschichte Hiobs Geschichte oder Dichtung sey, ist uns einerlei, gnug, er ist im Buche da."[40]

In der Beurteilung des Hiobbuches als *"consessus* einiger Weisen" sind Herder große Teile der deutschen Forschung gefolgt, u.a. Johann Gottfried Eichhorn (1787),[41] Johann Gottfried Hasse (1789)[42] und Johann Conrad Christoph Nachtigal (1799).[43] Dabei fehlte es auch nicht an Versuchen, Herders Begriff des "Morgenländischen" mit der Lowth'schen Kategorie der hebräischen *poemata dramatica* zu verbinden: das Hiobbuch wird in diesem Fall zum "morgenländischen Drama."[44]

2.4. Eine merkwürdige Zwischenstellung nimmt hier Wilhelm Martin Leberecht de Wette ein (1817). In Weiterführung von Lowth's poetischen Typen der hebräischen Poesie unterscheidet er zwischen lyrischer, lyrisch-elegischer, erotisch-idyllischer und didaktisch-gnomologischer Poesie. Zu letzterer zählt er das Buch Hiob. Gleichzeitig rekurriert de Wette auf Herders These von den Versammlungen der Weisen, denen das Hiobbuch sein dialogisches Grundmuster verdanke. Beides überführt de Wette dann aber in das Urteil, die "Aeltern" (unter denen er Th. Beza, J. Mercerus, J. Gerhard und R. Lowth nennt) hätten den Vergleich des Hiobbuches mit der Tragödie "zu ängstlich gefaßt"; man könne es durchaus "die hebräische Tragödie nennen."[45] Eindeutiger ist hier später

---

39. Ibid., 315.

40. Herder, S*tudium,* 132; ähnliches gilt nach Herder für das Buch Jona (*Studium,* 101–2).

41. J. G. Eichhorn, *Einleitung ins Alte Testament* (2d ed.; Leipzig, 1787), 3:492.

42. J. G. Hasse, "Vermuthungen über das Buch Hiob," *Magazin für die biblisch-orientalische Litteratur und gesamte Philologie* I, nos 3–4 (1789): 175–76.

43. J. C. C. Nachtigal, "Über die Weisen-Versammlungen der Israeliten," *ABBL* 9 (1799): 380–451: Die Gegengesänge, die sich unter der Aufschrift "Hiob" erhalten hätten, seien Proben von Vorträgen der Versammlungen von Weisen. Hiob sei in Samuels Sängerversammlung oder Prophetenschule entstanden.

44. W. F. Hezel, *Die Bibel Alten und Neuen Testaments mit vollständig-erk-lärenden Anmerkungen* (2d ed.; Lemgo, 1790), 3:463: "ein Drama in kunstloser Gestalt, ein morgenländisches und überdies noch das älteste in der Welt."

45. W. M. L. de Wette, *Lehrbuch der historisch-kritischen Einleitung* ([1817]; 3d ed.; Berlin, 1829), 409. In seinem Hiob-Artikel in der *Allgemeinen Enzyklopädie der*

Heinrich Ewald (1836), der das Buch Hiob zwar inhaltlich und intentional als Lehrgedicht bezeichnet, aber der "Kunst nach...als das göttliche Drama der alten Hebräer."[46]

2.5. Demgegenüber stehen Einordnungen des Hiobbuches in die von Lowth in der 24. Vorlesung behandelten *carmina didactica*, so beispielsweise bei Wilhelm Friedrich Hufnagel (1781), der zu den wenigen deutschen Alttestamentlern des ausgehenden 18. Jahrhunderts gehört, die Lowth ausdrücklich zitieren,[47] oder aber zum Epos.

2.6. Die umfassendste Begründung dieser Zeit für die Bezeichnung des Hiobbuches als *Epos* findet sich in einem frühen Werk des in der Pentateuchkritik glücklicher agierenden Carl David Ilgen (1789).[48] Der Vergleich mit den homerischen Epen (der im 17./18. Jahrhundert nicht ungewöhnlich war, denn auch Lowth konnte Hiob als "the Homer of the Hebrew Classics" bezeichnen[49]) führte Ilgen zu dem Ergebnis, es handle

Wissenschaft und Künste (ed. J. S. Ersch u. J. G. Gruber), 8/2 (1831): 296, und in der siebten (und letzten von eigener Hand verbesserten) *Auflage des Lehrbuchs* (Berlin, 1852), 383, wendet de Wette dann auch noch den Begriff des "Lehrgedichts" an.

46. H. Ewald, *Die poetischen Bücher des Alten Bundes, III. Theil, Das Buch Iob* (Göttingen, 1836), 60. In einer Anmerkung in der zweiten Ausgabe von 1854 fügt Ewald zur Unterstützung seiner Dramendeutung eine kuriose Entdeckung aus einer Handschrift von Leibniz an, dem das Hiobbuch "opernartig" vorgekommen sei (56–57).

47. W. F. Hufnagel, *Hiob neu übersetzt mit Anmerkungen* (Erlangen, 1781), Einleitung §2; ähnlich H. Sander, *Das Buch Hiob zum allgemeinen Gebrauch* (Leipzig, 1780), 32; G. F. Seiler, *Das grössere biblische Erbauungsbuch, aufgesetzt, zum Theil auch neu herausgegeben, Altes Testament* (9ter Theil; Erlangen, 1794), 1, und L. Hirzel, *Hiob* (KEH; Leipzig, 1839), 7.

48. C. D. Ilgen, *Iobi antiquissimi carminis hebraici natura atque virtutes* (Leipzig, 1789). Unmittelbare Vorgänger hatte Ilgen mit der epischen Klassifikation des Hiobbuches in den Werken von J. H. Stuss, *De Epopoeia Jobaea* (Gotha, 1753), und von A. A. H. Lichtenstein, *Num liber Jobi cum Odyssea Homeri comparari possit?* (Helmstedt, 1773).

49. R. Lowth, *A Letter to The Right Reverend Author of The Divine Legation of Moses Demonstrated* (1765), hier zitiert nach Smend, "Der Entdecker des Parallelismus," 190. Zum Vergleich alttestamentlicher Schriften mit Homer in der Forschung des 18. Jahrhunderts siehe generell D. Norton, *A History of the English Bible as Literature* (Cambridge: Cambridge University Press, 2000), 206, und speziell die zahlreichen poetologischen Parallelisierungen zwischen Homer und Jesaja in Lowths Jesajakommentar, p.e.: "Dies Gleichniß (sc. Jes 31,4) ist genau in dem Geiste und der Manier Homers, dessen Ausdruck es auch sehr nahe kommt (sc. Ilias, XII,299)" (J. B. Koppe, *Robert Lowth's Jesajas neu übersetzt, nebst einer Einleitung und kritisch philolog. erl. Anm. Aus dem Engl.* [Leipzig, 1781], 3:141).

sich um eine *Epopöe*, bestehend aus 27 Rhapsodien. Mit wenigen Ausnahmen fand Ilgens Einordnung des Hiobbuchs in die Epik (zunächst)
keine Gefolgschaft,[50] obgleich er mit der prinzipiellen Bezeichnung des
Hiobbuches als Epos in John Milton (1608–1674) einen prominenten
Vorgänger hatte.[51]

2.7. Moderner mutet demgegenüber die Einschätzung eines der ersten
Rezensenten von Ilgens Werk, Samuel Friedrich G. Wahl (1789), an.
Das Hiobbuch, so Wahl

> gehört offenbar zu einer Dichtungsart, welche in unseren beschränkten
> Poetiken noch keinen Namen und keine Stelle hat. Im Allgemeinen ist es
> ein Volks- oder Bardenlied, das mit den Liedern Ossians und der kelt-
> ischen Barden viel gemein hat... Muß das Kind einen Namen haben, so
> kann ich das Gedicht mit keiner Dichtungsart besser vergleichen, zu
> keinem näher bringen, als zu dem *Duan* der gallischen oder keltischen
> Dichtung.[52]

Im Hintergrund dieses Vergleichs, der u.a. auch von Karl Wilhelm Justi
(1794)[53] unternommen wurde, steht die 1762 von dem Schotten James
McPershon publizierte Sammlung keltischer Lieder *Fingal. An Ancient*

50. Zu den Ausnahmen gehört u.a. J. Chr. W. Augusti, *Grundriss einer historisch-kritischen Einleitung in's alte Testament* (Leipzig, 1806), 221, für den das
Hiobbuch einerseits ein "moralisches Epos" darstellt, andererseits das "ausführ-
lichste und gelungenste Lehrgedicht des AT" (185). Zur Annahme, daß zumindest
(literargeschichtlich zu differenzierende) Teile des Hiobbuches episch geprägt seien
(s.u. Abschnitt 4.1.), siehe für das 19. und 20. Jahrhundert: Cheyne, *Job*, 108; A.
Dillmann, *Hiob* (KEH; 4th ed.; Leipzig, 1891); K. Budde, *Das Buch Hiob übersetzt
und erklärt* (2d ed.; HK 2/1; Göttingen: Vandenhoeck & Ruprecht, 1913), x;
E. König, *Das Buch Hiob, eingeleitet, übersetzt und erklärt* (Gütersloh: Bertelsmann, 1929), 17–18; N. M. Sarna, "Epic Substratum in the Book of Job," *JBL* 76
(1957): 13–25; W. G. E. Watson, *Classical Hebrew Poetry: A Guide to its Techniques* (JSOTSup 26; repr. with corrections; Sheffield: Sheffield Academic Press,
2001), 85.
51. J. Milton, *The Reason of Church Government*, Book II, zitiert nach Cheyne,
Job, 107.
52. S. F. G. Wahl, "C. D. Ilgen, Iobi antiquissimi carminis hebraici natura atque
virtutes," *Magazin für alte besonders morgenländische und biblische Litteratur* 2
(1789): 192.
53. K. W. Justi, "Fragmente aus dem Hiob übersetzt und erläutert," *Memorabi-
lien* 5 (1794): 141–42. Als kompositionsgeschichtliche Analogien zur vermuteten
Entstehung des Hiobbuches aus sekundär verknüpften Liedsagen führte Justi
weiterhin die homerischen Epen, die *Hieroglyphika* des Horus Apollo von Neilopo-
lis (5. Jahrhundert n. Chr.) und die *Argonautika* des Orpheus von Kroton (6./5.
Jahrhundert v. Chr.) an.

Epic Poem in Six Books. Together with Severed Other Poems Composed by Ossian, the Son of Fingal, translated from the Gaelic Language, die zumindest bis zum Nachweis ihrer Fälschung einen bedeutenden Einfluß auf die europäische Literatur hatte.[54]

2.8. Angesichts dieser Einordnungen entschied sich Ernst Friedrich Carl Rosenmüller (1824)[55] in direktem Anschluß an Lowth, dessen *Praelectiones* er zusammen mit Michaelis' Noten und wenigen eigenen Anmerkungen 1815 herausgab, wieder für die Bestimmung des Hiobbuches als Werk *sui generis*—der bis heute am weitesten verbreiteten Klassifikation.[56]

2.9. Allen in diesem Abschnitt vorgestellten Kategorisierungen ist gemeinsam, daß sie die literarische Form des Buches primär von seinem eigentlich poetischen Teil in den c.3–42,6 her bestimmen. Daß dieses Verfahren zu einseitig sei, betonte daher zu Recht Friedrich Wilhelm Carl Umbreit (1824). Mit seiner Kritik, die Bezeichnung des Hiobbuches als didaktisches, religiöses, lyrisches oder dramatisches Gedicht greife zu kurz, traf er auch einen wunden Punkt der Hiob-Analyse von Lowth, der das Buch insgesamt als *poema* bezeichnete. Umbreit selbst wies das Hiobbuch dann aufgrund seiner Komposition aus Prolog, Dialog und Epilog, aufgrund seiner ("wenn auch nur mit dem Schwerte der Zunge"[57]) vollzogenen Handlung und aufgrund seiner inhaltlichen Abfolge von Knüpfung, Verwirrung und Lösung eines Knotens wieder dem *Drama* zu.

---

54. Vgl. nur den Ausruf des jungen Werther "Ossian hat in meinem Herzen den Homer verdrängt. Welch eine Welt, in die der Herrliche mich führt" (J. W. Goethe, *Die Leiden des jungen Werther*, zweites Buch, Brief vom 12. Oktober 1772, in *Werke* [ed. K. Alt], 10:67); zur Ossian-Rezeption in der deutschen Literatur des 18. Jahrhunderts siehe A. F. C. Vilmar, *Geschichte der Deutschen National-Litteratur* (26th ed.; Marburg: N. G. Elwert'sche Verlagsbuchhandlung, 1905), 360, 385.

55. E. F. C. Rosenmüller, *Scholia in Vetus Testamentum* (2d ed.; Leipzig, 1824), 5:25–26.

56. Vgl. dazu exemplarisch G. B. Gray und S. R. Driver, *A Critical and Exegetical Commentary on the Book of Job* (ICC; Edinburgh: T. & T. Clark, 1921), xxii; P. Dhorme, *Le livre de Job* (EtB; Paris: Gabalda, 1926), lxxix; M. H. Pope, *Job. Introduction, Translation, and Notes* (AB; Garden City, N.Y.: Doubleday, 1965), xxx; H. H. Rowley, *Job* (NCeB; London: Nelson, 1970), 5; J. E. Hartley, *The Book of Job* (NICOT; Grand Rapids: Eerdmans, 1988), 38; J. L. Crenshaw, "Job, Book of," *ABD* 3:865; H. Spieckermann, "Hiob / Hiobbuch," *RGG*[4] 3 (2000): 1777.

57. F. W. C. Umbreit, *Das Buch Hiob* (Heidelberg, 1824), xxviii.

3. *Die* reine *Form oder der Ort des Buches Hiob* in der Welt der Literaturen

Um 1800 sind alle wesentlichen Bestimmungen der literarischen Form des Hiobbuches als Gesamtkunstwerk in der Forschung vorhanden, die in unterschiedlichen Modifikationen bis heute vertreten werden. Neue Akzente erhielt die Frage nach der literarischen Gattung des Buches in der Mitte des 19. Jahrhunderts vor allem durch Heinrich Ewald, Konstantin Schlottmann und Ernst Heinrich Meier.[58]

3.1. Heinrich Ewald (1836ff.) unternahm erstmals den umfassenden Versuch, die Form des Hiobbuches nicht nur hinsichtlich seiner poetischen Struktur zu beschreiben und pauschal der morgenländischen Dichtung zuzuweisen, sondern im Gefolge von Herder diese genetisch aus einfacheren Formen der hebräischen Poesie und aus *der hebräischen Mentalität* abzuleiten. Als darstellende, d.h. als dramatische Dichtung sei das Hiobbuch letztlich aus dem hebräischen Singspiel hervorgegangen. Dieses habe sich in literarisch kunstvoller Form zunächst im Hohenlied niedergeschlagen: "Wäre das Hohelied oder vielmehr die wirkliche volksthümliche darstellung wovon wir jetzt im HL. ein beispiel haben in Israel nicht vorangegangen, so hätte in ihm nie ein B. Ijob entstehen können."[59]

Den Ursprung der hebräischen Spieldichtung, die sich in Gestalt des Hohenliedes als "Lustspiel" zeige, in Form des Hiobbuches als "Trauerspiel," sieht Ewald im Lied.[60] Während das Hohelied noch für eine "einfache bühne bestimmt" gewesen sei, könne dies für das Hiobbuch aus religiösen Gründen auf keinen Fall gelten. Denn im Gegensatz zu

---

58. Zur neuzeitlichen Geschichte der Erforschung des Strophenbaus und der Metrik der Hiobdichtung, die mit F. B. Köster, *Das Buch Hiob und der Prediger Salomos nach ihrer strophischen Anordnung übersetzt. Nebst Abhandlungen über den strophischen Charakter dieser Bücher* (Schleswig, 1831) beginnt, siehe die ausführliche Darstellung bei P. Van der Lugt, *Rhetorical Criticism and the Poetry of the Book of Job* (OTS 32; Leiden: Brill, 1995). Angesichts des handbuchartigen Charakters dieses Werkes überrascht allerdings die Nichtberücksichtigung der *Sacra Poesis* von Lowth (vgl. besonders dessen praelect. III. "מזמור sive de metris Hebraeis"; idem, "Metricae Harianae Brevis Confutatio," in idem, *De Sacra Poesi*, ed. Rosenmüller, 401–7; idem, *Isaiah* in *Works*, ed. Reibel, xxxiv).

59. H. Ewald, "Über liedwenden (strophen) im B. Ijob," *JBW* 3 (1850–51): 117. Zur unmittelbaren formgeschichtlichen Korrelierung von Canticum und Hiob vgl. Lowth, *De Sacra Poesi*, praelect. XXX-XXXI.

60. H. Ewald, *Die Dichter des Alten Bundes erklärt, I/1, Allgemeines über die hebräische Dichtkunst und über das Psalmenbuch* (2d. ed.; Göttingen, 1865), 69–70.

anderen Völkern sei es für Israel unmöglich, seinen Gott auf die Bühne zu bringen. Hiob erhebe die ernste Spieldichtung in geistige Höhen, "an welche keine irdische bühne und kein sinnliches auge reicht."[61] Das Hiobbuch stellt mithin die *reine* Form dramatischer Dichtung dar. "Weder die Inder noch die Griechen und Römer haben ein so erhabenes und so rein vollendetes gedicht aufzuweisen." Hiob ist für Ewald mehr als Oedipus oder Philoktet.[62] Denn, so Ewald weiter, "nur wo eine wahre religion herrschte, konnten so rein erhabene und vollkommene kunstwerke entstehen wie wir an dem B. Ijob das nirgends übertroffene große beispiel haben."[63] Reine Poesie und reine Religion gehören somit untrennbar zusammen. Angesichts dieses Urteils versteht es sich von selbst, daß Ewald die Korrelierung des Hiobbuches mit neuzeitlicher Literatur entschieden zurückwies: "Mit den werken neuerer dichter wie Dante Shakspeare [*sic*] Göthe kann man es schon deswegen nicht rein vergleichen weil es diesen selbst schon mehr oder weniger gut verstanden vorschwebte."[64]

Was den Vergleich mit neuerer Literatur anbelangte, hatte Franz Delitzsch (1864), der sich grundsätzlich der Ewald'schen Deutung des Hiobbuches als geistigem Drama und dessen Verständnis als der im Vergleich zu den Werken des Sophokles und Euripides reiferen Tragödie anschloß, weniger Vorbehalte, wenn er die dramatische Anlage des Buches mit Goethes *Iphigenie auf Tauris* und *Torquato Tasso* verglich.[65] Den Vergleichspunkt bildete für Delitzsch (wie kurz nach ihm für Th. K. Cheyne, 1887) die Substitution der Handlungen durch Gesinnungen (so in der *Iphigenie*) bzw. durch Charakterzeichnungen (so im *Torquato Tasso*): "The Colloquies [*sc.* of the book of Job] on the other hand are as undoubtedly a germinal character-drama, as the Song of Song is a

61. Ibid., 82.

62. Ibid., 80. Der Vergleich zwischen Hiob und dem sophokleischen Philoktet, den bereits Augusti, *Einleitung*, 223, vornimmt, dürfte letztlich unter dem Einfluß Lessings stehen, der im Laokoon Philoktet als Muster dramatisch dargestellten Affekts deutet (*Laokoon oder über die Grenzen der Malerei und Poesie* [1766], c. IV, in *Werke*, ed. Kurz, 4:24–35).

63. H. Ewald, "Neue bemerkungen zum B. Ijob," *JBW* 9 (1857–58): 27–28.

64. Ibid., 28.

65. F. Delitzsch, *Das Buch Iob* (BC 4/2; Leipzig, 1864); hier zitiert nach der 2d ed. (Leipzig, 1876), 17; vgl. auch E. Schrader in der *Neubearbeitung des Lehrbuchs von de Wette* (Berlin, 1869), 545. Fz. Delitzsch, dem die Forschung (neben Ewald) den philologisch und theologisch wichtigsten deutschsprachigen Hiobkommentar des 19. Jahrhunderts verdankt, würdigte ausdrücklich die Verdienste des von ihm ansonsten theologisch nicht geschätzten Rationalismus des 18. Jahrhunderts hinsichtlich der Betrachtung des Buches Hiob als poetisches Meisterwerk, ohne allerdings ausdrücklich auf Lowth, wohl aber auf Herder zu verweisen (33).

germinal stage-drama. The work belongs to the same class as Goethes's *Iphigenie* and *Tasso*."[66]

3.2. Die von Lowth u.a. ausgeführte literaturgeschichtliche Parallelis-ierung des Hiobbuchs mit der klassischen Tragödie und die von einzel-nen Forschern des ausgehenden 18. Jahrhunderts angestellten punktuellen Komparationen mit Schriften anderer Kulturen werden bei Konstantin Schlottmann (1851) in den bis dahin am breitesten angelegten Vergleich mit europäischen und asiatischen Texten von der Antike bis zur Gegenwart überführt. Für Schlottmann ist wie für Ewald das Hiobbuch ein "geistiges Drama, dessen einzelne Handlungen nicht äußere…son-dern tief innerliche sind."[67] Der literaturgeschichtliche Vergleich mit indischen, persischen, griechischen, ägyptischen und semitischen (d.h. assyrisch-babylonischen und phönizischen)[68] Parallelen läßt Schlottmann dann über Ewald hinausgehend zur Deutung des Hiobbuches als *Mensch-heitsdrama* kommen. Im Hiobbuch habe sich gesamtmenschheitliche Mythologie und Religion niedergeschlagen. Das Buch Hiob ist bei Schlottmann nicht nur heilige und reine Poesie, sondern Verdichtung der Urideen der Menschheit, der es den Weg zu ihrer ursprünglichen Einheit weist.

3.3. Bei Ewald (und noch stärker bei Schlottmann) wird deutlich, wie gerade die Einordnung des Hiobbuches in die dramatische Dichtung durch den Vergleich mit außerbiblischen Literaturen und durch inhalt-liche Erwägungen bedingt ist. Daher mußte sich Ewald von seinem ehemaligen Schüler, Ernst Heinrich Meier, an diesem Punkt "ein arges Miskennen der echten Kunstformen"[69] attestieren lassen. Meier urteilte in seiner *Geschichte der poetischen National-Literatur der Hebräer* (1856), in der er in bewußter Weiterführung von Lowth und Herder "den or-ganisch-geschichtlichen Entwicklungsgang der hebräischen Dichtung" nachweisen und "aus den konkreten Lebensverhältnissen jeder Zeit"

66. Cheyne, *Job*, 108.
67. K. Schlottmann, *Das Buch Hiob verdeutscht und erläutert* (Berlin, 1851), 41.
68. Schlottmann bezog sich dabei im wesentlichen noch auf Zeugnisse griech-ischer und römischer Schriftsteller, verwendete aber bereits die Berichte des Ausgräbers von Ninive, Sir Austen Henry Layard, *Niniveh and its Remains*, vols. 1–2 (London, 1849), und erhoffte sich "bei der bevorstehenden Entzifferung der assyrischen Keilinschriften wahrscheinlich bald eine neue Bestätigung" für seine Überzeugung von der wesentlichen Einheit der semitischen Religion (Schlottmann, *Hiob*, 83).
69. E. Meier, *Geschichte der poetischen National-Literatur der Hebräer* (Leipzig, 1856), 522.

erklären wollte[70]: Im Hiobbuch finden sich "die drei Grundformen aller Dichtung vereinigt: lyrische, epische und dramatische Elemente, und diese Vermischung...ist für das Lehrgedicht wie für die Idylle characteristisch."[71] Aufgrund der im Hiobbuch vorherrschenden Gattung und aufgrund der in 27,1 und 29,1 angegebenen Bezeichnung der Hiobreden als *Maschal* ordnet Meier das Hiobbuch der didaktischen Poesie zu.

4. *Das* eine *Buch Hiob und die Vielfalt seiner Formen*

4.1. Mit Ernst Meier deutet sich ein forschungsgeschichtlicher Neuansatz an, der dann über die literaturwissenschaftlichen Arbeiten von Richard G. Moulton (1896) und die gattungsgeschichtlichen Untersuchungen von Hermann Gunkel (1906) zu einer neuen Epoche der formgeschichtlichen Arbeit, auch am Buch Hiob führt.[72] Kennzeichnend für die formgeschichtliche Erforschung des Buches Hiob zu Beginn des 20. Jahrhunderts sind drei Phänomene:

1. die Konzentration auf die literaturgeschichtliche Einordnung der *im* Buch Hiob verwendeten Formen und Gattungen,

2. die differenzierte Betrachtung der literarischen Gattungen des narrativen Prologs und Epilogs und des poetischen Hauptteils. Hier wirkt sich vor allem die literarkritisch und stoffgeschichtlich problematisierte These von der ursprünglichen Selbständigkeit der Rahmenerzählung von der Dichtung aus, sei es, daß diese sekundär gerahmt wurde, wie es vereinzelt schon in der Forschung des 18. und frühen 19. Jahrhunderts vertreten worden war,[73] sei es, daß diese in ein bereits literarisch fixiertes "Volksbuch" eingeschrieben wurde.[74]

70. Ibid., viii.

71. Ibid., 523.

72. R. G. Moulton, *The Literary Study of the Bible. An Account of the Leading Forms of Literature Represented in the Sacred Writings* (London, 1896); Gunkel, "Die israelitische Literatur"; idem, "Die Grundprobleme der israelitischen Literaturgeschichte" (1906), in *Reden und Aufsätze* (Göttingen: Vandenhoeck & Ruprecht, 1913), 29–38; idem, *Genesis* (3d ed.; HK 1/1; Göttingen: Vandenhoeck & Ruprecht, 1910); idem, *Die Propheten* (Göttingen: Vandenhoeck & Ruprecht, 1917); idem und J. Begrich, *Einleitung in die Psalmen. Die Gattungen der religiösen Lyrik Israels* (Göttingen: Vandenhoeck & Ruprecht, 1933).

73. Vgl. die Übersichten bei Witte, *Vom Leiden zur Lehre*, 192, und bei Syring, *Hiob und sein Anwalt*, 25–28.

74. L. Laue, *Die Composition des Buches Hiob. Ein litterar-kritischer Versuch* (Halle 1895/96); Budde, *Das Buch Hiob*; B. Duhm, *Das Buch Hiob erklärt* (KHC 16; Tübingen, 1897); F. Delitzsch, *Das Buch Hiob. Neu übersetzt und kurz erläutert* (Leipzig: Hinrichs, 1902).

3.   das verstärkte Bemühen, die metrische und strophische Struktur
der Hiobdichtung zu erhellen.[75]

4.2. Gegenüber diesen drei Forschungsfeldern tritt die Frage nach der
literarischen Gattung des Gesamtwerkes zunächst etwas in den Hintergrund.[76] Charakteristisch für diese Entwicklung sind die Arbeiten von
Hermann Gunkel. In Weiterführung der gattungsgeschichtlichen Ansätze
von Herder, de Wette und Ewald,[77] hat Gunkel vor allem in der
Einleitung in die Psalmen der formgeschichtlichen Analyse der Reden
der Hiobdichtung wichtige Impulse verliehen.[78] Gleichwohl bleibt sein
Urteil über die literarische Gattung des gesamten Buches, das er als
"philosophisch-religiöses Streitgespräch" mit seinen nächsten Parallelen
in der ägyptischen Literatur bezeichnet,[79] recht blaß. Ähnliches gilt für
Norbert Peters (1928), der sich bis dahin am umfassendsten um eine
Zuweisung einzelner Redeteile der Hiobdichtung an einzelne Gattungen
(Sprichwörter, Sentenzen, Klagelieder, Elegien, Hymnen, Lehrpsalmen
u.a.) bemüht hatte und der wie Gunkel im Buch Hiob "ein in eine ältere,
später midraschartig ausgebaute Volkserzählung eingespanntes religionsphilosophisches Gespräch mit paränetischer Zielstellung" erkannte.[80]

75.   Vgl. dazu vor allem die Arbeiten von G. Bickell, *Carmina Veteris Testamenti
metrice. Notas criticas et dissertationem de re metrica hebraeorum adjecit* (Inns-
bruck, 1882); idem, *Das Buch Job nach Anleitung der Strophik und der Septuaginta
auf seine ursprüngliche Form zurückgeführt und im Versmaße des Urtextes übersetzt*
(Wien, 1894); J. Ley, *Das Buch Hiob nach seinem Inhalt, seiner Kunstgestaltung
und religiösen Bedeutung* (Halle, 1893); J. Hontheim, *Das Buch Job. Als stro-
phisches Kunstwerk nachgewiesen, übersetzt und erklärt* (BSt(F) 9; Freiburg i. Br.:
Herder, 1904); P. Vetter, *Die Metrik des Buches Job* (Biblische Studien 2/4;
Freiburg, 1897); und dazu Van der Lugt, *Rhetorical Criticism*, 2–30.
76.   Ausnahmen bilden u.a. Hontheim, *Das Buch Job*, mit einer detaillierten
Gliederung des Buches Hiob in Akte und Szenen, oder Moulton, *The Literary Study*,
471–72, der unter bewußter Absehung von literargeschichtlichen Fragen, das Hiobbuch in seiner Endgestalt als "dramatic parable in a frame of epic story" bezeichnete.
77.   Zum forschungsgeschichtlichen Hintergrund von Gunkel, für den das Werk
von Lowth im Gegensatz zu den Arbeiten von Herder offenbar keine Rolle, siehe W.
Klatt, *Hermann Gunkel. Zu seiner Theologie der Religionsgeschichte und zur
Entstehung der formgeschichtlichen Methode* (FRLANT 100; Göttingen: Vandenhoeck & Ruprecht, 1969).
78.   Gunkel, *Einleitung in die Psalmen*, 32–33, 50, 77, 172, 205–11, 265.
79.   Gunkel, "Die israelitische Literatur," 93. Zu den Gunkel bekannten ägyptischen Paralleltexten siehe A. Erman, "Die Ägyptische Literatur," in Hinneberg, ed.,
Die Kultur der Gegenwart, 28–38.
80.   N. Peters, *Das Buch Job. Übersetzt und erklärt* (EHAT 21; Münster i. W.:
Aschendorff, 1928), 60*.

4.3. Sowohl für Gunkel als auch für Peters führte das beobachtete Phänomen der Gattungsmischung weder zur Preisgabe der grundsätzlichen literarischen Einheitlichkeit des Hiobbuches noch zu einer formgeschichtlichen Neubestimmung des Gesamtwerkes—anders bei Paul Volz und bei Friedrich Baumgärtel. Für Paul Volz (1911) ist das Buch Hiob ein "Dom," der in mehreren Phasen und aus unterschiedlichen Bausteinen, die jeweils eigenen literarischen Großgattungen angehören, errichtet wurde. Beim Rahmen handele es sich um eine Erzählung, bei dem Hauptteil der Dichtung (c. 3–31) um eine Klage bzw. ein "lyrisches Wechselspiel" mit Elementen des Prozeßverfahrens und Analogien zum ägyptischen Gespräch eines Lebensmüden mit seiner Seele, bei den Gottesreden in weiten Teilen um einen rednerischen Wettstreit und bei den Elihureden um die Mahnschrift eines Weisen.[81] Wesentlich radikaler ging Friedrich Baumgärtel (1933) vor, der in großem Stil Klagelieder, Hymnen, Lieder auf die Gottlosen, Sentenzen, den Reinigungseid u.v.a. aus der ursprünglichen Dichtung eliminierte und die Hiobdichtung auf "ein lebendiges, gedanklich klar durchgeführtes... Wechselgespräch" mit nur einem Redegang und abschließendem Hiobmonolog reduzierte.[82]

4.4. Der Vorschlag Baumgärtels fand zu Recht keine direkte Gefolgschaft, zumal Baumgärtel es versäumte, ein literargeschichtliches Gesamtbild von der Entstehung des Hiobbuches zu entwerfen.[83] Dennoch übte sein Werk zusammen mit dem von Volz einen starken Einfluß auf zwei Thesen der fünfziger Jahre des 20. Jahrhunderts aus, die jeweils aus *einer* dem Hiobbuch immanenten und von diesem im wesentlichen benutzten Gattung auf die literarische Gattung des gesamten Werkes schlossen. Dazu gehören:

1.   der Vorschlag von Claus Westermann (1956), das Hiobbuch als eine "dramatisierte Klage" zu verstehen,[84] und

---

81. P. Volz, *Weisheit (Das Buch Hiob, Sprüche und Jesus Sirach, Prediger)* (SAT 3/2; Göttingen: Vandenhoeck & Ruprecht, 1911; 2d ed. 1921).

82. F. Baumgärtel, *Der Hiobdialog. Aufriss und Deutung* (BWANT 4/9; Stuttgart: Kohlhammer, 1933), 169.

83. In gewisser Hinsicht stellt das Buch von J. Vermeylen, *Job, ses amis et son dieu. La légende de Job et ses rélectures postexiliques* (StB 2; Leiden: Brill, 1986), eine redaktionsgeschichtlich modifizierte Weiterführung von Baumgärtel dar.

84. C. Westermann, *Der Aufbau des Buches Hiob* (CThM.A 6; Stuttgart: Calwer Verlag, 1956; 3d ed. 1978); neben Volz und Baumgärtel stand bei der Entfaltung dieser These vor allem A. Bentzen, *Introduction to the Old Testament* (2d ed.; Kopenhagen: Gads Forlag, 1952), 1:256, Pate. Rezipiert wurde sie u.a. von F. Horst, "Hiob," *EKL* 2 (1958): 169, und K. Seybold, "Poesie I. Bibel und antikes Judentum. 1. Altes Testament," *RGG*⁴ 6 (2003): 1418.

2. der Versuch von Hans Richter (1954/1959), das Hiobbuch auf-
    grund der in ihm quantitativ und inhaltlich dominierenden
    Gattungen des Rechtslebens als das Buch eines gerichtlichen
    Prozesses zu deuten.[85]

Forschungsgeschichtlich steht neben diesen beiden Ansätzen die von
Hartmut Gese (1958) unternommene Zuweisung des Hiobbuches an die
vor allem in der mesopotamischen Literatur, und hier besonders in der
Gestalt der babylonischen Dichtung *ludlul bel nemeqi* belegten Gattung
des Klageerhörungsparadigmas.[86]
     Während die Modelle von Westermann und Richter daran kranken,
daß *eine* als dominierend bestimmte Gattung im Buch im Blick auf die
Gattung des ganzen Buches generalisiert wird, überträgt Gese eine in der
Umwelt des antiken Israel vorgefundene Gattung auf das Buch Hiob,
ohne zuvor dessen Gattungen im einzelnen zu analysieren.[87]

5. *Die* Formen und ihre Funktionen *oder die* Frage nach dem Sitz im Buch Hiob

5.1. Die eigentliche, von Gunkel begründete Gattungstypologie verhalf
der weiteren Forschung zu einer exakteren Identifikation der im Hiobbuch verwendeten Formen. Die für Gunkel zentrale Frage nach dem *Sitz
im Leben* der einzelnen Gattungen trug aber für die Frage nach
Bedeutung der Formen im Hiobbuch zunächst noch nichts aus und führte
im Blick auf das Gesamtwerk lediglich zur Bestätigung der schon seit
Herder und Eichhorn vertretenen Zuordnung zu den weisheitlichen

     85. H. Richter, *Studien zu Hiob. Der Aufbau des Hiobbuches, dargestellt an den
Gattungen des Rechtslebens* ([1954]; ThA 11; Berlin: Evangelische Verlagsanstalt,
1959). Bereits hundert Jahre früher hatte Johann Gustav Stickel bemerkt, daß im
Hiobbuch der "Typus eines Gerichtsverfahrens" auf ein didaktisches Werk angewen-
det war (*Das Buch Hiob rhythmisch gegliedert und übersetzt, mit exegetischen und
kritischen Bemerkungen* [Leipzig, 1842], 277). Richter, der dieses Werk offenbar
nicht kannte, berief sich bei der Entfaltung seiner These vor allem auf Paul Volz und
Ludwig Köhler (s. Anm. 4).
     86. H. Gese, *Lehre und Wirklichkeit in der alten Weisheit. Studien zu den
Sprüchen Salomos und zu dem Buche Hiob* (Tübingen: J. C. B. Mohr/Paul Siebeck,
1958), 63–78. Die Gattungsbezeichnung wurde rezipiert von H.-P. Müller, "Keil-
schriftliche Parallelen zum biblischen Hiobbuch. Möglichkeit und Grenze des
Vergleichs" (1978), in idem, *Gesammelte Schriften* (BZAW 200; Berlin: de Gruyter,
1991), 148.
     87. Zu einer grundsätzlichen methodologischen Kritik an diesen Ansätzen siehe
K. L. Dell, *The Book of Job as Sceptical Literature* (BZAW 191; Berlin: de Gruyter,
1991), 89–73.

Dialogen bzw. zum "Lehrgedicht." An diesem Punkt führte die vor allem von Georg Fohrer (1959)[88] programmatisch aufgestellte Forderung weiter, nicht nur geschichtlich nach dem *Sitz im Leben* einer Gattung zu fragen, sondern auch inhaltlich nach ihrer Funktion in ihrem neuen literarischen Kontext, nach ihrem *Sitz im Buch.*

Mit der bereits von Johannes Hempel (1934) formulierten,[89] dann aber von Fohrer umfassend begründeten These einer bewußten *Gattungsmischung* wurden sowohl die einseitigen Beschreibungen des Hiobbuches als "dramatisierte Klage" oder "Gerichtsverfahren" abgewiesen als auch der spezifische Sitz einer Gattung in dem konkreten literarischen Werk aufgezeigt. D.h. der Hiobdichter hat Redeformen aus dem *Rechtsleben* ("Parteireden der Weisen"), dem *Kult* ("Hymnus und Klage") und der *Weisheit* ("Streitgespräche der Weisen") aufgenommen, verknüpft und durch direkte Eingriffe in die jeweilige Redeform oder deren Integration in einen neuen Sachzusammenhang modifiziert.[90] In der Auseinandersetzung um das richtige Verhalten im Leid, die nach Fohrer inhaltlich im Mittelpunkt des Hiobbuches steht, spielen die einzelnen Formen eine untergeordnete Rolle. Aus ihnen lasse sich, so Fohrer, weder eine Gesamtdeutung noch eine literarische Gattungsbestimmung für das Buch Hiob vornehmen. Dieses bilde vielmehr ein "Dichtwerk mit Rahmenerzählung."[91] Wie bereits Lowth verweist Fohrer dann auch auf Berührungen mit der griechischen Tragödie, in denen er lediglich Analogien und keine Beispiele für die beiderseitige Behandlung eines internationalen Themas sieht.[92] Die von Fohrer durchgeführte formgeschichtliche Einordnung aller Elemente der Hiobdichtung und die Bestimmung ihrer jeweiligen Funktion im Buch wurde von der Forschung breit rezipiert.[93]

88. G. Fohrer, "Form und Funktion in der Hiobdichtung" (1959), in idem, *Studien zum Buch Hiob* (Gütersloh: Gütersloher Verlagshaus Gerd Mohn, 1963), 68–86; idem, *Das Buch Hiob* (KAT 16; Gütersloh: Gütersloher Verlagshaus Gerd Mohn, 1963; 2d ed. 1989).

89. J. Hempel, *Die althebräische Literatur und ihr hellenistisch-jüdisches Nachleben* (Wildpark-Potsdam: Akademische Verlagsanstalt Athenaion, 1930–1934; 2d ed. 1968), 179: "Es wird dabei zu bleiben haben, daß der Reichtum literarischer Gattungen, die miteinander verschlungen sind, dem Dialogdichter selbst eigen gewesen ist."

90. Fohrer, *Das Buch Hiob*, 50–53.

91. Ibid., 53; ähnlich N. H. Tur Sinai, *The Book of Job: A New Commentary* (rev. ed.; Jerusalem: Kiryat-Sefer, 1967), lvi.

92. Fohrer, *Das Buch Hiob*, 47. Daneben bietet Fohrer natürlich auch eine Übersicht über die bis 1959 bekannten sumerischen, babylonischen, ägyptischen und aramäischen "Parallelen" zum Hiobbuch.

93. J. Kegler, "Hauptlinien der Hiobforschung seit 1956," in Westermann, *Aufbau* (2d ed.; Stuttgart, 1977), 9–12; Lévêque, *Job*, 1:230–36; R. E. Murphy,

5.2. Nun ist das Phänomen der Gattungsmischung und der damit verbundenen neuen Kontextualisierung nicht auf das Hiobbuch beschränkt, sondern findet sich in mehr oder weniger großem Umfang im gesamten Alten Testament und in anderen antiken Literaturen. Damit stellt sich erneut die Frage, ob sich aus der bewußten Mischung von Formen und ihren Funktionen nicht doch eindeutiger auf den literaturgeschichtlichen Ort und die Gattung des Hiobbuches schließen lasse. Genau an diesem Punkt setzt die breit angelegte formgeschichtliche Untersuchung von Katherine L. Dell (1991) an.[94] Die bewußte Rezeption und Verfremdung von Gattungen (*reuse* sowie *improper use / misuse of genre*) sei in literaturgeschichtlicher Hinsicht typisch für die Gattung der *Parodie* und verweise geistesgeschichtlich auf eine Verortung des Hiobdichters in skeptischen Kreisen, die der traditionellen Weisheit Israels kritisch gegenüberstünden. Das Buch Hiob stelle somit ein Beispiel für "sceptical literature" im Alten Testament dar. Kennzeichend für Dells Ansatz ist einerseits ihre Unzufriedenheit mit der formgeschichtlichen Bezeichnung des Buches Hiob als Werk *sui generis*,[95] andererseits ihr Versuch, mittels einer Analyse von Form und Funktion der "smallest genres" unter Berücksichtigung des Inhaltes zu einem formgeschichtlichen Gesamtbild zu kommen.[96]

Einen zweiten Entwurf, aus dem Phänomen der Gattungsmischung die Gattung des Gesamtwerkes zu skizzieren, legte in neuerer Zeit Marco Treves (1995) vor. Er korrelierte die Gattungsmischung im Hiobbuch mit den Komposittexten des Menippus von Gadara (3. Jahrhundert v. Chr.). In den dramatisch-philosophischen Dialogen des Menippus sah Treves obendrein die literaturgeschichtliche Vorlage des Hiobdichters, der sein Werk in Kenntnis der Poetiken von Aristoteles und Neoptolemos von Parion (3. Jahrhundert v. Chr.), aber auch der griechischen Tragödie geschrieben habe.[97] Das Hiobbuch sei mithin "a philosophical dialogue in

Wisdom Literature: Job, Proverbs, Ruth, Canticles, Ecclesiastes and Esther (FOTL 13; Grand Rapids: Eerdmans, 1981), 16–20; J. L. Sicre und L. Alonso Schökel, *Commentario teológico y literaria* (Nueva Biblia Española; Madrid: Ediciones Cristiandad, 1983), 83; Hartley, *Job*, 38–43; D. J. A. Clines, *Job 1–20* (WBC 17; Dallas: Word, 1989).
94. Dell, *The Book of Job*.
95. Ibid., 101, 107.
96. Ibid., 102, 109–38.
97. M. Treves, "The Book of Job," *ZAW* 107 (1995): 261–72. Mit seiner These, daß das Hiobbuch aus formgeschichtlichen Gründen weder vorhellenistisch noch nicht-griechisch beeinflußt sein könne, belebte Treves ein Diktum von Oskar Holtzmann, das Buch Hiob als "religionsphilosophisches Werk" sei für die Juden

verse or a dramatic poem" oder auch "a kind of philosophical tragedy."[98] So einseitig die Skizze von Treves ist, da sie die vorderorientalische Dialogliteratur ausblendet, so steht seine Analyse des Hiobbuches mithilfe griechischer und römischer Poetiken doch in Kontinuität zu Lowths Heranziehung von Aristoteles und Horaz.[99]

6. *Form und Zeichen* oder die Frage nach der Welt des Textes und der Leser

6.1. Die Frage nach dem *Sitz im Buch* und nach der Funktion der Gattungsmischung erlebte aber nicht nur eine literargeschichtliche Weiterführung, sondern seit den siebziger Jahren des 20. Jahrhunderts durch Impulse aus der Literaturwissenschaft[100] auch eine text- und leserorientierte Fokussierung. Charakteristisch für eine erste Phase der textorientierten Konzentration sind im Blick auf das Buch Hiob die vom Strukturalismus beeinflußten Arbeiten von William Whedbee (1977) und Norman C. Habel (1985).[101] Im Mittelpunkt des Interesses steht die Struktur des Endtextes. Dieser wird in *movements* und *segments* gegliedert, auf deren gegenseitiges Verhältnis hin analysiert und auf seinen

erst nach dem Kontakt mit den Griechen möglich und die dialogische Form sei eine "hebräische Nachbildung des philosophischen Dialogs bei Plato" (in B. Stade, *Geschichte des Volkes Israel*, vol. 1–2 [Berlin, 1887.1888], 2:351), ähnlich K. Fries, *Das philosophische Gespräch von Hiob bis Platon* (Tübingen: J. C. B. Mohr/Paul Siebeck, 1904), 58: "Das Buch Hiob ist ein philosophischer Dialog."

98. Treves, "The Book of Job," 261, 264.

99. Einen weiteren Versuch, das Phänomen der Gattungsmischung mittels der Annahme *eines* bewußt komponierenden Verfassers zu erklären, hat in jüngerer Zeit M. Oeming mit der These vorgelegt, das Hiobbuch sei ein poimenischer Traktat, der exemplarisch typische Erfahrungen aus der Seelsorgepraxis aufgreife und literarisch vielfältig reflektiere (in idem und K. Schmid, *Hiobs Weg. Stationen von Menschen im Leid* [BThSt 45; Neukirchen–Vluyn: Neukirchener, 2001], 35–56). Doch sprechen gegen eine solche Klassifikation als "Handbuch der Seelsorge" sowohl literargeschichtliche als auch sozialgeschichtliche Überlegungen. Auch wenn das Hiobbuch seelsorgerlich gelesen werden kann, so eignet sich die Bezeichnung Seelsorgetraktat nicht als literaturgeschichtliche Gattungsbezeichnung.

100. Vgl. dazu R. Alter und F. Kermode, eds., *The Literary Guide to the Bible* (London: Wilson, 1987), 1–8.

101. W. Whedbee, "The Comedy of Job," in *Studies in the Book of Job* (ed. R. Polzin und D. Robertson; Semeia 7; Missoula. Mont.: Scholars Press, 1977), 1–39; N. C. Habel, *The Book of Job: A Commmentary* (OTL; London: SCM Press, 1985); J. G. Janzen, *Job* (Interpretation, a Bible Commentary for Teaching and Preaching; Atlanta: John Knox, 1985); M. Greenberg, "Job," in Alter und Kermode, eds., *Guide*, 283–304.

code und seine *message* befragt.[102] Aus dem Wechselspiel zwischen *movements* und *segments* sowie der Verwendung und Verfremdung traditioneller Formen ließen sich sowohl der eigentliche *plot* als auch das literarische *genre* des Buches erheben.

Bei Whedbee, der als konstitutive Elemente im Hiobbuch einerseits eine *basic story* mit einem *happy end*, andererseits das Phänomen von Inkongruenzen im Gebrauch einzelner Redeformen und deren Funktionen, von Karikaturen (so vor allem in Gestalt der Freunde), Parodien (so vor allem in den Reden der Freunde) und Ironie (so vor allem in der Gottesrede) sieht, wird das Buch Hiob zur (ernsten) Komödie.[103] Trotz dieser so stark an der Textoberfläche interessierten Sicht fällt doch auf, daß die Zuweisung des Buches Hiob zur Komödie letztlich aus inhaltlichen (im einzelnen höchst problematischen) Erwägungen erfolgt.[104]

Für Habel hingegen spielen Redeformen des Rechts eine entscheidende strukturelle Rolle der insgesamt drei *movements*, die das Hiobbuch bestimmen.[105] Das Buch Hiob gerät damit gattungsmäßig in die Nähe des dramatisierten Rechtsstreits ("lawsuit drama"),[106] auch wenn für Habel die Vielfalt der verwendeten Formen letztlich die Zuordnung des Hiobbuches "to any single traditional genre structure" ausschließt.[107]

6.2. Für eine zweite Phase der textorientierten Interpretation und deren Bedeutung für die Frage nach der literarischen Gattung des Buches Hiob ist die Berücksichtigung semiotischer und intertextueller Fragen kennzeichnend. Exemplarisch ist hier die Untersuchung von Melanie Köhlmoos (1999).[108] Sie verbindet klassische form- und redaktionsgeschichtliche Fragestellungen mit einem vor allem im Schatten von Umberto

102. Vgl. dazu R. M. Polzin, *Biblical Structuralism. Method and Subjectivity in the Study of Ancient Texts* (Philadelphia: Fortress, 1977; zum Buch Hiob: pp. 54–125).

103. Whedbee, "The Comedy of Job," 4.

104. Siehe dazu auch die Kritik von Dell, *The Book of Job*, 95–102.

105. Habel, *The Book of Job*, 70–73: movement I. God afflicts the hero—the hidden conflict (1,1–2,10); movement II. the hero challenges God—the conflict explored (2,11–31,40); movement III. God challenges the hero—the conflict resolved (32,1–42,17).

106. Ibid., 54; vgl. dazu aber dezidiert S. H. Scholnick, *Lawsuit Drama in the Book of Job* (Ph.D. diss., Brandeis University, 1975).

107. Habel, *The Book of Job*, 45.

108. M. Köhlmoos, *Das Auge Gottes. Textstrategie im Hiobbuch* (FAT 25; Tübingen: Mohr Siebeck, 1999); zu einem stärker informationstheoretischen Ansatz siehe M. Cheney, *Dust, Wind and Agony. Character, Speech and Genre in Job* (CBOT 36; Lund: Almqvist & Wiksell, 1994).

Eco[109] stehenden semiotischen Zugang. Im Blick auf seine literarische Gattung als Gesamtkunstwerk wird das Hiobbuch einerseits als *erzählender Text* mit den Konstitutiva Akteuren, Handlung, Verlauf, Raum und Zeit verstanden, andererseits als ein Werk *sui generis*.[110] Das von G. Fohrer beobachtete und von K. L. Dell weiterentwickelte Modell der *Mischung von Gattungen* wird bei Köhlmoos weitergeführt zum Modell der bewußten und planvollen *Mischung von Texten*. Das Hiobbuch erscheint als Paradebeispiel für ein intertextuelles Werk, das mit zahlreichen Referenztexten arbeitet.[111] Das setzt beim Leser eine enorme Kenntnis (*Enzyklopädie*) von Formen, Traditionen und Texten voraus und fordert dessen gezielte Mitarbeit im Prozeß des Lesens und Verstehens. Der Leser des Hiobbuches wird bei einem solchen zeichentheoretischen Zugang, der wesentlich auf die Erhellung der Leserlenkung durch den Text selbst (*Textstrategie*) zielt, zum Mitspieler. Das Buch Hiob wird damit erneut zu einem Drama. Nicht umsonst spielt für Köhlmoos das Motiv des Auges Gottes eine zentrale Rolle bei der Deutung des Hiobbuches als ein dramatisches Geschehen zwischen Hiob, seinen Freunden, Gott und dem Publikum, das auf einer unsichtbaren Bühne stattfindet. Das bereits von Thomas Heath (1756), Heinrich Ewald (1865), Marco Treves (1995) u.a. vertretene Verständnis des Buches Hiob als ein vor dem inneren Auge stattfindendes Lesedrama, das sich letztlich auf eine Sentenz in der *Ars Poetica* des Horaz berufen kann,[112] findet durch diesen semiotischen Ansatz eine grundlegende Weiterführung.

7. Ausblick auf gegenwärtige Fragen zur Formgeschichte des Buches Hiob

Unter Rezeption und Modifikation der im 18. Jahrhundert durch Robert Lowth thematisierten Fragen nach der literarischen Gattung des Buches Hiob, kreist die gegenwärtige formgeschichtliche Arbeit an diesem Werk um fünf Themenfelder.

7.1. Die formgeschichtliche Klassifikation des Hiobbuches als Gesamtwerk: Hier herrscht in der neueren und neuesten Forschung eine ähnliche Vielfalt wie in der ersten Forschergeneration nach Lowth.[113]

---

109. U. Eco, *Lector in fabula: la cooperazione interpretativa nei testi narrativi* (Milano: Bompiani, 1979; 4th ed. 1989); idem, *I limiti dell' interpretazione* (Milano: Bompiani, 1990).

110. Köhlmoos, *Das Auge Gottes*, 24.

111. Ähnlich Spieckermann, "Hiob/Hiobbuch," 1178.

112. Horaz, *Ars poetica*, 180–82; vgl. dazu Treves, "The Book of Job," 269.

113. Siehe dazu auch die Forschungsberichte von C. Kuhl, "Neuere Literarkritik

7.2. Die Bestimmung der einzelnen im Hiobbuch selbst verwendeten Formen: Lowths grundsätzliche Typologie von einzelnen im Hiobbuch verwendeten Formen hat sich bis heute bewährt. Gleichwohl können die einzelnen Formelemente aufgrund der verfeinerten Analysen von J. G. Herder (1782/3), H. Ewald (1836ff.), E. Meier (1856), H. Gunkel (1906ff.), G. Fohrer (1963), R. E. Murphy (1981), J. E. Hartley (1988) und K. L. Dell (1991) sehr viel genauer bestimmt werden.[114] Entscheidend weiter führten die Fragen zunächst nach der soziokulturellen Verortung der jeweils verwendeten Form (*Sitz im Leben*), sodann nach der inhaltlichen und kompositionellen Funktion der jeweils verwendeten Form (*Sitz im Buch; Sitz in der Literatur*) und schließlich nach dem Verhältnis zwischen der jeweils verwendeten Form und dem Akt des Lesens, Verstehens und Deutens (*Sitz im Leser*).

7.3. Die Erhellung der Strophik und der Metrik des Hiobbuches: Trotz intensiver einschlägiger poetologischer Arbeiten und trotz des umfangreichen Vergleichsmaterials im Bereich der vorderorientalischen Literaturen ist die gegenwärtige Forschung weit entfernt von einer einheitlichen Beantwortung der Fragen nach der strophischen Gliederung der Hiobdichtung und der Metrik der einzelnen Verse. Als Minimalkonsens gelten hier weiterhin (1) das bereits von Johann Gerhard (1610/1622) geäußerte Diktum, das Buch Hiob werde zu Recht zu den poetischen Büchern gezählt, auch wenn sein metrisches Prinzip bis heute unbekannt sei,[115] und (2) die von Robert Lowth in der *Sacra Poesis* (praelect. XIX) und der *Preliminary Dissertation* zu seinem Jesajakommentar (1778)[116] entfaltete Erkenntnis des *Parallelismus membrorum* als Grundelement der hebräischen Poesie. Allerdings ist die Forschung durch die Arbeiten von Wilfred G. E. Watson (1984/2001), Robert Alter (1985/1987), Luis Alonso Schökel (1988) und Pieter van der Lugt (1995) zu einer vertieften Wahrnehmung der poetischen Stilmittel (nicht nur) im Hiobbuch gekommen.[117]

---

des Buches Hiob," *ThR* n.f. 21 (1953): 306–13; Dell, *The Book of Job*, 88–95; H.-P. Müller, *Das Hiobproblem* (EdF 84; Darmstadt: Wissenschaftliche Buchgesellschaft, 1978), 76–91; J. van Oorschot, "Tendenzen der Hiobforschung," *ThR* n.f. 60 (1995): 377–83.

    114. Fohrer, *Das Buch Hiob*; Murphy, *Wisdom Literature*; Hartley, *The Book of Job*, und Dell, *The Book of Job*.

    115. Gerhard, *Loci*, §140.

    116. Lowth, *Isaiah*, in *Works*, ed. Reibel, x–xxv.

    117. R. Alter, *The Art of Biblical Poetry* (New York: Basic Books, 1981); idem, "The Characteristics of Ancient Hebrew Poetry," in Alter und F. Kermode, eds.,

7.4. *Die literaturgeschichtliche Korrelation mit außerbiblischen Texten:*
Standen Lowth und seinen Zeitgenossen lediglich Werke aus der
klassischen Antike und vereinzelt aus dem arabischen, indischen und
persischen Raum zum Vergleich zur Verfügung,[118] so kann die gegenwärtige Forschung seit dem Ausgang der zweiten Hälfte des 19. Jahrhunderts in stetig steigendem Maß ägyptische und mesopotamische
Texte heranziehen. Dazu kommen mit den Textfunden von *Elephantine*
(seit 1909; vgl. vor allem die Fragmente des Achikar-Romans), *Ugarit*
(seit 1929; vgl. vor allem R.S. 25.460) und *Qumran* (seit 1947; vgl. vor
allem 11QTgJob; 4QTgJob; 4QOrNab) zusätzlich aramäische, ugaritische und nichtbiblische hebräische Texte.[119] Entsprechend dem von
Lowth in seiner 33. Vorlesung vorgelegten Verfahren des literaturgeschichtlichen Vergleichs zwischen dem Hiobbuch und den sophokleischen
Oedipus-Dramen finden sich gegenwärtig Korrelationen mit allen
inhaltlich und / oder formal verwandten Texten aus der Umwelt des
Alten Testaments. Dabei überwiegen die Vergleiche mit der ägyptischen
"Auseinandersetzungsliteratur"[120] und den mesopotamischen Theo-
dizeedichtungen und Streitgesprächen, die nach einem Vorschlag von
Dorothea Sitzler (1995) unter dem Terminus "Vorwurfdichtungen"[121]
subsumiert werden können. Die griechische Welt wird zu Recht nicht
völlig ausgeblendet. Die dabei erzielten Ergebnisse stehen in einer
direkten Beziehung zu den unter 7.1. bis 7.3. genannten Themen. Zu dem
Reichtum des literaturgeschichtlichen Vergleichs im engeren Sinn sind in
den letzten 25 Jahren schließlich über rezeptionsästhetische, semiotische

Guide, 611–24; Watson, *Classical Hebrew Poetry*; L. Alonso Schökel, *A Manual of Hebrew Poetics* (subsidia biblica 11; Rome: Pontificio Istituto Biblico, 2000); Van der Lugt, *Rhetorical Criticism*. Zur Forschungsgeschichte siehe auch Kugel, *Biblical Poetry*.

118.   Vgl. dazu W. Jones, *Poeseos Asiaticae Commentariorum libri sex cum appendice recudi curavit* Io. Gottfried Eichhorn (Leipzig, 1777).

119.   Zur Diskussion der einschlägigen Vergleichstexte siehe Lévêque, *Job*, 1:13–86; Müller, *Das Hiobproblem*, 49–72; M. Weinfeld, "Job and Its Mesopota-mian Parallels: A Typological Analysis," in *Text and Context: Old Testament and Semitic Studies* (ed. W. Claassen; JSOTSup 48; Sheffield: Sheffield Academic Press, 1988), 217–26.

120.   Zum Begriff siehe H. Brunner, *Grundzüge einer Geschichte der altägyp-tischen Literatur* (4th ed.; Grundzüge 8; Darmstadt: Wissenschaftliche Buchge-sellschaft, 1986), 22, und zur Anwendung dieser Gattungsbezeichnung auf das Hiobbuch: O. Kaiser, *Einleitung in das Alte Testament. Eine Einführung in ihre Ergebnisse und Probleme* (5th ed.; Gütersloh: Gütersloher Verlagshaus Gerd Mohn, 1984), 392.

121.   D. Sitzler, *"Vorwurf gegen Gott." Ein religiöses Motiv im Alten Orient (Ägypten und Mesopotamien)* (StOR 32; Wiesbaden: Harrassowitz, 1995), 119–37.

und wirkungsgeschichtliche Ansätze transhistorische Lektüreverfahren getreten, die das Buch Hiob nun mit literarischen (und nichtliterarischen) Werken aus den unterschiedlichsten zeitlichen und kulturellen Kontexten ins Gespräch bringen.[122] Tragen diese Vergleiche (zumindest primär) nichts zu einer form*geschichtlichen* Erhellung der Probleme des Hiob-buches und zur Frage nach seiner literarischen Gattung bei, so vermögen sie doch, zu dessen neuer Lektüre und neuen Formen der Wahrnehmung des Buches Hiob anzuregen—und entsprechen darin einem zentralen Anliegen von Robert Lowth.

7.5. Das Verhältnis zwischen der Gattungsbestimmung und der Gesamt-deutung: Über die Frage nach der literarischen Gattung und den Versuch, diese im Vergleich mit inhaltlich und/oder formal analogen Texten zu bestimmen, verändern sich das Wesen Hiobs und sein kulturelles Profil. Bildlich gesprochen, wechselt Hiob je nach Bestimmung der liter-arischen Gattung das Gewand. Sein rätselhaftes Heimatland Uz tritt den Schauplätzen Athen, Babylon oder Ägypten zur Seite. Die Gattungs-bestimmung bedingt die Wahrnehmung des Textes. Ein Drama liest sich anders als ein philosophischer Dialog, eine Klage anders als ein weis-heitliches Streitgespräch.

Methodisch heißt dies: Die formgeschichtliche Analyse des Hiob-buches muß fünf Punkte berücksichtigen:
1. die in diesem Buch verwendeten Gattungen, deren soziokulturelle Herkunft und buchimmanente Kontextualisierungen,
2. redaktionsgeschichtliche Erkenntnisse zur Literargeschichte des Buches Hiob und das Phänomen des Wandels der literarischen Gattung auf den unterschiedlichen redaktionellen Ebenen des Buches,
3. inhaltlich und formal vergleichbare Texte aus dem Vorderen Orient und dem griechischen Raum,
4. den im Buch verhandelten Inhalt,
5. die Beziehung zwischen den verwendeten Gattungen und der gewählten Gattungsbezeichnung für das gesamte Werk einerseits und dem Leser andererseits. Zu den Fragen nach dem *Sitz im Leben* (nach der Tradition oder Tiefenstruktur des Textes) und nach dem *Sitz im Buch* (nach der Funktion oder Oberflächenstruktur des Textes) muß die Frage nach dem *Sitz in der Welt des Lesers* (nach der Rezeption oder der Assoziationsfläche des Textes) treten.

122. Vgl. dazu exemplarisch U. Simon, "Job and Sophocles," in *Images of Belief in Literature* (ed. D. Jasper; New York: St. Martins, 1984), 42–51; Clines, *Job 1–20*, xxxiv–xxxviii, xlvii–lvi; J. Ebach, *Streiten mit Gott. Hiob*, vols. 1–2 (Neukirchen–Vluyn: Neukirchener, 1995.1996).

Die Exegese kann aus literaturgeschichtlichen Gründen nicht darauf verzichten, das Buch Hiob als Ganzes, aber auch seine einzelnen literar- und redaktionsgeschichtlich zu erhebenden Bausteine (A: eine ursprünglich selbständige, literarisch mehrschichtige Hiob-Erzählung, B: eine ursprünglich selbständige, literarisch mehrschichtige Hiob-Dichtung, C: das redaktionell aus A und B komponierte Hiob-Buch)[123] bestimmten literarischen Gattungen zuzuordnen. Gleichzeitig muß sie aufgrund der inhaltlichen Offenheit des Hiobthemas, aber auch aus rezeptionsästhetischen Gründen, die Antwort auf die Frage nach der Gattung flexibel gestalten. Denn die verschiedenen Gattungs*zuweisungen* sind jeweils auch Lese*anweisungen* und als solche eröffnen und begrenzen sie die Lesehorizonte. Für die literar- und redaktionsgeschichtlich ermittelbaren Elemente einer ursprünglich selbständigen Erzählung von der Bewährung des Frommen (A) bedeutet dies die Zuweisung zur Gattung der *weisheitlichen Lehrerzählung*,[124] die ihre nächsten innerbiblischen Parallelen in den Büchern Ruth und Jona findet. Für die (literarisch mehrschichtige) ursprünglich selbständige Hiobdichtung (B) bedeutet das in Analogie zu den Kompositionen der "Babylonischen Theodizee" oder des "Gesprächs eines Lebensmüden mit seinem Ba" eine Zuordnung zur *Theodizee- oder Vorwurfdichtung*. Für das aus der Lehrerzählung und der Dichtung erstellte Buch (C), das nun, wie bereits Lowth zutreffend formulierte, ein Werk *sui generis* darstellt, eignet sich sowohl aus literaturgeschichtlichen als auch aus rezeptionsästhetischen Gründen am besten der Begriff *Auseinandersetzungsliteratur*. Ihr Überlieferungsort dürfte die jüdisch-hellenistische Weisheitsschule gewesen sein.[125]

123. Zu dem hier vorausgesetzten kompositions- und redaktionsgeschichtlichen Modell der sekundären Verknüpfung einer ursprünglich selbständigen Hiob-Erzählung und einer ebenfalls ursprünglich selbständigen Hiob-Dichtung siehe Witte, *Vom Leiden zur Lehre*, 173–92, und Syring, *Hiobs Anwalt*, 154–67.

124. Vgl. dazu H.-P. Müller, "Die weisheitliche Lehrerzählung im Alten Testament und in seiner Umwelt," in idem, *Mensch—Umwelt—Eigenwelt. Gesammelte Aufsätz zur Weisheit Israels* (Stuttgart: Kohlhammer, 1992), 22–43; V. Maag, *Hiob. Wandlung und Verarbeitung des Problems in Novelle, Dialogdichtung und Spätfassungen* (Göttingen: Vandenhoeck & Ruprecht, 1982), 20–45; Syring, *Hiobs Anwalt*, 14, 154–58.

125. Erst nach dem Abschluß des Manuskripts bin ich auf die breit angelegte Studie von Françoise Mies, *L'espérance de Job* (BEThL CXCIII; Leuven: Leuven University Press, 2006), aufmerksam geworden, die das Buch Hiob selbst als (weisheitliches) Drama interpretiert. Auf das Werk von Mies wie auf ihren Aufsatz "Le genre littéraire de Job," *RB* 110 (2003): 336–69, sei hier in Ergänzung zu meiner Darstellung ausdrücklich hingewiesen.

THE STUDY OF HEBREW POETRY:
PAST—PRESENT—FUTURE

Wilfred G. E. Watson

1. *Introduction*

As is clear from its title, this article is concerned with classical Hebrew poetry as studied in previous centuries, now and in the near future. Obviously the considerable contribution made by Robert Lowth (1710–1787)[1] and his contemporaries in this area is of great significance. However, here the main concern is with the more recent past, that is to say, studies during the latter part of the twentieth century, for reasons that will become apparent. Some attention is also given to work currently being undertaken. At the close, some avenues of research for the future are listed, with brief discussion.

Although Robert Lowth was probably not the first scholar to be aware of parallelism in Hebrew verse (it had previously been recognized by A. S. Mazzocchi, J. D. Michaelis, C. Schoettgen and others), he was one of the first to make it widely known, drawing on the work of his fellow scholars. As Kugel puts it (1981, 273): "By Lowth's time all the elements of the puzzle he was to deal with had been laid out. His task was primarily that of arrangement and synthesis—but that was no small matter." Similar problems of precedence also occurred in the scientific world: Did Leibnitz invent calculus or was it Newton? Was Darwin the first to discover evolution? In fact, it seems that Lowth drew on work by Azariah de Rossi and David Kimchi, in their turn influenced by earlier Jewish scholars of the Middle Ages, such as Moshe Ibn Ezra (eleventh century) who analysed the Hebrew text, and by Renaissance scholars such as Fray Luis of León. However, his contribution has been well covered by other contributors to the present volume, so there is no need to say much more here.[2] Briefly, Lowth described the three types of

1. A brief account of Lowth's work is provided by Michael 1994.
2. See the summary in Collins 1978, 9–10, and the longer discussion in Kugel 1981, 273–92.

parallelism (synonymous, antithetic and synthetic) and had even referred to word-pairs, so much in vogue some thirty years ago, as "parallel terms." He isolated several small poems in the Pentateuch (cf. F. Andersen 1995, 54), a work that appears to be written in prose, yet he was sceptical about our recovery of Hebrew metre. There is no doubt that Lowth's influence is still felt today. This is expressed in the following quotation, which, in spite of the mixed metaphors it uses, is very apposite:

> Lowth suffered the normal eclipse of a century and a half after his death as more and more intricate types of parallelism and theories of Hebrew poetry swamped his thesis. However, in our own day, and especially with the discovery of the same phenomenon in Ugaritic literature, Lowth's original divisions and descriptions have come home to roost. (Baker 1973, 439)

2. *Previous Surveys*

Just over twenty-five years ago, in a paper presented at a meeting of the Society for Old Testament Study with the title "Trends in the Development of Classical Hebrew Poetry," a list was provided of recent books and articles on Hebrew poetry, including some reference to Ugaritic and Akkadian, as well as discussing a selection of topics also related to poetry.[3] At about the same time, several important books on Hebrew poetry were published. The first was a monograph by Collins (1978) on Hebrew poetry, more specifically, the poetry of the prophetic books, in respect of its grammatical structure. This involved an analysis of the individual verse-lines in terms of their components (noun clauses, verbs and modifiers) resulting in sets of patterns or line-forms.[4] The longest book on Hebrew poetry was by O'Connor (1980), an analysis based on modern linguistics, a groundbreaking but difficult work.[5] A year later, in 1981, Kugel wrote a significant book on parallelism which gave rise to a number of reviews and review articles,[6] particularly in view of his radical description of parallelism, namely, "A is so, and what's more, B" (Kugel 1981, 23), where "A" and "B" refer to the two parallel lines of a couplet.[7] Another work on parallelism by Berlin appeared in 1985 and is also

---

3. Published later as W. Watson 1982a; reprinted in W. Watson 1994a, 86–103.
4. The most critical review of this approach was by Niccacci 1980.
5. Reviews are listed in the second edition (O'Connor 1997, 660). Note also the comments by Holladay (1999a, 1999b).
6. E.g. Cooper 1987; P. Miller 1984; W. Watson 1983, 1984b.
7. See Kugel 1984 for a response to his critics.

important because of its focus on the linguistic aspect.[8] As a result of all these studies, several review articles were written, for example, the long article by T. Andersen, with the title "Problems in Analysing Hebrew Poetry" (1986), which was in effect another survey.[9] The following year, a collection of essays by sixteen contributors was published, with the title *Directions in Biblical Hebrew Poetry*, edited by Follis (1987). The main topics discussed were as follows: metre, types of parallelism, the *inclusio* or framing device, pseudosorites, the folktale, and the distinction between poetry and prose. The book also included several essays on single poems, but in spite of the title, there was no overall discussion of past work or even of future trends.[10] Kuntz (1993), according to whom the fundamental issues of the day are poetry vs. prose, parallelism, metre and rhythm, and figurative discourse, provides a survey of recent research on biblical Hebrew poetry.[11] He also provided a similar survey in 1998.[12] The latest such survey is W. Watson (2000).

In addition, there have been textbooks and encyclopaedia articles that provide accounts of work on Hebrew poetry. One is Alonso Schökel's *Manual of Hebrew Poetics* (1988). Another is Gillingham's *The Poems and Psalms of the Hebrew Bible* (1994), which provides a useful survey and critique of the issues dominating the study of Hebrew verse. The main topics in Part I of the book, "Identifying Hebrew Poetry," are as follows: poets as performing to an audience, the distinction between prose and verse, metre and parallelism. Also useful is Petersen and Richards' *Interpreting Hebrew Poetry* (1992). Cloete's book *Versification and Syntax in Jeremiah 2–25* (1989b), provides an excellent survey in the first hundred pages or so. Another survey is available in Raabe

---

8.   See also Berlin 1979.

9.   Geller 1982 is a review of Kugel 1981 and O'Connor 1980.

10.   See also Landy 1987. Several years ago, in another study, this time with the title "Problems and Solutions in Hebrew Poetry: A Survey of Recent Work," besides references to books and articles on Hebrew poetry, there was mention of studies in Ugaritic and Akkadian verse traditions and in addition, of work on Native American Indian tales which seem to straddle the boundary between verse and prose. Whatever the merits of that exposition, it did indicate that the problem of differentiating between verse and prose is not confined to the area of Semitic studies (see now W. Watson 1993, reprinted in W. Watson 1994a, 18–31 and in Orton 2000, 221–33).

11.   It is a review article of the following books: O'Connor 1980; Kugel 1981; W. Watson 1984a; Alter 1985; Alonso Schökel 1988; Fisch 1988.

12.   He evaluates and compares the contributions of O'Connor 1980; Kugel 1981; Krašovec 1984; W. Watson 1984a, 1994a; Alter 1985; Berlin 1985; Alonso Schökel 1988; Fisch 1988; Pardee 1988; Grossberg 1989; Petersen and Richards 1992; Gillingham 1994.

(1990, 9–28). A very succinct introduction is available in Chapter 2 of Gabel, Wheeler and York, *The Bible as Literature: An Introduction* (2000). More extensive, but aimed at a non-technical readership, is Fokkelman's book *Reading Biblical Poetry* (2001). The entries "Hebrew Poetry" (by Fitzgerald) in the *Jerome Biblical Commentary* (1968), and "Parallelism" (by Berlin) and "Psalms" (by Limburg) in the *Anchor Bible Dictionary* (1992) are also valuable. Similarly, the entries "Hebrew Poetry" (by Spicehandler) and "Hebrew Prosody and Poetics" (by Geller) as well as the entry "Parallelism" (by O'Connor) in the *New Princeton Encyclopedia of Poetry and Poetics* (1993) provide succinct surveys of these topics.[13]

In respect of the comparison between Hebrew poetry and ancient Near Eastern literature, Avishur, who has been publishing articles on North-west Semitic poetry for many years (e.g. Avishur 1984, on parallel pairs), provides a very brief survey in his book *Studies in Hebrew and Ugaritic Psalms* (1994). However, whether there are "psalms" in Ugaritic, as he claims, is a moot point. First, he examines Ps 29, the whole of Hab 3 and a few passages from the psalms, largely in terms of Ugaritic verse. Then he looks at three Ugaritic poems (which he labels as psalms) and points out similarities and parallels with the biblical psalms, and other passages in Hebrew poetry. There is much to be learned from this book even though it requires considerable updating from more recent work.

Some years earlier, in 1988, Pardee had compiled a book, incorporating a large number of tables and statistics, on the similarities and differences between Ugaritic and Hebrew poetry, with the title *'nt and Proverbs: A Trial Cut*. There, more logically, analysis of a Ugaritic text is provided first (a passage from the *Baal Cycle*)[14] followed by a detailed analysis of ch. 2 of the Hebrew book of Proverbs.[15] Of particular value is his application of the various approaches of O'Connor (1980), Geller (1979) and Collins (1978) to both these examples. Since Geller's analytical method is particularly difficult to follow, as he uses his own idiosyncratic system of notation, Pardee's explanation is certainly helpful. In addition, Pardee also applies the method of Kaiser, as set out in her unpublished dissertation with the title "Reconsidering Parallelism: A Study of the Structure of Lamentations 1, 2, and 4" (1983), to these two texts. Her approach is to analyse each line into verb, subject, object and modifier and draw up charts of the text so that they can be scanned

13. See also Payne 1994.

14. *KTU* 1.3 i 2–25, with the omission of the initial sequence *p rdmn*, considered to belong the previous syntactic unit. For a review of Pardee 1988, see Cooper 1990.

15. Parker 1989 also compares Hebrew and Ugaritic verse traditions.

almost at a glance.[16] He then applies his own analysis to these texts, and one of the many results of Pardee's own minute analysis was to show how even minor elements, such as prepositions and suffixes, formed parallel patterns within a poem. Another outcome was at the opposite end of the scale: there can also be parallelism between widely separated lines—a feature that has been called distant parallelism. In this respect, as Pardee himself acknowledges, the book complements conclusions previously reached by Dahood in a series of studies.[17] For various forms of parallelism in Hebrew and Ugaritic verse, Pardee's book is a mine of information, though the whole is often lost in the mass of detail.[18]

There now follows a closer look at the study of Hebrew poetry in the three phases as in the title: past, present and future, with more attention to the immediate past and to current work.

3. *Hebrew Poetry: Past*

Appraisals of early work on Hebrew poetry are provided by Kugel (1981, 96–286) and for the mediaeval period by Berlin (1991). Before Robert Lowth's time, scholars appear to have been involved in a series of philosophical and theological considerations, to the neglect of the literary meaning of the text, which was seen merely as a springboard for allegorical and other interpretations. Ocker provides a survey of such approaches in his book *Biblical Poetics Before Humanism and the Reformation* (2002). Then came Robert Lowth, whose contribution needs no emphasis here.[19] He was one of the earliest scholars to focus on the literary aspect of Hebrew poetry. According to Geller (1982, 66), Lowth's contribution, also felt by his contemporaries, is "the axiom that the Bible must be studied as literature." The other articles in the present volume show this judgment to be appropriate and indicate that the legacy of Lowth remains influential even today.

16. See Pardee 1988, 40–41. This is similar to the line-form analysis of Collins (1978); see above.

17. E.g. Dahood 1965, 1968, 1969, 1970.

18. See also W. Watson 1994a, 104–261. For an extensive bibliography up to 1992, see Hauser 1994.

19. G. B. Gray's classic critique of Lowth (1753) is his book, *Forms of Hebrew Poetry* (1915). See also Fokkelman 2001, 25–27. Besides parallelism, Lowth was also aware of several kinds of verse patterns, for example, "stanzas of five lines with an extra colon in the middle or at the end" (Buss 1969, 42).

4. *Hebrew Poetry: Present*

Modern study of Hebrew verse differs from such study in the time of Lowth in three ways. First, by the impact of ancient Near Eastern literature and languages on the study of Hebrew verse; second, by the application to Hebrew verse of studies on formula and theme from the study of Homeric verse; and third, by the application of modern linguistic analysis to Hebrew verse. These are considered in turn.

4.1. *The Impact of Ancient Near Eastern Literature and Languages on the Study of Hebrew Verse*

The discovery of ancient Near Eastern texts, including inscriptions in Hebrew and Phoenician, but especially in Egyptian and the languages of Mesopotamia, marked a turning point in the study of biblical literature. This is exemplified by the well-known similarity of the Flood Story with the account in Genesis, as first noticed by George Smith in 1873.[20] Up until then the only ancient literature that had been available for comparison with the bible was in Greek and Latin. Then, in the 1930s and 1940s, after Ugaritic[21] (the language of an ancient town in Syria) had been discovered and deciphered,[22] and texts began to be published, there came another decisive moment in the study of biblical literature and particularly of Hebrew poetry. The discoveries had provided texts that were written in a type of verse very similar to Hebrew poetry, and in a related language dating to about 1500–1200 BCE. As a result, now Hebrew poetry could be compared not only with the literature of Mesopotamia and Egypt[23] but also with Ugaritic. Enthusiasm engendered excess, in some respects, but overall the comparative method remains valid.[24] It is an approach used, with due caution, in works such as Gevirtz (1963), Stuart (1976), de Moor (1978a, 1978b, 1980), and W. Watson (1994a).[25]

For a long time, the main concern in the study of ancient Near Eastern texts has been with reading the text and with philology. At the present time our understanding of ancient Near Eastern texts has advanced

---

20. Not 1973, as in George 2003, 942, evidently a misprint.

21. A Semitic language written in alphabetic (not syllabic) cuneiform, very like Hebrew and Phoenician. For a brief description this language, see W. Watson 1994b.

22. For an account of the decipherment of Ugaritic, see Day 2002.

23. See, for example, Shupak 1983.

24. The excesses of Dahood in this approach were rightly criticized by de Moor and van der Lugt (1974), Loretz (1979), Craigie (1983, 49–56) and by others.

25. See also W. Watson 1997, on word pairs.

considerably, and text editions, translations and to a lesser extent literary studies of these texts are now available. In fact, in recent years, scholars of Mesopotamian literature have increasingly turned their attention to poetry, although in this respect they lag behind much that has been achieved in the study of classical Hebrew poetry. This has led to approaches that are literary and analytical and, in effect, the study of Hebrew verse has had an impact, both directly and indirectly, on the study of ancient Near Eastern literature. For example, broadly speaking, Black's *Reading Sumerian Poetry* (1998) is an attempt at making ancient Sumerian poetry intelligible to the modern reader, particularly in terms of its imagery. Parkinson's book on poetry and culture in Egypt (2002) does the same for Egyptian literature. Reiner, whose modest paperback has the subtitle "Poetry from Babylonian and Assyria" (1985), presents a variety of cuneiform texts (royal inscriptions, poems about the netherworld, a hymn, lyric poetry, etc.) and shows how they work, without going into too much technical detail.[26] A series called *Mesopotamian Poetic Language: Sumerian and Akkadian*, in effect the Proceedings of the "Groningen Group for the Study of Mesopotamian Literature," is now in its second volume,[27] and in 2002, Wasserman's *Style and Form in Old-Babylonian Literary Texts* was published.[28] In a recent article, West turned his attention to metre in Akkadian poetry[29] and concluded (1997, 186):

> From sometime before 2000 BC Amorite and Akkadian poetry was chanted in a particular way, or in some cases sung with harp or lyre accompaniment. The performers had a small repertoire of conventional but elastic intonational or melodic matrices to which they could fit their verses. These matrices were structured by means of certain fixed pauses or cadences... The singer or reciter stretched or shortened the matrix from verse to verse so that the accentual peaks fell at the appropriate points of its profile.

This agrees with the findings of Korpel and de Moor, that Hebrew and Ugaritic verse can also be expanded and contracted.[30]

---

26. See also Reiner 1993, Richardson 1993 and Westenholz 1997. On similes in Akkadian verse see Streck 1999. For a comparative study see Kämmerer 1998.
27. Edited by Vogelzang and Vanstiphout (1992, 1996).
28. See also Prinsloo 1992.
29. See also Edzard 1993–97.
30. Korpel and de Moor 1986, 174 (= 1988, 2–3). For expansion or contraction of text in the *Epic of Gilgamesh*, see Tigay 1982, 61–62, and George 2003, 423–24.

4.2. *The Application to Hebrew Verse of Studies on Formula and Theme from Analysis of Homeric Verse*

The work of scholars such as Milman Parry (1930, 1932)[31] and Lord (1960)[32] marked a change in the study of Greek literature. The Homeric poems were looked at in terms of oral composition and the building blocks were considered to be the formula and the theme in what Parry termed the "adding style." This approach was then applied to Hebrew poetry by several scholars, including Mowinckel (1962), Tsevat (1955), Culley (1967), Whallon (1969), Whitaker (1969) and Watters (1976). Much in vogue a few decades ago, little work has been done in this area since, though a recent writer such as Watkins, in his book *How to Kill a Dragon* (1995), is enthusiastic about this approach in respect of Indo-European poetics. Some discussion of formulae and formulaic images is available for Sumerian in Black's *Reading Sumerian Poetry* (1998, 124–43). Other work in this area concerns word pairs, which some scholars consider to be the Semitic equivalent of the formula.[33]

4.3. *The Application of Modern Linguistic Analysis to Hebrew Verse*

The final difference in approach is the use of modern linguistics to study Hebrew verse. This has taken several forms: syntactic analysis, as in O'Connor's *Hebrew Verse Structure* (1980), line-form analysis, as in the studies by Collins (1978) and Kaiser (1983), and a type of transformational analysis by Geller (1979). Cloete (1989b) also applied syntactic analysis to verse in Jeremiah, and Berlin (1985) has studied parallelism in terms of linguistics. These approaches have been mentioned above.[34]

5. *Hebrew Poetry: Current Work*

Recent work can be set out under a number of headings that describe the topics currently being discussed.

5.1. *The Differentiation Between Prose and Verse*

It was Robert Lowth who "introduced the practice of printing translations of biblical passages he had identified as 'poetic' in stichometric form. This practice is now universal, and has even spread to editions of the Hebrew text" (F. Andersen 1995, 53). A few years ago, a number of scholars were invited to contribute to a volume with the title *Verse in*

---

31. Milman Parry's work has been collected by Adam Parry (1971).
32. For an extensive bibliography, see Lord 1991, 245–57.
33. See especially Whallon 1969.
34. See also Segert 1987.

Ancient Near Eastern Prose, in an attempt at opening up debate concerning the distinction between prose and verse. Shortly before the book was
published (de Moor and W. Watson 1993), a conference was held in
Kampen, on the same topic. The purpose of these exercises was to determine how verse is to be differentiated from prose in the poetry of the
ancient Near East. As generally acknowledged, this is a difficult and
controversial topic. Some scholars, for example Niccacci (1997), were
simply sceptical about some of the conclusions reached, and perhaps
they are correct. One scholar who has devoted considerable energy to
this problem is Cloete (1993). He condensed the problem in the form of
three questions:

1.   Is there a distinction between prose and verse in the Hebrew Old
       Testament?
2.   If there is a distinction, which parts are verse and which are
       prose?
3.   What are the criteria for this distinction?

Cloete concluded that verse can be differentiated from prose on the basis
of structure, parallel word pairs and sound patterns (rhyme, alliteration,
etc.). As an example, he analysed 2 Kgs 19:14–19 and by applying these
criteria, showed that vv. 14–15a and 17–18 are prose and the remainder
is verse. Later, Niccacci (1997) proposed the following three special
characteristics that mark poetic texts:

1.   Segmented rather than linear communication.
2.   "Parallelism of similar bits of information" as against "sequence
       of different bits of information."
3.   Verbal systems that cannot be determined.

Talstra (1999) accepts the first two, with some reservations (and to some
extent they do overlap), but is unhappy with the third, claiming that
scholars are at fault in not being able to identify the verbal system in
poetry.

There are some clear differences between classical Hebrew and other
language traditions in respect of the use of prose and verse. Whereas in
Babylonian and Ugaritic literature all narrative is in verse, in Hebrew
this is not the case. Apart from a few exceptions, such as Ps 106 and the
Song of Songs, most narrative is in prose.[35] An explanation is required

---

35. As Pardee (2001, 142 n. 1) puts it: "In this respect, the two corpora are,
therefore, almost mirror-images of each other: there is very little narrative poetry in
the Hebrew Bible but much narrative prose, while in Ugaritic there is very little
poetry that does not have a narrational structure and nothing comparable to most of
the Pentateuch and Former Prophets in the Bible." See also Cloete 1988.

for this state of affairs. Could it be that some portions of what appears to be prose narrative in Hebrew are in fact in verse? Accordingly, several scholars have examined the prose sections of Hebrew and have attempted to analyse them as verse, for example, de Moor (1984 and 1986) on the book of Ruth, Koopmans on Josh 24 (1990), Kim (1993) on the Samson Cycle in the book of Judges, and Korpel (2001) also on the book of Ruth.

In Ugaritic, for example, the distinction is fairly clear: all narratives such as the tales of *Keret* and *Aqhat*, the *Baal Cycle*, the *Wedding of Dawn and Dusk*, to name the more well-known ones,[36] are in verse, and the rest (letters, legal documents, ritual texts) are in prose, a distinction based on genre. Yet even here, there are some grey areas and on at least one occasion, there is a prayer embedded within a ritual, namely, *KTU* 1.119: 26–36 (cf. Pardee 1993, 213–17; W. Watson 1996). As for Sumerian, "[w]ith very few exceptions, Sumerian literature is composed in poetic form, and Sumerian poetry can very broadly speaking be defined in extrinsic terms as a heightened form of language written in lines of verse" (Black 1998, 5). Much the same applies to Akkadian.[37]

The point is that, in both Sumerian and Ugaritic, literature is in verse, and other texts such as letters and legal documents, are in prose, whereas in Hebrew this is not the case. It is not a matter of "either/or." In Hebrew, passages can be in verse, in prose or in mixtures of both. This does not apply to texts such as psalms and proverbs, which are poetic by genre. However, it does apply to the prophetical books (notably Ezekiel) and to the so-called historical books (Samuel, Kings), which are mixtures of verse and prose. Of interest in this respect is the work by Watts, *Psalm and Story* (1992), since it concerns verse embedded in prose texts.[38] The Hebrew verse passages in Daniel (which is largely in prose) have also been discussed recently (Segert 1995).

In *Classical Hebrew Poetry* (W. Watson 1984a, 46–55), nineteen criteria are listed for differentiating verse from prose: the presence of line-forms, ellipsis, unusual vocabulary, conciseness,[39] archaisms, metre, regularity and symmetry, and then the use of parallelism, word-pairs, chiasmus, the envelope figure, break-up of a stereotype phrase, different forms of repetition, gender-matching parallelism, the tricolon and the omission of prose elements (notably the article and the object marker).[40]

36. That is, *KTU* 1.14–1.16, 1.17–1.19, 1.1–1.6 and 1.23.

37. For lineation etc. in Egyptian verse, see Parkinson 2002, 116–17.

38. Exod 15:1–21; Deut 32:1–43; Judg 5; 1 Sam 2:1–10; 2 Sam 22; Isa 38:9–20; Jonah 2:3–10; Dan 2:20–23; 1 Chr 16:8–36, etc.

39. Or, as Talstra (1999, 113) prefers, terseness.

40. Smith (1912, 11) had previously listed unusual word order, ellipsis, "a preference for archaic words or forms of words," omission of the definite article, the

To some extent these criteria, such as they are, overlap and of course they have been criticised by scholars in their reviews. Recently, Gillingham (1994, 23–28) has reduced them to twelve. While none is decisive, the presence of several of these elements together is indicative of verse. Ultimately, they are nothing more than simple indicators, to be applied with caution. Perhaps the presence of particular syntactical features may prove to be the decisive factor.

5.2. *Examination of the Masoretic Text and Manuscript Traditions for Indications of Colometry*

This approach entails the sophisticated analysis of Masoretic accents followed by attention to the layout in the manuscript tradition (Oesch 1979). Neither consideration is at all new, but both aspects have been considerably neglected in the study of Hebrew poetry. It has led to the discipline that has been called *"Gliederungskritik"* (by Oesch 2000) or "delimitation criticism" (by Korpel), that is, the study of text divisions in the MT and the manuscript traditions of the texts and versions, in order to determine the colometry of poetic texts.[41] Oesch (2000) argues that the text divisions *petuḥôt* and *setumôt* etc. are not related to reading within the liturgy, since they also occur outside the Torah. Rather, divisions of the text are an integral part of the tradition of writing down these texts. This is shown by the match in text-divisions between the MT and the oldest texts from Qumran, the Samaritan Pentateuch, etc. As Korpel (2000, 5) puts it: "The older the manuscripts, the more detailed the text divisions they have preserved." This approach has produced some interesting results, not only in terms of the divisions within the poetic books, as was to be expected, but also with respect to other topics, for example, the *qinah*-pattern. In the late nineteenth century, Budde (1882)[42] had noted the so-called *qinah*-pattern in Lam 1:9–10.[43] Supposedly characteristic of a dirge, this pattern comprises an alternating pattern of a long line followed by a shorter one, for example, Lam 3:19:

> $z^e kor$-'*onyî ûm^{e}rûdî*   Remember my anguish and roving,
> *la^{a}nâ w^{e}ro 'š* wormwood and poison.

However, by studying the divisions in the transmitted texts, as given in the MT and the versions, including the Septuagint, de Hoop (2000) has

relative and other particles, and the lengthening of pronominal suffixes as clear signs of poetry.

41. See Korpel and Oesch 2000, 2002, 2003 and 2005.
42. See also Budde 1883 and 1934.
43. And also in Lam 1:5a, 6, 8, 11–17; 2:1, 5, 6, 7a, etc.

shown that in fact no such pattern exists in Hebrew verse. Another example is provided by de Moor (2000), who has shown that H. Gunkel's interpretation of Mic 7:7–20, which he connects with the Northern Kingdom, is based on doubtful arguments since it ignores the *setumâ* after v. 8. As a result of his analysis, de Moor (2000, 158–60) has proposed some guidelines for the study of unit delimitation, which are worth repeating here:

1.   The relative age of the witnesses needs to be taken into account.
2.   Evidence from several traditions is better than evidence from only one.
3.   The structure of the immediate context needs to be checked.
4.   Alternative text divisions in terms of the wider context also need to be assessed.
5.   A plausible explanation for a false division is necessary.

Some years earlier, LaSor (1979) had been working along similar lines, and in 1985, Aronoff published a paper in the journal *Language*, with the title "Orthography and Linguistic Theory: The Syntactic Basis of Masoretic Hebrew Punctuation."[44]

In this connection, there is one aspect of comparing the Ugaritic poetic texts with Hebrew poetry that has been given less attention than, say, the similarity of poetic structure. It is the fact that the tablets from Ras Shamra (and elsewhere of course) usually remained untouched once they had been written on clay, whether as original compositions or as copies.[45] In contrast, the MT is several centuries later than the original texts—although the manuscripts from Qumran (the Dead Sea Scrolls) have confirmed their reliability—and in addition it is the result of re-editing and adaptation to the spoken languages of later times, namely, Late Hebrew and Aramaic. In other words, we cannot know whether Gen 49 or Exod 15, for example, assumed by many scholars to be early Hebrew poems if not two of the earliest,[46] are not in fact products of later periods or the result of earlier texts being reworked. Much the same happened to the Mesopotamian *Epic of Gilgamesh*, which was copied and recopied, translated into various languages, made into a single composition from several tablets, and so on. The lengthy process has to some extent been charted by Tigay (1982). It covers a period of about one and a half millennia, from the early Sumerian sources, through the Old Babylonian, Standard Babylonian and Middle Babylonian versions, and on to later

44.   See also Slotki 1931.
45.   There is some evidence that clay tablets were re-used, although this was not a question of later editing but due to lack of supply.
46.   Notably by Cross and Freedman 1975.

versions. The latest tablet of Gilgamesh dates to the first or second century BCE (Tigay 1982, 251). This means that, unlike the biblical books, in this instance we do have representative copies from many of the periods in question. By contrast, the Ugaritic tablets did not experience a long drawn out process of transmission and revision. They are as close to the originals as we are likely to get. The problem of why they were written down remains unsolved, as does the question of whether, as some scholars now maintain, all the tablets we have found really belong to the last phase of the city of Ugarit (c. 1200 BCE)[47]—evidently the two problems are linked.

Another aspect of these texts is the layout in lines of poetry for which the terms "colography" and "colometry" are used, which forms the subject of delimitation criticism mentioned above. In Sumerian poetry "[t]he lines are laid out on the clay tablet exactly as in modern European poetry: left-justified, with the continuation of an exceptionally long line indented to show that it is not the beginning of a new line" (Black 1998, 5). In the case of the Ugaritic tablets, many of the mythological and other poems have not been written out as poetry. Instead, the scribe has simply used all the surface of the clay as if it were in short supply (and possibly, it was) and written the lines irrespective of poetic lay-out (see W. Watson 1982b). An example is from *The Aqhat Tale*:[48]

[30]*yšu. gh w yṣḥ. knp. ṣml.*
[31]*b'l. ytbr. b'l. ytbr. diy*
[32]*hyt. tql. tht. p'ny. ibq'*
[33]*kbdh. w aḥd. hm iṯ. šmt hm iṯ*
[34]*'ẓm...*

[30]He raised his voice and cried: / "The wings of Samal
[31]may Baal break / May Baal break wings
[32]of her / May she fall beneath my feet / I shall split
[33]her entrails and see whether there is fat, whether there is
[34]bone/..."

Here the full stops in the transliterated text denote word dividers and the forward slash (/) marks in the translation the end of a line. One would have expected the following layout:

yšu. gh w yṣḥ.	He raised his voice and cried:
knp. ṣml. b'l. ytbr.	"The wings of Samal may Baal break,

47. As noted by Millard 1995, 121.
48. *KTU* 1.19 iii 30–33. It also seems that the scribe accidentally omitted the second *hm*, "if," here supplied in the text. For clarity, the rest of line 34 (*abky. waqbrnh. aštn*, "I will weep and I will bury him; I will place...") has been left out.

b'l. yṯbr. diy hyt.	May Baal break wings of her,
tql. tḥt. p'ny.	May she fall beneath my feet.
ibq' kbdh. w aḥd.	I shall split her entrails and see
hm iṯ. šmt hm iṯ 'ẓm.	whether there is fat, whether there is bone."

However, there are a few exceptions, notably the Ugaritic composition known as *Baal, the Heifer and Anat*,[49] where almost all the lines are set out colographically, that is, as poetry, so that each line on the tablet corresponds to a line of poetry or colon.[50]

5.3. *New Definitions of Terms such as "Parallelism"*

Kugel's definition of parallelism as "A, and what's more, B" (cited above) is rightly famous but has been criticized.[51] Similarly, Clines (1987) describes what he calls "parallelism of greater precision," that is, "the second half of a parallelistic line (line B) is often more precise or specific than the first half (line A)," and as an example he suggests Isa 40:26. Other scholars also define parallelism in radical terms, for example Nel, who prefers to speak of recurrence rather than parallelism. In his words: "recurrence is the dominant principle by which contiguity is established in a poetic text, and...parallelism is a language specific parameter for Biblical Hebrew versification" (1992, 138). Following Roman Jakobson, he lists several "modes of recurrence" such as repetition, equivalence, similarity, symmetry, congruence, opposition and analogy and he also explains chiasmus. Berlin (1985) also redefines parallelism in terms of grammar (morphology and syntax), in terms of semantics and lexis, and in terms of phonology, and discusses the interrelationship among these aspects. In his book on focus structure, Shimasaki (2002) prefers "simple juxtaposition of synonymous clauses" to "synonymous parallelism." As he explains, there is emphasis due to "the repetition of the same topic and similar predicate."[52] This is a long way from the definitions of Lowth (1753).

5.4. *Discussion of Metre*

In respect of metre, Freedman, who has worked for many years on syllable counting and metre, concluded as follows: "That Israelite poets had a system for counting seems both clear and inescapable, as otherwise it is impossible to explain how they produced poems of exactly equal length" (Freedman 1987, 27). More recently, Fokkelman has also used a

---

49. *KTU* 1.10; for a translation, cf. Wyatt 1998: 155–60.
50. Unfortunately, the text is incomplete. See also Mabie 2004.
51. See, e.g., Kugel 1981, 317–20; Clines 1987, 95.
52. On parallelism in Ugaritic and Akkadian verse, see Tropper 1998.

numerical approach, including syllable counting, in his detailed analysis of what he calls "major poems" in Hebrew, and has reached similar conclusions.[53] Earlier, Loretz had counted letters as an indication of analysis into lines of verse.[54]

On the other hand, many scholars deny the very existence of metre in Hebrew. O'Connor prefers to speak of syntactic constraints or constrictions.[55] Similarly, Pardee considers Ugaritic poetry not to be metrical.[56] In his article "Strophic Hebrew Verse as Free Verse" (1994), which is a response to Cloete's definition of verse as language written in lines,[57] Giese argues that without sustained metre, verse is really a kind of free verse and not metrical verse. He suggests (Giese 1994, 36) that "Hebrew verse may or may not have rhythm that is metrical (observable on the level of the line)." He therefore proposes a new definition of strophe as "a group of lines in which a cycle of rhythm is completed" (Giese 1994, 34). Within a cycle, comprising several strophes, each strophe corresponds in form to other strophes. However, the matter remains unresolved. This lack of consensus concerning metre indicates that Lowth's view regarding our inability to know Hebrew metre appears to be just as valid today as it was in his time.[58]

6. Recent Books

As an indication of current research, a few books on particular topics in Hebrew poetry that have been published recently can be listed.[59] In addition to the works by Kugel (1981) and Berlin (1985) on parallelism, the most recent work is by Ranieri (1993), part of a doctoral thesis.[60] For strophic structure, there is the book by van der Lugt (1995).[61] Besides W.

---

53. Fokkelman 1990, 1995, 1998, 2000, 2001, 2003.

54. See Loretz 1976, 1979, 1986, etc. Also, cf. Loretz and Kottsieper 1987.

55. For an extensive and detailed analysis and critique of O'Connor's monumental work, see Cloete 1989b, 80–98. Another appraisal is by Kugel (1981, 315–23) who concludes: "What is of undeniable value is the standard of precision and clarity set by this volume."

56. Pardee 1981, 116.

57. Cloete 1989a, 45 and 1989b, 5, following Hartman 1980.

58. The best survey still remains Cobb 1905.

59. Articles on various topics include: Greenfield 1990; Handy 1990; Levine 2002; Loretz 1989, 2001; O'Connor 1987; Paul 1992; W. Watson 1994c; Yaron 1986; Zevit 1992 and Zurro 2000. On the poetry of the psalms, see Seybold 2003.

60. See also O'Connor 1993; Howard 1997; Levine 2003; Veijola 2004; West 1992.

61. For enjambment, see Dobbs-Allsopp 2001.

Watson (1981),[62] Meynet (1998)[63] and Walsh (2001) have also written on chiasmus. However, the tendency to see the presence of chiastic patterns in verse (and prose) has recently been criticized by Boda (1996).[64] Refrains in the psalms are discussed in a monograph (Raabe 1990). Paronomasia is the subject of *Puns and Pundits: Word Play in the Hebrew Bible and in Ancient Near Eastern Literature*, edited by Noegel (2000), a volume that includes several essays on word play and alliterative allusions in Hebrew. There are also some contributions on word play in Egyptian, Sumerian, Akkadian and Ugaritic. The editor has also written extensively on so-called "Janus Parallelism," which, in spite of its label, is really a form of word play,[65] notably, *Janus Parallelism in the Book of Job* (Noegel 1996). Only one book has appeared on patterns involving sound, namely McCreesh, *Biblical Sound and Sense* (1991). Both Munro (1995) and Horine (2001) have written on imagery in the Song of Songs, and Abma (1999) has dealt with marriage imagery in Isaiah, Hosea and Jeremiah. Keel (1986/1994) also deals with the subject in relation to ancient Near Eastern images in his commentary on the Song of Songs.[66] There is only one work on similes, namely, Brensinger, *Simile and Prophetic Language in the Old Testament* (1996).[67]

7. *Hebrew Poetry: Future*

In spite of the many centuries of analysis of Hebrew poetry, there is still more to study and the following areas of research for the future can be listed.

7.1. *Analysis of Synthetic Parallelism*
One problem that remains unresolved is what Lowth called "synthetic parallelism," where the second line is not parallel to the first and often seems to be a continuation of it. For example, Job 9:31:

> Then in the pit you would dip me
> and my garments would loathe me.

Here there is no synonymous or even antithetic parallelism, and it is difficult to see how such couplets fit into a verse tradition that is principally

62. Reprinted in revised form in W. Watson 1994a, 328–89.
63. Also significant is Meynet, Pouzet, Farouki and Sinno 1998.
64. On verse patterns, see W. Watson 1995a.
65. The term was coined by Gordon (1978). Note also Paul 1992.
66. Geller (1990), Waldman (1989) and Walton (2003) have all written on the topic of imagery.
67. See also Parker 2004. On metaphors, see Weisberg 1991 and Korpel 1996.

based on parallelism.[68] Synthetic parallelism would appear to be related to problems of length of line, ellipsis[69] and enjambment.[70] Some couplets of this kind can be explained by invoking alternating parallelism, when they are combined with a similar couplet, as in Song 1:13–14:

(A)   A bundle of myrrh is my lover to me,
(B)   between my breasts he spends the night.
(A')   A cluster of henna is my lover to me,
(B')   in my vineyard Engedi

Here the (A) and (A') lines are parallel, as are the corresponding (B) and (B') lines. However, only a small percentage of lines with synthetic parallelism can be explained in this way[71] and a comprehensive explanation is still required.

7.2. *More Critical Comparison of Ancient Near Eastern Material with Hebrew Poetry*

Even though a considerable amount of work has been done in terms of comparing Hebrew verse with ancient Near Eastern texts, new editions of these texts are continually being published and new discoveries are being made. These, in turn, invite re-examination of the comparisons made earlier. Examples are provided by the many texts that have been compared to the Song of Songs. While the Sumerian love-songs have long been compared to the Song of Songs (Kramer 1962), a new edition of them, prepared by Sefati (1998), now provides reliable material for comparison. Similarly, although the standard and probably the best work on the comparison between the love poetry from Egypt and the Song of Songs is by Fox (1985), Egyptian love poetry is now available in a new edition, prepared by Mathieu (1996), so that the comparisons need to be evaluated anew. More recently, the Song of Songs has been compared with a New Assyrian composition called "Love Lyrics of Nabu and Tashmetu."[72] These poems comprise thirty-two lines divided into sections (marked by ruled lines on the tablet) spoken in turn by a Chorus, by Tašmetu (the female), by Nabu (the male) or by both Nabu and Tašmetu together. This means that the Song of Songs is not unique as a

---

68. One-line verses or monocola are frequent (e.g. Lam 2:12a), often as introductions to speech (cf. W. Watson 1994c), but tend to be short.

69. See O'Connor 1980, 401–7, Greenstein 1983, and C. Miller 1999 for some approaches to the problem.

70. For a possible explanation, see Greenstein 1983.

71. For discussion and further examples, see Willis 1987.

72. In fact, the title of Nissinen's article (1998) is: "Love Lyrics of Nabû and Tašmetu: An Assyrian Song of Songs?."

collection of love poems forming a single composition.[73] In addition, some well-known similarities between Hebrew and Egyptian compositions have recently been re-assessed, notably, the comparisons between the passage Ben Sira 38:24–39:11 and the Egyptian "The Satire of Trades" (Rollston 2001) and between Ps 104 and the Egyptian Hymn to the Aten (Niccacci 1994).

7.3. *Further Study of the Masoretic Text and of Its Ancient Manuscripts for Indications of Structure*

As shown above, it is quite clear that this is a profitable area of research, even though the results are uneven. Ancient traditions provide some guidance as to how the text is to be divided into poetic units and, while it cannot be followed slavishly, it cannot be ignored either.

7.4. *Further Application of Approaches used in Linguistics*

The innovative approaches by Berlin (1985), Collins (1978), O'Connor (1980) and others have shown us that we have much to learn from the application of linguistic analysis to the study of Hebrew verse, even though their work has yet to be more widely known. In an excursus written for the reprinting of his work, *Hebrew Verse Structure* (1997), O'Connor has tried to explain what he was attempting to do in that book and so make it more intelligible to the reader.[74] Other types of analysis involve the application of text linguistics and information theory to the Hebrew text: some work on parallelism in terms of word order and information structure has been presented by Shimasaki (2002, 185–204) indicating it to be a fruitful line of approach.

7.5. *Additional Study of Language*

The following aspects of Hebrew poetry can be listed as requiring further research. First comes the syntax of Hebrew poetry. As Gibson (1993, 141) notes: "Compared with the syntax of classical Hebrew prose…the syntax of classical Hebrew poetry has been seriously neglected." His own study (1993) is a discussion of the use of the verb. Here perhaps a refinement of the approaches pioneered by Collins (1978), Kaiser (1983) and O'Connor (1980), and the work by Niccacci (1997) and others, would be welcome. Such studies should also include an evaluation of word order, particularly in respect of the verb. Kaiser (1983), as presented in Pardee (1988), deals with word order in Hebrew poetry, but

73. See previously W. Watson 1995b.
74. With the title "The Contours of Biblical Hebrew Verse: An Afterword to *Hebrew Verse Structure*" (O'Connor 1997, 631–61).

further work is necessary.[75] Talstra (1999) provides a useful outline of
future study in this area, with a worked example (Isa 41:21–24), noting
that "the mechanism for reading poetry is in principle the same as the
mechanism for reading other text types" (p. 117), that is, prose.

As yet there is no comprehensive study of the lexicon peculiar to
poetry, not even for a single book. As mentioned above, it was given as
one of the indicators for distinguishing poetry from prose. For example,
there are over sixty words peculiar to Song and many more that are very
rare, and similar statistics apply to the book of Job.[76] This cannot be
accidental and has parallels in other traditions.[77]

The contribution of philology cannot be underrated. If the words that
comprise a poem are misunderstood or remain unknown, the poem is
more difficult to interpret. Fortunately, we now have reliable dictionaries
for Hebrew, notably the revision and translation of Koehler and Baumgartner's *Hebräisches und aramäisches Lexikon zum Alten Testament*
(1967–90) by Richardson (1994–2000) and the first six volumes of the
Sheffield *Dictionary of Classical Hebrew*, edited by Clines (1993–).[78] An
example of a misunderstood phrase is *bêt hayyāyin*, which only occurs in
Song (2:4). The literal translation of the expression is "house of wine."
Usually this is compared to *bêt mištê hayyāyin*, "house of drinking wine"
(Esth 7:8) or to *bêt mištê*, "house of feasting" (Qoh 7:2),[79] or else it is
compared to bowers in Egyptian paintings and love songs (Fox 1983,
201–2). In fact, although they do not refer to the Akkadian expression,
Bloch and Bloch (1995, 150) comment: "it is more likely to be a metaphor for a place in the fields or orchards where the lovers meet to make
love." I therefore suggest that it corresponds to Akkadian *bīt karāni*,
"tavern, wine-cellar, vineyard," literally, "house of wine." The Hebrew
expression, *bêt hayyāyin*, which also has the literal meaning "house of

75. For Ugaritic, some work is available in the article by Wilson (1982) on word-
order in the Ugaritic poem of Keret and syntactical analysis of many passages is
provided in Tropper's *Ugaritische Grammatik*, published in 2000.

76. For Aramaic loanwords in Job, see Greenstein 2003.

77. For example, the description of the manufacture of Baal's litter-throne or
palanquin (*KTU* 1.4 i 23–43) uses about forty different words of which about
seventeen are unique and twenty-three are rare or unique, many of them loanwords.
Similarly, Semitic words were borrowed in Egyptian verse (Loprieno 2000, 18).

78. In addition, for Ugaritic there is *A Dictionary of the Ugaritic Language in the
Alphabetic Tradition* (2003[1], 2004[1]), for North-West Semitic, the *Dictionary of
North-West Semitic Inscriptions*, and for Akkadian, besides the Chicago *Assyrian
Dictionary* which is nearing completion, there is the *Concise Dictionary of Akkadian*
(1999[1], 2000[2]).

79. E.g. by Munro 1995, 23 n. 5.

wine," here means "vineyard." The translation "vineyard" seems to fit the garden context of Song 2:4 better than "wine house":

> He brought me to the vineyard,
> and his intention over me was love.
> Put my bed among lush plants,
> spread it with apricots,
> for I am lovesick.

In addition, the findings of form criticism indicate that it would be very helpful if the original settings of poems were known, but since they are not, much remains conjectural, and to some extent, the same applies to ancient Near Eastern verse. In spite of the defects and excesses of H. Gunkel and others in attempting to determine a social setting (or *Sitz im Leben*) for passages in the Hebrew Bible, the form-critical approach remains valid, as shown recently by House (1992).[80]

There is still scope for further study on figurative language, particularly imagery, not simply as a separate topic but also as an inherent element of a poem. For example, Nwaoru (2004) has shown that the structure of Hos 7:8–8:4 is determined by its use of metaphors and similes. On the other hand, some topics, such as metre, seem to be dead ends and lead nowhere. Even though, as noted above, Fokkelman finds matching numerical patterns in respect of stanzas, strophes, verses and lines in the poems he has analysed, it is uncertain whether his analysis is to be understood metrically.

8. *Outlook*

As the verse of the ancient Near East becomes better understood and with the improved analysis of many aspects of Hebrew poetry, in the near future it may be possible to formulate a comprehensive theory for Hebrew poetry in terms of all levels: phonological, morphological (which may or may not include metre), structural and syntactical, not neglecting such components as the use of figurative language and the part played by the lexicon. In conclusion and to summarize, the following points can be mentioned:

1. There is a need for further application of the approaches used in linguistics, such as information theory and discourse analysis, to Hebrew poetry. A poetic text is language first, poetry second, and so should be studied, initially, in the same way that prose texts are studied (see Talstra 1999).

---

80. Also, cf. Diehl, Diesel and Wagner 1999.

2.   More analysis of complete books (or of sections of books) is required, principally in terms of their poetry. Mention has already been made of the work produced by the Kampen School in the form of monographs on single poems such as Gen 49 (de Hoop 1995) and Deut 32 (Sanders 1996), on sections of books (Korpel and de Moor, on Isa 40–55 [1998]) and on whole books such as the book of Job (van der Lugt 1995). To these can be added the recent analytical work by Fokkelman (1995, 1998, 2000, 2003) on the psalms and other poems.

3.   The application of computers to analyse data in respect of Hebrew poetry at levels beyond word processing and the compilation of concordances is needed. For example, Talstra (1999) is in the process of using computers for the syntactical analysis of Hebrew texts. This could be extended to include poetic texts.[81]

4.   Finally, a comprehensive investigation of the similarities and differences between Hebrew poetry and the poetic traditions of the ancient Near East is required in order to determine what is unique to the Hebrew tradition and to what extent Hebrew poetry contains shared features.[82]

Bibliography

Abma, R. 1999. *Bonds of Love: Methodic Studies of Prophetic Texts with Marriage Imagery (Isaiah 50:1–3 and 54:1–10, Hosea 1–3, Jeremiah 2–3)*. SSN 40. Assen: Van Gorcum.

Alonso Schökel, L. 1988. *A Manual of Hebrew Poetics*. Translated by Adrian Gaffy. Subsidia Biblica 11. Rome: Biblical Institute Press.

Alter, R. 1985. *The Art of Biblical Poetry*. New York: Basic Books.

Andersen, F. I. 1995. What Biblical Scholars Might Learn from Emily Dickinson. Pages 52–79 in Davies, Harvey and Watson 1995.

Andersen, T. D. 1986. Problems in Analysing Hebrew Poetry. *East Asia Journal of Theology* 4:68–94.

Aronoff, M. 1985. Orthography and Linguistic Theory: The Syntactic Basis of Masoretic Hebrew Punctuation. *Language* 61:28–72.

Avishur, Y. 1984. *Stylistic Studies of Word-Pairs in Biblical and Ancient Semitic Literatures*. Kevelaer: Butzon & Bercker; Neukirchen–Vluyn: Neukirchener.

———. 1994. *Studies in Hebrew and Ugaritic Psalms*. Publications of the Perry Foundation for Biblical Research. Jerusalem: Magnes.

Baker, A. 1973. Parallelism: England's Contribution. *CBQ* 5:429–40.

Berlin, A. 1979. Grammatical Aspects of Biblical Parallelism. *HUCA* 50:17–43.

81.   For the application of computer programs to ancient Near Eastern parallel word pairs, see Korpel and de Moor 1998, 11 n. 43.

82.   For an example of such a study, see W. Watson 1994c.

————. 1985. *The Dynamics of Biblical Parallelism*. Bloomington: Indiana University Press.

————. 1991. *Biblical Poetry Through Medieval Jewish Eyes*. Indiana Studies in Biblical Literature. Bloomington: Indiana University Press.

————. 1992. Parallelism. *ABD* 5:155–62.

Black, J. 1998. *Reading Sumerian Poetry*. London: Athlone.

Bloch, A., and C. Bloch. 1995. *The Song of Songs: A New Translation with an Introduction and a Commentary*. Berkeley: University of California Press.

Boda, M. J. 1996. Chiasmus in Ubiquity: Symmetrical Mirages in Nehemiah 9. *JSOT* 71:55–70.

Brensinger, T. 1996. *Simile and Prophetic Language in the Old Testament*. Mellen Biblical Press Series 43. Lewiston: Mellen Biblical Press.

Budde, C. 1882. Das hebräische Klagelied. *ZAW* 2:1–52.

————. 1883. Ein hebräisches Klagelied. *ZAW* 3:299–306.

————. 1934. Zum Ḳina-Verse. *ZAW* 52:306–308.

Buss, M. J. 1969. *The Prophetic Word of Hosea: A Morphological Study*. BZAW 111. Berlin: de Gruyter.

Clines, D. J. A. 1987. The Parallelism of Greater Precision. Pages 77–100 in Follis 1987.

————, ed. 1993. *The Dictionary of Classical Hebrew*. 6 vols. Sheffield: Sheffield Academic Press.

Cloete, W. T. W. 1988. Verse and Prose: Does the Distinction Apply to the Old Testament? *JNSL* 14:9–15.

————. 1989a. The Concept of Metre in Old Testament Studies. *Journal for Semitics* 1:39–53.

————. 1989b. *Versification and Syntax in Jeremiah 2–25: Syntactical Constraints in Hebrew Colometry*. SBLDS 117. Atlanta: Scholars Press.

————. 1993. Distinguishing Prose and Verse in 2 Kings 19:14–19. Pages 31–40 in de Moor and Watson 1993.

Cobb, W. H. 1905. *A Criticism of Systems of Hebrew Metre: An Elementary Treatise*. Oxford: Clarendon.

Collins, T. 1978. *Line-Forms in Hebrew Poetry: A Grammatical Approach to the Stylistic Study of the Hebrew Prophets*. Studia Pohl, Series Major 7. Rome: Biblical Institute Press.

Cooper, A. 1987. On Reading Biblical Poetry. *Maarav* 4:221–41.

————. 1990. Two Recent Works on the Structure of Biblical Hebrew Poetry. *JAOS* 110: 687–90.

Craigie, P. C. 1983. *Psalms 1–50*. WBC 19. Waco, Tex.: Word.

Cross, F. M., Jr., and D. N. Freedman. 1975. *Studies in Ancient Yahwistic Poetry*. Society of Biblical Study Dissertation Series. 2d ed., Grand Rapids: Eerdmans. Livonia, Mich.: Dove Bookseller, 1997.

Culley, R. C. 1967. *Oral Formulaic Language in the Biblical Psalms*. Near and Middle East Series 4. Toronto: University of Toronto Press.

Dahood, M. J. 1965. *Psalms I: 1–50*. AB 16. Garden City, N.Y.: Doubleday.

————. 1968. *Psalms II: 51–100*. AB 17A. Garden City, N.Y.: Doubleday.

————. 1969. Hebrew–Ugaritic Syntax and Style. *UF* 1:15.36.

————. 1970. *Psalms III: 101–150*. AB 17B. Garden City, N.Y.: Doubleday.

Davies, J., G. Harvey, and W. G. E. Watson, eds. 1995. *Words Remembered, Texts Renewed: Essays in Honour of John F. A. Sawyer*. JSOTSup 195. Sheffield: Sheffield Academic Press.

Day, P. 2002. *Dies diem docet*: The Decipherment of Ugaritic. *Studi epigrafici e linguistici sul Vicino Oriente antico* 19:37–57.

Diehl, J. F., A. A. Diesel, and A. Wagner. 1999. Von der Grammatik zum Kerygma. Neue grammatische Erkenntnisse und ihre Bedeutung für das Verständnis der Form und des Gehalts von Psalm xxix. *VT* 49:462–98.

Dietrich, M., and I. Kottsieper, eds. *"Und Mose schrieb dieses Lied auf." Studien zum Alten Testament and zum Alten Orient. Festschrift für Oswald Loretz zur Vollendung seines 70. Lebensjahres mit Beiträgen von Freunden, Schülern und Kollegen.* AOAT 250. Münster: Ugarit-Verlag.

Dobbs-Allsopp, F. W. 2001. The Enjambing Line in Lamentations: A Taxonomy (Part 1). *ZAW* 113:219–39.

Edzard, D. O. 1993–97. Metrik. *RA* 8:148–49.

Fisch, H. 1988. *Poetry with a Purpose: Biblical Poetics and Interpretation.* Indiana Studies in Biblical Literature. Bloomington: Indiana University Press.

Fitzgerald, A. 1968. Hebrew Poetry. Pages 238–44 in *The Jerome Biblical Commentary.* Edited by R. E. Brown, J. A. Fitzmyer and R. E. Murphy. London: Chapman.

Fokkelman, J. 1990. The Structure of Psalms 68. *OtSt* 26:72–83.

———. 1995. The Song of Deborah and Barak: Its Prosodic Levels and Structure. Pages 595–628 in *Pomegranates and Golden Bells: Studies in Biblical, Jewish, and Near Eastern Ritual, Law, and Literature in Honor of Jacob Milgrom.* Edited by D. P. Wright, D. N. Freedman and A. Hurvitz. Winona Lake, Ind.: Eisenbrauns.

———. 1998. *Major Poems of the Hebrew Bible at the Interface of Hermeneutics and Structural Analysis.* Vol. 1, *Ex. 15, Deut. 32, and Job 3.* SSN 37. Assen: Van Gorcum.

———. 2000. *Major Poems of the Hebrew Bible at the Interface of Hermeneutics and Structural Analysis.* Vol. 2, *85 Psalms and Job 4–14.* SSN 41. Assen: Van Gorcum.

———. 2001. *Reading Biblical Poetry: An Introductory Guide.* Louisville, Ky.: John Knox.

———. 2003. *Major Poems of the Hebrew Bible at the Interface of Hermeneutics and Structural Analysis.* Vol. 3, *The Remaining 65 Psalms.* SSN 43. Assen: Van Gorcum.

Follis, E., ed. 1987. *Directions in Biblical Hebrew Poetry.* JSOTSup 40. Sheffield: JSOT Press.

Fox, M. V. 1983. Scholia to Canticles (i 4b, ii 4, i 4a, iv 3, v 8, v 12). *VT* 33:199–206.

———. 1985. *The Song of Songs and the Ancient Egyptian Love Songs.* Madison: The University of Wisconsin Press.

Freedman, D. N. 1987. Another Look at Biblical Hebrew Poetry. Pages 11–28 in Follis 1987.

Gabel, J. B., C. B. Wheeler and A. D. York. 2000. *The Bible as Literature: An Introduction.* New York: Oxford University Press.

Geller, S. A. 1979. *Parallelism in Early Hebrew Poetry.* HSM 20. Missoula, Mont.: Scholars Press.

———. 1982. Theory and Method in the Study of Biblical Poetry. *JQR* 73:65–77.

———. 1990. The Language of Imagery in Psalm 114. Pages 179–94 in *Lingering Over Words: Studies in Ancient Near Eastern Literature in Honor of William L. Moran.* Edited by T. Abusch, J. Huehnergard and P. Steinkeller. HSS 37. Atlanta: Scholars Press.

————. 1993. Hebrew Prosody and Poetics, I. Biblical. *NPEPP*, 509–11.

George, A. 2003. *The Babylonian Gilgamesh Epic*. 2 vols. Oxford: Oxford University Press.

Gevirtz, S. 1963. *Patterns in the Early Poetry of Israel*. Studies in the Ancient Oriental Civilizations 32. Chicago: University of Chicago Press.

Gibson, J. C. L. 1993. The Anatomy of Hebrew Narrative Poetry. Pages 141–48 in *Understanding Poets and Prophets: Essays in Honour of George Wishart Anderson*. Edited by A. G. Auld. JSOTSup 152. Sheffield: JSOT Press.

Giese, R. L. 1994. Strophic Hebrew Verse as Free Verse. *JSOT* 61:29–38.

Gillingham, S. E. 1994. *The Poems and Psalms of the Hebrew Bible*. The Oxford Bible Series. Oxford: Oxford University Press.

Gordon, C. H. 1978. New Directions. *Bulletin of the American Society of Papyrologists* 15:59–66.

Gray, G. B. 1915. *The Forms of Hebrew Poetry: Considered with Special Reference to the Criticism and Interpretation of the Old Testament*. London: Hodder & Stoughton. Reprinted with a foreword and additional bibliography by D. N. Freedman. New York: Ktav, 1972.

Greenfield, J. C. 1990. The "Cluster" in Biblical Poetry. *Maarav* 5–6:159–68.

Greenstein, E. L. 1983. How Does Parallelism Mean? Pages 41–70 in *A Sense of Text: The Art of Language in the Study of Biblical Literature*. JQR Supplement 1982. Winona Lake, Ind.: Eisenbrauns.

————. 2003. The Language of Job and Its Poetic Function. *JBL* 122:651–66.

Grossberg, D. 1989. *Centripetal and Centrifugal Structures in Biblical Poetry*. SBLMS 39. Atlanta: Scholars Press.

Handy, L. K. 1990. Sounds, Words and Meaning in Psalm 82. *JSOT* 47:51–66.

Hartman, C. O. 1980. *Free Verse: An Essay on Prosody*. Princeton, N.J.: Princeton University Press.

Hauser, A. J. 1994. Rhetorical Criticism of the Old Testament. Pages 1–98 in Watson and Hauser 1994.

Holladay, W. L. 1999a. *Hebrew Verse Structure* Revisited (I): Which Words "Count"? *JBL* 118:19–32.

————. 1999b. *Hebrew Verse Structure* Revisited (II): Conjoint Cola, and Further Suggestions. *JBL* 118:401–16.

Hoop, R de. 1995. *Genesis 49 in Its Literary and Historical Context*. Leiden: Brill.

————. 2000. Lamentations: The Qinah-Metre Questioned. Pages 80–104 in Korpel and Oesch 2000.

Horine, S. C. 2001. *Interpretive Images in the Song of Songs: From Wedding Chariots to Bridal Chambers*. Studies in the Humanities55. New York: Peter Lang.

House, P. R., ed. 1992. *Beyond Form Criticism: Essays in Old Testament Literary Criticism*. SBTS 2. Winona Lake, Ind.: Eisenbrauns.

Howard, David M., Jr. 1997. *The Structure of Psalms 93–100*. Biblical and Judaic Studies 5. Winona Lake, Ind.: Eisenbrauns.

Kämmerer, T. 1998. *Šimâ milka: Induktion und Reception der mittelbabylonischen Dichtung von Ugarit, Emâr und Tell el-ʿAmārna*. Münster: Ugarit-Verlag.

Kaiser, B. 1983. *Reconsidering Parallelism: A Study of the Structure of Lamentations 1, 2, and 4*. Ph.D. diss., University of Chicago.

Keel, O. 1986. *Das Hohelied.* Zurich: Theologischer Verlag.

———. 1994. *The Song of Songs.* A Continental Commentary. Minneapolis: Fortress. Trans. of Keel 1986 by F. J. Gaiser.

Kim, J. 1993. *The Structure of the Samson Cycle.* Kampen: Kok Pharos.

Koehler, L., and Baumgartner, W. 1967–90. *Hebräisches und aramäisches Lexikon zum Alten Testament.* 5 vols. Leiden: Brill.

Koopmans, W. T. 1990. *Joshua 24 as Poetic Narrative.* JSOTSup 93. Sheffield: JSOT Press.

Korpel, M. C. A. 1996. Metaphors in Isaiah lv. *VT* 46:43–55.

———. 2001. *The Structure of the Book of Ruth.* Pericope 2, Scripture as Written and Read in Antiquity. Assen: Van Gorcum.

Korpel, M. C. A., and J. C. de Moor. 1986. Fundamentals of Ugaritic and Hebrew Poetry. *UF* 18:173–212.

———. 1988. Fundamentals of Ugaritic and Hebrew Poetry. Pages 1–61 in Van der Meer and de Moor 1988.

———. 1998. *The Structure of Classical Hebrew Poetry: Isaiah 40–55.* OtSt 41. Leiden: Brill.

———. 2000. Introduction to the Series Pericope. Pages 1–50 in Korpel and Oesch 2000.

Korpel, M. C. A., and J. Oesch, eds. 2000. *Delimitation Criticism: A New Tool in Biblical Scholarship.* Pericope 1: Scripture as written and read in antiquity. Assen: Van Gorcum.

———. 2002. *Studies in Scriptural Unit Division.* Pericope 3, Scripture as Written and Read in Antiquity. Assen: Van Gorcum.

———. 2003. *Unit Delimitation in Biblical Hebrew and Northwest Semitic Literature.* Pericope 4, Scripture as Written and Read in Antiquity. Assen: Van Gorcum.

———. 2005. *Layout Markers in Biblical Manuscripts and Ugaritic Tablets.* Pericope 5, Scripture as Written and Read in Antiquity. Assen: Van Gorcum.

Kramer, S. N. 1962. The Biblical "Song of Songs" and the Sumerian Love Songs. *Expedition* 5:25–31.

Krašovec, J. 1984. *Antithetic Structure in Biblical Hebrew Poetry.* VTSup 35. Leiden: Brill.

Kugel, J. 1981. *The Idea of Biblical Poetry: Parallelism and Its History.* New Haven: Yale University Press.

———. 1984. Some Thoughts on Future Research into Biblical Style: Addenda to *The Idea of Biblical Poetry. JSOT* 28:107–17.

Kuntz, J. K. 1993. Recent Perspectives on Biblical Poetry. *Religious Studies Review* 19:321–27.

———. 1998. Biblical Hebrew Poetry in Recent Research, Part I. *Currents in Research* 6:31–64.

Landy, F. 1987. Recent Developments in Biblical Poetics. *Prooftexts* 7:163–78.

LaSor, W. S. 1979. An Approach to Hebrew Poetry Through the Masoretic Accents. Pages 327–53 in *Essays on the Occasion of the Seventieth Anniversary of the Dropsie University (1909–1979).* Edited by A. I. Katsh and L. Nemoy. Philadelphia: Dropsie University.

Levine, N. 2002. The Curse and the Blessing: Narrative Discourse Syntax and Literary Form. *JSOT* 27:189–99.

Limburg, J. 1992. Psalms, Book of. *ABD* 5:522–36.

Loprieno, A. 2000. Puns and Word Play in Ancient Egyptian. Pages 3–20 in Noegel 2000.

Lord, A. B. 1960. *The Singer of Tales*. Harvard Studies in Comparative Literature 24. Cambridge, Mass.: Harvard University Press. London: Oxford University Press.

———. 1991. *Epic Singers and Oral Tradition*. Ithaca, N.Y.: Cornell University Press.

Loretz, O. 1976. Die Analyse der ugaritischen und hebräischen Poesie mittels Stichometrie und Konsonantenzählung. *UF* 7:265–69.

———. 1979. *Die Psalmen. Teil II. Beitrag der Ugarit-Texte zum Verständnis von Kolometrie und Textologie der Psalmen. Psalm 90–150*. AOAT 207/2. Kevelaer: Butzon & Bercker. Neukirchen–Vluyn: Neukirchener.

———. 1986. Kolometrie ugaritischer und hebräischer Poesie: Grundlagen, informationstheoretische und literaturwissenschaftliche Aspekte. *ZAW* 98:249–66.

———. 1989. Hexakola im Ugaritischen und Hebräischen. Zu KTU 1.3 IV 50–53 *et par. UF* 21:237–40.

———. 2001. Der Figur *Hysteron proteron* in KTU 1.14 I 28–30. *UF* 33:299–302.

Loretz, O., and I. Kottsieper. 1987. *Colometry in Ugaritic and Biblical Poetry: Introduction, Illustrations and Topical Bibliography*. Ugaritisch-biblische Literatur 5. Altenberge: CIS Verlag.

Lowth, R. 1753. *Lectures: De sacra poesi Hebraeorum*. Oxford.

Lugt, P. van der. 1995. *Rhetorical Criticism and the Poetry of the Book of Job*. OtSt 32. Leiden: Brill.

Lunn, N. P. 2006. *Word-Order Variation in Biblical Hebrew Poetry: Differentiating Pragmatics and Poetics*. Paternoster Biblical Monographs. Milton Keynes: Paternoster.

Mabie, F. J. 2004. The Syntactical and Structural Function of Horizontal Dividing Lines in the Literary and Religious Texts of the Ugaritic Corpus (KTU 1). *UF* 36:291–312.

McCreesh, T. P. 1991. *Biblical Sound and Sense. Poetic Sound Patterns in Proverbs 10–29*. JSOTSup 128. Sheffield: JSOT Press.

Mathieu, B. 1996. *La poésie amoureuse de l'Égypte ancienne: recherches sur un genre littéraire au Nouvel Empire*. Bibliothéque d'Étude 115. Cairo: Institut français d'archéologie orientale du Caire.

Meer, W. van der, and J. C. de Moor, eds. 1988. *The Structural Analysis of Biblical and Canaanite Poetry*. JSOTSup 174. Sheffield: Sheffield Academic Press.

Meynet, R. 1998. *Rhetorical Analysis. An Introduction to Biblical Rhetoric*. JSOTSup 256. Sheffield: Sheffield Academic Press.

Meynet, R., L. Pouzet, N. Farouki and A. Sinno. 1998. *Rhétorique sémitique. Textes de la Bible et de la Tradition musulmane*. Paris: Cerf.

Michael, I. 1994. Lowth. Page 2308 in vol. 4 of *The Encyclopaedia of Language and Linguistics*. Edited by R.E. Asher. Oxford: Pergamon.

Millard, A. 1995. The Last Tablets of Ugarit. Pages 119–24 in *Le pays d'Ougarit autour de 1200 av.J.-C. Actes du Colloque International Paris, 28 juin–1er juillet 1993*. Edited by M. Yon, M. Sznycer and P. Bordreuil. Ras Shamra-Ougarit 11. Paris: Éditions Recherche sur les Civilisations.

Miller, C. L. 1999. Patterns of Verbal Ellipsis in Ugaritic Poetry. *UF* 31:333–72.

Miller, P. D. 1984. Meter, Parallelism, and Tropes: The Search for Poetic Style. *JSOT* 28:99–106.

Moor, J. C. de. 1978a. The Art of Versification in Ugarit and Israel I: The Rhythmical Structure. Pages 119–39 in *Studies in the Bible and the Ancient Near East Presented to S. E. Loewenstamm on His Seventieth Birthday*. Edited by Y. Avishur and J. Blau. Jerusalem: Rubinstein's.

———. 1978b. The Art of Versification in Ugarit and Israel II. *UF* 10:187–217.

———. 1980. The Art of Versification in Ugarit and Israel III: Further Illustrations of the Principle of Expansion. *UF* 12:311–15.

———. 1984. The Poetry of the Book of Ruth (I). *Or* 53:262–83.

———. 1986. The Poetry of the Book of Ruth (II). *Or* 55:16–46.

———. 2000. Micah 7:1–13: The Lament of a Disillusioned Prophet. Pages 149–96 in Korpel and Oesch 2000.

Moor, J. C. de, and P. van der Lugt. 1974. The Spectre of Pan-Ugaritism. *BibOr* 31:3–26.

Moor, J. C. de, and W. G. E. Watson, eds. 1993. *Verse in Ancient Near Eastern Prose.* AOAT 42. Kevelaer: Butzon & Bercker. Neukirchen–Vluyn: Neukirchener.

Mowinckel, S. 1962. *The Psalms in Israel's Worship*. 2 vols. Oxford: Blackwell.

Munro, J. M. 1995. *Spikenard and Saffron: A Study in the Poetic Language of the Song of Songs*. JSOTSup 203. Sheffield: Sheffield Academic Press.

Nel, P. J. 1992. Parallelism and Recurrence in Biblical Hebrew Poetry. *JNSLL* 18:135–43.

Niccacci, A. 1980. Review of Collins 1978. *Liber Annuus* 30:450–53.

———1994. La lode del creatore. L'inno egiziano di Aton e la tradizione biblica. *Ephemerides Theologicae Zagrabienses, Bogoslovska Smotra* 64:137–59.

———. 1997. Analysing Biblical Hebrew Poetry. *JSOT* 74:77–93.

Nissinen, M. 1998. Love Lyrics of Nabû and Tašmetu: An Assyrian Song of Songs? Pages 585–634 in Dietrich and Kottsieper 1998.

Noegel, S. 1996. *Janus Parallelism in the Book of Job*. JSOTSup 223. Sheffield: Sheffield Academic Press.

———ed., 2000. *Puns and Pundits: Word Play in the Hebrew Bible and in Ancient Near Eastern Literature*. Bethesda, Md.: CDL Press.

Nwaoru, E. O. 2004. The Role of Images in the Literary Structure of Hosea vii 8–viii 14. *VT* 54:216–22.

Ocker, C. 2002. *Biblical Poetics Before Humanism and the Reformation*. Cambridge: Cambridge University Press.

O'Connor, M. 1997. *Hebrew Verse Structure*. Winona Lake, Ind.: Eisenbrauns. 2d ed. (1st ed. 1980).

———. 1987. The Pseudo-Sorites in Hebrew Verse. Pages 239–53 in *Perspectives on Language and Text: Essays and Poems in Honor of Francis I. Andersen's Sixtieth Birthday July 28, 1985*. Edited by E. W. Conrad and E. G. Newing. Winona Lake, Ind.: Eisenbrauns.

———. 1993. Parallelism. *NPEPP*, 877–79.

Oesch, J. 1979. *Petucha und Setuma: Untersuchungen zu einer überlieferten Gliederung im hebräischen Text des Alten Testaments*. OBO 27. Freiburg (Schweiz): Universitätsverlag. Göttingen: Vandenhoeck & Ruprecht.

———. 2000. Skizze einer synchronen und diachronen Gliederungskritik im Rahmen der alttestamentlichen Textkritik. Pages 197–229 in Korpel and Oesch 2000.

Orton, D. E., ed. 2000. *Poetry in the Hebrew Bible: Selected Studies from Vetus Testamentum*. Leiden: Brill.

Pardee, D. 1981. Ugaritic and Hebrew Metrics. Pages 113–30 in *Ugarit in Retrospect. Fifty Years of Ugarit and Ugaritic*. Edited by G. D. Young. Winona Lake, Ind.: Eisenbrauns.

———. 1988. *Ugaritic and Hebrew Poetic Parallelism: A Trial Cut (ʿnt I and Proverbs 2)*. VTSup 39. Leiden: Brill.

———. 1993. Poetry in Ugaritic Ritual Texts. Pages 207–18 in de Moor and Watson 1993.

———. 2001. Review of S. B. Parker, ed., *Ugaritic Narrative Poetry, JNES* 60:142–45.

Parker, S. B. 1989. *The Pre-Biblical Narrative Tradition*. SBLRBS 24. Atlanta: Scholars Press.

———. 2004. The Use of Similes in Ugaritic Literature. *UF* 36:357–70.

Parkinson, R. B. 2002. *Poetry and Culture in Middle Kingdom Egypt. A Dark Side to Perfection*. Athlone Publications in Egyptology and Ancient Near Eastern Studies. London: Continuum.

Parry, A., ed. 1971. *The Making of Homeric Verse: The Collected Papers of Milman Parry*. Oxford: Clarendon.

Parry, M. 1930. Studies in the Epic Technique of Oral Verse-Making I: Homer and the Homeric Style. *HSCP* 41:73–147.

———. 1932. Studies in the Epic Technique of Oral Verse-Making II: The Homeric Language as the Language of Oral Poetry. *HSCP* 43:1–50.

Paul, S. M. 1992. Polysensuous Polyvalency in Poetic Parallelism. Pages 147–63 in *"Sha'arei Talmon": Studies in the Bible, Qumran, and the Ancient Near East Presented to Shemaryahu Talmon*. Edited by M. Fishbane and E. Tov. Winona Lake, Ind.: Eisenbrauns.

Payne, G. 1994. Parallelism in Biblical Hebrew Verse: Some Secular Thoughts. *SJOT* 8:126–40.

Petersen, D. L., and K. H. Richards. 1992. *Interpreting Hebrew Poetry*. Guides to Biblical Scholarship, Old Testament Series. Minneapolis: Fortress.

Prinsloo, G. T. M. 1992. Poetic Conventions in an Old-Babylonian hymn to Ishtar. *Journal for Semitics* 4:1–21.

Raabe, P. R. 1990. *Psalm Structures: A Study of Psalms with Refrains*. JSOTSup 104. Sheffield: JSOT Press.

Ranieri, A. 1993. *Studio grammaticale e semantico del parallelismo in Proverbi I–IX*. Jerusalem: Studium Biblicum Franciscanum.

Reiner, E. 1985. *"Your thwarts in pieces, Your mooring rope cut": Poetry from Babylonian and Assyria*. Michigan, Ohio: Horace H. Rackham School of Graduate Studies at the University of Michigan.

Richardson, M. E. J., ed. 1994–2000. *The Hebrew and Aramaic Lexicon of the Old Testament*. 5 vols. Leiden: Brill.

———. 1993. Assyro-Babylonian Poetry. *NPEPP*, 104–5.

Rollston, C. A. 2001. Ben Sira 38:24–39:11 and the Egyptian *Satire of the Trades*: A Reconsideration. *JBL* 120: 131–39.

Sanders, P. 1996. *The Provenance of Deuteronomy 32*. Leiden: Brill.

Segert, S. 1987. Phonological and Syntactic Structuring Principles in Northwest Semitic Verse Systems. Pages 543–57 in *Proceedings of the Fourth International Hamito-Semitic Conference, Hamburg, 20–22 September, 1983*. Edited by H. Jungraithmayer and W. W. Müller. Amsterdam Studies in the Theory and History of Linguistic Science Series 4. Current Issues in Linguistic Theory 44. Amsterdam: John Benjamins.

————. 1995. Poetic Structures in the Hebrew Sections of the Book of Daniel. Pages 261–75 in Zevit, Gitin and Sokoloff 1995.

Sefati, Y. 1998. *Love Songs in Sumerian Literature: Critical Edition of the Dumuzi-Inanna Songs.* Ramat Gan: Bar-Ilan University Press.

Seybold, K. 2003. *Poetik der Psalmen.* Poetologische Studien zum Alten Testament 1. Stuttgart: W. Kohlhammer.

Shimasaki, K. 2002. *Focus Structure in Biblical Hebrew.* Bethesda, Md.: CDL Press.

Shupak, N. 1983. Stylistic and Terminological Traits Common to Biblical and Egyptian Literature. *Die Welt des Orients* 14:216–30.

Slotki, I. W. 1931. Typographic Arrangements of Hebrew Poetry: New Light on the Solution of Metrical and Textual Difficulties. *ZAW* 8:211–22.

Smith, G. A. 1912. *The Early Poetry of Israel in Its Physical and Social Origins.* The Schweich Lectures 1910. London: Oxford University Press.

Spicehandler, E. 1993. Hebrew Poetry. *NPEPP,* 501–9.

Streck, M. P. 1999. *Die Bildersprache der akkadischen Epik.* AOAT 264. Münster: Ugarit-Verlag.

Stuart, D. K. 1976. *Studies in Early Hebrew Meter.* Missoula, Mont.: Scholars Press.

Talstra, E. 1999. Reading Biblical Hebrew Poetry—Linguistic Structure or Rhetorical Device? *JNSL* 25:101–26.

Tigay, J. H. 1982. *The Evolution of the Gilgamesh Epic.* Philadelphia: University of Pennsylvania Press.

Tropper, J. 1998. Sprachliche Archaismen im Parallelismus membrorum in der akkadischen und ugaritischen Epik. *Aula Orientalis* 16:103–10.

————. 2000. *Ugaritische Grammatik.* AOAT 273. Münster: Ugarit-Verlag.

Tsevat, M. 1955. *A Study of the Language of the Biblical Psalms.* Philadelphia: Society of Biblical Literature.

Veijola, T. 2004. Zum Problem der Tempora in der Psalmenübersetzung. Pages 385–400 in *Verbum et Calamus: Semitic Studies in Honour of the Sixtieth Birthday of Professor Tapani Harviainen.* Edited by H. Juusola, J. Laulainen and H. Palva. Studia Orientalia 99. Helsinki: The Finnish Oriental Society.

Vogelzang, M., and H. L. J. Vanstiphout, eds. 1992. *Mesopotamian Epic Literature: Oral or Aural?* Lewiston, N.Y.: Edwin Mellen.

————. 1996. *Mesopotamian Poetic Language: Sumerian and Akkadian: Proceedings of the Groningen Group for the Study of Mesopotamian Literature,* vol. 2. Cuneiform Monographs 6. Groningen: Styx.

Waldman, N. H. 1989. The Imagery of Clothing, Covering, and Overpowering. *JANES* 19:161–88.

Walsh, J. 2001. *Style and Structure in Biblical Hebrew Narrative* (Collegeville, Minn.: Liturgical Press.

Walton, J. H. 2003. The Imagery of the Substitute King Ritual in Isaiah's Fourth Servant Song. *JBL* 122:734–43.

Wasserman, N. 2002. *Style and Form in Old-Babylonian Literary Texts.* Cuneiform Monographs 27. Leiden: Brill.

Watkins, C. 1995. *How to Kill a Dragon: Aspects of Indo-European Poetics.* Oxford: Oxford University Press.

Watson, D. F., and A. J. Hauser. 1994. *Rhetorical Criticism of the Bible: A Comprehensive Bibliography With Notes on History and Method.* BibInt Series 4. Leiden: Brill.

Watson, W. G. E. 1981. Chiastic Patterns in Biblical Hebrew Poetry. Pages 118–68 in *Chiasmus in Antiquity*. Edited by J. Welch. Hildesheim: Gerstenberg Verlag. Reprinted, with corrections, in Watson 1994a, 328–89.

———. 1982a. Trends in the Development of Classical Hebrew Poetry. *UF* 14:265–77.

———. 1982b. Lineation (Stichometry) in Ugaritic Verse. *UF* 14:311–12.

———. 1983. Review of Kugel 1981, *Biblica* 64:134–36.

———. 1984a. *Classical Hebrew Poetry: A Guide to Its Techniques*. JSOTSup 26. Sheffield: JSOT Press. 2d ed. 1986. 3d ed. 1994. Reprinted with corrections 1995, 2005.

———. 1984b. A Review of Kugel's *The Idea of Biblical Poetry*. *JSOT* 28:89–98.

———. 1993. Problems and Solutions in Hebrew Verse: A Survey of Recent Work. *VT* 43:372–84.

———. 1994a. *Traditional Techniques in Classical Hebrew Verse*. JSOTSup 170. Sheffield: JSOT Press.

———. 1994b. Ugaritic. Pages 4826 in vol. 9 of *The Encyclopaedia of Language and Linguistics*. Edited by R.E. Asher. Oxford: Pergamon.

———. 1994c. Introductions to Speech in Ugaritic and Hebrew. Pages 383–93 in *Ugarit and the Bible: Proceedings of the International Symposium on Ugarit and the Bible Manchester, September 1992*. Edited by G. J. Brooke, A. H. W. Curtis and J. F. Healey. Ugaritisch-Biblische Literatur 11. Münster: Ugarit-Verlag.

———. 1995a. Verse Patterns in the Song of Songs. *JNSLL* 21:111–22.

———. 1995b. Some Ancient Near Eastern Parallels to the Song of Songs. Pages 253–71 in Davies, Harvey and Watson 1995.

———. 1996. Verse Patterns in KTU 1.119:26–36. *Studi epigrafici e linguistici sul Vicino Oriente antico* 13:25–30.

———. 1997. Parallel Word Pairs in the Song of Songs. Pages 785–808 in Dietrich and Kottsieper 1997.

———. 2000. Hebrew Poetry. Pages 253–85 in *Text in Context. Essays by Members of the Society for Old Testament Study*. Edited by A. D. H. Mayes. Oxford: Oxford University Press.

Watters, W. R. 1976. *Formula Criticism and the Poetry of the Old Testament*. BZAW 138. Berlin: de Gruyter.

Watts, J. 1992. *Psalm and Story: Inset Hymns in Hebrew Narrative*. JSOTSup 139. Sheffield: JSOT Press.

Weisberg, D. B. 1991. Loyalty and Death: Some Ancient Near Eastern Metaphors. *Maarav* 7:253–67.

West, M. 1992. Looking for the Poem: Reflections on the Current and Future Status of the Study of Biblical Hebrew Poetry. Pages 423–31 in House 1992.

———. 1997. Akkadian Poetry: Metre and Performance. *Iraq* 59:175–87.

Westenholz, J. Goodnick. 1997. Studying Poetic Language. *Or* 66:181–95.

Whallon, W. 1969. *Formula, Character, and Context, Studies in Homeric, Old English, and Old Testament Poetry*. Washington: Center for Hellenic Studies.

Whitaker, R. 1969. A Formulaic Analysis of Ugaritic Poetry. Ph.D. diss., Harvard University.

Willis, J. T. 1987. Alternating (ABA'B') Parallelism in the Old Testament Psalms and Prophetic Literature. Pages 49–76 in Follis 1987.

Wilson, G. H. 1982. Ugaritic Word Order and Sentence Structure in Krt. *JSS* 27:17–32.

Wyatt, N. 1998. *Religious Texts from Ugarit: The Words of Ilimilku and His Colleagues.*
    The Biblical Seminar 53. Sheffield: Sheffield Academic Press.
Yaron, R. 1986. The Climactic Tricolon. *JSS* 37:153–59.
Zevit, Z. 1992. Cognitive Theory and the Memorability of Hebrew Poetry. *Maarav*
    8:199–212.
Zevit, Z., S. Gitin and M. Sokoloff, eds. 1995. *Solving Riddles and Untying Knots:
    Biblical, Epigraphic, and Semitic Studies in Honor of Jonas C. Greenfield.* Winona
    Lake, Ind.: Eisenbrauns.
Zurro, E. 2000. El *hysteron-proteron* en la poesía bíblica hebrea. *EstBíb* 58:399–415.

Part B

ON THE CONTEXT AND LEGACY OF JEAN ASTRUC'S
CONJECTURES ON GENESIS

JEAN ASTRUC: A PHYSICIAN AS A BIBLICAL SCHOLAR

Rudolf Smend

A German scholar is always delighted when he can begin with a fitting quotation from Goethe. For the present occasion such an introduction is facilitated by the fact that Goethe actually did say something about Jean Astruc. Disappointed by the limited resonance to his own scientific theories, he observed a demand on the part of his readers that everyone "remain within his subject," "that a talented person who has emerged as an expert in a particular field, whose ways are widely known and appreciated, should not leave his own circle, let alone make a leap into a remote realm." However, to quote Goethe further, "every energetic talent" is:

> a universal one, which gazes round about and performs its activities here and there exactly as it desires. We have physicians who love to build, design gardens and factories, surgeons who are numismatists and own priceless collections. *Astruc*, private surgeon to Louis XIV, first applied his scalpel and probe to the Pentateuch. After all, what do the sciences not already owe to interested connoisseurs and unbiased guests! Furthermore, we know businessmen who love to read novels or play cards, serious fathers who prefer farce on the stage to any other kind of entertainment. For many years the eternal truth has been repeated *ad nauseam* that life consists of both seriousness and play and that only those deserve to be called the wisest and happiest who can maintain a balance between the two, for everyone wishes to be, even involuntarily, the opposite of himself in order to be a whole![1]

The present German scholar is delighted that this quotation provides him the opportunity to remark most respectfully, but also triumphantly, "Here, Goethe is mistaken." Astruc's Louis was not the fourteenth, but the fifteenth. However, what pleases him the most—and he hopes his

---

1. J. W. Goethe, *Sämtliche Werke, Briefe, Tagebücher und Gespräche*. Vol. 24, *Schriften zur Morphologie* (ed. D. Kuhn; 40 vols.; Frankfurt a. M.: Deutscher Klassiker Verlag, 1987), 417–18.

audience agrees with him on this point—is the rather charming image of a surgeon who also treats the Bible with his medical instruments. The physician Astruc, the author of an imposing number of books and who, during his lifetime, was famous far beyond his narrow sphere of activity, is only known these days to specialists in the history of science, whereas the biblical scholar Astruc still occupies a place in every introduction to the Old Testament.

How were Astruc's pursuits related to each other? Certainly, his role in biblical scholarship was one of a connoisseur and guest. But was it something of a game of cards or a farce to him? Or were there deeper reasons for exactly this "opposite"? And did the two activities have anything in common, to use Goethe's image? In all of this, did he belong to the "wisest" and the "happiest"? We do not know Astruc, a figure from times long past, well enough to be able to answer these questions in a fully satisfactory way, but his biography and work do contain several hints.

I

Jean Astruc was born on March 19, 1684 in Sauve, a town in the Langue-doc—in the triangle, so to speak, formed by Nîmes and Montpellier. He always kept close ties to this region; his important achievements include a *Natural History of the Languedoc*[2] and a history of the Medical Faculty in Montpellier. The latter was completed long after he had moved to Paris and was published posthumously.[3] His surname appears often

2. J. Astruc, *Mémoires pour l'histoire naturelle de la province de Languedoc* (Paris, 1737).

3. J. Astruc, *Mémoires pour servir à l'histoire de la Faculté de Médecine de Montpellier* (Paris, 1767). It contains (p. 293) his own very short *curriculum vitae* and, secondarily prefaced (pp. xxxiii–lii), a detailed eulogy to Astruc from the pen of his younger colleague M. Lorry, which represents the basis for all prior biographical attempts and thus also for the following. Helpful are provided by E. Ritter, "Jean Astruc. Auteur des 'Conjectures sur la Genèse,'" *BSHPF* 65 (1916): 274–87 (274ff.); J. Alphandéry, "Jean Astruc (1684–1766)," *RHPhR* 4 (1924): 54–72 (54ff.); A. Lods, "Astruc et la critique biblique de son temps," *RHPhR* 4 (1924): 109–39, 201–27 (109ff., 201ff.); A.-M. Latour, "Astruc" 6–8, *DBF* 3 (1939): 1391–94 (1391ff.); J. Doe, "Jean Astruc (1684–1766): A Biographical and Bibliographical Study," *Journal of the History of Medicine* 15 (1960): 184–97 (184ff., with a bibliography); P. Huard and M.-J. Imbault-Huart, *Biographies médicales et scientifiques: 18e siècle* (Paris: Dacosta, 1972), 7ff. (with a bibliography); P. Huard, "Astruc, Jean," *Dictionary of Scientific Biography* 1 (1981): 322–24; A. M. Acosta, "Conjectures and Speculations: Jean Astruc, Obstetrics, and Biblical Criticism

among Jews in Spain and Southern France,[4] so that many have considered him to be of Jewish descent. If so, it would have been a motive for his interest in the Old Testament.[5]

However, this interest can be traced with greater probability to the influence of his father, Pierre Astruc,[6] who at the time of his son's birth was the minister of the Reformed church in Aigremont, a town near the family's hometown of Sauve. It was in these years that the freedom of the Huguenots to practise their religion, granted by the Edict of Nantes (1598), was coming to an end. Pierre Astruc was among the persecuted: in 1684, he was sentenced *in absentia* to death and executed in effigy. In early 1685, with his feet in chains, he was pardoned for the price of conversion to the Catholic faith. Because of this, the abolition of the edict in October 1685 did not affect him; his cousin, Jacques Astruc,[7] with whom he had studied theology in Geneva, was forced into exile, like many of his colleagues. In later years (1703–4), Pierre suffered the violent actions of the "camisardic" Huguenots, who took particular aim at the apostate ministers, and for a while, he escaped to Montpellier. Otherwise, he seems not to have had a bad life. For his conversion, he was paid a pension and worked as a lawyer. In his large and wide-ranging library, he pursued his scholarly interests, particularly in the field of antiquity.

His son Jean left a hidden memorial to him, namely there in the *Natural History of the Languedoc*, where he discusses the report of the Jewish traveller from the twelfth century, Benjamin of Tudela, and exhibits his acquaintance with the Hebrew language. This he inherited from his father, he says, for whom he has maintained his love and esteem. The elder Astruc's knowledge of languages was, according to his son, the smallest part of his erudition, and his erudition was infinitely surpassed by his virtue and honesty.[7] One often attributes his father's competence in Hebrew to the fact that, when he was studying in Geneva, Michel Turrettini was Professor of Hebrew. This scholar belonged to a famous family of theologians and wrote just one book, entitled significantly, *De Scripturae Sacrae auctoritate adversus Pontificios*.[8] "The

in Eighteenth-Century France," *Eighteenth-Century Studies* 35 (2001): 256–66 (256ff.).

4. See J. Heller, "Astruc," *EJ (D)* 3 (1929): 607–8.

5. See, e.g., Doe, "Jean Astruc," 186.

6. About him see Ch. Bost, "Les pasteurs Astruc—le père de Jean Astruc," *BSHPF* 66 (1917): 59–77 (59ff.).

7. Astruc, *Mémoires pour l'histoire naturelle*, 192.

8. Ritter, "Jean Astruc," 275–76.

theological virus, it seems, is difficult to rid from the blood" has been said by an individual experienced in this regard,[9] and thus Pierre Astruc must have retained something of the Geneva Theology and its biblicity and must have passed it on to both of his sons. He devoted the utmost care to their education; besides him, they had no other teacher. Jean reported that in his father's school they learned order and method, "without which science is often useless and always exhausting."[10] Not only did the older son, Jean, take advantage of this education, but also the younger one, Anne-Louis, became a well-respected lawyer and died as Professor of French Law at the University of Toulouse.

Jean went to study at Montpellier and decided, after being awarded the degree of *Magister artium* in 1700, to become a physician. In 1702, he received his baccalaureate and licence, and in 1703, not yet 19 years old, his doctorate. In the following years he distinguished himself to such an extent that his teacher—and former theologian—Pierre Chirac allowed him, with the consent of the faculty, to hold his anatomy lectures when he accompanied the Duke of Orléans to the Spanish War of Succession from 1706 to 1709. Following an interlude as Professor of Anatomy at Toulouse (1710/11), Astruc returned to his native Montpellier, again to assist Chirac. In 1716, he was granted a chair where he stayed until 1728. In 1720, the king endowed him with a pension and, in 1721, placed him in charge of the mineral water-plants of Languedoc. In later years, he was appointed to the high office of "Capitoul" in Toulouse. In 1728, he went to Paris from where King August II ("The Strong") of Poland (and Saxony) soon invited him to come and work as his personal physician. However, he was not happy there, and in 1730 he returned to Paris, now as Louis XV's personal physician, and a year later as Professor of Medicine at the Collège Royal de France. He gained his greatest satisfaction from the fact that in 1743 the Medical Faculty of the Sorbonne unanimously elected him as a member; until his death he was the most faithful attendee at their meetings.

Astruc's brilliant career was reflected in his social standing, which meant that many of his patients were wealthy and powerful. One of them was Madame de Tencin, who had been a nun, sister of a powerful cardinal, mistress of the Duke of Orléans (the "Regent"), mother of D'Alemberts (whom she abandoned as a baby on the steps of a church), successful author of novels, and not least was famous for her salon that was frequented also by Astruc. He even belonged to her select group of

9. Adrian Leverkühn in Th. Mann, *Doktor Faustus* (Gesammelte Werke in dreizehn Bänden 6; Frankfurt a. M.: S. Fischer, 1974), 472.
10. Lorry in Astruc, *Mémoires pour servir*, xxxiv.

the "seven wise men" that dined there every Tuesday. The other six were Fontenelle, Marivaux, Mairan, Mirabaud, de Boze and Duclos—all members of the Academie Française. Montesquieu and Marmontel were also guests there, as well as the Lords Bolingbroke and Chesterfield.[11] Astruc was one of the eldest in this circle and would probably have taken the conservative part in the discussions. He was particularly close to Madame de Tencin. She not only mentioned him in her will, but also arranged the marriage of his daughter to the multi-talented Etienne de Silhouette, who was a protégé of Mme. Pompadour and, for a while, the finance minister.

Besides a daughter, there was a son who also had a promising career ahead of him. Jean Astruc was a happy father and a loyal friend, noted his greatest eulogist, but he added that his father never had more than a few minutes for his children and friends, because he was always busy with serious and helpful studies and spent his whole life locked away in his "cabinet."[12]

II

In 1766, the year of his death, Astruc began his textbook on obstetrics with the admission that he had no practical experience in this field. However, he had, in 1745, been charged by the Parisian medical faculty to hold a course for midwives and had used the six months leading up to the course to read or reread all of the French and Latin literature that had been published in the last thirty years on the topic. Most of these works he found to be good as far as the facts were concerned, but they also lacked an order or method and were full of useless things, redundancies, vague or poorly described observations and pretentious discussions about difficult medical problems that did not belong there. His course was based on a "compilation" from these books that avoided their mistakes and which he then forgot. He claimed to be publishing them now in a new revised version in order to complete his work on women's diseases and to render them useful for midwifery courses throughout the provinces. He had three aims that he said were indispensable in didactic works: exact methods and order (everything in its place, progression from easy to difficult), brevity, clarity. For only two of the topics, namely for the History of Obstetrics and for Caesarean Sections, did he use a different

11. Cf. P.-M. Masson, *Une vie de femme aux XVIIIe siecle: Madame de Tencin* (Paris, 1909), 183–88 et passim; H. Nicolson, *The Age of Reason, 100–1789* (London: n.p., 1960) 214–33 (226).

12. Lorry in Astruc, *Mémoires pour servir*, li.

procedure: in these cases, he also included long quotations. The book begins with a motto both from Horace and from Genesis. As an addendum, it treats two, almost theological, problems that may appear curious to us, but at that time were matters of common interest, namely the validity of a baptism by injection and the procedure used by Adam and Eve with their first children.[13]

Mutatis mutandis, this swansong characterized Astruc's manner of writing for more than half a century. It included the entire field of medicine, just as Astruc's lectures covered the entire field in three-year cycles. Of all his talents, teaching was the one that others respected most. He was a professor "by nature and inclination." His imposing figure and his great charm impressed his listeners, and he lectured in such an elegant style that even the beginners could easily follow him and remember what was essential.[14] He dictated much and did not publish everything. Notes of his lectures were in circulation in many places, at home and abroad, yet only some exemplars did he ever see and, when appropriate, sanction. These transcripts (e.g. the very interesting lecture on geriatric diseases that he held in 1762 at the age of 78[15]) still come to light every now and then.

The oeuvre began in 1702 with the work of the 18-year-old, *Tractatus de motus fermentativi causa*. It provoked a reply from an anatomist called Vieussens, to which Astruc replied with *Brevis responsio criticis animadversionibus Francisci Renati Vieussens in Tractatum de causa motus fermentativi*, published also in 1702. The dispute went back and forth once more in 1703 beginning with Astruc's book, *Responsio ad secundam animadversionem in Tractatum de causa...* He carried on such scholarly disputes at later dates, while with several others he was even successful in settling them. After treating the subject of fermentation, he discussed the movement of the muscles in 1710, digestion in 1710 and 1714, and hydrophobia in 1719 (*Dissertatio medica de hydrophobia*). When the plague reached Marseille in 1720, he joined in on the medical discussion with several papers (among others "*Dissertation sur l'origine des maladies épidémiques, et principalement sur l'origine de la peste*," 1721), but unfortunately his theory that the plague was spread by contagion and his recommendations for prophylaxis and therapy were not accepted by the academic authorities. His most famous work, *De morbis venereis*, appeared in 1736 and underwent several editions. It was

13. See Acosta, "Conjectures and Speculations," 260–63.
14. Lorry in Astruc, *Mémoires pour servir*, xxxix–xl.
15. See F. D. Zeman, "Jean Astruc (1684–1766) on Old Age," *Journal of the History of Medicine* 20 (1965), 52–57 (52ff.).

also translated, not least into French, and was the last book Astruc published in Latin. "This book[...]is without doubt the most complete and most useful that has appeared on this topic hitherto" was the opinion of the *Göttingische Gelehrte Anzeigen*; the author shows "just as much erudition and diligence in his argumentation as modesty and keen discernment in his judgment of all opinions and statements that could be included here."[16] Later critics accused Astruc of not differentiating between syphilis and gonorrhoea, but in this regard he would have been far ahead of his time.[17] With proof that the leprosy of antiquity was a different phenomenon and that venereal diseases came from America to Europe and are spread by infection, he witnessed wide acceptance. In the year 1743 alone, no less than three of his lectures were published abroad without his permission, viz., a *Tractatus pathologicus* and a *Tractatus therapeuticus* in Geneva and *A treatise on all the diseases incident to women* in London. The latter publication occasioned his own writing on this topic, and, after a further *Traité des tumeurs et des ulcères* appeared in 1759, four volumes of a *Traité des maladies des femmes* were published in 1761, followed by two more in 1765, and then the work quoted above, *L'art d'accoucher*, conceived almost as a seventh volume.

How has Astruc's achievement in his field been assessed? Even a colleague who had once criticized him says in the end that he is *"le Médecin le plus consideré, le plus grand, et le plus heureux praticien de l'Europe."*[18] The latter does not seem to have been the unanimous opinion in Paris: Baron Friedrich Melchior Grimm, known to lovers of music from Mozart's biography, calls him *"un savant médicin," "un des meilleurs médicins de la Faculté de Paris quant a la théorie,"* but *"un praticien mèdiocre."*[19] Whatever the case may have been, he was unbeatable as a scholar. An *"homme des livres,"*[20] he had a very extensive library, part of which he inherited from his father, and the even larger libraries in Paris, after he had moved there, seem to have been very important to him.[21] For his own work, the substantial and well-organized information from new, but also from old, as well as from very old, literature is characteristic and seems to have influenced his judgment often. "Passion for the defence of traditional medical methods and also

16. (Anonymous), "Paris," *GGA* 1740, 828–32 (831) (probably A. v. Haller).
17. Doe, "Jean Astruc," 188.
18. (Anonymous), "Paris," *GGA* 1760, 1332–33 (1332).
19. M. Tourneux, *Correspondance littéraire, philosophique et critique par Grimm, Diderot, Raynal, Meister etc.* (16 vols.; Paris, 1877–82), vol. 4 (1878), 402; vol. 7 (1879), 37.
20. Alphandéry, "Jean Astruc," 61.
21. Lorry in Astruc, *Mémoires pour servir*, xlii.

for the survival of the accepted hierarchies" is ascribed to him.[22] He rejected not only inoculation or variolation, the risky precursor of preventive vaccination against smallpox,[23] but also the equality of surgeons and physicians.[24] He also does not seem to have taken part in the modernization of medicine in his time that was represented by such names as Boerhave, Morgagni, and Haller.[25] This, however, does not detract from his achievements as a physician and a professor.

The wide range of books found in his library shows what advantages he had over his colleagues. According to a saying about him, he was versed in everything, even in medicine.[26] When he prefaced the beginning of his book on midwifery with lines from Horace and the Bible, it was not an intellectual game as it may have been for many others; rather, it indicates in what worlds he lived and in which context he viewed his own work. And as far as the Bible is concerned, he made a discovery that anticipated the future. A nineteenth-century biblical scholar from Alsace picked up Goethe's image with which I began and called Astruc a *"véritable homme de l'art"* who, after reaching for the scalpel, hardly ever made better use of it during his entire career than on this occasion.[27] It is perhaps symbolic that in the very same year (1753) in which Albrecht von Haller published his treatise for the Academy of Sciences in Göttingen, *De partibus corporis humani sensilibus et irritabilibus,*[28] which has been called the "occasion for a dramatic change in the view of life,"[29] Astruc presented his contribution to biblical studies.

III

In 1753, the book was published whose title every student of theology should still memorize, *CONJECTURES SUR LES MEMOIRES ORIGI-NAUX Dont il paroit que Moyse s'est servi pour composer le Livre de la GENESE*, with the subtitle, *Avec des Remarques qui appuient ou éclair-cissent ces Conjectures*. The place of publication is given as Brussels; actually, however, it was Paris. The name of the author is missing, but

22. Alphandéry, "Jean Astruc," 65.
23. See R. Thomssen, *Schutzimpfungen* (Munich: Beck, 2001), 20–21.
24. Acosta, "Conjectures and Speculations," 259–61.
25. Doe, "Jean Astruc," 184–85.
26. Ibid. (Marquis de Rochefort).
27. A. Westphal, *Les sources du Pentateuque* (2 vols.; Paris, 1888), 1:104.
28. In A. v. Haller, "De partibus corporis humani sensilibus et irritabilibus," *Commentarii Societatis Regiae Scientiarum Gottingensis* II (1753): 114–58.
29. R. Toellner in R. Vierhaus, ed., *Wissenschaften im Zeitalter der Aufklärung* (Göttingen: Vandenhoeck & Ruprecht, 1985), 194.

soon everyone knew that it was Astruc. Under the title, there is a line from Lucretius: *Avia Pieridium peragro loca, nullius antè Trita solo* ("I roam through the pathless places of the Pierides which have never been touched by the sole of a foot"). The book was indeed something new for Astruc himself, but he had spent a long time preparing himself for it. He hesitated with the publication, as he noted at the outset in an *Avertisse-ment*, because he was afraid that those who pretend to be free thinkers (*les pretendus Esprit-forts*) could misuse the book to undermine the authority of the Pentateuch. However, a learned and pious man to whom he showed the manuscript was able to dispel his fears: others had already voiced the same opinion and this theory would not change the text of Genesis, but on the contrary, could remove or explain some of the diffi-culties arising from it. If his "suppositions" should turn out to be incor-rect or dangerous, he would let this be known. His predilection for his own ideas would never win a victory over his love for the truth and for religion.

As elsewhere in Astruc's writings, the train of thought here is a model of "order and method." It begins by stating several premises (*réflexions préliminaires*): Moses did not experience what he describes in Genesis. He knows it, therefore, from a revelation or from eyewitness reports. The first possibility can be ruled out because Moses does not mention a revelation (the reader is astonished how easily this possibility is dis-missed). If, therefore, it was eyewitness reports, then were they based on verbal or written tradition? If verbal, the accuracy of much of the information would have been questionable. Thus, it must have been written (*des relations ou mémoires laissez par écrit*). Here, Astruc quotes Clericus and Simon, while relying more on Abbé Fleury and François;[30] he carries their speculations even further with the claim:

> that Moses had access to old accounts (*mémoires anciens*) which con-tained the history of his ancestors beginning with the creation of the world; that, in order not to omit anything, he divided these reports into pieces (*morceaux*) according to the incidents described therein; that he collected all the pieces together one after the other; and that the first book of Moses originated from all these pieces.[31]

30. J. Clericus, "Dissertatio de scriptore Pentateuchi Mose," in *Genesis sive Mosis prophetae liber Primus* (Tübingen, 1730), xxv; R. Simon, *Histoire critique du Vieux Testament* (1780), l–li.; C. Fleury, *Les mœurs des Israëlites* (Paris, 1722), 7–8; M. L. L. François, *Preuves de la religion de Jesus-Christ, contre le Spinosistes et les Deistes*, vol. 1 (Paris, 1751), 458–63.

31. Astruc, *Conjectures*, 9, in the anonymous German translation: *Muth-massungen in Betreff der Originalberichte, deren sich Moses wahrscheinlicherweise bey Verfertigung des ersten seiner Bücher bedient hat* (Frankfurt a. M., 1783), 10f.

For this claim, he provides four points of support (*preuves*): (1) the repetition of the same events, (2) the alternation between God's names Elohim and Jehovah (which is how he read it), (3) the lack of this alternation, seen on the whole in the rest of the Pentateuch, from Exod 3 onwards where Moses no longer depends on tradition but gives an eyewitness account, and (4) the anachronisms (*antichronismes*).

Now, the path is free for the work on the text. Let us listen to Astruc's report, which belongs to the classical documents of our guild of biblical studies:

> Following these considerations, it was only natural to make an attempt to take the First Book of Moses apart (*decomposer*), to separate all the various mixed up pieces, to put back together those that were of the same kind and in all probability belonged to the same account and thus to bring those original accounts (*mémoires originaux*), which I believe Moses had at his disposal, back into their original order. This task was not as difficult as one might have thought; it was just a question of putting together all the pieces (*endroits*) in which God is always called Elohim. I set them in a column that I called A, and I considered them to be bits and pieces, or if you will, fragments (*fragmens*) of a first original account that I designate with the letter A. Next to them, in another column that I called B, I placed all the other pieces in which God was only called Jehovah. By this means, I had assembled all the pieces, or at least all the fragments of the second account B. In assigning these pieces, I took into consideration neither the division of the First Book of Moses into chapters nor the chapters in verses, because it is certain that these divisions are new and arbitrary.
>
> As I progressed, I became aware that I would have to assume the existence of further accounts. In the First Book of Moses, there are a few places, for example in the description of the Flood, where the same things are repeated even three times. Since the name of God is not mentioned in these places and there is, therefore, no reason to connect them with either of the first accounts, I considered it best to assume they belonged to a third account designated C and to include them in a third column, C.
>
> There are other places in which God is also not mentioned and which, therefore, belong neither to column A nor to column B. Where I assumed that the incidents did not belong to the history of the Hebrew nation, I put them in a fourth column, D, and related them to a fourth account. I actually doubt that all these pieces ever belonged to one and the same account, and I should probably have divided them up even more. But the treatment of this problem is not important enough to deserve that one should waste time on it. I shall address it elsewhere.[32]

I follow this translation here. It may be mentioned here that in 1999 P. Gibert prepared a useful new edition of the *Conjectures* in the *Classiques de l'histoire des religions*.

32. *Conjectures*, 17–18.

This is followed by the text of Gen 1–Exod 2 in French, and namely from the Geneva Bible of 1610. Astruc provides a practical reason for this decision,[33] but it may also be taken as a sign that he acknowledged his paternal tradition for his biblical studies.[34] He says that Moses had placed the accounts that he had at his disposal in columns next to each other in the style of the Tetrapla,[35] but in his own work they appear sequentially in the order of the present biblical text, only that A (the "Elohist") was on the left, B (the "Jehovist") on the right-hand side of the page, and the C and D parts in the centre. It is the same principle that was later followed especially by Eissfeldt in his *Hexateuchsynopse*, although just a brief glimpse at the appearance of the two synopses reveals how much the analysis had been refined in the scholarship subsequent to Astruc's.

The third part of the *Conjectures* is concerned with the objections that Astruc foresaw: first, nobody could write before Moses. To this Astruc replies that in the story of the Exodus, reading and writing were presupposed. The Phoenician Kadmos introduced the alphabet to Greece, and before that, there were hieroglyphics (I). Furthermore, it seems from Exod 6:2–3 ("I appeared to Abraham, to Isaac, and to Jacob as El Shaddai, but by my name 'Jehovah' was I not known to them") that the patriarchs did not yet know the name "Jehovah." To this Astruc responds that this passage means "that God was well known to the patriarchs in the full extent of the meaning 'Shaddai,' but not as 'Jehovah'" (II). Finally, if report D, which incidentally can be divided up into ten shorter reports, stemmed from neighbouring nations, how could Moses have presented it in Hebrew? Astruc's answer is that Hebrew was the language of all the people of Canaan and of Abraham's descendants; besides, Moses was capable of translating (III–V). In this context, Astruc adds an insightful remark relating the degree of certainty of his proposals:

> One can only make speculations (*conjectures*), which can freely be accepted or rejected. Thus, if deemed appropriate, one can restrict the last ten reports to a smaller number. In contrast, one can divide up the first reports (A and B) into more, since in the final analysis, there is nothing preventing the assumption that there could have been more than one report in which the author gave God the name Elohim, and also more than

33. Ibid., 18–21.
34. During Astruc's lifetime rumors were already circulating that the father had composed the *Conjectures* and that the son had only published them (cf. Huard and Imbault-Huart, *Biographies médicales et scientifiques*, 286); I find no support for this view.
35. *Conjectures*, 433.

one in which the author called God Jehovah. Since one should not assume anything without a reason or at least an apparent reason, one should also not reject anything without having at least plausible reasons.[36]

Having refuted all objections, Astruc developed, largely in recourse to the "proofs" in the introduction, four "advantages" (*avantages*) of his hypothesis: (1) "It saves (*sauve*) the peculiarity of the alternation between the usage of the two names for God." Here the exceptions are explained, with the result that they confirm the rule (VI, VII), (2) "It saves (*sauve*) most of the repetitions found in the First Book of Moses in that it separates them into different reports" (VIII, IX), (3) "It solves the problem of the antichronisms, i.e. disorder in the chronology" (X–XIII), and (4) "It exonerates (*disculpe*) Moses from any negligence or mistakes that anyone ventured to accuse him of and that some believe to be found in the First Book of Moses." These aspects derive from the fact that the scribes were negligent in combining the columns of Moses' texts and have in this way given the impression of a chronologically correct order (XIV, XV).

This point provides Astruc with a reason to discuss, in conclusion, a problem that he ignored at the beginning of the book when he tacitly assumes that Moses was the author of the Pentateuch. The "negligence" and "mistakes" in the text were cited as an argument by Spinoza in his criticism, which Astruc now believes to be refuted. He takes this opportunity to take on Hobbes, de la Peyrère, le Clerc and Simon by responding to their denial of the Mosaic authorship of the Pentateuch. In his opinion, the testimony of Philip (John 1:45), not to mention the testimony of Christ (John 5:46), which both explicitly refer to Moses, would actually have sufficed as a refutation. But he adds something of his own, following, as he says, the widow in the Gospel (Mark 12:41–44) who gave her two mites, and he hopes, like her, to be praised for it.

Against Spinoza, Astruc argues that Ezra could not have been responsible for the Pentateuch, because, after the Babylonian exile, the Samaritans could not have adopted it. Thus, it must have existed in its entirety before the Exile. But it could also not represent the work of the anonymous priest from 2 Kgs 17:28, as proposed by Richard Simon. Apart from the fact that this priest is unknown, how could he have had the original reports at his disposal of which the Pentateuch consists? (XVI). Almost as an addendum, but with an almost tormenting attention to detail (XVII), Astruc discusses the Edomite chapter Gen 36 (v. 31: "before there reigned any king over the children of Israel") with the result that

36. Ibid., 315.

also here "there is nothing that would be a problem, that would antedate the time of Moses and, therefore, nothing that provides the defenders of religion with the mistrust that they voice or would justify the triumphal tone of those who pretend to be freethinkers" (XVII).[37]

Thus, what Astruc had said elsewhere about his hypothesis, namely that through the "new arrangement" (*ce nouvel arrangement*) of the text of Genesis,

> Moses will be fully exonerated (*pleinement disculpé*) from all mistakes of negligence or inattentiveness that even the most cautious commentators have ascribed to him. It will strengthen respect and belief (*le respect et la foi*) for him as far as it is owed to the wisest legislator and one of the greatest prophets awakened by God. And at the same time, it must increase the belief in him as the clearest, most exact and most truthful of the "historians" (*le plus clair, le plus exact, et le plus vrai des Historiens*).[38]

IV

It can hardly be said more clearly than with Astruc's own words: his *Conjectures* follow an apologetic aim. The key word of the book is "*sauve*/save" (*Notabene*: also, the name of Astruc's birth place! And a second, more serious, *Notabene*: in the same year 1753/54 Gotthold Ephraim Lessing began the series of his "Rettungen"!). No one less than Ernest Renan doubted that Astruc was telling the truth in this regard. Might he not have intended, said Renan, "by loudly proclaiming his agreement with a traditional opinion on one point [the Mosaic authorship], to secure the right to express a new opinion on another point [the use of sources] that seemed to be a risk?"[39] Adolphe Lods has taken Astruc under his protection against this suspicion, and rightly so.[40] In questions of the Bible, religion and the church, Astruc was clearly on the side of tradition against the free thinkers, materialists and encyclopaedists. The opposition—D'Alembert, Grimm, Voltaire—paid him back with cutting invective long after his death.[41] However, his "*Avertissement*" reveals that he was indeed worried, and two years later he followed up the *Conjectures* with two philosophical treatises, one on the

37. Ibid., 495.
38. Ibid., 438 (489–90). See François, *Preuves de la religion de Jesus-Christ*, 458: "*Moyse est le premier Historien que nous connoissions.*"
39. Preface to A. Kuenen, *Histoire critique des livres de l'Ancient Testament*, vol. 1 (1866), xxiii.
40. Lods, "Astruc et la critique biblique," 206.
41. See Ritter, "Jean Astruc," 279–86; Huard and Imbault-Huart, *Biographies médicales et scientifiques*, 11.

soul and the other on freedom.[42] They appear to have been written with the secondary objective of removing, *comme un garant de sa foi*, any doubts in this regard.[43]

These concerns were unfounded, as was also the hope of the author, assuming that he had it, that the *Conjectures* would occasion a fruitful discussion in his fatherland; there, they produced almost no echo whatsoever.[44] On the other hand, a response was heard in Germany, although without mention of Astruc's name, from the pen of the unavoidable Johann David Michaelis. He reviewed the work in two Göttingen periodicals, in German and Latin, and the latter was especially verbose.[45] Michaelis treated the book "in very condescending manner."[46] Astruc's motto of the "un-tread paths" appeared to him "to be the fruit of not reading enough before writing," above all not enough of the products of the house of Michaelis.[47] The dispute in general is rather unproductive and shows that Michaelis had not noticed the importance of the possibility, discovered by Astruc, of solving the source-problem in Genesis with

42. J. Astruc, *Dissertation sur l'immatérialité et l'immortalité de l'ame. Dissertation sur la liberté* (Paris, 1755).

43. This opinion is already expressed by Lorry in Astruc (*Mémoires pour servir*, 1) and is countered by Alphandéry, "Jean Astruc," 67–68. Cf. Astruc's double explanation: "La hardiesse, avec laquelle le Matérialisme s'enseigne, m'a engagé à composer cette Dissertation" (*Dissertation sur l'immatérialité*, i). "Cette Dissertation, comme on voit, n'a été entreprise, que pour la défense de la Religion..." (*Dissertation sur la liberté*, vii–viii).

44. See J.-R. Armogathe, in Y. Belaval and D. Bourel, eds., *Le siècle des Lumières et la Bible* (Paris: Beauchesne, 1986), 437–38; B.-E. Schwarzbach, ibid., 764.

45. Michaelis, review of Astruc, *Conjectures*, *GGA* (1754): 973–76; idem, review of Astruc, *Conjectures*, *Relationes de libris novis* 11 (1754): 162–94. He confesses to be the author in his *Einleitung in die göttlichen Schriften des Alten Bundes*, vol. 1/1 (Hamburg, 1787), 268. His own copy of the *Conjectures*, which is located in the Tübingen Stiftsbibliothek (cf. H. Holzinger, *Einleitung in den Hexateuch* [1893], 41), contains, except for his name, no other notes from his own hand.

46. Holzinger, *Einleitung in den Hexateuch*; cf. Westphal, *Les sources du Pentateuque*, 1:116: "quelle hauteur"!

47. Michaelis, review of Astruc, 974 (the Dr. Christian Benedict mentioned there is Johann David's father). Neither Astruc nor Michaelis, who for geographical reasons had even less of an excuse, knew of the work of the scholar from Hildesheim, H. B. Witter, *Jura Israelitarum in Palaestinam* (Hildesheim, 1711), in which the repetitions and the alternation in the divine designations are noted; cf. A. Lods, "Un précurseur allemand de Jean Astruc: Henning Bernhard Witter," *ZAW* 43 (1925): 134–35.

the aid of the divine designations.[48] Perhaps it was this review that allowed the Abbot Jerusalem to feel legitimated in calling, with the naiveté of the dilettante (or from one dilettante to another!), Astruc's thesis "ungrounded and silly."[49] Yet Michaelis did not remain on his high horse for long. Decades later he returned to the thesis, now knowing that its author was the "famous medicus" whose "great perceptiveness" he praised.[50] He concluded a detailed, although not completely accurate, report with an outlook:

> For the second part of his *Introduction*, Herr Privy Councillor Eichhorn has reworked the Astrucian system, with which he is in more agreement than I, and has improved some pieces and presented it in a more plausible and pleasing way than Astruc himself. To quote sections of his work here would be unnecessary and would take us too far astray. One can read Herr Eichhorn's opinion for oneself.[51]

Having said this, Michaelis passed the staff on to his Göttingen successor, Eichhorn, who to be sure already possessed it and who, as he did elsewhere,[52] subtly concealed his connection to Astruc.[53] On this point, however, he advanced beyond Astruc and added to the "proofs" of the repetitions and the alternation in the names for God two others: the "evidence from the writing style" and "the difference of the characters."[54] Whereas for Astruc the "Jehovistic" and the "Elohistic" sources hardly began to assume an external and internal physiognomy, Eichhorn's criteria enabled a new and more thorough analysis of the sources in Genesis. Finally, it broadened the perspective to the entire Pentateuch, while abandoning the path taken by Astruc. "With the third chapter [of the book of Exodus], all the peculiarities cease that were characteristic for the historian in the First Book of Moses and in the first two chapters of the Second Book, and the work of a single individual continues until

48. See R. Smend, *Johann David Michaelis* (Göttingen, 1898), 6.
49. J. F. W. Jerusalem, *Briefe über die mosaischen Schriften und Philosophie*, vol. 1 (2d ed.; Braunschweig, 1772), 107; cf. 108.
50. Holzinger, *Einleitung in den Hextateuch*, 268.
51. Ibid., 301.
52. See R. Smend, *Deutsche Alttestamentler in drei Jahrhunderten* (Göttingen: Vandenhoeck & Ruprecht, 1989), 31–32.
53. See M. Siemens, "Hat J. G. Eichhorn die Conjectures von J. Astruc gekannt, als er 1779 seine Abhandlung über 'Mosis Nachrichten von der Noachischen Flut' veröffentlichte?," *ZAW* 28 (1908): 221–23.
54. J. C. Eichhorn, *Einleitung ins Alte Testament*, II (1781), 310ff., 319ff. Here he commissioned an assistant in Göttingen to collect further material: J. F. W. Möller, *Über die Verschiedenheit des Styls der beyden Haupt-Urkunden der Genesis* (Göttingen, 1792).

the end of the Books of Moses." This statement—formulated very à la Astruc—is found in the first three editions of Eichhorn's *Introduction to the Old Testament*,[55] the fourth of which from 1823 gives it precision and makes several changes:

> both of the chief designations for God alternate without any decipherable difference from this point on, until finally Jehovah is for the most part the only name used for God, since Israel, whose history is told here, has submitted to his reign and protection. Moses is from here on out the leading hero of the story. If we still have articles from his own hand, he could have guided the pen starting only at this point.[56]

It is thus no longer the work of a single individual, namely Moses, that renders source division from Exod 3 onwards superfluous, since we have only various "articles" from him. Henceforth, source criticism is no longer occupied with the two great "documents" of Genesis (and their subsidiary sources), but rather with diverse "articles," whether they derive from Moses or not. Here it begins to become apparent that a single hypothesis cannot do justice to the complex state of affairs in the Pentateuch. By 1823, the Fragmentary Hypothesis, and essentially also the Supplementary Hypothesis, had been around for some time. But the Documentary Hypothesis held, and still holds, its own, although with the source divisions that Astruc foresaw as he wrote in passing: in the end "nothing prevents the assumption that there was more than one report in which the author gave God the name Elohim..." This possibility was taken seriously by two scholars, Karl David Ilgen and Hermann Hupfeld, who as "Astruc's most important successors" (Wellhausen[57]) improved upon the "Elohistic Document" by dividing it into two. And as they replaced the "Older Documentary Hypothesis" with the "Newer Documentary Hypothesis,"[58] which is how one usually describes it, they paid homage to Astruc: "The physician who possessed unbelievable insights here as well as in his own profession" (Ilgen),[59] and "he was a layman, but a thinker with real critical gifts" (Hupfeld).[60]

55. Eichhorn, *Einleitung ins Alte Testamen*, II (1st ed., 1781) 409; (2d ed., 1787) 348; (3d ed., 1803) 387.

56. Eichhorn, *Einleitung ins Alte Testamen*, II (4th ed., 1823), 178.

57. F. Bleek, *Einleitung in das Alte Testament* (ed. J. Wellhausen; 4th ed.; Berlin, 1878), 655.

58. See O. Eissfeldt, *Einleitung in das Alte Testament* (3d ed.; Tübingen: J. C. B. Mohr [Paul Siebeck], 1964), 213–14, 216–17.

59. C. D. Ilgen, *Die Urkunden des Jerusalemischen Tempelarchivs in ihrer Urgestalt*, vol. 1 (Halle, 1798), x.

60. H. Hupfeld, *Die Quellen der Genesis* (Berlin, 1853), 11.

These assessments sound almost like Wellhausen's description of de Wette: he is "a bright fellow," to which he added, one can find in his works everything he himself wrote on the Old Testament.[61] Wellhausen could not have said the latter about Astruc inasmuch as historical criticism was foreign to his studies. It was first introduced—apart from exceptional pioneers in this, as in every, field—by de Wette and then integrated with literary criticism by Wellhausen himself—again apart from the few exceptional pioneers. Astruc's argumentation with respect to historical questions, above all in his defence of Mosaic authorship, "is in details unusually naive, even for his age." By "recognizing historical connections," his hypothesis represents "a retrogression from the views of le Clerc and especially of Spinoza."[62] Considering the influence exerted by the *Conjectures*, one could laugh these days about "*cette solution*" even more than Père de Vaux already did in his 1953 jubilee address.[63] Yet, de Vaux had explicitly recognized the importance of this "solution" for research leading up to Wellhausen. And as far as Astruc's apologetic aim is concerned, Wellhausen should have the last word. About his predecessor's *Conjectures* he said: "This criticism is indeed the only way to understand and defend the biblical books."[64] The fact that we must apply the scalpel differently than Astruc did, does not lessen his merit. According to Voltaire's last comment on the *Conjectures*, uttered in 1776, "This book did not live up to its promise."[65] In the introduction to this paper, I remarked respectfully: "Here, Goethe is mistaken." Now I add respectfully: Here, Voltaire is mistaken.

61. Cf. Smend, *Deutsche Alttestamentler in drei Jahrhunderten*, 38.

62. M. Soloweitschik, "Astruc, Jean," *EJ (D)* 3 (1929): 611–13.

63. R. de Vaux, "A propos du second centenaire d'Astruc—réflexions sur l'état actuel de la critique du Pentateuque," in *Congress Volume: Copenhagen, 1953* (VTSup 1; Leiden, Brill, 1953), 182–98 (183).

64. Bleek, *Einleitung in das Alte Testament*, 655.

65. *La Bible enfin expliquée par plusieurs aumoniers de S. M. L. R. D. P.* (1777): *Oeuvres complêtes de Voltaire, nouv. ed.* (52 vols.; Paris, 1877–85), vol. 30 (Paris, 1880), 50 n. 1.

DE L'INTUITION A L'EVIDENCE:
LA MULTIPLICITE DOCUMENTAIRE DANS LA GENESE
CHEZ H. B. WITTER ET JEAN ASTRUC

Pierre Gibert

Parler de « théorie documentaire » ou de « principe documentaire » pour rendre compte de la composition du Pentateuque, revient à parler de l'histoire d'une longue intuition dont S. Jérôme serait un des premiers témoins. Mais ce n'est qu'au XVIIe siècle, en France en particulier, que la question de documents antérieurs à la composition du Pentateuque est devenue pressante. Ainsi, lorsque Richard Simon, dans l'*Histoire critique du Vieux Testament* (1678), affirme que « Moïse ne peut être l'auteur de tout ce qui est dans les livres qui lui sont attribués » (Liv I, chp. V), il invoque ici comme prédécesseurs contestataires Maesisus, La Pereyre et Bonfrère. Le premier argument est alors classique, et tient au principe de vraisemblance littéraire: Moïse n'a pu écrire le récit de sa mort ! Corrélativement, deux autres arguments sont aussi avancés, celui de la différence des genres littéraires et des styles qui laissent supposer l'utilisation d'autres ouvrages ; et aussi l'argument de la vraisemblance historique excluant l'anachronisme,—les « antichronismes » dira Astruc: Moïse ne pouvait, par ex., parler des Cananéens qu'il ne connaissait pas.

Ainsi, selon les intuitions et déductions du maître de Dieppe, le Pentateuque est pris entre, d'une part, des rédactions et même des livres antérieurs à l'activité scripturaire de Moïse, et, d'autre part, des rédactions et additions qui lui seraient postérieures.

R. Simon accorde là une place importante à ceux qu'il appelle des « écrivains publics »—ce que nous dirions aujourd'hui « écrivains officiels »—de la « République des Hébreux », écrivains qui, dans ce cadre culturel, auraient donc préparé et conditionné le travail de Moïse, mais aussi assuré d'éventuelles additions à son œuvre.

Le XVIIe siècle n'ira pas plus loin. Ainsi, de Maesius à Simon, sans oublier Spinoza et Le Clerc, on se contenterait alors d'argumenter à partir des principes de cohérence, de non contradiction, voire de vraisemblance historique, sans oublier l'exigence littéraire d'unité de style et d' « ordre »—ce sont alors des obsessions bien françaises, on dira plus tard « cartésiennes »—avec le rejet de la répétition et de toute forme de « désordre ».

Il appartiendra donc au XVIIIe siècle de dépasser le stade de l'intuition, des idées et principes généraux, grâce en particulier à Witter et Astruc qui descendront, pour ainsi dire, sur le terrain du texte, tels des laboureurs, pour le retourner.

Ce qui va se passer avec ces deux auteurs de génie et qui ne pouvaient que s'ignorer, a cependant quelque chose d'étrange: la différence et la complémentarité de leurs approches aboutissant à une forte convergence de résultats et d'ouvertures.

Avant de faire l'analyse comparatiste de ces approches et résultats, je voudrais souligner ce « mouvement » des esprits qui, entre le premier tiers du XVIIe siècle dans les Pays-Bas de l'époque et le nord de la France, et la seconde moitié du XVIIIe siècle en Allemagne, en Suède et bientôt en Angleterre, convergent dans le même questionnement et le même type de réponses. Certes, demeurent les différences de points de départ, des divergences pouvant aller parfois jusqu'à la polémique, notamment entre catholiques et protestants, en France notamment. Mais, dès la fin du XVIIe siècle, une « République des lettres » se met en place qui transcendera ces « partis » tant politiques et culturels que religieux.

En effet, tous témoignent alors de cet « esprit du temps » dont parlera Tocqueville au XIXe siècle, esprit qui se manifeste dans la convergence d'idées, de questions et de réponses dans des lieux et milieux qui peuvent d'abord n'avoir aucune communication. Witter et Astruc, de par leurs situations respectives, géographiques, sociales, religieuses, témoignent avec Lowth de cet « esprit du temps » que chacun respire et partage, sans nécessairement se connaître ni s'être jamais rencontrés, fut-ce par livre interposé.

Ils sont assez exactement contemporains: Witter naît en 1683, et Astruc en 1684, mais l'un à Hildesheim, au sud de Hanovre, l'autre près de Nîmes, à Sauve, dans le sud protestant de la France. Mais lorsque Witter meurt en 1715, à 32 ans, ayant déjà donné son grand œuvre, Astruc pense d'abord à sa carrière médicale qui en fera l'un des plus grands médecins du Royaume, et le fera bientôt désigner médecin du roi Louis XV, tandis que Witter fut, de 1707 à sa mort, pasteur luthérien à Hildesheim.

Si Astruc a lu Richard Simon et Spinoza entre autres, il n'a pas eu la moindre connaissance de l'ouvrage de Witter paru en 1711. C'est pourtant à cet ouvrage que 40 ans plus tard il fera plus que donner un écho. Ainsi allait l'esprit du temps…

Pourtant grande est la différence entre les deux démarches qui vont aboutir à une étape décisive dans l'intelligence de la composition du Pentateuque et donc de sa nature.

Dans une brève note des ZAW de 1925 (p. 134–135), A. Lods, qui fut l'un des rares historiens biographes d'Astruc, établit ainsi le rapport entre celui-ci et Witter:

> …ayant à étudier les idées qui avaient cours avant 1753 sur les moyens d'information dont avait disposé l'auteur de la Genèse, j'ai eu l'occasion de signaler un auteur peu connu, qui, quarante ans avant le médecin français, a esquissé clairement la méthode que ce critique d'occasion allait appliquer d'une façon si géniale: c'est Henning Bernhardt Witter, pasteur à Hildesheim. (p. 134).

La question qu'on peut d'abord se poser est celle de « l'esquisse claire » de la méthode, et surtout celle de la proximité des deux approches. Autrement dit: quel est le degré exact de similitude entre la méthode d'Astruc et celle de Witter ?

L'ouvrage de Witter est, selon la mode du temps, longuement intitulé: *Jura israelitarum in Palaestinam Terram Chananaeam Commentatione in Genesin Perpetua sic demonstrata ut idiomatis authentici nativus sensus fideliter detegatur, Mosis autoris primaeva intentio sollicite desiniatur, adeoque corpus doctrinae et juris Cum antiquissimum, tum consumatissimum tandem eruatur.*

En fait, ce long titre met l'accent sur une sorte d'a priori: le « droit des Israélites en Palestine » entendu dans le double sens d'une légitimité et légitimation de la possession de la « Terre de Canaan », et d'un ensemble de lois à y observer.

L'ouvrage est donc rédigé en latin, un latin redondant et parfois grandiloquent, surtout dans la longue dédicace et la préface. Malgré cela, il ouvre assez vite à sa problématique et à sa méthodologie.

La problématique n'est pas radicalement originale. Si l'on passe sur les « indications » et « affirmations générales »,[1] on peut situer Witter dans la mouvance, voire au terme, d'une généalogie d'auteurs au questionnement plus précis ou aux hypothèses plus argumentées que celle des La Peyrère, Spinoza et Richard Simon. Ici, trois ou quatre noms méritent d'être évoqués.

---

1. Selon les expressions d'Adolphe Lods dans *Jean Astruc et la critique biblique au XVIIIe siècle, avec une notice biographique par Paul Alphandéry* (Strasbourg: Librairie Istra, 1924), 49. Voir aussi H. Bardtke, « Henning Bernhard Witter. Zur 250. Wiederkehr seiner Promotion zum Philosophiae Doctor am 6. November 1704 zu Helmstedt », *ZAW* 66 (1954): 153–81.

Au premier rang, il faut citer Campegius Vitringa (1659–1722), hollandais, qui, dans ses *Observationes sacrae* (1683), au livre I, chap. IV, parle des Patriarches, les *Patres Ecclesiae*, qui ont laissé l'expression des révélations divines qui leur avaient été adressées, ou des récits d'autrui, le tout sous forme de « mémoires » et de « recueils », « conservés chez les Israélites », et que Moïse « a réunis, disposés, développés et complétés là où ils présentaient des lacunes », et grâce auxquels « il a composé le premier de ses livres »[2].

Dans la ligne directe de ce qui fera l'originalité de Witter, Vitringa dit clairement qu'en Gn 2,4, « sont répétées quelques-unes des choses qui avaient été dites au chapitre précédent sur la création du ciel et de la terre, la production des herbes et leur mode d'apparition, la formation de l'homme fait d'une âme et d'un corps… » Et la femme, qui avait été créée le 6e jour, n'avait pu l'être après le 7e !

Certes, les arguments de Vitringa restent faibles, notamment pour le repérage de différents documents, par des formules stéréotypées notamment

Plus proches du travail de Witter, il faut citer ici Jean Le Clerc et Dom Calmet, dont il ne semble pas qu'il ait eu connaissance des œuvres.

Le plus explicite, le plus prudent aussi, est Jean Le Clerc. Echaudé par ses désaccords avec les frères Turetini qui régnaient en maître à l'Académie de Genève, il dut quitter la cité de Calvin pour se réfugier à Amsterdam. Ainsi prend-il un luxe de précautions pour affirmer ce qui lui paraît malgré tout sauter aux yeux. Dans les *Sentimens de quelques théologiens de Hollande sur l'*Histoire critique du Vieux Testament *composée par le P. R. Simon de l'Oratoire* (1685), il confirme la plupart des principes et résultats des recherches de Simon et reconnaît explicitement que dans le Pentateuque il y a « trois sortes de choses, dont les unes étaient postérieures au temps de Moïse, les autres devraient avoir été écrites de son temps, et les autres enfin, avant le temps même de Moïse. »[3].

Ainsi parle-t-il de « l'auteur du Pentateuque », comme s'il plaçait implicitement Moïse parmi les auteurs de ces « vieux mémoires » qui composent le Pentateuque. A la base de sa réflexion, Le Clerc place dix-huit passages qui prouvent soit l'antiquité, soit l'anachronisme (postérieur) par rapport à Moïse. Son argumentation est donc de type historique et corrélativement de cohérence littéraire.

2. Cité par Lods, *Jean Astruc et la critique biblique*, 50
3. Ibid., 107.

Mais dans sa *Dissertatio* de 1693, il semblera se rétracter en faveur de l'authenticité mosaïque totale, en fait sans grande conviction ni surtout arguments décisifs !

Si je cite ici Dom Calmet, et même Bossuet dans son *Discours sur l'Histoire universelle* (1707), c'est surtout pour confirmer cet « esprit du temps » dans lequel s'exprime Witter. Tous deux reconnaissent que des textes ont été utilisés par Moïse, qui ont pu le précéder depuis une haute antiquité. Retenons que pour ces très orthodoxes auteurs, la chose paraît alors aller de soi...

En résumé, avant d'aborder vraiment la réflexion de Witter et son apport méthodologique, constatons le caractère général et parfois hésitant de ces affirmations dont le processus de production est plus d'ordre intuitif que vraiment rationnel, même si étaient avancés des arguments pris dans le texte. Manquait encore, au seuil du XVIIIe siècle, une véritable méthodologie, compte tenu cependant du fait que les principes d'une épistémologie avaient été nettement mis en place par Spinoza et Richard Simon, ce dernier relevant dans le texte biblique un certain nombre de données propres à fonder ou justifier ses questions et ses hypothèses.

A mon sens, l'originalité de Witter est d'arriver plus minutieusement, pourrait-on dire, sur le terrain du texte en tant que le texte n'est pas seulement « relation historique » ; pour lui, il ne suffit donc par d'apprécier sa cohérence et sa véracité de ce seul point de vue. Car le texte a pour lui une *dimension littéraire* tout aussi révélatrice de sa complexité.

Cette dimension littéraire tient, lointainement, à l'idée générale que Witter se fait de la rédaction du Pentateuque dominée par l'expression des « Droits des Israélites sur la Palestine ». C'est pourquoi,

> Moïse fait remonter le début de ses écrits à celui du monde afin de justifier par un repère certain dans le temps le point de départ de ses commentaires sur les générations humaines, leurs successions, leurs âges, destins et actions, et dont découleraient les droits de son peuple hébreu. (Exegesis capitis primi, § 1, p. 19[4])

Si donc « rien n'est plus ancien que sa création entière par le Tout-Puissant », ce qui explique que « Moïse entame son Pentateuque par son

---

4. *Moses Jura Israelitarum in Palaestinam ab ipsa mundi origine derivat. (...) Unde Moses exordium scripturae suae ab exordio mundi derivat, quo de certo aloquo temporis, mundique principio constateret, a quo hominum geneses, successiones, aetates, fata et facta computarentur, atque Jura gentis suae Hebraeae derivarentur.*—La traduction, inédite, du latin au français est de R. Vandamme. La numérotation des paragraphes (§) et la pagination sont celles de l'édition originale de Witter.

évocation » (§ 4, p. 21), « à la vérité, Moïse semble voir rapporté l'histoire de la création, moins avec ses propres mots qu'avec ceux de quelque poète ancien. »[5] (§ 5, p. 21).

Par rapport à ceux qu'on peut considérer comme ses prédécesseurs, Simon y compris, il faut ici souligner l'introduction que fait Witter du concept de poésie, même s'il ne s'agit d'abord que de « quelque poète ancien ».

Rejoignant par d'autres chemins l'idée de documents antérieurs initiés par ses prédécesseurs—et que nous retrouverons chez Astruc sous la désignation de « Mémoires » -, l'intérêt et l'originalité de cette position sont donc de faire une place particulière et particulièrement forte à la poésie.

> Il est indiscutable, en effet, que, chez les Hébreux, de nombreux cantiques ou poèmes ont été composés bien avant la rédaction du Pentateuque et introduits dans le culte sacré pour proclamer les bienfaits et miracles divins. Myriam pousse vivement son peuple à célébrer l'admirable pouvoir de Dieu manifesté contre les Egyptiens en magnifiant par des hymnes la bienveillance de la Divinité, sans faire mention d'un cantique en particulier (Ex 15,21). Et ce n'est absolument pas étonnant que l'origine de la poésie remonte à des temps si anciens puisque l'on avait commencé à pratiquer la musique elle-même déjà avant le déluge. (Gn 4,21)

« Ainsi donc, les humains, dépourvus de l'usage des lettres composèrent d'abord des poèmes plus simples, et ensuite rimés et rythmés pour être plus facilement mémorisés (Ex 15,1 ; Gn 3,24 et 7,11). »[6] (§ 5 p. 21–22).

Witter part, lui aussi, de l'intuition de l'antériorité de documents au travail de Moïse, mais en valorisant particulièrement la poésie qu'il associe d'abord à la pratique conservatoire de l'oralité, idée d'ailleurs assez courante dans le XVIIIe siècle germanique.

---

5. *Unde..., ab istius delineatione Pentateuchum suum Moses orditur (§4)— Creatiois vero historiam non tam suis, quam antique alicujus poetae verbis videtur tradere Moses (§5).*

6. *Inter Hebraeos enim plurima cantica vel poemata jam ante Pentateuchi consignationem a piis viris concinnata, atque in usum sacrum depraedicandis beneficiis miraculis divinis adhibita fuisse, negari nequit. Mirjam mirabilem Dei potentiam in Aegyptos exertam celebratura gentem suam concitat, ut canticis benevolentiam Numinis efferat, nulla singularis cantici injecta mentione (Ex 15,21). Neque sane mirum, poeseos initia ad tam prisca tempora referri, cum ipsa musica jam ante diluvium excoli coeperit (Gn 4,21). Unde poemata, cum literarum usu destitueruntur mortals, confecerunt primum simpliciora, deinde, quo facilius memoriae mandarentur, et rythmica (Ex 15,1 ; Gn 3,24 ; 7,11)*

De ces œuvres transmises de père en fils et répandues par la tradition
orale, Moïse, avec le soutien de Dieu, tirera l'ensemble du Pentateuque.
A ces cantiques peut-être, et à ce que j'appelle 'poèmes', décrivant
sommairement la naissance du monde, il faudra rapporter ce qu'ensuite a
rédigé Moïse. Ce sont, d'après mon sentiment, des considérations très
sérieuses. »[7] (§ 5, p. 22)

On sait le sort que réservera Astruc à cette fameuse « tradition
orale »[8]. Retenons pour l'instant l'accent mis sur la poésie, et avant de
continuer, comme il le fait, sur la désignation de « Dieu » en Gn 1 (et
non point de « YHWH »), citons la question que pose Witter et qui
induit, sans conscience claire, la distinction de deux récits de création:

> Pourquoi Moïse a-t-il renvoyé dans le deuxième chapitre seulement ce
> qui, à l'évidence, regarde l'histoire du deuxième et du sixième jour (Gn
> 2,5ss), alors que dans le premier chapitre il avait achevé et parfait
> l'histoire de la création (Gn 2,1)? Quelle liaison, quelle explication
> donnera-t-on de cette disposition? A moins de supposer que Moïse, pour
> des raisons du plus grand sérieux, n'a, pour son projet, mis en lumière
> qu'après coup ce poème antique, parce qu'il ne répondait pas entièrement
> à son intention.

Et d'ajouter cet argument qui peut nous paraître aujourd'hui étrange-
ment pédagogique:

> Notre hypothèse ne comprend rien d'absurde, sauf si je m'égare en tout
> point. Il a préféré commencer par ce cantique, ou 'poème' si l'on préfère,
> qui serait sur les lèvres de tous et très connu de son peuple, pour l'inciter
> ainsi à une lecture empressée de son Pentateuque.[9] (§ 5 p. 23).

---

7. *E quibus monumentis et orali traditione propagatis, Deo adminiculante,*
Pentateuchum collegit Moses. Ad quae cantica fortassis hoc quoque, quod dico,
poema, creationem mundi summatim exhibens, postea a Mose literis mandatum
referendum erit. Sunt enim, ut ita sentiam, rationes gravissimae.

8. « Ceux » qui pensent que « la connaissance des faits antérieurs ait pu être
transmise à Moïse…par une tradition purement orale, c'est-à-dire de bouche à
bouche…ne manquent pas de profiter de la longue vie des patriarches pour faire
remarquer que cette tradition orale a pu se transmettre d'Adam jusqu'à Moïse par un
très petit nombre de personnes… Ils prétendent par là rendre la tradition plus facile
et plus sûre, en évitant de la faire passer par un trop grand nombre de mains où elle
aurait pu s'obscurcir, s'affaiblir, s'altérer. Mais le nombre de ceux par qui les faits
ont pu parvenir de main en main jusqu'à Moïse, fût-il plus petit, il est difficile de se
persuader que, dans une tradition plusieurs fois répétée, on ait pu se souvenir
exactement de la description topographique du Paradis terrestre…de l'âge de chaque
Patriarche, du temps précis où ils ont commencé d'avoir des enfants, et de celui où
ils sont morts… » etc *Conjectures sur la Genèse* [(1753); ed. P. Gibert; Paris:
Noésis, 1999), 133–34.

9. *Denique, quare, quae ad secundi sextique diei historiam aperre spectant, in*
secundum caput demum digessisser Moses? (Gn 2,5ss) cum intra primum caput

Revenons à l'évocation de traditions orales qui ont assuré la transmission du poème, évocation que Witter clôt par sa conviction selon laquelle ce sont des « considérations très sérieuses » qui de la part de Moïse font suite à ce poème. Et d'abord la précision du nom divin, YHWH, qui surgit en Gn 2.

> D'abord, en effet, dans tout ce que je nomme le 'cantique de Moïse', embrassant la perspective très courte du monde, le nom de Dieu en quatre lettres YHWH n'apparaît jamais, alors qu'il sera par la suite habituel chez Moïse.[10] (§ 5, p. 22)

Witter rappelle que la différence des désignations divines entre Yhwh et Elohim trouble depuis longtemps les commentateurs tant juifs que chrétiens. Cependant, quoi qu'il en soit des difficultés et tentatives d'explication, en ce qui concerne le chapitre premier de la Genèse, rien « ne fait absolument obstacle à cette opinion que la rédaction de Moïse soit inspirée de Dieu », et que « notre poème a obtenu la caution divine par la recommandation de Moïse » (§ 5, p. 23).

> Et, en effet, il ne faut pas penser que Moïse, Dieu lui tenant la main, a transcrit dans l'Ecriture sainte autre chose que ce qu'il avait reconnu comme vrai. Ensuite, même la grande diversité de style, qui apparaît à l'évidence entre ce premier chapitre et les suivants de Moïse, rend cela probable.[11] (§ 5, p. 23)

Il y a donc, pour Witter, une différence d'écriture qui se révèle ici, ce qu'il confirme un peu plus loin en parlant de ce qui est désormais pour nous un second récit de création. A propos de Gn 2,7 rapportant que « Jehova Dieu ayant formé l'homme de la poussière de la terre, insuffla dans ses narines le souffle de vie… », il écrit, se référant à Gn 1,27:

> Dans l'intervalle, pour que la vraie genèse de l'homme ainsi créé apparaisse au mieux, Moïse l'a développée plus précisément [en Gn 2,7], sans doute transmise par un ancien historiographe… Le style de Moïse,

historiam creationis absolverit et consummaverit (Gn 2,1). Quae connexio, quae ratio contextus dabitur ? nisi supponas ex tot gravissimis rationibus, Mosem antiquum hoc poema, quod ex asse non responderet intentioni suae, postmodum pro scopo suo paululum illustrasse. Neque enim absurdi quicquam, nisi me omnia fallunt, hypothesis nostra complectitur. Maluit autem ab ipso hoc cantico, vel, si mauis, poemata exordiri, quod in omnimum ore versaretur, atque genti suae notissimum, quo illam ad sedulam Pentateuchi sui lectionem sic invitaret.

10. *Primum enim in toto hoc, quod ita nuncupo, Mosis cantico, orbis perbrevem complexo, nomen Dei, Yhwh, nuspiam occurrit, quod posthac Mosi ordinarium.*

11. *...poema ex commendatione Mosis autoritatem divinam obtinuit. Neque enim, nisi quae vera deprehendit, Deo manuducentel, in scripturam sacram transtulisse Mosem existimandum est.*

complètement différent du reste de l'histoire des êtres vivants créés, suggère qu'il s'est soumis plus étroitement aux paroles dont il se souvenait. Dieu [en Gn 1] avait confié la genèse des autres vivants à la *vertu de la terre*, alors qu'absolument rien n'existait encore. Moïse utilise cependant une phrase similaire au sujet du mode de création de l'homme. Mais *celle-ci revient à Dieu sans intermédiaire: Jéhova créa l'homme*. Il faut donc nécessairement que la génération de l'homme soit de beaucoup différente, ce que Moïse a raconté de manière significative et de diverses façons.[12] (Exegesis capitis II, § 20, p. 85, *soulignés par Witter*)

Il est aujourd'hui tentant de sourire de ce que nous pourrions considérer là comme un mélange, sinon un entremêlement plus ou moins inextricable, de naïvetés et de justes intuitions que l'avenir se chargerait de séparer. En fait, nous saisissons là, sur le vif pour ainsi dire, l'émergence d'un processus d'intelligence d'un texte qui laisse percevoir tantôt sa complexité, tantôt l'évidence de ses différentes composantes.

Après Simon et avant Astruc pour la question des sources de Moïse, avant Lowth pour la poésie, Witter part, lui aussi, de l'intuition de l'antériorité de documents par rapport au travail de Moïse ; mais il introduit ici, en les renforçant, non seulement l'idée de traditions antérieures orales puis écrites, mais aussi celle de la spécificité de la poésie et du langage poétique.

Autrement dit, il se dégage d'une conception plus ou moins exclusivement narrative et historique du Pentateuque, pour intégrer le poème et le cantique dans l'héritage biblique, et donc dans les traditions orales et écrites reçues par Moïse.

Ainsi donc, Moïse a composé le Pentateuque avec de tels « monuments hérités des Pères et transmis par tradition orale. »

On peut penser que l'hypothèse qu'il émet ainsi relève d'abord de l'intuition, une intuition qui paraît quelque « peu hasardée » au dire de A. Lods[13]. Mais les « preuves » qu'il apporte, ajoute Lods, « sont des plus remarquables » !

---

12. *Interea vero, quo hominis ita conditi vera genesis apertissime constaret, Moses plenius illam edisserit, a priore Historiographo nimium concise traditam* (Gn 1,27). *Videlicet,* condidit Jehova Deux hominem pulverem de terra (*quod Latini dicerent* e pulvere terra) eique animam vivam inspiravit, ut animal vivum esset. *Stylus Moses plane a reliqua animantium generatorum historia alienus altius quippiam verbis memoratis subesse, suggerit. Reliquorum animantium genesin* terra virtuti *demandaverat Deus, ut nihilominus* viva *exstiterint. Qua simillima tamen phrasi de homine ita condito modo utitur Moses. At* hominis creatio Deo immediate *tribuitur:* Condidit Jehova hominem. *Necesse igitur est, longe diversam hominis generationem esse, quam adeo et significanter et diverse tradidit Moses.*

13. Lods, *Jean Astruc et la critique biblique*, 54.

De fait, et c'est sans doute la supériorité de Witter sur ses prédé-cesseurs, il argumente à partir des composantes du texte, c'est-à-dire de ce qu'il impose immédiatement. Aussi, dans son intuition d'abord, il « remarque » comme quelque chose d'immédiat que Gn 1 est un poème. Là encore, ainsi que le fait Lods, on peut s'étonner de cette reconnais-sance poétique faiblement argumentée. Mais c'est, à mon sens, la conception poétique de Lods qui est un peu courte: « à part quelques lignes rythmées (1,27) », tout lui paraît de « style purement prosaïque », et lui semble donc moins poétique que le « récit populaire » qui le suit, c'est-à-dire l'histoire d'Adam et Eve.

Lods est, lui aussi, de l' « esprit » de son « temps », où les études folkloriques projetées sur la Bible battaient leur plein en Allemagne, en Angleterre et bientôt en France. Pourtant, c'est ici que Witter révèle ce qu'on pourrait considérer comme l'ampleur de sa perception poétique: construction même du texte, avec le « rythme » des jours dans leurs répétitions et leurs différences, l'espèce de contemplation qui s'en dégage et donc, malgré la progression du « discours », l'absence d'intrigue, de drame, et de narratif typique de Gn 2, 3 et 4. C'est tout cela qui, à mon sens, permet à Witter de voir dans ce premier chapitre de la Genèse autre chose et plus qu'un « récit » ou un « narratif », autre chose et plus que du prosaïque, c'est-à-dire du poétique !

« Ce qui rend encore notre opinion probable, écrit-il, c'est la très grande différence de style qui éclate entre ce premier chapitre du livre de Moïse et les suivants. »

A cette thèse qui, selon moi, n'a rien d' « un peu hasardé » (ainsi que le dit Lods), Witter apporte des arguments précis.

En premier lieu, il y a ce que nous avons déjà cité, à savoir que « dans tout ce que je nomme le 'cantique de Moïse', embrassant la perspective très courte du monde, le nom de Dieu en quatre lettres YHWH n'apparaît jamais, alors qu'il sera par la suite habituel chez Moïse. » (§ 5, p. 22).

On reconnaît là ce qui apparaîtra longtemps comme le premier pilier du principe documentaire ; et même si aujourd'hui nous en avons une autre perception que celle héritée d'Astruc, puis de Wellhausen, le constat fait ici par Witter est parfaitement pertinent.

En second lieu, il invoque ce que nous avons déjà également évoqué, la différence de style entre Gn 1 et la suite des récits.

Enfin, Witter renforce sa thèse d'auteurs différents entre Gn 1 et la suite, que confortent déjà les différences de désignations divines, par les répétitions entre Gn 1 et Gn 2: quelles raisons avait Moïse d'ajouter quelque chose à ce premier chapitre dans lequel « il avait… terminé et parachevé l'histoire de la création », ainsi que le dit explicitement Gn 2,1 ?

Malgré ses développements et dans le redondance de son écriture, Witter a tout mis en place dans ces premières pages de son ouvrage, la suite étant un commentaire de Gn 1–17.

***

Le rapport entre Astruc et Witter nous renvoie maintenant, avec sa part de mystère ou d'énigme, à ce que j'ai évoqué avec le concept tocquevillien d' « esprit du temps ».

En principe, quarante deux années séparent l'ouvrage d'Astruc de celui de Witter. Mais l'importance de ce chiffre peut être illusoire et mérite d'être relativisée: dans la mesure où Astruc n'a pas attendu le seuil des années 1750 pour se mettre au travail ni pour assumer l'important héritage paternel.

Car il me faut rappeler ici l'importance de cet héritage.

Le pasteur calviniste Pierre Astruc, le père de notre auteur, fait ses études à l'Académie protestante de Genève en pleine crise de la pensée calvinienne des années 1670. Dans ces mêmes années, J. Le Clerc va se reconnaître dans les idées de R. Simon dont il lit l'*Histoire critique du Vieux Testament*.

Dans mon édition des *Conjectures de la Genèse*[14], j'ai émis l'hypothèse selon laquelle l'évolution du pasteur Pierre Astruc vers le catholicisme, après sept ans de persécutions concrètes assumées, a sa cause profonde, plutôt que lointaine, dans cette double crise, théologique et biblique, de la Genève des années 1670.

En tout cas, si J. Astruc cite J. Le Clerc à côté de Richard Simon au seuil de ses *Conjectures*, il n'y a pas à douter du lien, soit intellectuel, soit de maître à élève, entre Pierre Astruc et l'exilé d'Amsterdam.

Autrement dit, J. Astruc a dû très tôt partager cet « esprit du temps » exégétique qui cerne, pour ainsi dire, les décennies entre 1660 et 1750.

En tout cas, il reçoit une solide formation humaniste de son père qui fut son premier précepteur. Celui-ci, encore fraîchement issu du Protestantisme calviniste, lui inculque un fort intérêt pour la Bible. Et même s'il est très tôt pris par ses études de médecine qui aboutiront à une brillante carrière de professeur, Astruc ne cessera de s'intéresser à la Bible, et pas seulement pour la lire.

Ce sera un catholique fervent, parfois craintif vis-à-vis de l'autorité de l'Eglise. Et sa passion biblique relève tout autant de l'ambiance catholique du moment que des antécédents paternels.

14. Jean Astruc, *Conjectures sur la Genèse* (Introduction et notes de Pierre Gibert; Paris: Noésis, 1999), 21ss.

Les *Conjectures sur la Genèse* sont publiées en 1753, alors qu'il a 68 ans, loin du jeune âge de Witter, dont il n'aura jamais entendu parler, alors qu'il connaît Simon, Le Clerc et Spinoza.

Faute de documents, il est difficile de dire la genèse de son ouvrage. On peut avancer qu'il y a longuement travaillé, à ses moments perdus sans doute, mais avec ténacité et sans doute selon une perspective pressentie depuis longtemps.

Qu'est-ce qui permet de dire cela ? Sa considérable œuvre médicale !

Autant que médecin, Astruc est un scientifique de son temps, très attentif aux réalités immédiates auxquelles il est toujours soumis, au risque de s'opposer à des collègues éminents et surtout puissants: ainsi s'opposa-t-il, au début de sa carrière, à son professeur et maître, Chirac, qui niait alors que la peste bubonique fût contagieuse !

Astruc se soumet pareillement au texte biblique, à ses richesses, mais aussi à ses difficultés, appliquant le principe de R. Simon qu'il ne pouvait qu'approuver: « Ceux qui font profession de critique ne doivent s'arrêter qu'à expliquer le sens littéral de leurs auteurs, et éviter tout ce qui est inutile à leur dessein. » (Livre III, chp. XV, p. 441).

Mais Astruc est également conditionné dans sa recherche biblique par son approche médicale, originale pour l'époque: par l'histoire de la maladie étudiée ou de la pratique défendue. Celui qui le célèbrera après sa mort, son élève Lorry, qui publiera une *Histoire de la Faculté de médecine de Montpellier*, notera cette approche historienne quasi systématique chez lui, et établira par là un lien entre son étude de la Bible et ses publications médicales.

Assez vite, me semble-t-il, dut s'imposer à Astruc que, comme pour Richard Simon, le texte biblique était le produit d'une histoire. Ainsi, l'idée des « Mémoires » dont il « paraît », c'est-à-dire dans le français des XVIIe et XVIIIe siècles, dont il est « manifeste » que Moïse s'est servi, est-elle une idée de quelqu'un qui a un sens historique fondamental. Et puisque j'établis une comparaison avec Witter, je dirais déjà que nous avons affaire là à deux esprits différents, l'un, Witter, sensible à la dimension littéraire, poétique, du texte qu'il va révéler par là composite, l'autre, Astruc, sensible à la dimension historique, ce qui, redisons-le, ne les empêchera nullement de converger quant aux résultats.

Cet esprit historique se marque dès les « Réflexions préliminaires »: il dénonce ainsi les invraisemblances tenant à la chronologie tant interne qu'externe au livre de la Genèse, et à la propre chronologie de la vie de Moïse. Parallèlement, nous l'avons vu, l'ordre de l'invraisemblance tenait, pour Witter, à la spécificité des genres littéraires, et donc à la différence entre poésie et récit prosaïque. Une nécessité s'impose à ces deux esprits: réduire cette invraisemblance et donc rendre justes et positives les différences perçues, acceptées et non plus niées ou gommées.

C'est donc de l'histoire, et d'une méthodologie historienne, que Astruc va produire la première étape de sa démonstration: seul un héritage informatif peut expliquer le savoir de Moïse. Ainsi l'arrache-t-on à l'invraisemblance d'une histoire due au fait qu'il aurait été exclusivement seul à pouvoir écrire. Pour cela, Astruc commence par exclure une quelconque inspiration divine directe, car si cela avait été, Moïse l'eût dit, ainsi que le disent d'autres auteurs bibliques. Il exclut également la tradition orale d'Adam à Abraham: notons ici qu'il le fait au nom des limites mêmes de toute tradition orale un peu trop invoquée, en France notamment, ces dernières décennies. Enfin, il reconnaît que seuls des documents écrits sont susceptibles de porter une longue mémoire.

« Je prétends donc que Moïse avait entre les mains des Mémoires anciens contenant l'histoire de ses ancêtres depuis la création du monde. »[15].

Ce disant, il reconnaît qu'il ne fait que mettre ses pas dans ceux de J. Le Clerc, de R. Simon, des abbés Fleury et François, mais ajoute-t-il: si, « dans le fond, je pense comme ces auteurs,… je porte mes conjectures plus loin, et je suis plus décidé. »

Parallèlement à Witter, et selon son point de départ propre, il va procéder en deux temps.

Tout d'abord, il note les répétitions et doublets, à commencer par ceux des récits de création ! Quelque chose s'impose donc à lui, quasi immédiatement, avec la force de l'évidence, comme s'imposent les doublets du Déluge. Sans doute n'est-il pas le premier à avoir plus ou moins clairement perçu cela. Un Lemaistre de Sacy, par ex., un siècle plus tôt, lorsqu'il traduit Gn 2,4, témoigne d'un effort manifeste pour *limer la soudure* sur la ligne de séparation de deux récits qu'il perçoit dans ce verset.

Quoi qu'il en soit, Astruc, dans un second temps, procède analogiquement à la manière de Witter: ayant déterminé ces doublets et donc ces deux récits de création et du Déluge, il s'appuie sur les différences de désignation de Dieu, en Elohim et Jehovah.

Là aussi, comme chez Witter, l'essentiel de la perception des choses semble dit, et pour une part, c'est vrai ; mais pour une part seulement. Car, me semble-t-il, Astruc va aller ici plus loin que Witter ; il sera plus systématique pour tirer les conséquences de ces différences de désignations.

---

15. Astruc, *Conjectures*, 137.

De façon schématique, je dirai qu'à partir de cette double détermination de textes, par le jeu des répétitions et doublets comme par le jeu des désignations divines, il va entamer une double démarche. De cette double démarche, on retient généralement la première, celle, relativement évidente, de la détermination de quatre « mémoires » principaux, en fonction des textes qui portent le nom de Elohim, de ceux qui portent le nom de Jehovah, de ceux qui ne portent ni l'un ni l'autre tout en concernant Israël, et enfin de ceux qui sont étrangers à Israël.

Ainsi, on réduit ses intuitions et sa démonstration à l'expression de la théorie telle que Wellhausen a contribué à la fixer, et telle qu'elle fut reçue jusqu'au début des années 1970 du XXe siècle[16].

Mais vous savez comment Rendtorff, entre autres[17], a mis à mal cette expression, relevant une série d'objections qui n'avaient guère été entendues depuis la fin du XIXe siècle. On pourrait croire que du fait de leurs contestations, Astruc n'avait plus qu'à entrer dans une sorte de Panthéon sinon de morgue pour y être définitivement oublié.

Or, le second temps de la thèse d'Astruc, et là il dépasse définitivement le projet de Witter, dit les limites de la première perception des « Mémoires » utilisés par Moïse. Dans le chapitre III de ses longues « Remarques » conclusives[18], il oriente son lecteur et, j'ai envie d'oser ajouter: les générations à venir d'exégètes, vers ce « qu'il paraît », c'est-à-dire ce qui est manifeste, « qu'on peut y en distinguer jusqu'à douze, mais dont la plupart ne sont que des fragments. » De façon générale, il procèdera là par argument de relation historique ; autrement dit, il jugera de différents « Mémoires » par le rapport plus ou moins étroit qu'ils entretiennent vis-à-vis d'Israël et les uns vis-à-vis des autres.

Au terme de ce chapitre, il dira à la fois prudemment et audacieusement: « Au reste, dans le détail qu'on vient de faire des douze différents mémoires dont il paraît que Moïse s'est servi, on n'affirme rien, comme je crois l'avoir dit. On ne fait que proposer des conjectures qu'on est maître de recevoir ou de rejeter. On peut donc, si on le juge à propos, réduire les dix derniers mémoires à un moindre nombre. On peut au contraire partager les deux premiers, A et B [nos traditionnels E et J], en plusieurs ; car enfin rien n'empêche qu'il y ait eu plus d'un Mémoire, où

---

16. Ainsi qu'en témoigne, pour la France, l'article « Pentateuque » du DBS, signé Henri Cazelles (1962).

17. Rolf Rendtorff, *Das überlieferungsgeschichtliche Problem des Pentateuch* (Berlin: de Gruyter, 1977). Un bon tableau de la situation est fourni pour le public francophone dans Albert de Pury et Thomas Römer, éd., *Le Pentateuque en question* (3d ed.; Genève: Labor et Fides, 2002).

18. Jean Astruc, *Conjectures sur la Genèse*, 395–401.

les auteurs aient donné à Dieu le nom d'*Elohim*, et plus d'un aussi, où les auteurs lui aient donné le nom de *Jéhovah* ; mais comme on ne doit rien avancer sans quelque raison, du moins apparente, on ne doit pas non plus rien condamner que sur des raisons pour le moins plausibles. »[19].

***

Qu'en est-il aujourd'hui de ces itinéraires croisés qui ont en commun d'être allés de l'intuition à l'acquis objectivement établi ? L'acquis est-il définitif qui semble parfois avoir été relativisé sinon vraiment contesté ? Le surgissement de méthodes nouvelles d'approches des textes bibliques, du Pentateuque et de la Genèse en particulier, font parfois douter de la pertinence de cette « théorie documentaire » que semble fragiliser la remise en question des années 1970. Sans doute n'est-ce pas le moment de poser de telles questions. Je voudrais seulement rappeler deux choses que contraint à prendre en compte cette étape importante de l'histoire de l'exégèse critique au point où l'ont laissée les travaux de Witter et d'Astruc.

Tout d'abord, la longue généalogie des noms qui, entre les XVIIe et XVIIIe siècles, illustrent et concrétisent des efforts convergents malgré les inévitables hésitations, manifeste une nécessité. S'il n'y avait pas eu le caractère inévitable de la question, s'il n'y avait pas eu urgence à trouver des réponses, s'il n'y avait eu que jeu esthétique, on ne saurait s'expliquer cette sorte de constance et même de ténacité dans la recherche. Qui plus est, celle-ci fut le fruit d'esprits très divers, aux origines les plus opposées, et provenant aussi bien de la France que de la Suède, de l'Allemagne que de l'Angleterre, même si telle ou telle région comme les Pays-Bas de l'époque mérite une mention particulière. Ce qu'il est convenu de désigner par l' « exégèse critique », ou moins pertinemment par l' « exégèse historico-critique », n'est pas de l'ordre du choix plus ou moins arbitraire, mais de la nécessité étant donné les questions posées par le texte biblique.

En second lieu, pour en revenir au comparatisme et à la complémentarité de ces deux critiques que furent Witter et Astruc, dans la distance même qui sépare leurs parcours respectifs sans contacts réciproques, nous avons là un témoignage de ce que peut être la quête et la mise au point d'une épistémologie. L'intuition, et même le bricolage, sont au départ, c'est-à-dire au moment où la question se pose dans son immédiateté, son urgence, voire sa brutalité. Doit venir un moment où des esprits particulièrement perspicaces, partant de points acquis, font le même

---

19. Ibid., 400–401.

chemin: de l'intuition à la démonstration. Dans l'héritage des hésitations, des impasses et des conquêtes de leurs prédécesseurs, et donc libérés de questionnements dépassés, ils proposent un acquis qui peut alors être considéré comme définitif. Il me semble que Witter et Astruc ont été de ces esprits perspicaces dont nous vivons des acquis.

Enfin, dans le prolongement de ce que j'ai évoqué avec l' « esprit du temps », je ne voudrais pas totalement ignorer celui qui avec Astruc nous réunit et partage la même année de célébration. Car Lowth rejoint Astruc et Witter qu'il n'a sûrement pas connus, mais en leur faisant un écho que nous pouvons entendre. Evoquant l'inspiration poétique des hébreux, et dressant la liste de leurs images, au chapitre VIII de son *Cours de poésie sacrée*, il souligne l'importance du « chaos » et de la « création qui, écrit-il, forment, pour ainsi dire, l'exorde de l'Histoire Sainte ». Ainsi:

> C'est à l'un ou à l'autre, [le chaos et la création], que les poètes font constamment allusion lorsqu'ils veulent exprimer quelque changement remarquable, soit heureux, soit malheureux dans les affaires publiques, tels que la chute ou la restauration des royaumes et des nations. Les images tirées de ces deux objets sont très communes dans les livres poétiques des prophètes ; ils s'en servent toutes les fois qu'ils traitent quelque sujet dont l'exécution demande beaucoup de hardiesse…L'un et l'autre prophète ne font pas seulement allusion au chaos dont parle Moïse ; ils se servent encore des expressions mêmes de cet historien. Tous les poètes hébreux ont amplifié et agrandi ce sujet par une accumulation de circonstances et de détails.[20]

Comme Witter voyait dans Gn 1 le grand poème introductif au Pentateuque, et comme Astruc voyait dans Moïse l'historien qui avait su exploiter des documents antérieurs, Lowth nous confirme par les siennes leur intelligence et leurs intuitions de l'écriture poétique et de l'œuvre d'historien, qui, même aujourd'hui dépassées, nous ont permis d'avancer dans la connaissance biblique.

---

20. *Cours de poésie sacrée* par le Docteur Lowth, traduit pour la première fois du latin en français par F. Roger (Paris, 1813), 75 et 76.

JEAN ASTRUC AND SOURCE CRITICISM
IN THE BOOK OF GENESIS*

Jan Christian Gertz

Within the scope of the "Sacred Conjectures Conference" that gave rise to the present volume, experts on biblical research in the eighteenth and the nineteenth centuries addressed Jean Astruc's contribution to the beginning of historical-critical work on the Pentateuch. The *Conjectures sur les Mémoires originaux*—frequently cited in literature but presumably rarely read—were published several years ago in a new critical edition.[1] Pierre Gibert's introduction and commentary present the essentials about this work and its origin. In what follows, one should not expect substantially new information. Here I shall take the liberty of representing the perspective of an interested layman who knows only little about the eighteenth century but who shares with Astruc a field of research: the history of the origin and development of the book of Genesis. In what follows I would therefore like to read Astruc as an exegetical contemporary.

If this approach seems anachronistic, it should be pointed out that research on the Pentateuch is a *"Disziplin, wo der Stoff im wesentlichen keine Veränderung erfährt und seit Jahrhunderten von vielen Leuten über ihn nachgedacht worden ist, die nicht dümmer waren als wir..."*[2]

---

* I would like to thank Dr. Jacob L. Wright for his assistance in translating this essay.

1. J. Astruc, *Conjectures sur la Genèse. Introduction et notes de Pierre Gibert* (Paris: Noésis, 1999). The title of the original version, anonymously published in 1753 in Brussels, is: *Conjectures sur les Mémoires originaux dont il paroit que Moyse s'est servi pour composer le Livre de la Genèse*. In what follows, the quotations are taken from the new edition of P. Gibert.

2. "[A] discipline in which the material essentially does not change and which has been contemplated for centuries by people who were not more ignorant than we are...," according to R. Smend, *Deutsche Alttestamentler in drei Jahrhunderten* (Göttingen: Vandenhoeck & Ruprecht, 1989), 9.

Moreover, in our discipline there is a growing scepticism about dia-chronic questions. And this scepticism applies especially to the source criticism of the Pentateuch established by Astruc. In German research on the Pentateuch, critics of diachronic analysis like to appeal to the work of Benno Jacob (1862–1945), whose commentary on the books of Genesis and Exodus from 1934 and 1942 have undergone a remarkable renais-sance.[3] It is an interesting coincidence that at a congress for ancient Near Eastern studies in 1928, 175 years after the publication of Astruc's *Conjectures*, Jacob took the offensive against source criticism here in Oxford with a lecture about the Flood:

> *Das größte Hemmnis für das wahre Verständnis des Pentateuch ist die heute noch fast unumschränkt herrschende Quellenscheidung. Sie bedarf unter allen Umständen einer gründlichen Revision. Diese kann aber nur von einer Exegese geleistet werden, die sich von allen literarkritischen Dogmen freihält und jede Behauptung der Quellenkritik mit unnachsichti-ger Schärfe nachprüft.*[4]

In the context of this quotation, Astruc is explicitly mentioned. Thus the debate between Astruc (I) and Jacob (II) can begin here. Thereafter (III) I will provide a short evaluation.

I

Astruc's contribution to the formation of the "Older Documentary Hypothesis" is fundamental to Hebrew Bible scholarship. Essentially adhering to the Mosaic authorship of the Pentateuch, Astruc explains the

3. B. Jacob, *Das erste Buch der Tora Genesis, übersetzt und erklärt* (Berlin: Schocken, 1934; repr., *Das Buch Genesis*, hg. in Zusammenarbeit mit dem Leo-Baeck-Institut [Stuttgart: Calwer, 2000]); idem, *Das zweite Buch der Tora Exodus, übersetzt und erklärt*, masch. 1942 (Engl. edition: *The Second Book of the Bible*; trans. with an introduction by W. Jacob in association with Y. Elman; Hoboken: Ktav, 1992]; German edition: *Das Buch Exodus* (ed. S. Mayer, J. Hahn and A. Jürgensen; Im Auftrag des Leo-Baeck-Instituts; Stuttgart: Calwer, 1997). These new editions reflect the great interest in Jacob's work). See B. S. Childs, "The Almost Forgotten Genesis Commentary of Benno Jacob," in *Recht und Ethos im Alten Testament—Gestalt und Wirkung* (FS H. Seebass; ed. S. Beyerle et al.; Neukirchen–Vluyn: Neukirchener, 1999), 273–80; W. Jacob and A. Jürgensen, ed., *Die Exegese hat das erste Wort. Beiträge zu Leben und Werk Benno Jacobs* (Stuttgart: Calwer, 2002).

4. "The greatest obstacle for the proper understanding of the Pentateuch is source criticism, which today reigns with almost no restraints. This approach absolutely requires a thorough revision. Such a task can be assumed only by an exegesis which distances itself from all literary-critical dogmas and tests each assumption of source-criticism with the strictest analysis" (B. Jacob, *Die biblische Sintfluterzählung. Ihre literarische Einheit* [Berlin: Schocken, 1930], 1).

origin of the book of Genesis (and Exod 1–2) as a secondary connection of two continuous documents and another ten fragmentary documents. While Moses arranged these documents side by side in four columns, a later hand has woven them into a single narrative. Astruc's criteria for source criticism are repetitions, the variation of divine names and chronological discrepancies. He aligns these two sources into columns A[5] and B.[6] In column C, he groups texts which report single details for the third time and which, because they do not mention God by name, cannot be assigned to one of the two main sources.[7] The latter also applies to the texts of column D except that they present additional material not contained in A and B. These texts need not originally have belonged to the same source. For reasons of content, Astruc even thinks that they could have originated among Israel's neighbours.[8]

In evaluating Astruc's work, it is important to remember that neither his basic observations on the character of the text nor his explanations are completely new. Astruc refers to a number of scholars who both agree and disagree with him, such as Thomas Hobbes (1588–1679),[9] Isaac de la Peyrère (1594–1676),[10] Baruch Spinoza (1632–1677),[11] Richard Simon (1638–1712),[12] Claude Fleury (1640–1723),[13] Johannes

---

5. Gen 1:1–2:3; 5; 6:9–22; 7:6–10, 19, 22, 24; 8:1–19; 9:1–10, 12, 16, 17, 28, 29; 11:10–26; 17:3–27; 20:1–17; 21:2–32; 22:1–10; 23; 25:1–11; 30:1–23; 31:4–47; 31:51–32:2; 32:24–33:16; 35:1–27 (Cf. *Conjectures sur la Genèse*, 504; on p. 294, however, v. 27 is assigned to D); 37; 40–48; 49:29–33; 50; Exod 1–2.

6. Gen 2:4–4:26; 6:1–8; 7:1–5, 11–18, 21, 24; 8:20–22; 9:11, 13–15, 18–29; 10:1–11:9; 11:27–13:18; 15:1–17:2; 18:1–19:28; 20:18–21:1; 21:33–34; 22:11–19; 24; 25:19–26:33; 27:1–28:5; 28:10–22; 29; 30:24–43; 31:1–3, 48–50; 32:3–23; 33:17–20; 38; 39; 49:1–28.

7. Gen 7:20, 23, 24; 34 (?).

8. Gen 14; 19:29–38; 22:20–24; 25:12–18; 26:34–35; 28:6–9; 34(?); 35:28–36.43 (according to ibid., 294, Gen 35:27 also belongs to D). Astruc distributes the texts of column D over the source-fragments E to M (pp. 96ff.).

9. T. Hobbes, *Leviathan, or the Matter, Form, and Power of a Commonwealth Ecclesiastical and Civil* (London, 1651), quoted by Astruc, *Conjectures sur la Genèse*, 507. See the recent English edition, T. Hobbes, *Leviathan* (ed. R. Tuck; (Cambridge: Cambridge University Press, 1991).

10. I. de la Peyrère, *Systema Theologicum ex praeadamitarum hypothesi, pars prima* (anon. and n.p., 1655), quoted by Astruc, *Conjectures sur la Genèse*, 507.

11. B. Spinoza, *Tractatus theologico-politicus*, anon. (Amsterdam, 1670), quoted by Astruc, *Conjectures sur la Genèse*, 491, 506–7.

12. R. Simon, *Histoire critique du Vieux Testament* (Paris, 1678; 2d ed., Rotterdam, 1685), quoted by Astruc, *Conjectures sur la Genèse*, 135, 523–24.

13. C. Fleury (very probably), *Les Mœurs des Israélites et des Chrétiens* (Paris [?], original edition 1681/82) (thereafter published in several editions); quoted by Astruc, *Conjectures sur la Genèse*, 136.

Clericus (Jean le Clerc; 1657–1736)[14] and Laurent Francois (1698–1782).[15] Although these authors stand in a long tradition of critical research which has always accompanied the reading of the Pentateuch in Christianity and in post-biblical Judaism, they are responsible for transforming the study of the Pentateuch from the answers provided by the Church Fathers, Philo and the rabbis to a methodical and scientific inquiry. In this context we must also regard Astruc's service, whose hypothesis, while characterized by a remarkable inner coherence and consistency,[16] leaves room for integrating new insights.

The historical basis of Astruc's hypothesis is the assumption of the Mosaic authorship of the Pentateuch, which he adopted from the traditional way of reading the Bible. He defends this assumption against contemporary counter-positions,[17] and it contributes much to the heuristic value of his model. Ascribing the Pentateuch to Moses demands first of all that one distinguish the account of Moses' time from that of the pre-Mosaic period. Accordingly, Astruc limits his analysis to Gen 1–Exod 2. Whereas the narrative beginning in Exod 3 is evaluated as a report of the mature Moses written after the exodus, this is definitely out of question for Gen 1–Exod 2 (p. 132 [hereafter bracketed page references refer to Astruc's *Conjectures*]). The question arises: Where did Moses gather his

14. J. Clericus, "Dissertatio de scriptore pentateuchi Mose," in idem, *Genesis sive Mosis prophetae liber primus ex translatione Joannis Clerici* (Amsterdam. 1693), where he retracts his former thesis on the formation of the Pentateuch in idem, *Sentimens de quelques théologiens de Hollande sur l'histoire critique du Vieux Testament composée par le P. Richard Simon de l'Oratoire* (Amsterdam. 1685). Clericus' work is quoted by Astruc, *Conjectures sur la Genèse*, 135, 408, 473ff., 507–8, 523–24, 561. Concerning Clericus, cf., among others, M. C. Pitassi, *Entre croire et savoir. Le problème de la méthode critique chez Jean Le Clerc* (Leiden: Brill, 1987).

15. It probably concerns the work L. François, *Les Preuves de la religion de Jésus-Christ contre les Spinosistes et les Déistes* (n.p., 1751), a work which was not available to me, quoted by Astruc, *Conjectures sur la Genèse*, 136.

16. This is also to be emphasized in view of the older H. B. Witter (1683–1715) who was recently rediscovered and was probably unknown to Astruc. In his unfinished Genesis commentary, Witter also undertakes a source criticism of Gen 1–3 by means of the divine name as well as by factual and stylistic differences, but he does not apply the consequences of his discoveries to more than just this text. Concerning Witter, cf. H. Bardtke, "Henning Bernhard Witter," *ZAW* 66 (1954): 153–81 and the contribution of P. Gibert to the present volume.

17. See Astruc, *Conjectures sur la Genèse*, 506–15, concerning the Ezran authorship of the Pentateuch claimed, for example, by Hobbes (*Leviathan*), de la Peyrère (*Systema Theologicum*) and Spinoza (*Tractatus theologico-politicu*), or to the priest mentioned in 2 Kgs 17 by Clericus ("Dissertatio de scriptore").

knowledge of history from the creation of the world until his own birth? The possibility of a revelation is denied by Astruc on the basis of several form-critical arguments. Moses speaks as "simple historian" in the book of Genesis; in contrast to the prophets, he does not employ the customary formulas to introduce a revelation; and finally his diction in Genesis differs clearly from that of the Sinai narration where he appears as the mediator of the divine law (pp. 132–33). Astruc's conclusion from this is that Moses drew upon older sources, which poses the question about how this information was transmitted. An exclusively oral transmission is conceivable inasmuch as the number of generations from Adam until the descendants of Jacob's son Levi in Egypt was small. However, this assumption is rendered unlikely given the formal peculiarities of the text with its numerous genealogies and topographical details (pp. 133–34). Thus, the process of transmission must have been literary. Moses could have employed written reports from contemporary witnesses. Moreover, there must have been several parallel reports. Against the alternative that the account is historically unreliable, Astruc emphasizes the written character of the documents, their contemporaneity with the reported incidents, and their substantiation of each other:

> *Je prétends donc que Moïse avait entre les mains des Mémoires anciens contenant l'histoire de ces ancêtres depuis la création du monde; que pour ne rien perdre de ces Mémoires, il les a partagés par morceaux suivant les faits qui y étaient racontés; qu'il a inséré ces morceaux en entier les uns à la suite des autres, et que c'est de cet assemblage que le Livre de la Genèse a été formé.* (p. 137)

In order to test his hypothesis, Astruc arranges what many had already observed into this interpretational framework and demonstrates its heuristic value. The structure of the *Conjectures* corresponds to this procedure. In the introductory portion, "Réflexions préliminaires" (pp. 131–48), Astruc cites the textual observations made by earlier scholars as four proofs for his hypothesis. After completing the source criticism of Gen 1–Exod 2, he refers to these observations again in the last part of the work, the "Remarques sur la distribution de la Genèse en différents Mémoires" (pp. 375–537), in order to demonstrate the heuristic value of his hypothesis. In this context Astruc speaks about the four advantages (*"avantages"*) of his hypothesis. In what follows, I subdivide the argument into three steps:

1.   The first proof for the existence of different continuous documents is provided by the repetition of identical events, which one finds difficult to attribute to a single author. That they both have been transmitted can be explained only by the effort of a

historian such as Moses to be thorough (pp. 137–38). In addition to the two reports about the creation in Gen 1:1–2:3(!) and 2:4–3:24 (Table of Nations in Gen 10 and the alliance between Laban and Jacob in Gen 31), the story of the Flood in Gen 6–8 is a prominent example of parallel accounts (pp. 432ff.). The argument of repetition gains strength when Astruc considers those cases which cannot be explained by the thesis of several documents. Aside from post-Mosaic comments (pp. 438–39), Astruc allows for repetitions that were caused either by the stylistic peculiarities of Hebrew (pp. 439–41, 442–44) or by the influence of oral speech on the early written form (pp. 445–47). If the modern literary taste should not be used in isolating disturbing repetitions in the "divine Homer," then why should it play a role for the older and not less "divine Moses" (pp. 445–47)? Finally, the repetitions in the legal sections of the books from Exodus to Deuteronomy are of a completely different nature. They are to be explained by their pedagogical aim, and this again illustrates the necessity of a special treatment Gen 1–Exod 2 (pp. 441–42).

2. The second proof for the hypothesis is provided by the alternation between the Tetragrammaton—which at that time was vocalized as Jehovah—and Elohim, which Astruc understands as the proper name of the highest being (pp. 138, 395 etc.).[18] Since this source-critical criterion has been recently placed into doubt,[19] we must pay particular attention to how Astruc uses it. For the most part he treats the variation in the names for God as evidence for different documents. Nevertheless it should be noted that Astruc excludes the alternative explanation that the divine names have been employed arbitrarily in both of his main sources, because the linguistic usage is uniform in entire chapters or at least in longer segments (pp. 139–40). In this respect the findings for Genesis differ considerably from the one of Moses' own presentation. From Exod 3 on lengthy segments do not alternate in their use of Elohim and Jehovah. Rather, the language usage is mixed. As a rule Moses uses the proper names, while inserting the name Elohim merely for stylistic reasons (pp. 140–42). In the

18.   For a new approach, cf. A. de Pury, "Gottesnamen, Gottesbezeichnung und Gottes begriff," in *Abschied vom Jahwisten. Die Komposition des Hexateuch in der jüngsten Diskussion* (ed. J. C. Gertz, K. Schmid and M. Witte; BZAW 315; Berlin: de Gruyter, 2002), 25–47. De Pury rightly points out that P in its programmatic text, Gen 1, introduces the use of the former appellative as the universal *name* of God.

19.   See E. Blum, *Die Komposition der Vätergeschichte* (WMANT 57; Neukirchen–Vluyn: Neukirchener, 1984), 471–75.

discussion of this thesis, Astruc also addresses the exceptions in
both of his main sources. He explains them all by recourse to
conceptual reasons such as the appellative usage of Elohim or an
etymologizing context (pp. 415–32 about Gen 28). Finally
Astruc recognizes in each case different theological accents yet
does not wish to have this point used as an argument against
source criticism (p. 387).[20]

3. Astruc finds the third and for him most important proof in the
    chronological discrepancies in the course of the narration, which
    he refers to as "antichronisms." Their existence definitely seems
    to contradict the assumption of a unified authorship, but they
    could be explained just as well as a secondary connection of
    documents (pp. 142, 447–70).[21] In order to safeguard Moses from
    the accusation that he edited the documents in a haphazard and
    incorrect manner, Astruc resorts to the assumption that the texts
    arranged by Moses into a synopsis were subsequently fused
    together (pp. 486–505). This assumption is of course not justified
    either by the source-critical argument or by the basic histo-
    riographic supposition of Mosaic authorship. Apart from text-
    critical evidence of later editors, the assumption derives solely
    from an apologetic interest in defending the credibility of the
    Pentateuch against Spinoza and other critics. And at this time the
    credibility of the Pentateuch is closely related to the person of
    Moses (pp. 506–15). Nonetheless, Astruc has insightfully noted
    that incoherencies appear precisely where later authors employed
    a *Vorlage*.

A description of Astruc's arguments would be incomplete without at
least a brief appreciation of its openness. The utility of a model proves
itself in its flexibility to integrate new and even conflicting evidence.
Examples of Astruc's openness are his refusal to use the criterion of the
divine name in a rigid manner and the way he deals with two conceivable
objections to the attribution of Gen 1–Exod 2 to two continuous documents. The incompleteness and the non-uniformity of these sources
constitute still today the fundamental criticism of source criticism.

20. This question is discussed by Astruc with regard to Exod 6 and Yhwh's
declaration that he did not reveal himself to the fathers with his name. Because this
statement contradicts the use of the Yhwh-name in source B, Astruc looks for a
difference in the meaning of the two designations of God. See Astruc, *Conjectures
sur la Genèse*, 387ff.

21. Ibid., 470–85. Astruc mentions some controversial passages within the two
main sources, but in his opinion, the anachronisms in question can be removed.

With respect to the lacunae in the sources, one must consider whether they are not merely due to the expectations of modern readers. Moreover, Astruc provides a redaction-historical model. Against the supposition that the documents have been transmitted intact, one must reckon with the possibility of omissions even where there is complete conformity. For this reason Astruc attributes some texts to both sources (pp. 146–47).[22]

According to Astruc, the disunity of the two main sources is conditioned by the fact that they are the result of a process of *Fortschreibung*. Thus, he attributes the stylistic differences between the relatively unified Joseph story and the preceding narratives to a different cultural environment for the historical Joseph, the author of the Joseph story (p. 403).[23] Furthermore, Astruc does not wish to fundamentally exclude a further differentiation of the sources into parallel reports, yet finds this difficult to prove (pp. 400–401). The reason for this uncertainty is both that Astruc does not, with the exception of the alternation of the divine name, deal with stylistic differences, and that he did not keep up with the research of that time.[24] It should be mentioned in passing that reception and continuation of Astruc's source criticism by Johann Gottfried Eichhorn shows how much the plausibility of the hypothesis is enhanced by a detailed analysis of the stylistic differences and character of the documents.[25]

The openness of Astruc's model is augmented finally by the insight that a late dating of the complete work does not necessarily preclude the assumptions of an early composition and of the existence of older sources. Here Astruc is ahead of his time, even if he does make this discovery merely by distinguishing between the periods of Adam, Noah and the Patriarchs, on the one hand, and Moses, on the other.

---

22. Gen 7:24 is assigned to A, B and C, Gen 9:28–29 to A and B.

23. Astruc ascribes the history of Joseph to column A. In his opinion, only Gen 39 comes from another source: Joseph—as a subtle person—would have left out the episode with Potiphar's wife, but Moses—correct as he was—had added it from report B (Jehovah).

24. See J. D. Michaelis, *Göttingsche Anzeigen von gelehrten Sachen*, vol. 1 (1754), 973–75, who simply failed to appreciate the achievement of explanation and the importance of Astruc's hypothesis.

25. Concerning the *Quellenscheidung* in Gen 1–Exod 2, where the analysis of the Flood narration is of crucial importance, cf. J. G. Eichhorn, *Einleitung in das Alte Testament*, vol. 2 (2d ed.; Reutlingen, 1790), 245–348 (1st ed. [1781], 294–409). Page 246 (1st ed. [1781], 297) supplies the often quoted reference to Astruc.

II

Astruc's source criticism manifests a clear apologetic aim. The proof of the documents in Genesis is intended as a defence of the authority of the Pentateuch and transformation of the traditional belief in the Mosaic authorship into a tenable scientific thesis. If Moses' work as a collector and editor of the documents is thought to be inspired (p. 133), it calls for a historicizing reformulation of the doctrine of inspiration. This reformulation was provided a little later by Johann Friedrich Wilhelm Jerusalem (1709–1789),[26] the one who supposedly mediated Astruc's ideas to Eichhorn.[27] Astruc's work made history in laying the literary-critical foundation for a historical and independent view of the Hebrew Bible and its religion that was for the most part independent of the tradition. In so doing, Astruc became unwillingly one of the fathers of higher criticism.

The situation is completely different when we turn to Benno Jacob. His insistence upon the unity of the Pentateuch and his attack on source criticism does not take its point of departure from the belief in its Mosaic authorship. In this sense, the aim of his exegesis is not apologetic, but rather an interpretation which does methodological justice to the demand of the transmitted text of Genesis to be read as *"eine Einleitung zur Geschichte Israels unter Mose."*[28] Trying to understand the text in its completeness and not to explain it historically, Jacob looks for coherence in the text at almost any price.[29] Both the starting point for and the aim of

26. J. F. W. Jerusalem, *Briefe über die Mosaischen Schriften und Philosophie* (Braunschweig, 1762), in particular p. 110. On pp. 107–8, he directly refers to Astruc's work (see the note by C. Bultmann, *Die biblische Urgeschichte in der Aufklärung. Johann Gottfried Herders Interpretation der Genesis als Antwort auf die Religionskritik David Humes* [BHTh 110; Tübingen: Mohr Siebeck, 1999], 82 n. 148). With regard to Jerusalem, see W. E. Müller, "Legitimation historischer Kritik bei J. F. W. Jerusalem," in *Historische Kritik und biblischer Kanon in der deutschen Aufklärung* (ed. H. Graf Reventlow, W. Sparn and J. D. Woodbridge; Wolfenbüttler Forschungen 41; Wiesbaden: Harrassowitz, 1988), 205–18 (209–12). Of course also here Astruc had predecessors such as H. B. Witter. For the contemporary discussion, see E. Hirsch, *Geschichte der neuern evangelischen Theologie*, vol. 1 (Gütersloh: Bertelsmann, 1949), 221–44 ("Die Ermäßigung der Inspirationslehre und die veränderte Fragestellung hinsichtlich der christlichen Religion").

27. Concerning Eichhorn's dependence on Astruc, cf. the notes of Smend, *Deutsche Alttestamentler*, 30–31.

28. "...an introduction to the history of Israel by Moses" (Jacob, *Das Buch Genesis*, 689).

29. Cf. S. Gesundheit, "Bibelkritische Elemente in der Exegese Benno Jacobs," in *Die Exegese hat das erste Wort. Beiträge zu Leben und Werk Benno Jacobs* (ed.

his exegetical enterprise is the proof of the text-critical integrity of the Masoretic text, of its literary unity and of its freedom to pose contradictions. This also applies to the narrative of the Flood in Gen 6–8, which is often treated as the parade example for source criticism and which Jacob thus quite justifiably selects as his point of attack on source criticism.[30]

With regard to the source criticism of the Flood story, Astruc employs the criteria of the names for God and literary repetitions. The details are not important here; it suffices to note that Astruc's analysis does not always correspond to the classical division of the text into Priestly and a non-Priestly strands.[31] He does not observe the contradictions between sources since he believes they represent historically reliable eyewitness reports which of necessity must concur with each other. Jacob's attack on the "prized possession [*Glanzstück*—viz. of source criticism]...since Astruc–Eichhorn"[32] has accordingly a more developed model in view. Nevertheless, this model—with its division of documents based upon the names for God and repetitions—are inseparably connected to Astruc's work. In keeping with rabbinical exegesis, Jacob attributes the switch between Elohim and Yhwh to a single author's theology inasmuch as this switch corresponds to a change of perspective:

W. Jacob and A. Jürgensen; Stuttgart: Calwer, 2002), 98–110 (100). See there also notes to the following.

30. The "parade example" of the source-criticism; see H. Gunkel, *Genesis* (3d ed.; HK 1/1; Göttingen: Vandenhoeck & Ruprecht, 1910 [= 9th ed. 1977]), 137, on Gen 6–9: "Source criticism...is a jewel of modern criticism... The beginner can observe the way which one should do source criticism in this pericope") represents the exception: only in Gen 6–9 and Exod 14 have the sources been completely integrated. Otherwise the redactor prefers to juxtapose the individual sources. The reasons for the variation in Gen 6–9 and Exod 14 are clear: The flood and the crossing of the Red Sea are unique events that can only be portrayed once.

31. See Astruc, *Conjectures sur la Genèse*, 434–36. Astruc mentions the following repetitions: the description of the world's corruption in Gen 6:1–8 (B) and 6:11–14 (A), the order to load the ark including the remark on Noah carrying it out in Gen 6:19–21, 22 (A) and 7:1–4, 5 (B), the chronological information in Gen 7:6 (A) and 7:11 (B), the account of the animals entering the ark in Gen 7:8–10 (A) and 7:14–16 (B), and the coming of the Flood in 7:18 (A) and 7:19 (B). Finally, the destruction of the world by the Flood is depicted three times, and that is why Astruc reckons, in addition to Gen 7:21 (B) and 7:22 (A), with the existence of a further narrative about the Flood in 7:23 (C), even if this third one is only extant in a fragmentary form. Gen 7:6 and 7:11 as well as 7:18 and 7:19 are usually not distributed to two different layers. Basically, Astruc's source A corresponds to priestly texts. Differences can be found especially in Gen 7:8–10 (A) or 7:14–16 (B).

32. See Jacob, *Sintfluterzählung*, 1.

In unserer Erzählung liegt die Lösung in der zweifachen Natur Noahs.
Einerseits ist er Mensch und Vertreter des Menschengeschlechts, das er
als zweiter Adam nach der Flut erneuern soll. Dafür ist der Gottesname
Elohim, der Gott der Schöpfung c. I. Andererseits ist er ein Frommer, und
darum wird die Menschheit gerade in ihm gerettet. Dafür ist der
Gottesname Jhvh.[33]

While Astruc recognized that within one document the alternative designation for God can be employed for reasons of content,[34] in Jacob's
analysis of the Flood story the varying names for God serve to demonstrate the integrity of the text. Yet I doubt whether the change of perspectives can be maintained with respect to both prologues of the Flood and
the order to enter the ark in Gen 6:5–8; 7:1–5 (Jehovah) and in Gen 6:9–
22 (Elohim). God's reflections on the state of the world and his direct
address to Noah are found in both sections, yet the change of perspectives does not correspond to a change in the name for God.[35] Jacob's
second objection relates to contradictions within the story of the Flood. It
should be pointed out that factual contradictions, which are resolved
when one postulates several sources, support Astruc's literary model
considerably. But at the same time this runs contrary to Astruc's apologetic intention. With regard to the contradictions, I will focus on the
different chronologies according to which the Flood lasts either forty
days (Gen 7:4, 12, 17; 8:6) or 150 days (Gen 7:24; 8:3b).[36] Jacob solves

33. "In our story the solution is to be found in the two-fold nature of Moses. On
the one hand, he is a human and representative of humanity, which as a second
Adam he renews after the flood. For this function the author uses the divine name
Elohim, the God of creation in ch. 1. On the other hand, he is a righteous person, and
for that reason humanity is saved by him. In this respect, the name Yhwh is used"
(my translation of Jacob, *Sintfluterzählung*, 3). See idem, *Genesis*, 78. The assumption that the use of "Yhwh" is aimed at God's mercy, whereas mere "Elohim" would
refer to God as a judge, can already be found in Philo's work (*De vita Mosis* 2.99;
De Somniis 1.162–63).

34. Thus Astruc mentions in the closer context of the Flood narrative that in the
speech of the snake, the divine name "Yhwh" would have been avoided for
theological reasons. See *Conjectures sur la Genèse*, 418.

35. The same applies to the orders to enter the ark in 7:1 (Yhwh) and to go out of
it in 8:15 (Elohim).

36. The chronology in detail is more differentiated: P dates the beginning of the
Flood on 17th day of the second month of the 600th year of Noah's life (Gen 7:11)
and the end on 27th day of the second month of the 601st year of his life (Gen 8:14),
so that the Flood lasts one lunar year (354 days from 17th day of the second month
until 16th day of the same month a year later) and eleven further days, which corresponds exactly to a solar year of 365 days. The highest level of the Flood, when the

the problem by resorting to a complicated calculation: "And the *mabbul* was forty days upon the earth" (Gen 7:17) refers solely to the duration of the rain; "And the waters prevailed upon the earth one hundred and fifty days" (Gen 7:24) describes conversely the increase of the water and the duration of the highest water level after the rain stopped. The problem with this approach is, first, that one must reduce the meaning of *mabbul* to the arrival of the water.[37] It does not agree with the notice of the decision to destroy life in 6:17, with the chronological data in 7:6; 9:28;

mountains were covered with water 15 cubits high (Gen 7:20), was reached on the 150th day (Gen 7:24). If five months with 30 days each are assumed, this will have been on 17th day of the seventh month. On this day, the ark came to rest on the mountains (Gen 8:4). The ark is 30 cubits high (Gen 6:15) and half of it is under water, and so it had to come to rest when the level just slightly decreased (Gen 8:3b). On the first day of the tenth month the mountain-peaks were visible (Gen 8:5), on first day of the first month of the following year, the waters on earth had disappeared (Gen 8:13a), and on 27th day pf the second month, the ground was dry. But the problem of this calculation remains that 150 days only correspond to five months, when there is a solar year. If there is a lunar year, there will only be 147/8 days between 17th day of the second month and 17th of the seventh month. Probably, the 150 days are to be considered as an inexact but a "round" designation for five months. See Gunkel, *Genesis*, 147. This problem of calculation will not arise if Gen 8:4 is read following the LXX: ἑβδόμῃ καὶ εἰκάδι τοῦ μηνός ("27th day of the month"). In this case, MT לחדש יום עשר־שבעה ("17th day of the month") would have to be attributed to a haplography of an original יום ושרים־שבעה. In this reading, the waters increase for 150 days, that is, until 20th day of the seventh month following a lunar year. After the waters have decreased seven days, the ark comes to rest on 27th day of the second month (Gen 8:4 LXX). See H. Seebass, *Genesis I. Urgeschichte (1,1–11,26)* (Neukirchen–Vluyn: Neukirchener, 1996), 219. However, against this neat solution one should observe that the chronology of the LXX dates the beginning of the Flood in a different way, namely, on 27th day of the second month. The chronology in the non-Priestly text, which is based on 100 days in all, is simpler: seven days from Yhwh's speech until the beginning of the Flood (Gen 7:4); 40 days of rain (7:12; cf. 7:17; 40 days of waiting until Noah sent out a dove for the first time (Gen 8:6, 8); seven days each of waiting till the second and third sending out of the dove (Gen 8:10, 12); and finally the discovery that the earth was dry on the 101st day (Gen 8:13b). See also M. Rösel, "Die Chronologie der Flut in Gen 7–8. Keine neuen textkritischen Lösungen," *ZAW* 110 (1998): 590–93. For a new proposal, see J. C. Gertz, "Beobachtungen zum literarischen Charakter und zum geistesgeschichtlichen Ort der nichtpriesterschriftlichen Sintfluterzählung," in *Auf dem Weg zur Endgestalt: Festschrift Hans-Christoph Schmitt zum 65. Geburtstag* (ed. U. Schorn and M. Beck; BZAW 370, Berlin: de Gruyter, 2006), 41–57; see also idem, "Noah und die Propheten. Rezeption und Reformulierung eines altorientalischen Mythos," forthcoming in *Deutsche Vierteljahrsschrift für Literaturwissenschaft und Geistesgeschichte* 2007.

37. Jacob, *Sintfluterzählung*, 8.

10:1, nor with the promise of the covenant with Noah in Gen 9:11, 15, where the word *mabbul* clearly designates the totality of the flood. On the other hand, the assumption that it rained for forty days and that the highest water level remained for 110 days cannot be reconciled with the statement in Gen 8:2–3 according to which the water starts sinking with the end of the rain.[38]

These two examples suffice to show that a number of observations on the story of the Flood are easier to explain on Astruc's source-critical model than on Jacob's thesis of literary unity.[39] If Astruc's source-critical analysis has proved itself worthy regardless of its refuted historiographic assumption (i.e. the Mosaic authorship of the Pentateuch), one must ask with respect to Jacob whether his "close reading" does justice to the text.

III

As already mentioned, the reconstruction of the redaction history, beginning with the compilation of documents by Moses and ending with their integration by only moderately talented redactors, belongs to the weak points of Astruc's hypothesis. Even if subsequent research has not followed Astruc in detail, it shared for a long time his devaluation of later redactors and editors of the Pentateuch and his favour for the original documents. Fortunately, these values have radically changed. Few would oppose Jacob's view that the redactor could not have been the "*Schwachkopf*" (idiot) that he is usually presented as being and that he should rather be designated "*Verfasser*" (author).[40] Although it is difficult to understand the intention of that redaction responsible for the combination of both main sections of the Pentateuch (the Priestly and the

38. See J. A. Emerton, "An Examination of Some Attempts to Defend the Unity of the Flood Narrative in Genesis," *VT* 37 (1987): 401–20 (Part I); *VT* 38 (1988): 1–21 (Part II): here pp. 402–5. Jacob tries to cover up the problem by translating v. 2 with a past perfect (cf. idem, *Genesis*, 213; similarly G. J. Wenham, "Method in Pentateuchal Source Criticism," *VT* 41 [1991]: 84–109). Given the temporal structure of 7:23–8:4, this is, however, difficult. Jacob's reference to Ezek 31:15 and Hag 1:10 (*Genesis*, 213) lacks weight because of the different syntactical construction.

39. Recent contributions that consider one of the two strands within the Flood narrative to be a revision layer of the other must emphasize the double restraint on the redactors: the redactors were not free with their additions. Rather, they integrated transmitted material into the text that was to be revised. These analyses thus call for a modification of Astruc's source-model.

40. B. Jacob, *Die Thora Moses, Volksschriften über die jüdische Religion 1/3.4* (Frankfurt am Main, 1912–13), 93.

non-Priestly text), one does have reason to believe that the redaction attempted to combine the available texts into an independent and original literary composition. The presupposition of this new literary composition is the redactor's belief that the available materials reliably report one and the same "true" story. This is also Astruc's view. In keeping with such a presupposition, the literary evidence should be treated less as repetitions, stylistic deviations, *antichronisms*, etc. than as different perspectives which complete and modify each other. Here the redactor's inner biblical exegesis comes into contact with Jacob's search for coherence, which unwillingly contributes to a better understanding of redaction history. Jean Astruc's apologetic aims unfortunately hindered him from participating in this search.

The *Memoires* of Moses and the Genesis of Method in Biblical Criticism: Astruc's Contribution

Aulikki Nahkola

The purpose of this study is to argue—and hopefully go some way towards demonstrating—that what we have in Astruc's *Conjectures* on Genesis is also the genesis of method in biblical scholarship. It is in Astruc's work that we see the first systematic, if embryonic, presentation of the procedures for determining compositional layers in biblical traditions, which became the hallmark of Old Testament criticism for nearly two centuries, as well as an articulation of the presuppositions on which these procedures are based.

In the following I will outline Astruc's critical approach and assess its contribution to the developing Old Testament scholarship. I will do this by employing three perspectives. First, I will look at the paradigm shift in the study and use of the Bible which took place at the time of the Enlightenment and which for the first time brought the Bible to the focus of academic scrutiny for its own sake, rather than as source material for other disciplines or theological interests, and which culminates in Astruc's work. Secondly, I will focus on the specific contribution of *Conjectures* as a "first case" of explicitly articulated method in biblical studies and for the study of a biblical book. And finally, I will reflect on the notion of method in biblical studies and the nature of the discipline as a quintessentially Enlightenment, that is, modern, enterprise.

Paradigm Shift

By Astruc's time, and still in eighteenth-century France, the Bible had been studied for many purposes. Since the adoption of Christianity as an official religion in the late fourth century by Roman emperors, the Bible had had an unprecedented role in influencing human affairs. In the political realm, Christian rulers regarded their earthly powers as divinely ordained, as did their subjects and ecclesiastical establishments—based on such texts as Rom 13:1–7.[1] Similarly, in the pursuit of knowledge, whether in what we today call sciences or what we call humanities, the Bible had dominated to an astonishing extent, and had been used both as direct data for areas as varied as physics, government, law, history and linguistics, and as a backdrop for any discussion and a test for accepting any innovation—a fact witnessed in a spectacular way as late as 1616, when Galilei found to his cost that his thesis of heliocentric cosmology "expressly" contradicted "the doctrines of Holy Scripture."[2] At the same time, on the more overtly religious front, in the myriad of doctrinal and ecclesiological debates that followed the Reformation, all sides appealed to "what is written," while in church life the application of *Quadrica* to the Bible still provided spiritual guidance for many.

And even when sciences ceased to be directly derived from Scripture, then at least most people still thought, as Basil Willey famously put it, that "'truth' was not all of one order," and that "the older order of numinous truth was still secure in its inviolate separateness": that is, "Scripture...was a numinous book, and horror must be felt towards any attempt to apply to it the usual scientific tests."[3] Thus, when the Enlightenment started to push the boundaries of other realms of knowledge, the Bible was largely exempted. That explains why, when comments were eventually made concerning the Bible or its claims, such as miracles, there was such outrage. By the same token, and more so, the Bible had not been studied in any significant way for its own sake, that is, for understanding its own history, its composition and authorship. And when we talk about biblical criticism, that is of course what we mean, the study of the Bible itself, as a book, in its own right. Subjecting the Bible to

1. While the intimacy between the "two powers," the Church and the monarchy, fluctuated, the assumption of the biblical foundation for the model was not in doubt. This was still the case in Astruc's France, where the Gallican doctrine dictated "a profound union of two sources of legitimacy," one political, the other religious, in which "kings derived their authority directly from God and stood immediately below him in rank"; see D. Roche, *France in the Enlightenment* (trans. Arthur Goldhammer; Cambridge, Mass.: Harvard University Press, 1998), 353–54, 356. See also J. Grès-Gayer, "Gallicanism," in *The Papacy: An Encyclopedia* (ed. P. Levillain; 3 vols.; London: Routledge, 2002), 2:615–18.

2. J. J. Langford, "Galilei, Galileo," *New Catholic Encyclopedia* (15 vols.; 2d ed.; Washington, D.C.: The Catholic University of America, 2003), 6:58–64 (62). Bible texts used to defend a geo-centric view included Josh 10:12–13; Ps 103:5 and Eccl 1:5, see, for example, Langford, "Galileo, Galilei," 61.

3. B. Willey, *The Seventeenth Century Background: Studies in the Thought of the Age in Relation to Poetry and Religion* (repr.; London: Chatto & Windus, 1942 [1934]), 59.

scientific scrutiny was therefore not an obvious thing to do even in the context of the age. Thus it took place only sporadically at first and mainly fairly late in the Enlightenment, and was often carried out by unlikely practitioners. When it did finally happen, however, its consequences were momentous.

The Enlightenment was a time of rapid and sometimes cataclysmic change in the intellectual landscape. Pierre Chaunu has characterized the Enlightenment paradigm shift in human inquiry as the time when "the rational acquisition of knowledge was superimposed, in the minds of many, on the Christian notion of revealed knowledge."[4] This "rational acquisition of knowledge" was characterized by a focus on nature as both the source of knowledge and the model for it, and empiricism as the means of inquiry.[5] The eighteenth-century watch-words are sometimes encapsulated as secularism, rationalism and naturalism.[6]

Already in the centuries preceding the eighteenth century and the golden age of French Enlightenment, in which the work of Astruc also falls, a "science of nature" had emerged.[7] Nature had ceased to be looked upon as mythical, unpredictable and impenetrable, and instead it was discovered to be well-ordered, subject to laws and open to human

---

4. P. Chaunu, *La Civilisation L'Europe des Lumières* (Arthaud: Paris, 1971), 299. Similarly B. Willey, *The Eighteenth Century Background: Studies in the Idea of Nature in the Thought of the Period* (repr.; London: Chatto & Windus, 1980 [1940]), 3: "During the Christian centuries religion had rested upon revelation; now it rested largely upon 'Nature,' and even the orthodox, who retained the supernatural basis, felt that faith must be grounded firmly upon Nature before one had recourse to super-nature."

5. Ana Acosta, another historian of ideas, has aptly described the Enlightenment paradigm shift in the means of inquiry as a shift from "scholasticism to empiricism"; see A. M. Acosta, "Conjectures and Speculations: Jean Astruc, Obstetrics, and Biblical Criticism in Eighteenth-Century France," *Eighteenth-Century Studies* 35 (2002): 256–66 (258).

6. A. Wolf, *A History of Science, Technology, and Philosophy in the Eighteenth Century* (London: Allen & Unwin, 1938), 34.

7. For the difficulty of defining science, see D. C. Lindberg, *The Beginnings of Western Science: The European Scientific Tradition in Philosophical, Religious, and Institutional Context, 600 B.C. to A.D. 1450* (Chicago: University of Chicago Press, 1992), 1–20. For the general concepts of "science of nature" and "human science," see C. Fox, "Introduction: How to Prepare a Noble Savage: The Spectacle of Human Science," in *Inventing Human Science: Eighteenth-Century Domains* (ed. C. Fox, R. Porter and R. Wokler; Los Angeles, London and Berkeley: University of California Press, 1995), 1–30 (1–6), and for the development of "natural history" to "natural science," see G. S. Rousseau and R. Porter, *The Ferment of Knowledge: Studies in the Historiography of Eighteenth-Century Science* (Cambridge: Cambridge University Press, 1980), 263–78.

observation: there emerged, as A. Wolf has pointed out, "a belief in the 'natural order' of things and events, or a faith in the intrinsic orderliness of the processes of Nature (including human nature), without any magical or supernatural interference."[8] This paradigm shift ultimately influenced all realms of inquiry, biblical studies included, and it forms the proper context for the current discussion on the work of Astruc.

Just as there were discovered to be laws of physics and an ordered solar system,[9] so it was now thought that humankind and its actions, as part of nature, would be found to be similarly well-structured, perhaps even similarly predictable. The eighteenth century, particularly in France, was, then, a time when "thinkers sought to cap" the advances already made earlier in physical sciences "with a science of human nature," that is, "those sciences...the object of which is man himself."[10] Disciplines such as sociology, anthropology and psychology trace their roots to the eighteenth century in particular and regard themselves as a further stage in the Scientific Revolution, building on the already better-established natural sciences and their methodology.

While a wealth of scholarly literature now exists on how these "human sciences" in the conventional sense of the term emerged,[11] and how they relate(d) to natural science(s), and how obvious or complicated that relationship may have been, nowhere near as much attention has been given to the fact that the disciplines whose object is the *products* of human nature, of human creativity, such as literary criticism and aesthetics,[12] also emerged at the same time and from the same context. What is important for my argument here and for the study of Astruc's work, is the recognition of the close kinship between the human sciences and the disciplines studying their creative products, and the indebtedness of both to the "science(s) of nature." The emergence of the "criticisms," whether of biblical literature or of such classical works as the Homeric epics, is

8. Wolf, *A History of Science*, 34.

9. Much of this thanks to the work of "natural philosophers from Copernicus to Newton," who "had forged a science of nature" (Fox, "Introduction," 3).

10. Ibid., 1, 3. Fox is citing the famous eighteenth-century definition of human sciences already suggested by Marquis de Condorcet, who regarded by many as the "Father of Sociology."

11. For the possibilities in defining human sciences and a suggestion that theology should be included in them, see J. Christie, "The Human Sciences: Origins and Histories," *History of the Human Sciences* 6 (1993): 1–12 (1–3).

12. For the origin and development of aesthetics as a disciplines, see, for example, P. Mattick, Jr., "Introduction," in *Eighteenth-Century Aesthetics and the Reconstruction of Art* (ed. P. Mattick, Jr.; Cambridge: Cambridge University Press, 1993), 1–15.

thus not an isolated phenomenon, but part and parcel of the Enlightenment revolution and best understood in that context.[13] This explains both
the wide portfolios of interest and publication many scholars of the time
had, Astruc being a case in point, and both the philosophical and
methodological indebtedness of the early biblical scholarship to many
other types of contemporary inquiry.[14]

  This close kinship of disciplines is well illustrated by one of the most
notable characteristics of Enlightenment scholarship, namely, the lack
of clear lines of demarcation between various disciplines, even at times
their practitioners.[15] All the disciplines shared, as Ferro has argued,
"modes of functioning…similar for activities as far apart as historical
analysis, political thought, the social sciences, medical research."[16] Ferro
goes on to argue that this sharing of modes of functioning in each case
"resulted at the same time in the institutionalization of a profession and
the establishment of a discipline."[17] Wolf, in a similar vein, sees a common denominator between various disciplines in the fact that they shared
an "attitude of confidence in the competence of the human understanding, confidence in private judgement, as distinguished from reliance on
the dogmatic authority of others."[18] In other words, all the emerging
disciplines shared methods, underlying presuppositions and even practical ways of functioning in society.

  13. A great deal has been written recently on human sciences, their origin,
development and methodology, with several journals dedicated to the matter; see
especially *History of the Human Sciences* and also *Journal of the History of Ideas*.
Similar work is still largely left undone in biblical studies.
  14. Even a quick perusal of biblical scholarship betrays the extent of excursions
biblical studies have always made to other disciplines, be they anthropology,
folkloristics, linguistics or sociology, even if the meaning and implications of such
forays may not have often been explored, even recognized.
  15. This is in stark contrast to today's often excessively strict specialization,
where inferences are regularly left un-drawn between related areas of humanities, let
alone between humanities and sciences. That this is not necessarily the best, let alone
the only, possible state of affairs, is witnessed by the growing interest in inter-
disciplinary studies, as well as an outright challenge in some quarters to the rigid
disciplinary boundaries; see A. Grafton and N. Siraisi, "Introduction," in A. Grafton
and N. Siraisi, eds., *Natural Particulars: Nature and the Disciplines in Renaissance
Europe* (Cambridge, Mass.: MIT Press, 1999), 1–21.
  16. M. Ferro, *L'Histoire sous surveillance:Science et conscience de l'histoire*
(Paris: Calmann-Lévy, 1985), 115, cited in S. Bann, "History and Her Siblings: Law,
Medicine, and Theology," *History of the Human Sciences* 1 (1988): 7–21 (8).
  17. Ferro, *L'Histoire sous surveillance*, 115, cited in Bann, "History and Her
Siblings," 8. It may be of some interest here that Bann's article deals specifically
with the three disciplines, cum professions, of law, theology and medicine.
  18. Wolf, *A History of Science*, 34.

Besides the fact of shared roots, the lack of demarcation between disciplines and their modes of functioning in the Enlightenment is not surprising on several other accounts. Pre-Enlightenment, various realms of study were not well differentiated either. First, all knowledge was seen as welling from one source, revelation, and besides, practically all higher education was the realm of clergymen.[19] In the Universities, not only were teachers clergy, but students, whatever else they might study, all pursued a certain amount of divinity curriculum as well. In that sense there was no secular knowledge. In the Enlightenment reversal of fortunes, it was quite natural then that the new paradigm of "reason and nature" became equally pervasive: as much as one paradigm, revelation, had previously provided knowledge for all realms of inquiry—from doctrine to astronomy—so all disciplines now turned to the newly discovered, and it seemed, legitimized, sources of knowledge.

Secondly, concurrent with the move to the "reason and nature" paradigm there was a change in the demographics of the pursuit of knowledge. A phenomenon sometimes intriguingly labelled as "secular theology" emerged.[20] Theology became secular as "matters divine" ceased to be the sole domain of professional clergymen and started to be discussed by men without advanced divinity degrees, who took the centre stage, not only in advancing sciences and philosophy in general, but also in entering into debate about the nature of the Bible both as a document and as revelation. "Never before or after," Funkenstein points out, "were science, philosophy, and theology seen as almost one and the same occupation."[21] At the same time, theology became "secular" also in another way. It became orientated "toward the world, *ad speculum*."[22] This new outlook was secular at this stage in the sense of its "lively interest in this world and in our earthly life, as distinguished from the attitude of other-worldliness and a concentration of interest on a life hereafter."[23] The agenda of "earthly life" included the study of the Bible for itself.

The contribution of "secular theologians" becomes very obvious in the budding biblical scholarship. While "professional" theologians and clergymen occupied themselves with doctrinal controversies and the

19. "Except medicine and sometimes law," everything was taught by clergy, although even more qualifications than ordination was needed to teach theology; see A. Funkenstein, *Theology and the Scientific Imagination: From the Middle Ages to the Seventeenth Century* (Princeton, N.J.: Princeton University Press, 1986), 4.
20. For this term, see ibid., 3.
21. Ibid., 3.
22. Ibid., 3.
23. Wolf, *A History of Science*, 34.

practical aftermath of the Reformation, people such as Spinoza[24]—and Astruc—turned to the study of the Bible. It is not far-fetched to suggest that Astruc himself was a quintessential "secular theologian," a medical man of some considerable public stature—publications accredited to him by the end of his life numbered over a hundred—turning his hand to an apparently different field, biblical studies. And in doing so he transferred his scientific knowledge and mindset to the new, emerging discipline.

The fact that the accolade "Father of Biblical Criticism" has been regularly attached to the name of Astruc, a physician, rather than a theologian, has puzzled not only biblical scholars but many historians of science as well, familiar with Astruc from his medical context, where he left no similar legacy.[25] Seeing his work in the context of secular theology may go some way towards explaining how such interdisciplinarity was possible. To what extent Astruc's work on the Bible mirrors his medical publications, is also a relevant question and may throw light on Astruc's unique contribution to Enlightenment scholarship.

Even with no contributions of *Conjectures'* calibre to medicine, Astruc nevertheless had a stellar career in science. Most recently, Pierre Gibert has written about Astruc's medical work in most laudatory terms, and historians of medicine largely join the chorus. Thus Gibert describes him as a "brilliant student of the medical faculty of Montpellier," and describes his scientific work as "rigorous" and Astruc himself as possessing "authentic curiosity" and demonstrating a "clear and precise spirit."[26] In a similar vein, Laurence Brockliss and Colin Jones, leading historians

---

24. Funkenstein names people such as Galileo, Descartes, Leibniz, Newton, Hobbes and Vico. He also sees secular theology emerging "to a short career" in the sixteenth and seventeenth centuries. I would like to extend both his list of secular theologians and his timeframe, to include the eighteenth century and its scholars as well. See Funkenstein, *Theology and the Scientific Imagination*, 3.

25. In the history of medicine Astruc is not an unknown figure, but he is commented upon normally only in connection with fairly specialized, French, eighteenth-century issues, such as his contribution to midwifery and the treatment of venereal diseases; see L. Brockliss and C. Jones, *The Medical World of Early Modern France* (Oxford: Clarendon, 1997), 45–46, 417, 446–50, 468. There are also a few biographically inclined articles by scientists introducing his biblical work, in very general terms, to a scientist audience, and one exploring his works from the perspective of history of ideas. See, e.g., Acosta, "Conjectures and Speculations," 256–66; W. J. Osler, "Jean Astruc and the Higher Criticism," *Canadian Medical Association Journal* 2 (1912): 151–52; and A. Simpson, "Jean Astruc and His Conjectures," *Edinburgh Medical Journal* 14 n.s. (1915): 461–75.

26. P. Gibert, "Introduction et Notes de Pierre Gibert," in J. Astruc, *Conjectures sur la Gènese* (Paris: Editions Noêsis, 1999), 9–119 (9, 34–35) (my translation).

of medicine, label him as "the Montpellier *érudit.*"[27] However, Astruc was not always in the vanguard of medical progress—opposing, for instance, vaccination against smallpox and clinging to a "mechanistic view" of the human body much longer than most.[28] And when Astruc did focus on the more avant-garde causes—such as he did in his work on syphilis—this may have been as much for moral, as for scientific, reasons.[29]

The picture that emerges of Astruc in the medical field is a curious combination of erudition, encyclopaedic learning—his bibliography for a book on venereal diseases alone included over 600 works—and conservatism. In his professional field, Astruc may not have been as much an innovator and a creative thinker as he was an analyst and processor of a vast range of current ideas.

Contrary to some interpretations which see the Enlightenment spirit—and the above-mentioned secularization of knowledge—as intrinsically atheistic,[30] the shift to rationalism and naturalism, even secularism, was not necessarily antireligious, let alone atheistic in essence, particularly not early in the Enlightenment and never for the majority of its thinkers.[31]

27. Brockliss and Jones, *The Medical World*, 631.
28. Ibid., 470. The mechanical view of the body, or iatromechanism, seems to be one of the main reasons for Astruc's medical conservatism, and may have led him to see inoculation merely as "deliberately giving a healthy person a dose of small-pox"—an idea which he regarded as "absurd and dangerous."
29. Ibid., 45–46.
30. Some, including Paul Hazard, go as far as to argue that "the eighteenth century was not content with a Reformation. It wanted to topple the Cross. It wanted to eliminate the idea of a revelation, a communication between God and man. It wanted to destroy the religious conception of life" (P. Hazard, source unspecified, cited in Roche, *France in the Enlightenment*, 579). However, as Roche (*France in the Enlightenment*, 579) himself observes, this view portrays "unwarranted generality." It is more generally held that what appear as strong anti-religious sentiments generally target the Church as the mouth-piece of God, doctrines or forms of religious observance, rather than the idea of a divinity itself. And even when unambiguously atheistic, A. C. Kors has suggested, "quantitatively, of course, atheism was a narrowly circumscribed current of thought"; see A. C. Kors, *Atheism in France, 1650–1729.* Vol. 1, *The Orthodox Sources of Disbelief* (Princeton, N.J.: Princeton University Press, 1990), x.
31. Although the word "atheism" was certainly liberally used in religious works/tracts during the Enlightenment, it is far from certain that it actually designated people who truly denied the existence of any form of divinity. It was much more likely to be used to define opponents of all sorts, those one regarded "heretics," the ones considered to be "less pious," even those "who made light of the superstitions they knew"; see W. R. Ward, *Christianity Under the Ancien Régime, 1648–1789* (Cambridge: Cambridge University Press, 1999), 148–50.

Rather, it was a shift from revealed, special revelation to nature as God's general revelation, equally meant for humankind to study as the Bible, the special revelation, had always been. As Rousseau and Porter have pointed out, still in "the first half of the eighteenth century natural history was written mainly for religious purposes," to study "the wisdom of God," not to undermine belief in the Creator.[32] Nature's laws may have been discovered, but "the world" was still viewed very much "as the work of God."[33] This certainly seems to be the context and spirit of Astruc's work.

Astruc's Contribution

When it comes to his work on the Bible, Astruc stands on the shoulders of many great thinkers, in fact, thinkers much greater than himself. Just as in his scientific publications, Astruc had done his homework. *Conjectures* betrays a great deal of reading and an intimate familiarity with the intellectual landscape of the time. In *Conjectures* Astruc makes overt reference to more than a dozen Enlightenment scholars of various persuasions—church men (and ex-church men), philosophers and humanists. Most famous among the authors that he had read are Baruch Spinoza, Richard Simon, Jean le Clerc, Thomas Hobbes, Hugo Grotius and Isaac de la Peyrère.[34] Although there are many more people who wrote on problems in the Bible, this group is in fact representative of the innovative ideas of the time. Astruc also refers to a number of church fathers, Latin and Greek classical sources and ancient and medieval Jewish writers,[35] but his handling of biblical and historical issues suggests theological sophistication beyond his obvious sources.[36]

The Pentateuch, and particularly Genesis, was capturing the imagination of the Enlightenment. Many of the scholars Astruc refers to had pointed out problems in the biblical composition: inconsistencies, anachronisms and duplications. These "disturbances" in the text seem to have

32. Rousseau and Porter, *The Ferment of Knowledge*, 263.

33. Ibid., 263.

34. Others include Jean Pascal, Samuel Bochart, Pierre Huët, Claude Fleury, Laurent François and Thomas de Vio. Most of these authors appear in Astruc's index to the work, the rest in footnotes.

35. E.g. Augustine, Tertullian, Origen, Cicero, Homer, Josephus, Philo and Ibn Ezra.

36. The fascinating religious sojourn of the Astruc family—father Pierre's conversion to Catholicism having already trained as a Protestant pastor, his own theological training and what of that he seems to have passed on to his son Jean—is recounted by Gibert, "Introduction," 19–30.

crystallized into two main questions[37] at the time, which also vexed Astruc and which he set out to answer in *Conjectures*—and to that extent, the agenda for Astruc's *Conjectures* seems to have been set entirely by others. The questions were: Was Moses the author of the Pentateuch? Astruc thought "yes" and his work was a defence of this fact. Secondly: Had Moses used sources? And again Astruc answered "yes" and arguing and demonstrating that this fact did not amount to negating the Mosaic authorship emerges as the central contribution of his *Conjectures*. Thus, far from being an attempt to undermine Mosaic authorship or Penta-teuchal authority, *Conjectures* is in fact an apology for them.

On a certain level, then, very little of essence in Astruc's work is original to him: the confusing elements in the biblical text—repetition, inconsistencies, possible sources, perhaps even the different names of God, in fact, the observations that Astruc's work is remembered for—had all been pointed out by others.[38] Indeed, at least two of his prede-cessors, Baruch Spinoza and Richard Simon, have at times vied for the title "Father of Biblical Criticism."[39] At least in Simon's case, this could be quite justifiable, as Simon's critical work on the Bible had certainly been the most extensive up to that time, encompassing the entire Bible and also pioneering work in textual criticism. On the other hand, Spinoza was one of the most innovative thinkers of his time, besides also being a prolific writer with a command of several disciplines. He was also one of the first to point out problems which were difficult to reconcile with the traditional views of biblical authorship.

In contrast, Astruc does not emerge as an innovative thinker. He was a methodical man and *Conjectures* bears the hallmark of vast and ency-clopaedic learning, but he also impresses the reader as cautious, even conservative in his ideas. And yet it is Astruc's work that comes to be remembered as a vehicle for a new form of scholarship. And rightly so, for I would like to argue that *Conjectures* is the most significant work on

37. See, e.g., J. Astruc, *Conjectures sur les Mémoires originaux don't il paroit que Moyse s'est servi pour composer le Livre de la Genèse* (Brussels: Fricx, 1753), "Avertissement" and pp. 3–4. The third question was "whether Hebrew was the common language of the Canaanites," on which see Astruc, *Conjectures*, 323. Again, Astruc answered in the affirmative. The issue here really was the extent of the use of Hebrew in ancient times and therefore whether Moses' sources were in Hebrew.

38. Astruc himself acknowledges that both le Clerc and Simon had already pointed out that "it is very apparent that Moses, when writing Genesis, had had the help of some old documents (*Mémoires anciens*)"; see Astruc, *Conjectures*, 7.

39. See, e.g., A. Nahkola, *Double Narratives in the Old Testament: The Founda-tions of Method in Biblical Criticism* (Berlin: de Gruyter, 2001), 86.

the Bible at the time, because what was before him were basically *obser-vations*, comments on various individual quirks in the text, often of a very haphazard and disconnected nature. In contrast, Astruc was the first to construe a theory of *why* the inconsistencies and other disturbances were in the text, and to attempt to demonstrate the correctness of his theory by an extensive and consistent treatment of the texts in question. Astruc's work thus amounts to the first theory of biblical composition and an outline of a method of studying compositional features in the text. Both his theory and his method are assumed, in essence unchanged, when Julius Wellhausen brought the documentary theory to full bloom a little over a century later.

Thus, although much had already been written on the issues of Mosaic authorship and Pentateuchal composition, Astruc's predecessors had only been able to highlight the problem and offer hypothetical solutions to it. In his *Tractatus Theologico-Politicus* of 1670, for instance, Spinoza points out how in the five books of Moses "one and the same story is often met with again and again, and occasionally with very important differences in the incidents." This, together with the fact that "precept and narrative are jumbled together without order, and there is no regard to time," should lead the reader to the conclusion that "in the Pentateuch we have merely notes and collections to be examined at leisure, materials for history rather than the digested history itself." Spinoza goes on to suggest that in "the seven books which remain, down to the destruction of Jerusalem" (Joshua, Judges, Ruth, 1–2 Samuel and 1–2 Kings), the same characteristics appear as in the Pentateuch.[40] Spinoza's reasons for rejecting Mosaic authorship are mainly logical—the Pentateuch does not appear coherent as it repeats itself and includes events from both before and after Moses' birth.

Richard Simon in his *Histoire critique du Vieux Testament* of 1678, observes much the same confusion of repetitions and anachronisms and states as the cause the fact that what we now have in the Bible is "only an Abridgement of the Acts (*des Actes*)" originally "preserv'd intire in the Registery of the Republick."[41] In the process of abridgement, "many repetitions of the same things" may have been preserved as they did not seem to those that joined together the records "altogether superfluous, because they serv'd for explanation."[42] Simon moots a number of possible

40. B. Spinoza, *Tractatus Theologico-Politicus* (Hamburg, 1670) 117; ET *Tractatus Theologico-Politicus* (London: Trübner & Co., 1862), 189.

41. R. Simon, *Histoire critique du Vieux Testament* (Paris, 1678), Preface, p. * 6; ET *A Critical History of the Old Testament* (London, 1682), Preface, p. a 4.

42. Ibid., Preface, p. ** 1; ET, Preface, p. a 6.

reasons for problems in the text, such as "the Genius of the Hebrew tongue," which was prone to repetition, and the fact that "the Hebrews were not very polite (*polis*) writers" but "transpos'ed, or repeated the same thing."[43] There could also have been a mechanical reason: the biblical record was at first written on "little Scrolls or separate sheets" and the order of these could have changed.[44]

Thomas Hobbes, in his *Leviathan* of 1651, irritated by the anachronistic Mosaic claims for all of the Pentateuch, thunders that "it were a strange interpretation, to say *Moses* spake of his own sepulchre (though by Prophecy)" and that "it is therefore manifest, that those words were written after his interrement." He then goes on to enumerate similar instances in the rest of the Pentateuch.[45] Hobbes also dismisses conventional claims to authorship on the account of titles of works by arguing that, on that basis, Moses was no more the author of the book of Moses than Ruth was the author of the book of Ruth or the kings were the authors of the books of the Kings.

La Peyrère in his wonderfully titled *Men Before Adam* solves inconsistencies by suggesting "that *Moses* made a Diarie of all those wonderful things which God did for the people of *Israel* under the conduct of *Moses*," but that the Pentateuch was written from "a copy of a copy" of that "Diarie." In much copying—there was "a heap of copy confusedly taken"—it was inevitable that things got "confus'd, and out of order, obscure, deficient."[46] Otherwise, la Peyrère's basic argument is that some duplications—or at least the Creation stories—arose from two separate events: there had been two separate creations of humanity.[47]

What is different with Astruc is that, while he observes these very same disturbances in the text, he looks at the phenomenon comprehensively throughout Genesis and Exod 1–2,[48] and attempts to demonstrate that the study of the text bears out his suspicions of why the problems exist. Although Astruc does not explicitly call his approach a "method" or use all the relevant labels, *Conjectures* does provide all the steps required for a method, and they can be easily reconstructed.

43. Ibid., Preface, pp. ** 1, 1:38–39; ET, Preface, pp. a 6–7, 1:40.
44. Ibid., 1:38–39; ET, p. 1:40.
45. T. Hobbes, *Leviathan, or, the Matter, Forme & Power of a Commonwealth, Ecclesiasticall and Civill* (London: Andrew Crooke, 1651), 200.
46. I. de la Peyrère, *Men Before Adam* (London, 1656), iv, 205–6.
47. Ibid., iv, 208.
48. The history of the "adult" Moses starts with Exod 3, so these events he could, in Astruc's view, have recounted from his own experience.

Thus, first, Astruc observes the problem and moots a hypothesis. This is done in a fairly oblique fashion, by suggesting already in the title of the book that Moses appeared to have used sources (*mémoires*) in his composition of Genesis—and that this work was Astruc's "surmises" (*Conjectures*) about them—and by expressing in the Foreword the concern that *Conjectures* might provide "ammunition" "for the self-styled Free-thinkers" (*esprits-forts*), who "might use it to diminish the Pentateuch."[49] The problem Astruc appears to present is thus not the presence of inconsistencies in the text, but the fact that there have been attacks on the authority of the Pentateuch.[50] However, as it is these inconsistencies that had led to the undermining of Pentateuchal authority, that is, Mosaic authorship, the appearance of inconsistencies in the text is the real problem Astruc is tackling. The hypothesis Astruc presents to solve the problem is that Moses used sources in composing Genesis.

Secondly, Astruc enumerates his proofs, or evidence (*preuve*), for the use of sources. These are four in number. The first arises "from the repetitions which are in Genesis."[51] The second proof arises from the fact that "God has been given two different, alternative names in Genesis," "Elohim" and "Jehovah."[52] The third proof consists of the fact that in a study of Genesis "one finds this alternation in the names of God," while in the rest of the Pentateuch, "which Moses composed himself," "one does not find anything similar."[53] Finally, the fourth proof arises from the fact that there are "anachronisms and reversals of order" in Genesis.[54]

These proofs both describe the main points of contention in the text of Genesis and suggest the number and limits of the main documents. Proofs 1, 2 and 4 point out inconsistencies in the Genesis account and imply that such inconsistencies are not expected to be found in an account written by a single author.[55] Proof 4 argues that an application of proof 2, the different names of God, to the rest of the Pentateuch demonstrates that this phenomenon, so evident in the "repetitions" of Genesis, does not occur elsewhere in the Pentateuch—thus implying that in the rest of the Pentateuchal books *mémoires* are not used.

49. Astruc, *Conjectures*, "Avertissement."

50. This is suggested in the Foreword ("Avertissement") where Astruc hopes his work will not give ammunition to those who "might use to diminish the authority of the Pentateuch."

51. Astruc, *Conjectures*, 10.

52. Ibid., 10–11.

53. Ibid., 13–14.

54. Ibid., 16.

55. Astruc also states this explicitly, ibid., 12.

Astruc's third step is to apply these proofs to Genesis and Exod 1–2 and arrange in columns the resulting delineations of the documents. This results in four main documents, and displaying them in full forms the bulk of *Conjectures*.[56] Astruc characterizes this process as "decomposing" (*décomposer*) and explains the process of laying them out as "not all that difficult" since he "only needed join together all the places where God is consistently called *Elohim*," place them in one column, and then do the same to "all the other places where God is consistently called *Jehovah*."[57]

Finally, Astruc argues the correctness of his theory from four "advantages" (*advantages*) which it offers in solving the problems of Genesis. These advantages are in part similar to the "proofs," in that they explain the problems identified by them. The first advantage "redeems" (*sauver*) "the peculiarity" (*singularité*) of finding alternating names of God in Genesis, while the second advantage similarly explains repetitions and the third anachronisms that are found there.[58] Finally, the fourth advantage of Astruc's theory on composition, crucially for Astruc's main purpose of the book, "exonerates Moses from the errors which have been imputed to him."[59]

Method in Biblical Studies

The foregoing is in outline Astruc's method, which consists of comparing duplicate passages and the variations that occur in them in a few practical steps. This method eventually became the template in biblical criticism for discerning sources in biblical literature and determining their limits. This brings me to the most interesting aspect of not only Astruc's work, but of the notion of method in biblical studies as such. For although we commonly think of method as "steps" or "procedures" which we "apply" to a text to "find out" something about it—that is, its unity—these steps are only a mirror image of what we think the text "should be like." This is a key observation that, for instance, John Barton makes in his seminal work on biblical methodology, *Reading the Old*

---

56. Document A contains the name "Elohim" and document B the name "Jehovah." Document C consists mainly of Patriarchal matters, while D has much of the rest, although Astruc also suggests a further eight minor documents. See ibid., 25–290.

57. Ibid., 17.

58. Ibid., 332–438.

59. Ibid., 431 : "Elle disculpe Moyse des négligences et mêsme des fautes, qu'on ose lui imputer."

Testament, where he states that "no method can be used until there is some prior understanding of the text."[60]

Astruc, or anyone else, only "registers" repetitions, inconsistencies, anachronism, and the like in a composition as something unusual, because he already has a notion of "what a text should be like." Such notions are usually held unconsciously and are therefore regarded as self-evident, and as such are very difficult to challenge. It may be of significance that Astruc nowhere addresses the question of why he expects such coherence from biblical accounts. In turn, the fact that Astruc's work has had such a lasting legacy perhaps indicates, above all, how deeply held and widely shared this model of literature has been in the Western world since the Enlightenment.

But how did Astruc acquire this notion of literature? The model of literature Astruc adheres to is that of a treatise, a scientific or a historical document.[61] Enlightenment historians generally see Spinoza as the originator of this concept of literature, and certainly as the one to apply it to the Bible. As Yirmiyahu Yovel has pointed out, "humanists had turned the Bible from a mere story into a 'text,' whilst Spinoza's second revolution turned it into a 'document'"—and crucially, "a *secular* document."[62] The Bible became "a literary document like any other,"[63] and one that reflected the inherently rational, continuous experience of the Enlightenment.

The point in reflecting on Asruc's work is not to arbitrate whether his model and/or method are right or wrong, but to understand how they arose and what presuppositions are inherent in them. That Astruc's model is not the only possible model, even in the Enlightenment, is witnessed to by the fact that this very volume celebrates the work of another eighteenth-century scholar, Robert Lowth, whose *De sacra poesi Hebraeorum* was published in the same year as Astruc's *Conjectures*, but implies a very different concept of literature, where repetition is seen as an

60. J. Barton, *Reading the Old Testament: Method in Biblical Study* ([1984]; new ed.; London: Darton, Longman & Todd, 1996), 5. For a further synopsis on discussion of method in biblical scholarship, see Nahkola, *Double Narratives*, 73–79.

61. I have elsewhere called Astruc's model of literature, which he shares with, among others, Simon, that of an "archivist-historian," a slight development from Spinoza's "nature"-model; see Nahkola, *Double Narratives*, 86–93.

62. Y. Yovel, *Spinoza and Other Heretics*. Vol. 2, *The Adventures of Immanence* (Princeton, N.J.: Princeton University Press, 1989), 19; Yovel is here reflecting P. F. Moreau, "La méthode d'interprétation de l'Ecriture Sainte," in *Spinoza, science et religion* (ed. R. Bouveresse; Actes du Colloque, Cerisy-la-Salle, 1982; Paris: Vrin, 1988), 109–14.

63. L. Strauss, *Spinoza's Critique of Religion* (New York: Shocken, 1965), 35.

artistic device. However, it is also a fact that Astruc's model has dominated biblical studies until relatively recently, when first the "Bible as literature" approach offered a different model of literature (if not a different method of studying it) and then post-modern approaches mooted a new hermeneutical perspective, one with the emphasis on the reader.

When we attempt new vistas in biblical studies, it may, however, be worth remembering that any insights are only as good as the method that procures them, and that any method is only as valid as the presuppositions that underline it: it is not possible to produce something truly new by simply "tinkering with the corners." But if and when something truly new does arrive, one hopes that it is presented with as much flare and clarity as Astruc's *Conjectures*.

AN HEIR OF ASTRUC IN A REMOTE GERMAN UNIVERSITY: HERMANN HUPFELD AND THE "NEW DOCUMENTARY HYPOTHESIS"

Otto Kaiser

Der Kampf für Wahrheit und Recht ist nichtig
ohne Wahrhaftigkeit und Gerechtigkeit.[1]

1. *Hermann Hupfeld as founder of the*
New Documentary Hypothesis

In looking for the influence of Jean Astruc's *Conjectures sur les mémoires originaux dont il paroit que Moyse s'est servi pour composer le livre de la Genèse* on German Old Testament scholarship, we should mention not only Johann Gottfried Eichhorn, but also Hermann Hupfeld, the founder of the so-called New Documentary Hypothesis. In his study, *Die Quellen der Genesis und die Art ihrer Zusammensetzung. Aufs neue untersucht,*[2] which was published in 1853 and formerly communicated in four articles in the *Deutsche Zeitschrift für christliche Wissenschaft und christliches Leben* (cf. Hupfeld 1853, iii), he found that most scholars understood the books of the Pentateuch in the frame of the so-called Development Hypothesis.

According to its basic form, the Pentateuch is the result of the supplementation of a primary Elohistic document by Yahwistic texts. In its most frequently occurring variant, this happened by one redactor introducing the Yahwistic texts into the older document. Influential representtatives of this theory include Wilhelm Martin Leberecht de Wette (1780–1849),[3] Friedrich Tuch (1806–1867)[4] and Friedrich Bleek

---

1. "The fight for truth and justice is nothing without honesty and fairness." According to Riehm (1867, 140), Hupfeld put this motto under his lithography.
2. "The sources of Genesis and the way of their compilation. Examined again."
3. Cf. de Wette 1845, 214–15; for more on de Wette, see Smend 1989, 38–52.
4. Cf. Tuch 1838 (= 1871), xli–xlv; for Tuch's biography, see Ryssel 1908.

(1793–1759).[5] It was the particular achievement of Hermann Hupfeld, then professor at the University of Halle, to clarify the textual situation, making a distinction between a primary Elohistic *Urschrift* and a newer Elohistic source. Additionally, he demonstrated that the Yahwistic texts (or "Jhvhistic," as he preferred to say) (cf. Hupfeld 1853, 5 n. 1) should be understood as parts of a special document, whose relationship to mythology and popular legends is responsible for their special flair (cf. Hupfeld 1853, 93–97). In addition, he observed that virtually all the Elohistic narratives have Yahwistic parallels and that they are more tolerant than those with their rather nationalistic orientation.

In spite of this, he judged the Elohistic document to be older than the Yahwistic one, for he thought its theology related more to the *Urschrift* than to the other source (cf. Hupfeld 1853, 33–43, 47–48, 98 and esp. 193–95). He attributed the combining of the three files to one late redactor, who, if necessary, smoothed the transitions and added, at most, short sentences.[6] Hupfeld's particular observations are most compelling within the realms of Genesis,[7] but somewhat dubious in his tabulation of the

5. Cf. Bleek 1860, 252–60; for Bleek's biography, see Kamphausen 1897; Smend 1989, 71–84. For the varieties of the *Ergänzungs*, Development Hypothesis, see Holzinger 1893, 54–60.

6. Cf. Hupfeld 1853, 200–203, and the summary at p. 163 n. 69.

7. Cf., for example, his source analysis of the story of the Flood (1853, 81, 136) with that of Martin Noth (1948, 17, 29) as representative of an adherent to the classical documentary hypothesis and that of Christoph Levin (1993, 103–17) as representative of redactional criticism. Levin distinguishes between JR (the Yahwistic Redaction), JQ (the Pre-Yahwistic Source), JS (the Post-Yahwistic Additions), R (the Final-Redactor) and RTh (the late Theodicy-Redaction) as follows:

The Story of the Flood according to the Primary Document or P:

Hupfeld PD: 6:9–22; 7:6, 11, 13–16a, 17–22, 24; 8:1a, 2a, 3b–5, 6b, 13–19; 9:1–17 (+28–29).

Noth P: 6:9–22; 7:6, 11, 13–16a, 18–21, 24; 8:1, 2a, 3b–5, 7, 13a, 14–19; 9:1–17, 28, 29.

Levin P: 6:9–22; 7:6–9, 11, 13–14bα, 15–16a, 18–21, 23b–24; 8:1–2a, 3b–5, 13a, 14–19; 9:1–17 (+28–29).

The Story of the Flood according to the Yahwistic History:

Hupfeld J: 6:5–8; 7:1–5 (7–9), 16b, 10a, 12, 23; 8:(1b), 2b, 3a, 4aαb; 7:6, 7, 8–12, 20–22.

Noth J: 6:5–8; 7:1, 2, 3b, 4, 5, 10, 7*, 16b, 12, 17b, 22, 23aαb; 8:6a, 2b, 3a, 6b, 8–12, 13b, 20–22.

Levin JR: 6:1–2, 5a, 6–8; 7:1a–2, 4, 5, 16b, 23aα; 8:8, 9aα, 6b–11a, 12–13b, 20–21aα, 21b–22; 9:18.

JQ: 7:10a, 12, 17b, 22*, 23aβ; 8:6a, 2b–3a, 6b–7.

JS: 7:3b; 8:9aβ, 11b.

R: 7:10b, 17a.

RTh: 6:5b, 9*; 7:1b; 8:21aβ.

primary Elohistic document, his *Urschrift*, in the book of Exodus. Here, for example, he reckons the Ten Commandments and the Covenant Code hail from this older document.[8]

When Hupfeld had finished his research, he became aware of the work of two other scholars. In his 1798 *Urkunden des Jerusalemischen Tempelarchivs* I,[9] Karl David Ilgen had already given some evidence that two different Elohistic documents must have existed. So too de Wette, in his 1807 *Kritik der Mosaischen Geschichte*,[10] had observed that there were, at least as far as the Sinaitic lawgiving, some independent Elohistic texts which had not been part of the primary Elohistic document and were similar to the Yahwistic narratives. Unfortunately, these observations became overshadowed by newer publications and theories so that even Hupfeld had forgotten them. He declared that he usually preferred to read the texts for themselves rather than what other people had written about them. Later on, we shall see that this sincerity is a significant part of his character. However, before we examine Hupfeld's education and his further career, we have to confirm genuinely his merits as the founder of the New Documentary Hypothesis. To do this, I quote Robert H. Pfeiffer's 1941 *Introduction to the Old Testament*:

> If we call his Primary Document the Priestly Code and his later Elohistic source the Elohist it is obvious that Hermann Hupfeld has been the founder of the New Documentary Hypothesis. The chief weakness of Hupfeld's theory was the chronological sequence of his three sources. It was eventually found that the order was not P, E, J, as Hupfeld had it, but J, E, P. (Pfeiffer 1941, 189)

2. *The Contribution of Eduard Riehm*

In the interest of the completeness of the picture, let me add some remarks on the book, *Die Gesetzgebung Mosis im Lande Moab*,[11] written

---

8. Cf. Hupfeld 1853, 80–86; there he also offers a division of the *Urschrift* or Primary Document into four periods: (1) from the creation to the beginning of the flood (Gen 1:1–5* +, 9:28–29); (2) from the flood to Abraham (Gen 6:9–11:26*); (3) from the history of the divine guidance of the elected fathers of his holy people Israel in Canaan and Egypt (Gen 11:27–Exod 2:25*); and (4) from the deliverance out of Egypt and its conclusion to the covenant at Mount Sinai and the mediation of the basic laws of the kingdom of God by Moses (Exod 6:2–24:8) and the following revelation to the cultic orders, the second part of the march through the wilderness and the distribution of the country in Canaan.

9. *Documents from the Jerusalemian Archives of the Temple I*; cf. also Seidel 1993, 222–24, 229–30, 239.

10. *Critic of the Mosaic History*.

11. *The Legislation of Moses in the Land of Moab*.

by Hupfeld's master's student, later his colleague and his true successor, Eduard Riehm (1830–1888).[12] Riehm's work was published in 1854 only one year after Hupfeld's book. It also had its own prehistory, for it had been the reworked and augmented edition of his Heidelberg dissertation, which he had written under the supervision of Friedrich Wilhelm Karl Umbreit, editor of *Theologische Studien und Kritiken*, the organ of the so-called Mediation Theology,[13] to which he dedicated his study (in addition to dedicating it to Hupfeld). It is well known that, due to this investigation, the idea—which de Wette had already published in his 1803 *dissertatio critica* and which he repeated in every edition of his successful *Lehrbuch der historisch-kritischen Einleitung*[14]—became almost commonly accepted. It is conspicuous that Riehm refers only briefly and vaguely to de Wette's 1806 *Kritischer Versuch über die Glaubwürdigkeit der Bücher der Chronik mit Hinsicht auf die Geschichte der mosaischen Bücher und Gesetzgebung*, and not at all to the sixth edition of his *Introduction* from 1845, which includes a special chapter on the characteristics of Deuteronomy and its late origin that also includes Riehm's main arguments.[15] The primary partner in his discussion was instead the *Geschichte des Volkes Israel I–III* of Heinrich Ewald (1803–1875).[16]

Riehm's principal arguments for the determination of Deuteronomy's age of origin are: (1) that a book containing such laws as that for the king in Deut 17:14–20 could be written neither by Moses nor in the time of King Solomon;[17] (2) that the law on the installation of judges in Deut

12. For Riehm's biography, see Pahncke-Pforta 1905. In 1862, Riehm became extraordinary professor in the theological faculty of the University at Halle. He became ordinary professor after Hupfeld's death in 1866.

13. Cf. to him Hirsch 1949 (= 1964), 375. It may have been through the influence of *Umbreit* that Riehm finished his book with a chapter on the difference between the meaning of the Law in the Old and the New Testaments, using a typically Protestant, if not Lutheran, argument; cf. Riehm 1854, 126–30 (129–30).

14. *Manual of the Historical and Critical Introduction* (6th ed. 1845).

15. Cf. de Wette 1845, 213–42, and for the dating of the time of Josiah, pp. 220–21.

16. For more on Ewald, see Perlitt 1987, and Reventlow 2001, 290–94.

17. Cf. Ewald 1843, 160–61 and 1847. Dtn was written in the second part of King Manasseh's reign (1845, 20–21): it cannot be Mosaic (1847, 279–82) since it has been written by a Jew who fled during the time of Manasseh's horrific deeds to Egypt, where he was later confronted with his compatriots, whom Manasseh had sold to the Egyptian king Psammetich—a romance which Ewald based on Deut 17:16 and 28:68 and which Riehm did not accept. However, he agreed with Ewald that the lawbook, which was found during the time of King Josiah, was identical to the Pentateuch as a whole; cf. Riehm 1854, 81–85.

17:8–13 could not have been written before the time of King Jeho-
shaphat;[18] and (3) that the laws on the limitation of the public worship to
Jerusalem in Deut 12 and those on the tithe in Deut 18:1–8 could not
have been designed before the reform introduced by King Hezekiah
(Riehm 1854, 36, 49). On the other side, the law already existed in the
eighteenth year of Josiah and must, therefore, have been composed some
time earlier. Reflecting that some interval was needed to draw the consequences of the new cultic conditions introduced by Hezekiah and its
effects on the Levites,[19] Riehm argued in principal agreement with Ewald
for a date in the second part of the government of King Manasseh (pp.
98–105). Lastly, we should mention that Riehm became aware that the
Deuteronomic Law is something like a new edition of the Covenant
Code in Exod 20:22–23:33 (pp. 62–64 with 116–26). Riehm's discussion
of whether the author of Deuteronomy's putting on of the clothes of
Moses is a forgery or is justified (pp. 114–15) and his final chapter on its
salvation-historical meaning (pp. 126–30) give us a hint that he was
strongly influenced by the post-Schleiermacher Theology of Mediation,
which had its roots in the Prussian Awakening Movement and was
ecclesiastically oriented (Hirsch 1949 [= 1964], 375). Let me pass over
the not-yet-finished discussions on the literary history of the Tetrateuch
and the unity and age of Deuteronomy (Kaiser 2000), but underline that
Riehm has rounded the New Documentary Hypothesis down and may be
remembered with gratitude for this.

3. *The Historical Context of Hupfeld's Life*

What does the scientific contribution of Hermann Hupfeld and Eduard
Riehm have to do with the beginnings of historical criticism at the
University of Marburg and, moreover, what does it have to do with the
subject of the legacy of Jean Astruc? The answer to this queston is very
simple: Hupfeld has been *de facto* the first documented representative of
the new method in the history of the Philipps-University at Marburg and
its theological faculty, which was stimulated by Astruc's well-known
monograph and, of course, by Eichhorn's development of it. The following pages shall not only prove this, but also remind us that the way from
belief in the verbal inspiration of biblical scriptures to the liberty to read
them according to the same principals used in other literature of the past
has, for many of them, been a difficult one. For this, we may take Hupfeld's development as an example.

18. Cf. Deut 17:8–13 with 2 Chr 19:8–11; see Riehm 1854, 86–89.
19. Cf. Deut 14:22–29; 26:1–11.

Hupfeld was born on March 31, 1796 in Marburg, which is situated in the Landgrafschaft Hessen and became an electorate only in 1803,[20] and he died on April 24, 1866 in Halle. His life spanned the time between the last decade of the Old German Empire, which ceased to exist upon the relinquishment of its crown by the Habsburg Emperor Franz II on August 6, 1806 (cf. von Aretin 1997, 522–31; respectively Schmidt 1999, 329–46), until just a few months before the Prussian Parliament decided upon the annexation of the Hessian electorate in 1866.[21]

However, before we may compare the yet-to-be-famous student with his then-famous academic teacher, we must review the main dates of Hupfeld's life. Hermann (Christian Carl Friedrich) Hupfeld was the first of ten children. His father, Bernhard Carl Hupfeld (1765–1823),[22] a man of piety but also of mild rationalism, then held the office of priest in the small village of Dörnberg in the county of Holzappel situated northwest of Limburg at the Lahn.[23] Anxious about an expected French attack on the eastern bank of the Rhine, Bernhard Hupfeld sent his pregnant wife to his parents' house in Marburg.[24] As a result, the boy was born in the city where he would later live for nearly a quarter of a century as a student and as a professor of its Philipps University.[25] His father was

20. Cf. Losch 1922, 1–19; and for its politics to 1806, Seier 1998 (= 2003), 12–14.
21. For the Prussian annexation of the electorate, see Losch 1922, 376–428, and Seier 1998 (= 2003), 176–81.
22. For the dates of the families of Hupfeld's grandfather, Bernhard Hupfeld, his father and his own, see Stahr 1957, 15–16, Nr. 18597–602. In his father's dates (18599) his position as a pastor in Melsungen is missing, in those of Hermann Hupfeld the place of his birth is probably under influence of Gundlach (1927, Nr. 61) erroneously given as Spangenberg, but according to Hupfeld (1831, 271) to change in Marburg.
23. For more on the "Herrschaft Esterau-Holzappel," see Lau 1943, 51–56, 135–36, 154–55.
24. Situated in the Augustinergasse; cf. Stahr 1957, 15, Nr. 18597 Hupfeld, Bernhard.
25. Hupfeld 1831, 271: "*Ich bin der Erstgeborene des im J.1823 zu Spangenberg verstorbenen Metropolitans Bernhard Karl Hupfeld und dessen noch lebender Witwe Ernestine geb. Sigel, aus dem Württembergischen; und wurde den 31. März 1796 dahier zu Marburg in meinem großväterlichen Hause geboren, wohin mein Vater—damals Pfarrer in Dörnberg, einem Anhalt-Bernburg-Schaumburgischen Dörfchen unweit Holzappel—meine Mutter wegen der dortigen Kriegsunruhen beim Herannahen ihrer Niederkunft in Sicherheit gebracht hatte*" ("I am the firstborn of the Metropolitan Bernhard Karl Hupfeld, who died 1823 at Spangenberg, and his still-living widow, Ernestine born Sigel, from Württemberg, and was born here at Marburg in my grandfather's house, where my father—then pastor at Dörnberg, a small Anhaltinian-Bernburgian-Schaumburgian village not far from Holzappel—had my mother brought because of martial unrest and her expected delivery"). Indeed, in

minister in Melsungen from 1802, and in Spangenberg from 1804 until
his untimely death in 1823, two places situated some thirty miles into the
beautiful mountain country southeast of Cassel. His mother, Ernestine
Eberhardine Catharine, born Sigel (1773–1864), was the daughter of the
Württemberg Pastor and Magister Georg Christian Sigel at Laichingen.
Bernhard Carl Hupfeld's decision, in 1809, to stop teaching his eldest
son himself and to send him to his wife's brother, Magister Carl Christian Ferdinand Sigel might be attributed not only to the father's limited
educational abilities, but also to his intention to secure for Hermann
quieter surroundings, for his brother-in-law ministered as Lutheran
pastor at Siglingen, a small village on the Jagst, a northern tributary of
the Neckar.

Uncle Sigel was deeply influenced by the pietistic ideals and practices
of Nikolaus Ludwig, Count of Zinzendorff (1700–1760) (cf. Wallmann
1990, 108–23), and he did his best during the two years he was responsible for Hermann's education to lead his open-minded nephew along
the same path. Later Hupfeld confessed that Sigel planted in him *"eine
Begeisterung für das Christenthum"* and the *"Predigerberuf"* ("an enthusiasm for Christianity" and "the wish to became a preacher"), both of
which would subsequently be decisive in his life. Another heritage,
equally influential upon him, was his uncle's opposition to every variety
of rationalism (Hupfeld 1831, 279). After a year and a half, Hupfeld's
father sent him to the well-attended grammar school at Hersfeld in the
east of the electorate, where Hermann was a student from November
1811 to Spring 1813 and where he met, as a fellow pupil, his younger
brother Gustav.

4. *The Eve of Suprarationalism and Rationalism*
in the Theological Faculty of Marburg and Its
Leading Figure Professor Jacob Albert Arnoldi

When at Easter of 1813 Hupfeld began his studies at Marburg, Albert
Jacob Arnoldi[26] was one of the most influential members in the senate of

the same year a French army crossed the Rhine and reached Wetzlar, where it was
defeated by the Archduke Karl and forced to retreat; see Straganz 1914, 72.

26. Born on October 1, 1750 in Herborn, died on November 4, 1835 in Marburg,
professor at the University of Marburg from 1789 to 1829; honorary citizen of
Marburg for his merits at the University of Marburg on December 9, 1834; cf. Akten
des Stadtarchivs Marburg D 1123: Verzeichnis der Ehrenbürger der Stadt Marburg
Nr. 8 resp. Ehrenbürger (1978), 41, Nr. 8. For more on Arnoldi, see Gundlach 1927,
35–36, Nr. 55, Kähler 1927, 511; for his biography, see Strieder 1781, 179–81, and
further Maurer 1930, 2:48–50, and Kaiser 2005, 29–42.

the university and also, as the Professor Primarius, in the theological faculty. Arnoldi had studied theology and Oriental languages at the Universities of Herborn and Groningen, and in 1789 was appointed third full professor of theology at Marburg, where he was further promoted to second and then, in Autumn of 1792, to the Primarius of his faculty. He was a three-time prorector of the university, twice a second prorector, and an eight-time dean of the theological faculty. He was also co-director of the philological seminar from 1811 to 1815.[27] His vote for Hupfeld's appointment, on March 8, 1825, was consistent with his conviction that a good knowledge of classical antiquity is the best foundation for all true scholarship (cf. Acta 1825), an opinion which G. R. Driver still promoted in his Presidential Address at the Strassbourg Congress in 1956 (cf. Driver 1957, 5–6). Heidelberg's theological faculty in 1795 and its philosophical faculty in 1822 respectively awarded Arnoldi an honorary doctoral degree.

However, in spite of his rhetorical abilities[28] and his comprehensive education, Arnoldi published only three booklets: one on difficult passages in the book of Proverbs,[29] a second on the same in the book of Isaiah (cf. Arnoldi 1796), and a third on the Syrian Chronicle of Abulfaragi (cf. Arnoldi 1805). As an excellent Orientalist, he is recorded as a contributor to the eleventh volume of the *Thesaurus Syriacus* published in Oxford in 1879 by Payne-Smith (cf. Arnoldi 1897). The catalogue of his personal library has 190 pages and lists about 7000 items. The small number of philosophical books, among them one by Descartes and seven by Christian Wolff,[30] offers just a hint as to his rationalistically broken supranaturalism, as does the fact that in 1790 he edited the second edition of the *Compendium theologiae dogmaticae*, written by his predecessor Samuel Endemann (1727–1789),[31] which he used, together with

27. Cf. Gundlach 1927, Nr. 55, and Münscher and Wachler 1817b, 79, 86, 92, 98.

28. For which his special vote for the appointment of Hupfeld to an extraordinary professor of the theological faculty on April 14, 1825 may be quoted as a testimony; cf. Acta 1825. He begins with a modest antithesis to the opinion of his opponents and then takes their arguments to the extreme in an ironical fashion so that his own position seems, in the end, to be the only natural one; cf. Kaiser 2005, 56–57.

29. Cf. Arnoldi 1781 with the shorter Latin translation of 1783.

30. Katalog 1836, Nr. 2171–77. For more on Wolff's time as a professor in Marburg, see Kähler 1927, 332–62, 374–87; for his intellectual supranaturalism, see Dorner 1867, 687–93.

31. Unfortunately, the Marburg University library lost this book at the end of the Second World War, while other German libraries have only a former edition. Therefore his systematic convictions were only documented by a transcript of his

the 1789 *Epitome Theologiae Christianae* of the Lutheran theologian
Samuel Friedrich Nathanael Morus, as a manual for his lectures in
dogmatics.[32]

As testimony to his exegetical erudition, we may mention that works
standing on Arnoldi's shelves included many of Johann David Michaelis' publications, but also Robert Lowth's *De sacra poesi Hebraeorum*
with notes by Michaelis,[33] and, of course, the anonymous German translation of Astruc's *Conjectures* (published at Frankfurt in 1783),[34] Johann
Gottfried Eichhorn's *Einleitung in das Alte Testament I–III* (Leipzig,
1780–1783),[35] and last, but not least, Johann Gottfried Herder's *Vom
Geist der ebräischen Poesie I–II* (Dessau, 1782–83).[36]

According to Hupfeld's statements regarding his primary academic
teacher, Arnoldi's lectures must have been influenced by Endemann's
differentiation between the *revelatio naturalis* and the *revelatio supranaturalis* with a special ethical emphasis (cf. Maurer 1930, 1:49–50 with
9). This mixture of naturalistic and supranaturalistic ideas, eclectically
combined with historical criticism, should have led his young student,
Hermann Hupfeld, to severe doubting.[37] However, hastily judging Arnoldi
as a backward-oriented scholar would be wrong. It would be more just to
see him as a scholar in the period of transition from a late rationalised
supranaturalism to historical criticism.

lectures on *Christliche Glaubenslehre* written by A. F. C. Kilmer during the summer
term of 1820; cf. StAMR 340 Nachlaas (August) Vilmer No. 262). See Gundlach
1927, 35, Nr. 54. For the suspicion that he had caused the interdict of the Landgraf
in 1786 and 1788 to treat Kant in the University, cf. Kähler 1927, 428–38 (437) and
Sieg 1989, 17–18. For Arnoldi's biography, see Münscher and Wachler 1817b,
69–71; for the judgment Endemann's systematic position, see Wagenbach 1877
(= 1968), 105, and also Maurer 1930, 1:3–10 (5–6). According to them, Endemann
distinguished between a *revelatio naturalis* and a *revelatio supranaturalis*, which
caused Maurer to attest to Endemann (1930, 10) that he possessed a strong systematic power to combine as a whole the different aspects of Christian doctrine.
Endemann's anti-Kantian conviction was shared by Arnoldi and Münscher, both of
whom lost parts of their audience to the pro-Kantian theologian Johann Lorenz
Zimmermann (1762–1834), who was appointed in 1792 as third professor of the
theological faculty; cf. Münscher and Wachler 1817, 35; Gundlach 1927, Nr. 57; and
Kaiser 2005, 30–34.

32. Cf. Maurer 1930, 1:49–50; for Endemann's system cf. pp. 3–10.

33. Katalog 1836, Nr. 2773: Robert Lowth, praelectt. de s. poesi hebraeorum c.
not. et epimetr. J. D. Michaelis, Altendorf und Nürnberg 1770.

34. Katalog 1836, Nr. 3587.

35. Katalog 1836, Nr. 2719–2721.

36. Katalog 1836, Nr. 2774–2775.

37. Cf. below, 228–29.

Unfortunately, we do not have Hupfeld's scripts of Arnoldi's exegetical lectures, but only the catalogue of his library and a note by Arnoldi in the files concerning Hupfeld's appointment as a *professor extraordinarius* in the theological faculty at Marburg from April 14, 1825, that he had lectured in the summer term of 1823 on the topic of "Historical and critical introduction to the scriptures of the Old and New Testament" (Acta 1825, StAMR 305a AIV 1b 32). That he did not use in his lectures what he had read in his above-mentioned modern exegetical books is hardly imaginable. When Hupfeld tells that he later studied Astruc, Lowth, Michaelis, Ammon, Herder and de Wette privately, one may assume that he had became aware of their importance to Old Testament scholarship by Arnoldi's lectures.

In the records of Hupfeld's appointments between 1825 and 1830, Arnoldi appears as an experienced and self-confident member of the senate's commission who achieved, through prudent and skilled arguments, his aims of promoting his former student (Acta 1825, StAMR 305a AIV 41). When Hupfeld was dean of the theological faculty in 1836—more than a year after the death of Arnoldi—he wrote a note in the faculty register, describing Arnoldi as "one of the best Oriental scholars of our time and, especially in the classics, one of the most educated and beloved teachers the faculty and the university has ever had."[38]

5. *Hupfeld as a Student in 1813–17*

In the matriculation catalogue for the summer term of 1813, Hupfeld was registered under Nr. 2: "*30. April: Herrmanus Christianus Carolus Fridericus Hupfeld, Melsungen-Guestphalus, Theologius.*" With his registration as a student, Hupfeld simultaneously became a member of the Nether-Hessian College, where, seventeen years later, he would become Ephorus.[39] Now called Hessische Stipendiatenanstalt, this college was housed until 1811 in the Collegium at the Plan and reacquired a building of its own only in 1946—a building situated adjacent to the castle, high over the city.[40]

---

38. *"Ein(n) der ersten Orientalisten unserer Zeit und einer der gelehrtesten, namentlich klassisch gebildeten und beliebtesten Lehrer, welche die Facultät und die Universität überhaupt gehabt hat.*" Cf. Protocollum (StAMR 307 a 1a 31.1–537), December 6, 1836, 333, quoted also by Heppe 1873, 62. For more details, see also Hupfeld's letter to his friend, W. Bickell, dated June 10, 1832, StAMR 340 Nachlass Hupfeld.

39. Cf. Senats-Protokoll (der Universität Marburg) sessions from February 13, and March 22, 1834 (AtAMR Annalen).

40. Cf. Meyer zu Ermgassen 1977, 108–17; Stephan 1977.

The university was founded in 1527 by the Landgraf of Hessia, Philipp II, as a Protestant institution without a special confessional obligation. This status continued until 1653, when Wilhelm VII made it a Reformed institution. After that time the Lutheran students had to visit the Ernestina at Rinteln, which was closed by King Jérome in 1809 and, after the reinstitution of the electorate late in 1817, was never reopened.[41] This event led to a weakening of the confessional state of the University of Marburg, whose theological faculty became officially responsible for the education of Lutheran and Reformed students in 1822.[42] Hupfeld himself was from a Reformed denomination, but this would not keep him, later as a professor, from fighting against a moderation of the obligation on pastors of the Lutheran *Confessio Augustana* and from insisting on its permanent status as the true expression of the Christian message.[43]

In his studies, Hupfeld focused on theology and classics. In the field of classical studies, Hupfeld's first and most influential academic teacher was Professor Georg Ludolf Dissen (1784–1837), only ten years his elder. Unfortunately, Dissen moved from Marburg to Göttingen in the winter term of 1813,[44] and Christoph Andreas Leonhard Creuzer (1768–1844)[45] became his second classics teacher.

Among Hupfeld's theological teachers, he was especially attracted to the Old Testament lectures of Albert Jacob Arnoldi. Scripts of three Arnoldi lectures were found in the Hupfeld estate: ones on Psalms

41. For more on the Period of Jérome's Kingdom of Westphalia, see Seier 1998 (= 2003), 18–28.

42. Cf. Hermelink and Kähler 1927. For the change in 1653, see Kähler (1927, 282) and Demandt (1972, 265). For the history of the University Ernestina of Rinteln, a foundation of Count Ernst of Schaumburg-Lippe, see Münscher and Wachler 1817b, 91; Demandt 1972, 548; and, comprehensively, Schormann 1982 on its liquidation by the decree of King Jérome in 1809, who ordered the merging of the universities of Helmstedt and Rinteln with those of Goettingen, Halle and Marburg (see pp. 296–302). For the change in responsibilities of the Marburg theological faculty in 1822 during the course of the fundamental reorganisation of the country in 1821/22, see Demandt 1972 549–51; Heppe 1873, 55–58; 1876, 2:385–89, and Kähler 1927, 510–11.

43. Cf. also his publication of the Augsburgian Confession, together with the preface of Luther's lectures on the epistle to the Romans in 1840, see also Kaiser 2005, 104–9.

44. Professor in Marburg 1812 to 1813; cf. Gundlach 1927 (= 1977), Nr. 584, 385–86.

45. Professor in Marburg from 1803 to 1844; cf. Gundlach 1927 (= 1977), Nr. 500, 392), not to be confused with his famous cousin Friedrich Creuzer; who became famous through his romantic interpretation of myth as symbol; cf. Baeumler 1965, 103–14.

(1814), Isaiah (1816), and Job (1816/17).[46] "*In der Exegese*," he confessed in his 1831 autobiographical sketch,

> *wählte ich Arnoldi zu meinem Führer, und ich wendete besonders an die alttestamentlichen Vorlesungen, zu denen ich auch schon mit einiger Kenntnis der Dialekte ausgerüstet war, ungemeinen Fleiß...aber um mich ganz für dieses Fach zu entscheiden, wirkte—bei aller Neigung, die ich schon damals dafür fühlte—die große Gelehrsamkeit meines Führers vielleicht mehr abschreckend als anlockend auf mich, indem sie das Bild eines alttestamentlichen Exegeten in eine Höhe stellte die für wenige andere erreichbar schien.*[47]

While the lectures fascinated the prospective theologian, they also raised deep doubts in him about the authority of the Bible. The suprarationalist Arnoldi had taught on one side *theopneusty*, the inspiration of the Holy Scripture, but delimited it on the other side: he taught his students that the Bible's authority is limited to its religious truth, but that it is incompetent in all questions of nature. In addition, he compared the biblical stories of creation with the ancient cosmologies.

Hupfeld sensed the inconsistent position of his teacher, but, to the end of his studies, had no idea how to resolve the tension between belief in the religious authority of the Bible and knowledge of nature (Hupfeld 1831, 281; cf. also Riehm 1867, 14). Only in his aversion to the rationalists did he remain unshakable, a point which became significant in his subsequent position.[48] The same tension existed with regard to his pietistic devotion: even later when Hupfeld lost his belief in the verbal inspiration of the Bible, he did not lose his piety.[49] A deep and honest

46. Cf. the *Catalogus librorum* (1866, 130, Nr. 4177a–c).

47. "In exegesis I elected Arnoldi as my guide, and I have been especially industrious in regard to the Old Testamental lectures, for which I owned some previous experiences in the field of the dialects...but to decide for myself on this subject, of which I had already become fond, I was prevented by the immense knowledge of my guide, who put the picture of an Old Testament exegete in such a high position that it seemed reachable by only a few people" (Hupfeld 1831, 280). That Arnoldi recognized the scientific talent of his student is documented by his vote in the Acta for the appointment of Hupfeld as an extraordinary professor in 1825 from May 8 (StAMR 305a AIV 1b 32): "*Ich kenne den Dr. Hupfeld, da er in den Jahren 1813–1817 mein Zuhörer und Schüler war. Schon damals bemerkte ich ein vorzügliches Talent an ihm, und ermunterte ihn, sich zu einem akademischen Lehramt vorzubereiten*" ("I am well-acquainted with Dr. Hupfeld for he has been my student and pupil during the years 1813–1817. Even then I observed his special talent and admonished him to prepare himself to be an academic teacher").

48. According to Hupfeld's letters to his Uncle Sigel; see Riehm 1867, 14–16.

49. For Alberti's pious personality, see Maurer 1930, 1:49. In his vote for Hupfeld's application of March 9, 1825, Alberti described Hupfeld "einen

piety, together with an aversion to Kantian moral theology, would remain throughout his life the heritage of his uncle's teaching.[50]

We may pass over Hupfeld's activities as a founder, in December 1816, of the "allgemeine Studentenvereinigung," afterwards called the *Landsmannschaft Teutonia*. This organization was the Marburg version of the "Burschenschaft" or German students' union.[51] This organization desired a free revival of the spirit of fraternity and piety among the German people, but in 1819 was prohibited in the German states by the "Karlsbader Beschlüsse."[52] Even so, we must remember that Hupfeld's lifelong political ideals were deeply influenced by these years. If his father had agreed, Hupfeld would have been a voluntary soldier in the army by 1814. His father, instead, asked him to follow through and finish his studies. Indeed, Hupfeld took his theological examination in autumn 1817,[53] followed several days later by his doctoral disputation in the

achtungswerthen Charakter und echten religiösen Sinn" ("as a worthy person with true religious conviction").

50. Cf. also Kamphausen 1900, 462. However, he alluded positively to Kant's categorical imperative in voting for de Wette in his statement to the senate on April 23, 1832 (cf. StAMR 305 A IV 1b Nr. 41). This is in agreement with the fact that he owned, according to the *Catalogus librorum*, 117 Nr. 3587ff. the following moral-philocophical publications: *Kritik der praktischen Vernunft* (2d ed.; Riga, 1792); *Kritik der Urteilskraft* (2d ed.; Berlin, 1793); *Die Religion innerhalb der Grenzen der bloßen Vernunft* (Königsberg, 1793); *Zum ewigen Frieden* (Königsberg, 1795); *Der Streit der Fakultäten* (Königsberg, 1798); *Metaphysik der Sitten* (Königsberg, 1803) and *Vermischte Schriften I–II* (Königsberg, 1792). He also owned the most important publications of Johann Gottfried Fichte, cf. *Catalogus librorum*, 117–18, Nr. 3886–3895, for example, *Versuch einer Critik aller Offenbarung* (Königsberg, 1792); *Bestimmung des Menschen* (Frankfurt and Leipzig, 1805); *Wissenschaftslehre* (Berlin, 1810) and *Grundzüge des gegenwärtigen Zeitalters* (Berlin, 1806). In 1817, Hupfeld defended, in theses I–IV of his doctoral disputation, the difference between necessity and freedom—a post-Kantian position (cf. Hupfeld 1818, 56–58), presumably influenced by his philosophical teachers Johann Bering and Wilhelm Gottlieb Tennemann; cf. Sieg 1989, 21–22, 24–26.

51. Cf. StAMR 267 Nr. 3 and the corresponding dossiers with the speech of Hupfeld in the foundation assembly, reproduced in Kaiser (2005, 232–37, cf. Plate 274); cf. also Riehm 1867, 19. For the context, see Kähler 1927, 520–21, and especially Heer 1927, 105–16. On the *Karlsbader Beschlüsse* in 1819, see Kähler 1927, 522–23, and on its return to the public in the procession at the occasion of the 300th anniversary of the Philipps-University (p. 538); see now also Speitkamp 1986, 412–17. For the awakening of the national consciousness in Germany during the Napoleonic period, see Nipperdey 1983 (= 1987), 303–5.

52. Cf. above, n. 51; also Hupfeld in Gerland 1863, 314–15; Kaiser 2005, 42–44.

53. Cf. Protocollum Facultatis Theologiae Marburgensis A. MDCCXII (1712–1910), 295: *Anno MDCCCXVII Decano Maurtio Jo.Henr. Beckhaus III. Novembris 5.)*

philosophical faculty.[54] The substance of his philosophy dissertation, "Animadversiones philologicae in Sophoklem," was text-critical reflections on selected Sophoclean tragedies.[55]

6. Excessive Demand and Retreat: On the Way to Becoming an Old Testament Scholar (1817–24)

Afterwards, Hupfeld needed some years to find his way professionally. He used the time to resolve his personal position on the relationship between faith and knowledge. First, he wanted to take a long hike to southern Germany in preparation for becoming a Swabian pastor. Therefore, he remained in his father's house at Spangenberg during the winter of 1817–18 and did not accept appointments as a classics teacher at the Göttingen and Heidelberg grammar schools, positions for which Dissen and Creuzer respectively had recommended him. However, when he got a governmental order to go to Marburg as second major (*zweiter Repetent*) of the Nether-Hessian College and assistant to the pastor *primarius* at the university church, he decided that he could not refuse to work for his country.

In a short time he learned that he would be under excessive demands. Throughout his life, he was unable to write quickly (Kamphausen 1900, 462), and would begin again and again until he found the exact expression. His manner of speaking, at least in his Halle lectures, was the same, with the consequence that superficial students mocked him, while diligent ones became fascinated by his scientific honesty.[56] In any case, after a brief time, he completed his duties at Marburg. When he went as a

Hermanus Hupfeld, Spangenbergensis alumnus elect. optime stetit. Text: 1 Joh. IV, 20–21. and StAMR 307a I A Nr.35:Kandidatenprüfung 1817.

54. Cf. the relevant pages in StAMR 307d I A Nr. 55, and Kaiser 2005, 44–46.

55. Published Marburg 1818. For the longeivity of Hupfeld's interest in classical Greek and Latin the *Catalogus librorum*, 72–79, Nr. 2230–2491 with 263 relevant editions and studies a convincing witness.

56. Cf. Riehm 1867, 97, who reports about Hupfeld's manner of lecturing during his time at Halle, that it has "*äußerlich nichts anziehendes; er mußte oft mit dem Ausdruck ringen, und manchmal gelang es ihm erst nach wiederholten Versuchen das rechte Wort zu finden. Zum eigentlichen Redefluß kam es selten; meist behielt die Rede etwas zerstückeltes und zerhacktes. Und doch wußte er seine Zuhörer, wenn ihnen anders das Interesse an der Sache nicht fehlte, in hohem Maaße zu fesseln*" ("formal, nothing attractive; he has to search for the right expression, succeeding sometimes after repeated attempts. His speech rarely flowed; mostly it was disjointed and interrupted. In spite of this fact, he has been able to interest his audience as far as it has been interested in the subject").

teacher to the Hohe Landesschule (grammar school) at Hanau in April
1819, the same things happened (Hupfeld 1831, 283), and in the spring of
1822, after two years, he had a nervous and physical breakdown. That
summer he was able to realize his earlier desire and he hiked through
Switzerland and Württemberg. Afterwards, he returned to his parents'
house at Spangenberg (cf. Riehm 1867, 21–23; Kaiser 2005: 48–49).

He used this time to overcome his doubts, and he studied thoroughly
Johann Gottfried Eichhorn's *Einleitung in das Alte Testament*,[57] the two
volumes of Johann Gottfried Herder's *Vom Geist der ebräischen Poesie*,
Jean Astruc's *Conjectures*, Robert Lowth's *De sacra poesi Hebraeorum*,
and a selection of books written by Johann David Michaelis. These men
demonstrated, as Hupfeld wrote from Halle to his Uncle Sigel in July
1824 while reflecting back on these years, how beautiful, splendid, and
true the biblical scriptures are if one reads them as Oriental poetry and
without any prejudice regarding their inspiration (Riehm 1867, 28–29).
However, he learned first from Herder, about whom he had already
written enthusiastically to his uncle in February 1823,[58] that his *Geist der*

57.   The *Catalogus librorum* (1866) lists twelve of Eichhorn's books: .9, Nrs.
262–265: Eichhorn's *Einleitung in das Alte Testament*, I–V (4th ed.; Göttingen,
1823–24); *Einleitung in das Alte Testament*, I–III (Leipzig, 1803); *Einleitung in die
apokryphischen Schriften des Alten Testaments* (Leipzig, 1795); *Einleitung in das
Neue Testament*, I–V (Leipzig, 1804–27); 21, Nr. 684: *Commentarius in apocalypsin
Johannis*, I–II (Göttingen, 1791); 30, Nrs. 977 u. 978: *Repertorium für biblische und
morgendländische Lit*, I–X (Leipzig, 1777–86); *Allgemeine Bibliothek der biblischen Litteratur*, I–IX (Leipzig, 1887–1900); 115, Nr. 3784: *Geschichte der Künste
und Wissenschaft*, I–II (Göttingen, 1796); 82, Nr. 2624: *Monumenta antiquissima
historiae Arabum* (Gotha, 1775); S.86: *Weltgeschichte*, I–III (Reutlingen, 1818–20);
88, Nr. 2799: *Geschichte der drei letzten Jahrhunderte*, I–V, VII (Supplement für
das 19.Jh.; Hannover, 1817); 81, Nr. 2581 his translation of W. Jones, *Poeseos
Asiatiacae commentarii* (Leipzig, 1777); for Eichhorn's biography, see Smend 1987,
71–81; 1989, 25–37; Reventlow 2001, 209–26.
58.   According to the *Catalogus librorum*, Hupfeld had in his library no less than
sixteen of Herder's books, cf. 8, Nr. 213: *Vom Geist der ebräischen Poesie* I–II
(Dessau, 1782); 12; Nr. 363: *Aelteste Urkunde des Menschengeschlechts* I–II (Riga
1774–76); 30, Nr. 1001: *Aussichten zu künftigen Aufklärungen über das Alte
Testament in Briefen* (Jena, 1785); 54, Nr. 1684–88: *Von der Gabe der Sprachen am
ersten christlichen Pfingstfest* (Riga, 1794); *Von der Auferstehung* (Riga, 1794); *Gott*
(Gotha, 1787); *Vom Erlöser der Menschen* (Riga, 1796); *Christliche Schriften* III–IV
and V (Riga, 1797; bzw. Leipzig 1798); 102, Nrs. 3270–76a–d: *Zerstreute Blätter*,
1–6 (Gotha, 1790); *Ideen (zur Philosophie der Geschichte der Menschheit)* I-IV
(Riga, 1785); *Briefe zur Beförderung der Humanität* I-IV (Riga, 1793); V–VI
(1795); VII–VIII (1796); IX–X (1797); *Zur Philosophie der Geschichte* 1–22 in XI.
(Stuttgart, 1827); *Adrastea* Lfg.1–12 (Leipzig, 1801–3); *Zur Religion und Theologie*,
I–XVIII (Stuttgart, 1827–30; Nachlass hg. v. Düntzer und F.G. Herder 1–3, 2. Aufl.,

ebräischen Poesie has more merits for Christianity than all the books on doctrine taken together.[59] Yet, in resolving his doubts, he may have already been helped by the books of the anti-Kantian philosophers Friedrich Heinrich Jakobi (1743–1819), *Von den göttlichen Dingen und ihrer Offenbarung*,[60] and Jacob Friedrich Fries (1773–1843), *Wissen, Glaube und Ahndung*.[61] Editions from 1811 and 1805 respectively are registered in his estate.[62] However, we have to mention especially Wilhelm Martin Leberecht de Wette, who had adapted their basic ideas and had been one of the most influential Protestant scholars of these decades.[63] In a letter

Frankfurt a. M., 1856–57); 117, Nr. 3384; *Verstand und Erfahrung. Eine Metakritik zur Kritik der reinen Vernunft* (Leipzig, 1799). For Herder's religious and theological development, see Zippert 1994, 289–96; Reventlow 2001, 189–99, and about his life, see Zaremba 2002.

59. "*Meiner Meinung nach hat dieses Buch dem Christenthum einen größeren Dienst geleistet, als alle Dogmatiken zusammen genommen*" ("In my opinion this book has greater merits for Chrstianity than all dogmatics together)." Cf. Riehm 1867, 23–25.

60. *On the Divine and Its Revelation.* It may be noted that the Marburg philosopher, Suabedissen, Hupfeld's later father-in-law, also shared Jacobi's anti-Kantian attitude; cf. Ballauff 1942, 361.

61. *Knowledge, Faith and Premonition.*

62. Cf. *Catalogus librorum* 1866, 117, Nrs. 3875 and 3883.

63. For the reception of Fries' philosophy by de Wette, see Rogerson 1992, 92–101. According to his statement to de Wette in the files of the senate from April 23, 1832, he was able to characterize the idealistic position of de Wette's systematic and ethical concept as a reconciliation of the true aspects of Rationalism and Supranaturalism on a higher level; cf. SMA 305a A IV 1b Nr.41. In Hupfeld's library stood not only de Wette's romance, *Theodor oder des Zweiflers Weihe* (2d ed.; Hamburg, 1828), and his *Lehrbuch der christlichen Dogmatik I: Biblische Dogmatik* (2d ed., 1818) (cf. *Catalogus librorum* 1866, 55, Nrs. 1728 and 1716a), but also *Christliche Sittenlehre I–II* (Berlin, 1819/21); *Vorlesungen zur Sittenlehre I/1–2 and II/1–2* (Berlin, 1823/4); *Lehrbuch der christlichen Sittenlehre in ihrer Geschichte* (Berlin, 1833); *Über die Religion* (Berlin, 1827); *Über Religion und Theologie* (2d ed., Berlin, 1821) (cf. *Catalogus librorum* 55, Nr. 1712–17); *Zur christlichen Belehrung und Ermahnung* (Berlin, 1819) (*Catalogus librorum* 40, Nr. 1299); and, of course, the 2d, 4th, 5th and 6th ed. of his *Lehrbuch der hist.-krit. Einleitung in die Bücher der heiligen Schrift I: AT* (Berlin, 1820, 1833, 1840, 1846); the 3d and 4th ed. of his *Lehrbuch II: New Testament* (Berlin, 1834, 1842) (*Catalogus librorum* 11, 312–317a); *Lehrbuch der hebräisch-jüdischen Archäologie* (2d ed.; 3d ed., 4th ed., Leipzig, 1830, 1832 and [ed. Rack] 1864) (*Catalogus librorum* 26, 873–75); *Opuscula theologica* (Berlin, 1830) (*Catalogus librorum* 40,1299); *Der nachmosaische Pentateuch* (Karlsruhe, 1841) (*Catalogus librorum* 13, 409) the 1st–5th ed. of his *Commentar über die Psalmen* (Heidelberg, 1811, 1823, 1829, 1836 and [ed. G. Baur], 1856). (*Catalogus librorum* 18, 581–83); *Ueber die erbauliche Erklärung der Psalmen* (Heidelberg resp. Basel, 1836) (*Catalogus librorum* 18, 580 and 584); and

written to him on December 10, 1825, Hupfeld underlined that he and Fries had been his main helpers to overcome his doubts and to get down to his historical work with confidence in the Lord:[64]

> *Es fiel mir wie Schuppen von den Augen, die Nebelgestalt, die ich früher aus heiliger Ferne betrachtet hatte, bekam klare menschliche Umrisse und zeigten aber auch wie wenige Züge, die mir den ehrwürdigen Gesetzgeber des Alterthums, oder auch nur eine rohe und reine Menschheit verrathen hätten! die meisten gemeine, widrige Priesterzüge, nur zu kleinlich durch Fanatismus, Blutdurst, schnöden Eigennutz und unedle Gesinnung. Ich bedurfte keines Beweises mehr, daß das weder göttlich noch mosaisch seyn könne, ich fühlte es mit aller Stärke des getäuschten Vertrauens und des beleidigten sittlichen Gefühls. Selbst Herder vermochte mich daüber nicht mehr zu trösten.*
>
> *So hätte de Wettes Schriften keine Überraschung mehr für ihn dargestellt, so daß er "im strengsten Sinne" sein Schüler geworden sei—einschließlich in der Vorliebe für die Fries'sche Philosophie.*[65]

Willingly, then, the young pietistic theologian and philosopher accepted Jacobi's, Fries's and de Wette's recourse to "feeling" (*Gefühl*) as solid basis for the religion that they judged to be threatened by Kant's moral theology.[66] Especially important in this context is the distinction Jacobi made between "reason" (*Verstand*) and "speculative reason" (*Vernunft*). Reason (*Verstand*) has the function of comprehending the causal coherence of nature, but out of the divine depth of speculative reason (*Vernunft*) emerges "faith." This belief is rooted in a certainty which is independent of "knowledge," but faith and knowledge are adhered together by feeling (*Gefühl*), which opens the gates of the finality of the infinity of God.[67] Later on he would characterize de Wette's systematic

last but not least Dr. Martin Luther's *Briefe, Sendschreiben, Bedenken I–V* (Berlin, 1825–28; VI [ed. Seidemann], Berlin, 1856).

64. UBMR Ms 963:1 = Hupfeld 1963, Nr. 1.57–59, spec. 58–59. For Hupfeld's failed efforts to manage de Wette's appointment to a chair at the Marburg Theological Faculty in 1831/32 cf. Kaiser 2005, 166–212.

65. That this "conversion" did not stop his aversion to "the so-called naturalism" may be proved by his letter to de Wette from August 6, 1827, UB Marburg Ms. 967; cf. Hupfeld 1963, ##61–64.

66. Cf. Smend 1991b, 145–54; Reventlow 2001, 227–39.

67. Cf. Jacobi 1816 (= 1968), 3:413–15; Hagenbach 1850, 24–26; and further in Frischeisen-Köhler and Moog 1924 (= 1953), 616–19 (618); and Bollnow 1933 (= 1966), 244–50. Fries (1805 [1905]) distinguishes between knowledge, belief and presentiment, whereby the source of knowledge is experience, that of belief the ideas, and that of presentiment the determination of feeling (*Gefühl*). It is the presentiment that is the cause of the sentiment of the eternal in the realm of finity, cf. pp. 61–63, 235–39 and 327 and further on also Oesterreich 1924 (= 1951), 147–56

position as the reconciliation on a higher level of rationalism and supra-naturalism.[68] This religious philosophy was for Hupfeld the release of his doubts. Reading his vote of April 16, 1832, on de Wette's theological and moral respectability and his attraction to the students, one cannot fail to hear the personal note for de Wette, in whom Hupfeld's doubts had found their healer in 1823.[69] When he has found an answer to his theological problems, the way lay open for Hupfeld to become a criti-cal interpreter of the Old Testament without losing his personal piety.[70] His resolution is, of course, a typically Romantic one, demonstrating that this movement, which had been so influential in German art, poetry and philosophy, had even reached theology.

Now Hupfeld could read the Old Testament as *"Urquelle des Chris-tenthums und aller Religion,"* as "the primary fountain of Christianity and all religion." However, this meant for him that one has to read it as an historical book and, after Herder's advice, as an Oriental one. The young doctor summarized with enthusiasm bolder than that of the later professor, when he wrote to his uncle:

> *Wenn ich auch zum Orthodoxen auf immer verdorben bin, so ist doch mein Glauben an eine göttliche Offenbarung in Geschichte und Schriften der Israeliten felsenfest geworden, und wenn ich fest überzeugt bin, daß das kirchliche System einst nicht mehr zu retten sein wird, so glaube ich ebenso fest, daß dadurch die Bibel in der allgemeinen Achtung gewinnen und ihre Anfeindung sich verlieren wird. Mein Leben soll fortan dem Schöpfen und Mittheilen aus dieser Quelle des Lebens geweiht sein.[71]*

and Hirsch 1949 (= 1964), 5:358–59, and for the special Romantic understanding of feeling or sentiment, cf. also Taylor 1975 (= 1978), 21: "Feeling here is not what it was for the mainstream of the Enlightenment, a passive state of affect only contin-gently linked with what provokes it on one hand, and with the action it motivates on the other. Rather we have a notion of feeling in the pregnant sense as inseparable from thought, just as thought, if it truly engages with reality, is inseparable from feeling." Cf. also p. 421: "The Romantics…put faith in sentiment in the spontaneous love of good and of fellow, something which could not be grasped or planned by reason," and for the Romantic world view, pp. 9–10.

68. Cf. his vote for de Wette's theological, moral and political integrity of April 23, 1832 (Bericht, 1832, StAMR 305a A XIV 16 Nr. 41).

69. Cf. Bericht, 1832, StAMR 305a A IV 1b Nr. 4; de Wette 1822 (= 2d ed. 1828).

70. Cf. Kaiser 2005, 49–55; Hupfeld, *Nachwort*, in Bickell, *Über die Reform der Kirchenverfassung* (Marburg, 1831), 56–57, quoted by Riehm 1867, 34–35; cf. also Maurer 1930, 2:85–86, and for Hupfeld's later distance from Bickell's ideas, pp. 269–72; for the problem of the transition from reason to revelation by feeling for God in de Wette's thought (and also in that of Hupfeld), cf. Barth 1947, 432–41 (439–41).

71. "Although I am corrupted forever as an orthodox person, so is my faith in the divine revelation by the history and the scriptures of Israel unshaken like a rock, in

His new liberty found its expression in a letter he wrote in July 1824, while in Halle, to his uncle. The fact that Eichhorn defended the credibility of the book of the Chronicler and the historical books, without considering their national prejudice, now seemed to Hupfeld nothing more than a sign of inconsistency.[72] Mockingly he asked "*Aber muß denn nicht auch B sagen, wer A gesagt hat?*" ("But does the one who has said A not also have to say B?"). He then added that, according to his conviction, attacks on the dogma of inspiration are not identical to such attacks against religion, and made the following statement:

> *Wie dem auch sei, ich habe ganz den Grundsatz de Wettes, für den "einzelnen Menschen giebt es nichts Höheres und Heiligeres als die Wahrheit; was auch daraus entstehen mag, mögen auch hier und da die Folgen scheinbar nachtheilig sein—und wir übersehen ja nur was das Nächste und Oberflächlichste ist- Gott wird schon eine Kirche schützen; er weiß allein den Weg, den sie zu nehmen hat; der Einzelne kann nichts andres thun, und hat keine andre Pflicht, als seiner Überzeugung und seinem Gewissen treu zu sein.*"[73]

Furthermore, with regard to the centre of Christianity, faith in Jesus Christ, he could say that—disregarding the metaphorical speech about Jesus as the son of God, the mythical narratives of his arrival on earth, and all the speculations on his nature and celestial relations—he honoured him as mystery,

> *vor dem alle meine philosophische und historische Kritik verstummt; ich weiß nicht wie ich das Wesen nennen soll, zu dem ich sonst in der ganzen*

spite of the fact that I am as firmly convinced that the churchal system shall not be the one to save, so I believe likewise that by this the respect for the Bible shall increase in the common estimation and lose its animosities. My further life shall be consecrated to scooping up and partaking of this fountain of life." Quotations after Riehm 1867, 23–24; cf. also Kaiser 2005, 52–54.

72. That Hupfeld had in his library the main works of Schleiermacher, beginning with his *Reden über die Religion an die Gebildeten unter ihren Verächtern* (Berlin 1827), and taking in *Der Christliche Glaube nach den Grundsätzen der evangelischen Kirche* (Berlin, 1821–22), vols. 1 and 2, up to the ethical and philosophical publications, is substantiated by the *Catalogus librorum* 1866; cf. f .ex. 53, Nrs. 1715–16 and .118 Nrs. 2922–29.

73. "However it might be, I agree completely in the principles of de Wette, that there is for the individual nothing higher and more holy than the truth, be its consequences even if they seem to be negative, but we have insight only into the nearest and superficial—God will protect his church; he alone knows the way she has to follow; and the individual can do nothing more and has no other duty than to be faithful to his convictions and his conscience." Quoted by Riehm 1867, 30.

Menschengeschichte kein Analogon finde; aber ich finde, daß die ganze
Menschengeschichte vor ihm und nach ihm auf ihn hinweist, und in ihm
ihren Mittelpunkt, ihre Lösung findet.[74]

7. Hupfeld's Developed Ideas on the
Relationship Between Historical Criticism
and the Christian Meaning of the Old Testament

Interested in his developed resolution to the theological problem caused
by historical criticism, we turn now to look at Hupfeld's programmatic
writing *Ueber Begriff und Methode der sogenannten biblischen Einlei-*
tung, which was published only in 1844, although the manuscript was
already finished before he left Marburg and went to Halle in Autumn
1843. Its second paragraph is a digression on the consequences of criticism for the theological interpretation of the Holy Scriptures (Hupfeld
1844, 4–27). According to Hupfeld's view, the problem is caused by the
historian becoming aware that scripture is not the result of divine
inspiration but of human efforts, and that consequently its interpretation
becomes a mundane task (Hupfeld 1844, 17). This concerns, as Hupfeld
rightly observed, not only biblical exegesis, but also the other historical
disciplines of theology, as is obvious in the case of church history and
dogma. In changing the divine pragmatism into a human one, they seem
to lose their theological character (Hupfeld 1844, 17). Asking whether
the dogmatic and the historical-critical views are compatible, the inevitable answer is a clear "No!" (Hupfeld 1844, 18). According to the
dogmatic views, the writers of Scripture are only mechanical tools of the
divine spirit, and their product, the Holy Bible, is unchanging. While this
radical and uncompromising Protestant variant of the inspiration hypothesis may be a necessary consequence of the Protestant principle of *sola*
scriptura and may correspond to a religious need (Hupfeld 1844, 20), it
is nevertheless incompatible with all the known facts of the history of the

---

74. Translated: "before whom all my philosophical and historical criticism
becomes silent; I don't know what I shall call this being for whom there is no analogy in the entire history of men, but I am convinced that the entire history of men
before him and after him is refering to him and has its centre in him and its
solution." Quoted by Riehm 1867, 31; cf. also de Wette 1823 1/2:336: "*Christus ist*
das vollendete Vorbild der Tugend, Wahrheit und Gerechtigkeit, der sündlose,
vollkommene Mensch, in welchem kein Trug und kein Mangel war. Was der Mensch
dunkel in sich trägt, das erscheint hier klar in lebendiger, thatsächlicher Wirk-
lichkeit in Christi Leben und Lehre" ("Christ is the perfect example of morality,
truth and justice; the perfect man without sin, without lies and flaw. What every man
unconciously knows appears in the life of Christ as a living reality").

biblical text. Moreover, its contents are not free from contradictions, vagueness and errors. This is valid not only with regard to the history of the saviour but also with that of religious concepts and doctrines—with the exception of the one who has been without sin and whose picture, in its pure divinity, is shining through its incompletely written cover.[75] In consequence, it is beyond doubt, "*daß die heilige Schrift auch eine menschliche Seite, und in dieser Hinsicht vor andern menschlichen Schriften nichts voraus hat.*" Its human element is not only its cover, but also reaches deeply into its content. Therefore, the divine element is only discernable by a spiritual examination and view (Hupfeld 1844, 22; cf. also 23–24). This appellation to the spiritual experience is (as in the case of Johann Salomo Semler[76]), on the one hand, a transformation of the criterion for the divine origin of the biblical message by the *testimonium Spiritus Sancti internum*[77] and the effective reduction of the Old Testament's revelation to the moral law, the Decalogue and the predictions of a saviour—both of which became essential to Protestant orthodoxy in the course of the seventeenth and early eighteenth centuries.[78] However, it is, on the other hand, also a hint of the importance which personal piety achieved for theology during the next century, especially in its Romantic branch.

However, Hupfeld was not content only with an internal experience: according to his conviction, an external dimension is also necessary one too. He recognized the message of the kingdom of God on earth as such: God has established this by his special revelations to his chosen people, to educate for himself a holy congregation and to stimulate, through his ideas of salvation, the whole of humankind. For he wanted—when it became needed—a great banner of atonement and salvation to be erected, which would be destined to assemble all the peoples of the earth and to lead them back to their God.[79] Corresponding to the two natures of Christ, the divine and the human, the Old Testament also has two aspects: according to the outer nature it is an assembly of Jewish scriptures, but

75. Cf. Hupfeld 1844, 21; Kaiser 2005, 128–35

76. Cf. Dorner 1867, 706–7; Lüder 1995, 135–38; and for Semler's differentiation between the scripture and the word of God, Hornig 1996, 237–39. For Semler's biography, see Hornig 1996, 1–85.

77. Cf., for example, Hollaz, *Examen theologicum acroamaticum* (1707 [repr. Rostock, 1725]), 1:129, quoted by Hirsch 1937, 317.

78. Cf. Lüder 1995, 138–48, and his excursus (pp. 148–55) on the meaning of the Old Testament as medium *salutis* in the Protestant orthodoxy exemplified by Johann Friedrich König's *Theologia positiva acraomatica* (Rostock 1619 [repr. 1699]).

79. Cf. Hupfeld 1844, 24.

according to the inner nature they are awaiting the response of faith.[80] The Roman Catholic acceptance of tradition has its relative rights,[81] but the difference remains that for Protestants, the spirit, which is working in the history of the kingdom of God, is presented only by the Bible, which therefore remains fundamental for the life of the church (Hupfeld 1844, 27). If we recall what has already been said on Hupfeld's estimation of the Augsburg Confession, it becomes obvious that for him its fourth article, *De justificatione*, is the summary of the testimony of scripture and the Christian faith.[82]

Devotion to truth and honesty accompanied exegetical accuracy in Hupfeld's academic career. Through this he was given confidence that the results of his scientific work could reckon (as he declared to the reader in the Preface to his 1853 *Quellen der Genesis*) with the consent of any unbiased and unbribed, honest reader,[83] as Jean Astruc had done in his *Conjectures*: "*Ains, ou l'on doit renoncer à prétendre rien pouvoir jamais dans auqune question de critique, ou l'on doit convenir avec moi, que la preuve qui résulte de la réunion de ces faits forme une démonstration complette de ce que j'ai avancé sur la composition de la Genèse.*"[84]

Files of Archives

Annalen (Protokoll der Senatssitzungen der Universität Marburg) 1789–1829 (StAMR)

Annalen (Protokoll des Senatssitzungen der Universität Marburg) 1829–1876 (StAMR).

Protokollum Facultatis Theologiae Marburgensis.. MDCCXII (1712–1900) (StAMR 307d 1a. Bl. 1–537).

80. This judgment is compatible with de Wette's differentiation between the particularistic and the universal aspect of the Bible, cf. de Wette 1813, 103–4, and for his Christological remarks p. 251; cf. also Fries 1805 (= 1905), 237, where he argues that the presentiment, the *Ahndung*, with its reverent sentiment reveals the eternal in the finite.

81. Hupfeld 1844, 26. Cf. also the letter from de Wette to Hupfeld from March 1, 1826 (UB MR Ms. 967: 2; Hupfeld 1963, Nr. 2, 60–61, quotation 60), and his answer from August 6, 1827 (UBMR Ms. 967:3; Hupfeld 1963, Nr. 3, 61–64, quotation 64).

82. "*Item docent, quod homines non possint iustificari coram Deo propriis viribus, miritisaut operibus, sed gratis iustifcentur propter Christum per fidem, quam credunt se in gratiam recipi et peccata remitti propter Christum, qui sua morte pro nostis peccatis satisfecit. Hand fidem imputat Deus pro iustitia coram ipso, Rom 3 et 4.*"

83. Hupfeld 1853, 1. For Hupfeld's further academic career and his involvement not only in academic and ecclesiastical politics, cf. Kaiser 2005.

84. Astruc 1753, 2 (repr. 1999, 146); quoted by Hupfeld 1853, 1 n. 1.

Protokoll der Philosophischen Fakultät Marburg Marburg 1760–1844. (StAMR 307d1d).

Universität Marburg. Rector und Senat: Acta die Berufung des Prof. Arnoldi betrf. 1789 (StAMR 16 5664)

Kürfürstl. Universität Marburg: Acta Berufung und Anstellung theol. Professoren betrf. 1793–1834 (StAMR 307a. Acc. 1895/63.Nr.8).

Kommission zur Untersuchung staatsgefährdender Unternehmungen: Acta: Die hier bestandenen hessische, rheinländische und wesrtfälische Landsmannschaft und dem unter den Namen Teutonia hier gewesenen Verein betrf. (StAMR 263, Nr. 3).

Kurfürstl. Universität Marburg. Theologische Fakultät: Acta die Zulassungen zum Facultatsexamen 1817 betrf. (StAMR 16/5645).

Kurfürstl. Universität Marburg. Theologische Fakiultät: Das Examen der theol. Kandidaten 1817 (StAMR 305a IVc Nr. 12).

Kurfürstl. Universität Marburg. Theologische Fakultät. Kandidatenprüfungen 1817 (StAMR 307a I A 35).

Acta des Ministeriums des Innern: Die Ernennung des Hr. Dr. Hupfeld zum Professor extraord. in der Theol. Fakultät betreffend 1825 (StAMR 305a A IV 1b 32).

Universitäts Kuratorium Marburg: Akten betref. den außerordentlichen Professor der Theologie Dr. Hupfeld zum ordentl. Professor der oriental. Sprachen ernannt den 2. Mai 1827 desgl. zum ordentl- Profesor der Theologie am 1.Okt. 1830. 1825–1843 (StAMR 16. 5622).

Bericht über den theol.- und moral. und polit. Charakter des 1831 zur Berufung nach Marburg vorgeschlagenen Professors de Wette zu Basel (StAMR 305a A IV 4b 41).

StAMR 340 Nachlaß Hupfeld (enthaltend den Briefwechsel zwischen H. Hupfeld und J. W. Bickell vom April 1832 bis Februar 1848)
Quoted:

Letter from J. W. Bickell to H. Hupfeld April 9, 1832
Letter from H. Hupfeld to J. W. Bickell April 11, 1832
Letter from H. Hupfeld to J. W. Bickell April 16, 1832
Letter from H. Hupfeld to J. W. Bickell May 8, 1832
Letter from H. Hupfeld to J. W. Bickell June 10, 1832
Letter from J. W. Bickell to H. Hupfeld July 20, 1832

Briefwechsel W. M. L. de Wette und H. Hupfeld. Universitätsbiblothek Marburg (UBMR MS 967; cf. R. Hupfeld, 1963)
Quoted:

Letter 1 from H. Hupfeld to W. M. L. de Wette November 10, 1825
Verzeichnis der Ehrenbürger der Stadt Marburg nach §29 der Gemeinde Ordnung vom 23ten Oktober 1834: Akten des Stadtarchivs Marburg D 1123.

Published Documents

Birt, Th., Hg. ([1903–1914] ND 1980), *Diem natalem augustissimi et potentissimi principis Guilelmi II imperatoris regis ab Academia Marpurgensi die XXVII. M. Januari hora XI oratione in universitate aula habendo celebranda* (Catalogus studiosorum Marpugensium) Fasc.1–12 [1659–1882], (Marburg) Nenden u.a.: Kraus.

Ehrenbürgerbrief der Universitätsstadt Marburg für den Bundesminister a. D. Gerhard Jahn, (mit einem Verzeichnis der Ehrenbürger von 1834–1978) (1978) Marburg; Presseamt des Magistrats der Universitätsstadft Marburg.

Bibliography

Aretin, K. O. von. 1997. *Das Alte Reich 1648–1806*, Vol. 3. *Das Reich und der öster-reichischpreußische Dualismus (1745–1806)*. Stuttgart: Klett-Cotta.

Arndt, M. 1996. *Militär und Staat in Kurhessen 1813–1866. Das Offizierskorps im Spannungsfeld zwischen monarchischem Prinzip und liberaler Bürgerelt.* Quellen und Forschungen zur hessischen Geschichte 102. Marburg: Historische Kommission für Hessen.

Arnoldi, A. J. 1781. *Anmerkungen über einzelne Stellen der Sprüche Salomos.* Zur Exegese und Kritik des Alten Testaments 1. Frankfurt: Fleischer, 1781.

———. 1783. *Observationes ad quaedam loca Proverbiorum Salomonis.* Ex Germanico in Latinam conversae, Lugdunum Bataviorum: Ad Petrum Phygers.

———. 1796. *Pr. Observationes ad quaedam Jesaicae loca.* Marburg: Krieger.

———. 1805. *De Chronico Syriaco Abulfaragino ex scriptoribus graecis emendato, illustrato.* Marburg: Krieger.

———. 1897. *Thesaurus Syriacus.* Colleg. S. M. Quatremare, A. J. Arnoldi, G. W. Lorbach et al. Edited by R. Payne-Smith. Fasc. 10/1. Oxford: Clarendon.

(Arnoldi), N N. 1836. *Katalog der Bibliothek des zu Marburg verstorbenen Herrn Dr. A.J. Arnoldi, Prof. Primar. der Theologie, welche am Montag am1. August d.J. und folgende Tage öffentlich zu Marburg versteigert wird.* Marburg: N. G. Elwert.

Astruc, J. 1753. *Conjectures sur les mémoires originaux dont il paroit que Moyse s'est servi pour composer le livre de la Genèse.* Reprinted in 1999 *Conjectures sur la Genèse.* Introduction et notes P. Gibert; Paris: Editions Noèsis.

Baeumler, A. 1965. *Das mythische Baeumler Weltalter.* Bachofens romantische Deutung des Altertums. Reprint. Munich: Beck [1926].

Bainville, J. 1950. *Napoleon.* Translated by L. Laporte. Munich: Beck.

Ballauf, Th. 1942. David Theodor Suabedissen (1773–1835). Pages 345–61 in Schnack 1942.

Barth, K. 1947. *Die protestantische Theologie im 19. Jahrhundert.* Zollikon/Zurich: Evangelischer Verlag.

Bickell, J. W. 1831. Selbstdarstellung. Pages 24–30 in Justi 1831.

———. mit einem Nachwort von H. Hupfeld. 1831. *Über die Reform der protes-tantischen Kirchenverfassung in besonderer Beziehung auf Kurhessen,* Marburg: N. G. Elwert.

Bleek, F. 1860. *Einleitung in das Alte Testament.* Edited by J. F. Bleek and A. Kamp-hausen. Berlin: Georg Reimer.

Bollnow, O. F. 1933 [2d ed. 1964]. *Die Lebensphilosophie F. H. Jacobis.* Stuttgart: W. Kohlhammer.

Craig, G. A. 1974. *Europe Since 1815.* New York: Dryden. Trans. *Geschichte Europas 1815–1980.* Vom Wiener Congress bis zur Gegenwart. Translated by Marianne Hopmann. Munich: Beck, 1989.

Cobb, J. D. Die Philipps-Universität in der westfälischen Zeit 1807–1813. Pages 353–66 in Dettmering and Grenz 1980.

244   *Sacred Conjectures*

Demandt, K. E. 1972. *Geschichte des Landes Hessen*. 2d ed. Kassel: Bärenreiter Verlag.
Dettmering, E., and Grenz, R., eds. 1980. *Marburger Geschichte*. Rückblick auf die Stadtgeschichte in Einzelbeiträgen. Marburg: Presseamt der Stadt Marburg.
Dorner, J. A. 1867. *Geschichte der protestanischen Geschichte besonders in Deutschland.* Geschichte der Wissenschaft in Deutschland, Neuere Zeit 5. Munich. Cotta'sche Buchhandlung.
Driver, G. R. 1957. Presidential Address. Pages 1–7 in *Congress Volume: Strassbourg, 1956*. VTSup 6. Leiden: Brill.
Eichorn, J. G. 1780–83. *Einleitung in das Alte Testament*, vols. 1–3. Leipzig: Weidmann's Erben & Reich.
Ewald, H. 1843, 1845, 1847. *Geschichte des Volkes Israel bis Christus*, vols. 1–2 + 3/1. Göttingen: Deuerlich'sche Buchhandlung.
Fleckenstein, J. Grundlagen und Beginn der deutschen Geschichte. 1985. Pages 3–186 in *Deutsche Geschichte*. Vol. 1, *Mittelalter*. Edited by J. Fleckenstein, H. Fuhrmann, and J. Leuschner. Göttingen: Vandenhoeck & Ruprecht.
Fries, J F. F. 1805 [repr. 1905]. *Wissen, Glaube und Ahndung*. Edited by L. Nelson. Göttingen: Vandenhoeck & Ruprecht.
Frischeisen-Köhler, M., and W. Moog. 1924 [repr. 1953]. *Friedrich Ueberwegs Grundriss der Geschichte der Philosophie*. Vol. 3, *Die Philosophie der Neuzeit bis zum Ende des XVIII. Jahrhunderts*. 12th = 13th ed. Berlin: Mittler & Sohn. Darmstadt: Wissenschaftliche Buchgemeinschaft.
Gerland, O. ed., 1863. *Grundlage zu einer Hessischen Gelehrten-, Schriftsteller- und Künstler Geschichte von 1831 auf die neueste Zeit*. Kassel: August Freyschmidt.
Grimm, J. L. K. 1831. Selbstdarstellung. Pages 148–64 in Justi 1831.
Gundlach, F., ed. 1927 [repr. 1977]. *Catalogus Professorum Academiae Marburgensis. Die akademischen Lehrer der Philipps Universität in Marburg von 1527 bis 1910*. Marburg (Hessen): N. G. Elwert.
Hagenbach, K. N. 1850. *Wilhelm Martin Leberecht de Wette. Eine akademische Gedächtnisrede mit Anmerkungen und Beilagen*. Leipzig: Weidmann'sche Buchhandlung.
Hauck, A., ed. 1896–1913. *Realenzyklopädie für die protestantische Theologie und Kirche*. 24 vols. Leipzig. Hinrich'sche Buchhandlung.
Heer, R. 1927. *Marburger Studentenleben 1527–1927. Eine Festgabe zur 400 jährigen Jubelfeier der Universität Marburg*. Marburg: N. G. Elwert (G. Braun).
Heinemeyer, W., ed. 1977. *Studium und Stipendium. Untersuchungen zur Geschichte des hessischen Stipendiatenwesens*. Veröffentlichungen der Historischen Kommission für Hessen 37. Marburg: Historische Kommission für Hessen.
Heppe, H. 1873. *Geschichte der Theologischen Facultät zu Marburg*. Marburg: Erhardt's Universitätsbuchhandlung.
———. 1876. *Kirchengeschichte beider Hessen*, vol. 2. Marburg: Carl Kraatz.
Hermelink, H., and S. A. Kähler, eds. 1927. *Die Philipps-Universität Marburg 1527–1927. Die Universität Marburg 1527–1866 in Einzeldarstellungen*. Marburg: N. G. Elwert.
Heinemeyer, W., ed. 1977. *Studium und Stipendium. Untersuchungen zur Geschichte des hessischen Stipendiatenwesens* (Veröffentlichungen der Historischen Kommission für Hessen 37). Marburg: Historische Kommission für Hessen.
———. ed. 2003. *Die hessischen Staaten bis 1945*. Handbuch der hessischen Geschichte 4.3. (Veröffentlichungen der Historischen Kommission Hessen 63). Marburg: N. G. Elwert.

Hirsch, Emanuel. 1937. *Hilfsbuch zum Studium der Dogmatik.* Repr., Berlin: de Gruyter.
————. 1949 (= 3d ed. 1964). *Geschichte der neuern evangelischen Theologie im Zusammenhang mit den allgemeinen Bewegungen des europäischen Denkens.* 5 vols. Gütersloh: Gütersloher Verlagshaus Gerd Mohn.
Holzinger, H. 1893. *Einleitung in den Hexateuch.* Mit Tabellen über die Quellenscheidung. Freiburg: J. C. B. Mohr.
Hornig, G. 1996. *Johann Salomo Semler.* Studien zu Leben und Werk des Hallenser Aufklärungstheologen (Hallesche Beiträge zur Europäischen Aufklärung 2). Tübingen: Max Niemeyer.
Hupfeld, H. 1818. *Animadversiones philologicae in Sophoclem.* Marburg: Krieger.
————. 1831. Selbstdarstellung. Pages 277–85 in Justi 1831.
————, ed. 1840. *Die Lehrartikel der Augsburgischen Confession.* Nach der ersten Ausgabe Melanchthons mit den wichtigsten Eigenheiten der übrigen Ausgaben nebst einer einleitenden Vorerinnerung und dem allgemeinen Theil der Vorrede Luthers zum Brief an die Römer. Marburg: N. G. Elwert.
————. 1844. *Ueber Begriff und Methode der sogenannten biblischen Einleitung nebst einer Übersicht ihrer Geschichte und Literatur.* Marburg: N. G. Elwert.
————. 1853. *Die Quellen der Genesis und die Art ihrer Zusammensetzung. Von neuem untersucht.* Berlin: Verlag von Wiegandt & Grieben.
Hupfeld, N. N. 1866. *Catalogus librorum quos collegit et reliquit beatus Hermanus Hupfeld.* Philos. et Theol. Dr. huisque in acad. Frid. P. P. O. Halis: Typis Ploetzianis.
Hupfeld, R. 1963. W. M. Leberecht de Wette und Hermann Hupfeld: ein Briefwechsel aus theologisch und politischer bewegter Zeit. *NZSTh* 5: 54–96.
Ilgen, Karl David. 1798. *Die Urkunden des Jersualemischen Tempelarchivs*, vol. 1. Halle: Hemmerde.
Jacobi, F. H. [1816] 1968. *Von den göttlichen Dingen und der Offenbarung.* Pages 247–462 in *Werke.* Edited by F. Roth and F. Köppen. 6 vols. in 7. Repr., Leipzig: Gerhard Fleischer der Jüngere. Darmstadt: Wissenschaftliche Buchgesellschaft.
Justi, K. W. 1831. *Grundlage einer Hessischen Gelehrten- Schriftsteller und Künstler-Geschichte vom Jahre 1806 bis zum Jahre 1831.* Marburg: Chr. Garthe.
Kähler, S. A. 1927. Die Philipps Universität Marburg 1652–1866. Pages 225–568 in Hermelink and Kähler 1927.
Kaiser, O. 2000. The Pentateuch and the Deuteronomistic History. Pages 289–322 in Mayes 2000.
————2005. *Zwischen Reaktion und Revolution. Hermann Hupfeld—ein deutsches Professorenleben.* Abhandlungen der Akademie der Wissenschaften in Göttingen, Philologisch-Historische Klasse. Bd. 268. Göttingen: Vandenhoeck & Ruprecht.
Kamphausen, A. 1897. Bleek, Friedrich. Pages 254–57 in vol. 3 of Hauck 1896–1913.
————. 1900. Hupfeld, Hermann. Pages 462–67 in vol. 8 of Hauck 1896–1913.
Kraus, H.-J. 1969. *Geschichte der historisch-kritischen Erforschung des Alten Testaments.* 2d ed. Neukirchen–Vluyn: Neukirchener.
Lau, R. 1943. Territorialgeschichte der Grafschaft Diez samt den Herrschaften Limburg, Schaumburg, Holzappel. Ph.D diss., Marburg.
Levin, C. 1993. *Der Jahwist.* FRLANT 157. Göttingen: Vandenhoeck & Ruprecht.
Losch, P. 1922. *Geschichte des Kurfürstentums Hessen 1803 bis 1866.* Marburg: N. G. Elwert (G. Braun).

Lüder, A. 1995. *Historie und Dogmatik. Ein Beitrag zur Genese und Entfaltung von Johann Salomo Semlers Verständnis des Alten Testaments*. BZAW 233. Berlin: de Gruyter.

Maurer, W. 1930. *Aufklärung, Idealismus und Restauration. Studien zur Kirchen- und Geistesgeschichte in besonderer Beziehung auf Kurhessen 1780–1850*. Vol. 1, *Der Ausgang der Aufklärung*. Vol 2, *Idealismus und Rastauration*. SGNP 13/14. Giessen: Töpelmann.

Mayes, A. D. H., ed. 2000. *Text in Context. Essays by Members of the Society for Old Testament Study*. Oxford: Oxford University Press.

Meyer zu Ermgassen. 1977. Tisch und Losament in Verköstigung und Unterbringung der Stipendiaten. Pages 101–240 in Heinemeyer 1977.

Moeller, B., ed. 1987. *Theologie in Göttingen. Eine Vorlesungsreihe*. Göttinger Universi-tätssitätsschriften A: Schriften 1. Göttingen: Vandenhoeck & Ruprecht.

Münscher, W., and W. Wachler, ed. 1817a. *D. Wilhelm Münscher's Lebensbeschreibung und nachgelassene Schriften*. Frankfurt am Main: Verlag der Hermannschen Buchhandlung.

———. 1817b. Beyträgezur neuerenGeschichte der Universität Marburg. Pages 67–98 in Münscher and Wachler 1817.

———. 1817c. DieVerschwörung vom 24sten Juny 1809. Pages 198–102 in Münscher and Wachler 1817.

———. 1817d. Ende des Königreiches Westphalen. Pages 103–14 in Münscher and Wachler 1817. Verfassungsgeschichte Kurhessens in der Reaktionszeit (1850–1859), (Hessische Forschungen zur geschichtlichen Landes- und Volkskunde 28), Kassel: Verein für hessische Geschichte und Landeskunde e.V.

Nipperdey, Th. 1983 (= 1987 [4th ed.]), *Deutsche Geschichte 1800–1806. Bürgerwelt und starker Staat*. Munich: C. H. Beck.

Nowak, K. 2001. *Schleiermacher. Leben, Werk, Wirkung*. Göttingen: Vandenhoeck & Ruprecht.

Noth, M. 1948 (= 1960), *Überlieferungsgeschichte des Pentateuch*. Stuttgart: W. Kohlhammer; Darmstadt: Wissenschaftliche Buchgesellschaft.

Oesterreich, K. 1924 (= 1951). *Die deutsche Philosophie des XIX. Jahrhunderts und der Gegenwart*. 13th = 12th ed. Berlin: Mittler & Sohn; Darmstadt: Wissenschaftliche Buchgemeinschaft.

Pahncke-Pforta, K. H. 1905. Riehm, Eduard. Pages 776–83 in vol. 16 of Hauck 1896–1913.

Pannenberg, W. 1997. *Problemgeschichte der neueren evangelischen Theologie in Deutschland*. Göttingen: Wandenheock & Ruprecht.

Perlitt, L. 1987. Heinrich Ewald: Der Gelehrte in der Politik. Pages 157–212 in Moeller 1987.

Pfeiffer, R. H. 1941 (= 1949). *Introduction to the OldTestament*. New York: Harper & Brothers.

Reventlow, H. Graf. 2001. *Epochen der Bibelauslegung*, Vol. 4, *Von der Aufklärung bis zum 20. Jahrhundert*. Munich: C. H. Beck.

Riehm, E. 1854. *Die Gesetzgebung Mosis im Lande Moab. Ein Beitrag zur Einleitung in's Alte Testaments*. Gotha: Friedrich Andreas Perthes.

———. 1867. *D. Hermann Hupfeld. Lebens- und Charakterbild eines deutschen Professors*. Halle. Verlag von Julius Fricke.

Rogerson, J. W. 1992. *W. M. L. de Wette, Founder of Modern Biblical Criticism: An Intellectual Biography*. JSOTSup 126. Sheffield: JSOT Press.

Ryssel, V. 1908. Tuch, Friedrich. Pages 147–48 in vol. 20 of Hauck 1896–1913.

Schmidt, G. 1999. *Geschichte des Alten Reiches. Staat und Nation in der Frühen Neuzeit.* Munich: C. H. Beck.

Schnack, Ingeborg, ed. 1942. Lebensbilder *aus Kurhessen und Waldeck 1830–1930.* Veröffentlichungen der Historischen Kommission für Hessen und Waldeck 20/3. Marburg: N. G. Elwert.

(Schneider, H.) (o.J.[1994]), *Die Marburger Professoren für alttestamentliche Exegese und fürHebräische Sprache 1527–1994*. Eine Dokumentation. Marburg: Private publication.

Schormann, G. 1982. *Academia Ernestina. Die schaumburgische Universität zu Rinteln an der Weser*. Academia Marburgensis 4. Marburg: N. G. Elwert.

Seidel, B. 1993. *Karl David Ilgen und die Pentateuchforschung im Umkreis der sogenannten Älteren Urkundenhypothese*. BZAW 213. Berlin: de Gruyter.

Seier, H. 1979. Kurhessen und die Anfänge des Deutschen Bundes 1816–1823. Pages 98–161 in *Hessisches Jahrbuch für Landesgeschichte* 29. Marburg: Hessisches Landesamt für geschichtliche Landeskunde.

———. 1998. Das Kurfürstenstum Hessen 1803–1866. Pages 1–184 in Heinemeyer 1998 (= 2003).

Sieg, U. 1989. *Das Fach Philosophie an der Universität Marburg 1785–1966*. Hessische Forschungen zur geschichtlichen Landes- und Volkskunde 18. Kassel: Verein für Hessische Geschichte und Landeskunde e.V.

Smend, R. 1987. Johann David Michaelis und Johann Gottfried Eichhorn. Pages 58–81 in Moeller 1987.

———. 1989. *Deutsche Alttestamentler in drei Jahrhunderten*. Göttingen: Vandenhoeck & Ruprecht.

———. 1991a. *Epochen der Bibelkritik*. Gesammelte Studien 3. BevTh 109. Munich: C. Kaiser.

———. 1991b. De Wette und das Verhältnis zwischen historischer Bibelkritik und philosophischem System im 19. Jahrhundert', Pages 145–54 in Smend 1991.

Speitkamp, W. 1986. *Restauration als Transformation. Untersuchungen zur kurhessischen Verfassungsgeschichte 1813–1830*. Quellen und Forschungen zur hessischen Geschichte 67. Marburg: Historische Kommission Hessen.

Stahr, K. with O. Lange. 1957. *Marburger Sippenbuch 1500–1850,* XIII: Hube-Lizerich (Familiennummern 18577–20406), Archiv der Stadt Marburg.

Stephan, K.-D. Die Hessische Stipendiatenanstalt von 1946–1976. Pages 247–74 in Heinemeyer 1977.

Straganz, M. 1914. *Von der großen französischen Revolution bis zum Jahre 1913*, in P. Fischer and W. Felka, Illustrierte Weltgeschichte der Neuesten Zeit IV, Wien/ Leipzig: Verlag der Leo-Gesellschaft (d. F. Wagner, Leipzig).

Strieder, F. W. 1781. *Grundlage zu einer Hessischen Gelehrten und Schriftsteller Geschichte. Seit der Reformation bis auf gegenwärtige Zeiten*. Cassel: Cranzische Buchhandlung.

Taylor, C. 1975 [repr. 1978]. *Hegel*. Cambridge: Cambridge University Press.

Tuch, F. ([1838] 1871), *Commentar über die Genesis*. 2d ed. Halle: Buchhandlung des Waisenhauses.

Verzeichnis der Ehrenbürger der Stadt Marburg nach § 29 der Gemeinde Ordnung vom 23ten Oktober 1834: Akten des Stadtarchivs Marburg D 1123.

Wagemann. 1877 (= 1968). "Endemann, Samuel." Page 105 in *Allgemeine Deutsche Biographie*, VI. Berlin: Duncker & Humblot.

Wallmann, J. 1990. *Der Pietismus*. Göttingen: Vandenhoeck & Ruprecht.

Wette, W. M. L. de. 1807. *Beiträge zur Einleitung in das Alte Testament*. Vol. 1, *Kritik der mosaischen Geschichte*. Halle: Schimmelpfennig.

————. 1813. *Die christliche Dogmatik I: Biblische Dogmatik Alten und Neuen Testaments oder kritische Darstellung der Religionslehre des Hebraismus, des Judenthums und Urchristenthums. Zum Gebrauch in Vorlesungen*. Berlin: Realschul Buchhandlung.

————. 1822 (= 2d ed. 1828). *Theodor oder des Zweiflers Weihe: Bildungsgeschichte eines evangelischen Geistlichen*. Berlin: G. Reimer.

————. 1823–24. *Vorlesungen über die Sittenlehre*. 2 Theile in 4 vols. Berlin: George Reimer.

————. 1845. *Lehrbuch der historisch-kritischen Einleitung in die kanonischen und apokryphischen Bücher des Alten Testamentes*. 6th ed. Berlin: G. Reimer.

Zaremba, Michael. 2002. *Johann Gottfried Herder. Prediger der Humanität. Eine Biographie*. Köln: Böhlau.

Zippert, Thomas. 1994. *Bildung durch Offenbarung. Das Offenbarungsverständnis des jungen Herder als Grundmotiv seines theologisch-philosophisch-literarischen Lebenswerks*. MThSt 39. Marburg: Elwert.

INDEXES

INDEX OF REFERENCES

INDEX OF AUTHORS